EDUCATING THE GIFTED

A Book of Readings

EDUCATING THE GIFTED

❧❦❧

A BOOK OF READINGS

Edited by

JOSEPH L. FRENCH

UNIVERSITY OF MISSOURI

A HOLT–DRYDEN BOOK

HENRY HOLT AND COMPANY · NEW YORK

PREFACE

INTERNATIONAL COMPETITION, increased technological demands, the pressure of a greatly increased school-age population on existing school facilities, and the demand for expanded public-school programs have aroused widespread public interest in the education of our talented youth. Once the "forgotten" element in our schools, the gifted student has become the center of controversy. The great debate in education is now focused on how to teach gifted students for their role as technological and political leaders. As a result more articles concerning the gifted have appeared in the last three years than in the preceding thirty years.

Drawn primarily from professional journals, the articles in this collection present a balanced view of what is being done for the gifted, pose the problems inherent in educating such a group regardless of the special program—if any—selected, and report basic research findings in the field. The selection of articles for this collection was quite difficult, since many current publications are either rewritings of previously known information or emotionally written opinion pieces; but wherever possible I have included original studies so that the reader may become familiar with the data upon which later conclusions and opinions have been based. When editorials and opinions were necessary to round out the presentation, the work of analysts with considerable personal experience has been included.

These readings can fully provide the materials for a one-semester course on the gifted and can also be selectively used for guidance institutes or courses which discuss the problems of special education.

The articles have been arranged topically. After the first introductory section, Section 2 specifically considers the characteristics of gifted individuals throughout their lives. The articles in Section 3 cover a great variety of the programs provided for the gifted in public schools throughout the country. Descriptions of the four classical special programs appear in Section 4, while other programs are described in Section 5. In describing specific programs, the authors have dealt with many of the problems inherent in initiating any new program.

In recent years acceleration has been so neglected that a special section (Section 6) has been provided to help clear up many of the unfortunate misconceptions that now exist. Of course, the mention of special classes and acceleration raises questions about personal and social adjustment, overachievement and underachievement, and teachers of gifted children. The significant articles in these areas have been grouped in Sections 7, 8, and 9. Section 10 is devoted to generalized evaluative studies of special programs and schools.

It is not the purpose of the editor of this book to advocate any one provision for gifted children unless it is to meet the needs of each child to the best of our ability. Each community requires a unique program tailored to the needs of the children in that community, and any one community might use portions of all known provisions. It is hoped that this collection of readings reflects what is now known about gifted children and that those interested in the education of all children can find here ideas to help them improve their over-all educational program. It is by putting good ideas into controlled experimentation and then into general practice that we improve.

ACKNOWLEDGMENTS

Special thanks are certainly due to many people who helped make this collection possible, but two men stand above the rest: Dr. Dean A. Worcester and Dr. Charles O. Neidt. Dr. Worcester, professor emeritus and formerly chairman of the Department of Educational Psychology and Measurements at the University of Nebraska, introduced the editor to the study of gifted children. Now a visiting lecturer at the University of Wisconsin, Dr. Worcester still searches for new evidence, just as he has pioneered in so many of the fields related to his main interest—the application of psychology to people. Professor Neidt, chairman of the Department of Educational Psychology and Measurements at the University of Nebraska, is a researcher and leader of extraordinary capability. Without Professor Neidt's encouragement, enthusiasm, and support, the titles of these readings would still be on a reading list in Nebraska instead of in the Table of Contents for this text.

Special thanks are also due to Professor Galen Saylor, chairman of the Department of Secondary Education at the University of Nebraska. Dr. Saylor persistently surveys all literature in education and offered several valuable suggestions to the editor.

The secretarial, clerical, and proofreading chores were greatly reduced by Mrs. Sally Wagner and Mrs. Margaret French. Their identification with the project and their attention to detail went far beyond that usually expected of a typist and a wife.

And, of course, a book of readings could not be issued if it were not for the gracious owners of copyrighted material who make individual papers available for reprinting.

J. L. F.

Columbia, Missouri
January 1959

CONTENTS

SECTION 3

GENERAL PROVISIONS

Page 139

SECTION 4

CLASSIC ELEMENTARY-SCHOOL PROGRAMS
Page 209

SECTION 5

MORE SPECIAL PROGRAMS AND PROVISIONS

Page 233

SECTION 6

ACCELERATION

Page 277

SECTION 7

ADJUSTMENT

Page 327

SECTION 8

UNDERACHIEVEMENT
Page 391

SECTION 9

THE TEACHERS
Page 427

SECTION 10

EVALUATION AND RESEARCH
Page 457

INDEX
Page 545

EDUCATING THE GIFTED

A Book of Readings

I

INTRODUCTION

Concerning the Nature and Nurture of Genius

Intellectual Resources

Are We Shortchanging the Gifted?

SOME CHILDREN of great intellectual ability become very productive adults. Many others of equal potential, however, do not fulfill the promise of their youth to the satisfaction of either themselves or society. The United States wastes much of its talent, primarily because many of its brightest youth do not secure the education that would enable them to work at levels for which they are potentially qualified. With no loss in quality, the number of graduating college seniors could be doubled. Only half of the students with above-average ability who graduate from high school enter college; only 35 percent of all high-school graduates enter college.

But college attendance alone does not indicate an efficient use of manpower. While an IQ of 110 may be considered the minimum desirable for college students, all colleges do not adhere to such a standard. In a typical year, an analysis of the intelligence test scores of entering freshmen in several hundred colleges revealed a wide range of average student scores. In recent years the group at the highest ranking college had a median score equivalent to an IQ of 122 while the group at the lowest ranking college had a median score corresponding to an IQ of 94. One fourth of the freshmen in the lowest ranking college have IQs of less than 90, whereas in the most selective colleges the majority have IQs of 120 or more.

It is encouraging to note that, as the guidance services of secondary schools improve, a larger percentage of the students with high academic ability enter college. But intelligence alone does not guarantee success in college. For example, high-school students who fall in the top 20 percent of the population when intelligence is measured are too often judged to have about equal potential for college careers. If one breaks down the top quintile on the intellectual scale into scholarship ratings, one finds that the brightest 20 percent of high-school graduates who go to college will have ranged all the way from the lowest quintile in scholarship to the highest. For 25 years Dr. W. R. Carter of the University of Missouri has collected data that is pertinent. Dr. Carter has evidence that the 1½ percent of the college freshmen who ranked in the bottom quintile in scholarship, in spite of a highest quintile ranking in intelligence, have practically no possibility of profiting academically from enrolling in college. Again, of this

2

high-ranking group, state universities find that from 1½ to 3 per-cent of the freshman class range from a percentile rank of 21 to a percentile rank of 40 in high-school scholarship. Only about one in five of this group survives the first college year with average grades.

Our educational system is doing a good job with most of the students, but a better job must be done if we are to continue our rapid development. The United States Central Intelligence Agency has estimated that the Soviet Union is producing four trained technicians to our three. If we disregard international competition and concern ourselves only with improving our living conditions, it has been reliably estimated that each year we need to train 25,000 more engineers, 200,000 more new public-school teachers, and 20,000 more new college teachers to maintain our present rate of development. Our population is not filling all of the re-quirements for manpower.

To meet the demands as best we can will require a better use of our wasted manpower and a more efficient use of our re-sources. The fact that intellectually capable people fail in college may indicate that the colleges should modify their instructional procedures; it does indicate that preparatory schools have not met the needs of these individuals. It can then be hypothesized that cer-tain changes in our educational programs would encourage the in-tellectually capable, high-achieving individual to become more use-ful to himself and to society.

Our particular concern is with the so-called gifted child. There are no standard definitions of brightness or giftedness. Many of the definitions adopted by individual research workers, by school per-sonnel, and by community committees are based on measures of in-telligence. The lower limit is sometimes as low as an IQ of 110 or the top quarter of the age group, or sometimes as high as an IQ of 150, which describes the top one tenth of 1 percent of the popula-tion. When an IQ is used to define the lower limit of giftedness, what is really referred to is a percentage of the population who earn an IQ that high or higher. Since scores of those at the uppermost end of the IQ distribution vary so dramatically, it is preferable to define the gifted as a percentage of the population rather than on an IQ basis.

Leta Hollingworth defined the gifted as children in the top 1 percent of the juvenile population in general intelligence, but her greatest fame has come from studying those very few children in the top one tenth of 1 percent of the population. The late Lewis Terman included in his monumental study individuals whose IQs fell within the highest 1 percent in general intelligence (and consequently he had to use different IQ levels for different age groups). If the definition is to be restricted to an IQ qualification, support for the use of almost any figure above 110 can be found. If IQ is omitted, several sources for a definition are available. National Education Association publications have defined giftedness as "a high order of ability to handle ideas, to produce creatively, and to demonstrate social leadership" and a gifted child as "one of the million and a half academically talented boys and girls . . . in the upper 15 to 20 percent of the secondary-school students. . . ." Dr. Paul Witty of Northwestern University, the most vocal spokesman for the gifted, referred to a gifted child as "one whose performance in a potentially valuable line of human activity is consistently remarkable."

In their recent book Robert Havighurst and Robert DeHaan identified children in the upper one tenth of 1 percent as "first-order" or extremely gifted children and the remaining children in the upper 10 percent as "second-order" gifted children. They went on to identify several characteristics of the gifted, such as intellectual ability, scientific ability, leadership ability, artistic talent, creative-writing talent, dramatic talent, musical talent, dancing talent, mechanically skillful, and physically skillful. But when they identified the top 10 percent in each area, they had only identified about 15 percent of the population. The great overlap of talent among gifted children gives a strong support to the use of general intelligence measures as the criterion for defining giftedness.

Considerable attention has been given to academic achievement in addition to intelligence. When only the students who are already achieving quite well are selected for special enrichment sessions, we do not make as much use of our wasted manpower as we might. High-achievers are the easiest students with whom to work. When we take them from a situation in which they are already quite successful and put them into a different environment, only limited improvement can be shown. Is this really the way to help the gifted? What happens to the person with high intellectual potential who is not accomplishing as much as some of his intellectual peers? He remains in an environment in which he has established a pattern of failure or at least something less than outstanding success. The underachieving gifted student is a difficult one to work with; yet he is the one who needs the most help.

The question of democracy in public education becomes a major issue whenever suggestions for special education are made. Confusion and strong emotion center around the word equal: To some, equal means "the same learning experiences for all"; to others, equal means "the same opportunities for all to learn." In this context opportunity suggests that each child in school should have the opportunity to develop to the limit of his ability and that all children cannot profit equally from the same learning experiences. For all students to have equal opportunity to develop, different learning experiences must be provided. This is in keeping with our knowledge of individual differences and at the same time is more democratic than providing each child with the same experiences, which will be beyond the reach of some and only a tease to others.

The introductory articles were written by noted scholars. Professor Sidney L. Pressey, a psychologist at The Ohio State University since 1921, has long been aware of the inadequate methods used to handle gifted students in our schools. His personal investigations and those he has stimulated have done a great deal to counter many of the misconceptions about the gifted. Pressey's plea for effective identification and real provision for individual differences has gained increasing acceptance through the years. Dr. Dael L. Wolfle, Executive Officer of the American Association for the Advancement of Science, is perhaps the foremost authority on manpower needs and his suggestions for its maximum utilization have played a major role in our increasingly effective employment of human resources. The data reported by Wolfle was collected when he was Director of the Commission on Human Resources and Advanced Training. Dr. A. Harry Passow is currently the Director of the Horace Mann-Lincoln Institute of School Experimentation, a part of Teachers College, Columbia University. From this vantage point Dr. Passow has had a helping hand and critical eye for a vast number of contemporary research projects. In "Are We Shortchanging the Gifted?" Dr. Passow discusses the compatibility of democracy with special provisions for selected children.

≈§§≈

CONCERNING THE NATURE AND NURTURE
OF GENIUS

by Sidney L. Pressey

OHIO STATE UNIVERSITY

It has been well said that "in the present international tug of war, survival itself may depend upon making the most effective use of the nation's intellectual resources." [1] Means of better identifying young people of superior intellectual capacities, and of getting more of them into present programs of advanced training, have been widely discussed. However, there has been relatively little consideration of whether present educational programs are best suited to the needs of our most brilliant young people. Superior abilities are now generally considered so predominantly a product of innate constitution that certain "educational" factors, possibly of very great importance in the growth of such abilities, are overlooked. It is sometimes well to get outside of current habits of thought and try to look at a topic in a reappraising way. This paper attempts so to do. It focuses attention on that most extraordinary type of very superior intellect—the precocious genius—as possibly exhibiting especially clearly both innate capacities and developmental influences involved in extraordinary accomplishment. It presumes to suggest that there may be ways by which many more "geniuses" might be not only discovered but even, to a substantial degree, *made* and brought to fruition.

MAJOR FACTORS MAKING FOR PRECOCIOUS MARKED SUPERIORITY

An informal search for instances of marked precocity suggests that such cases have been especially frequent (or, at least, espe-

[1] D. Wolfle, *America's Resources of Specialized Talent*, New York: Harper, 1954.

[Reprinted from *Scientific Monthly*, 68, September 1955, 123-129, with the permission of *Scientific Monthly*, the American Association for the Advancement of Science, and the author.]

cially noted and featured) in certain fields and in certain localities at certain times. In the Europe of 100 to 200 years ago there were outstanding musicians of whom most were precocious. Handel played on the clavichord "when but an infant" and was composing by the age of 11. Haydn "played and composed at the age of 6." Mozart played the harpsichord at 3, was composing at 4, and was on a tour at 6. Chopin played in public at the age of 8; Liszt, at 9; Verdi, at 10; Schubert, at 12; and Rossini, at 14. Mendelssohn was playing publicly and also composing by the age of 9, as was Debussy at 11, Dvořák at 12, and Berlioz at 14. Wagner conducted one of his own compositions in public when he was 17.[2]

Recently, and especially in this country, there have been many precocious athletes. Thus, Bobby Jones was state golf champion at 14.[3] Marlene Bauer was playing notable golf at 13.[4] Sonja Henie was figure-skating champion of Norway at 10 and world champion at 15. Barbara Anne Scott was Canadian figure-skating champion at 15.[5] Vincent Richards was national tennis singles champion at 15, and Maureen Connolly was woman's singles champion at 16. Mel Ott was in big-league baseball at 16; Bob Feller, at 18. Eddie Lebaron was an intercollegiate football star at 16. Bob Mathias won an Olympic gold medal in track and field events at 17.[6] The reader may doubt whether athletic champions are relevant to the topic of this paper, but he can hardly question that they are very competent in their fields. Moreover, precocity in athletics and in musical performance might seem especially extraordinary because finger reach and dexterity on a musical instrument and strength, as well as skill and endurance, in athletic competition would seem especially to call for physical maturity.

An especially remarkable type of athlete must also be noted: the champion whose superiority emerged after great and persistent efforts to overcome a crippling handicap. Walt Davis, holder of a world's record in the high jump, was a former polio victim.[7] Glenn Cunningham, the Olympic runner, was burned so severely in the

---

[2] F. Barlow, *Mental Prodigies*, New York: Philosophical Library, 1952; M. Davenport, *Mozart*, New York: Scribner, 1942; and F. Schwrimmer, *Great Musicians as Children*, New York: Doubleday, 1930.
[3] A. J. Stump, *Champions against Odds*, Philadelphia: Macrae Smith, 1952.
[4] *Life*, March 20, 1950, p. 95.
[5] *Time*, February 2, 1948.
[6] See Stump, *op. cit.*
[7] *Time*, July 6, 1953.

legs when he was 8 years old that it was doubted that he would ever walk again. At the age of 8, Nancy Merki had polio and at 10 was further paralyzed, but at 13 she was high-point scorer in a national swimming meet.[8] Other well-known athletes have had polio. In all these instances, athletic prowess was the final result of very persistent (and usually expertly guided) efforts to overcome the handicap. There was no evidence before the injury or illness of notable athletic potential.

The first question, then, is why there should have been a rash of notable precocious musicians in the Europe of a century and more ago and a spate of youthful athletic champions in this country now. Certain major factors seem evident. In the Europe of that time, music was the major popular interest, reaching practically all social classes and all ages, and offering even to underprivileged youngsters the possibility of wide popular acclaim. Athletics is a similar interest in this country now. The second question is more specifically how, in such favorable total situations, have these prodigies come about. A study of their careers suggest that the following factors are important.

1. Precocious musicians and athletes usually had excellent early opportunities for the ability to develop and encouragement from family and friends. Mozart's father was a musician; his older sister was his companion in music; family and friends admired and encouraged the boy. Schubert's father was musical and fostered Franz's musical aptitude; soon Franz became a member of a string quartet with his father and two brothers. Of the athletes, Bobby Jones lived next to a golf course. When he was still a little boy, he was given small clubs and followed his father around the links. From early childhood, Barbara Anne Scott's skating was fostered by her father, and soon her whole life was so centered.

2. Usually individuals who developed precocious excellence had superior early and continuing individual guidance and instruction. From the age of 3, Mozart was taught, guided, and managed in his career by his father, who sought practically from the beginning to make his son an outstanding musician. Mendelssohn, also from the age of 3, was taught by his mother and other good musicians. Marlene Bauer's father, a golf professional, began to teach her the game when she was 3. Nancy Merki had an expert swimming coach.

[8] See Stump, *op. cit.*

3. Precocious individuals have had the opportunity frequently and continuingly to practice and extend their special ability and to progress as they were able. From the age of 3, Mozart practiced with his older sister; he had the opportunity to play the violin, the harpsichord, and the organ, to perform frequently in public, and a little later to conduct. From the age of 11, Maureen Connolly practiced tennis at least three hours a day. The climate of southern California made this possible at all seasons. She took on more able opponents and entered more important tournaments, as she was able. Nancy Merki was "in the water for hours at a time, just trying to master the trick of fluttering her legs." Under the guidance of her coach she moved forward in her aquatic accomplishments as she was ready.

4. The special precocious ability usually brought a close association with others in the field, which greatly fostered the abilities of all concerned, and led to a still wider stimulating acquaintance. Mozart lived from early childhood in a world of musicians who listened to and watched one another, played together, cooperated, competed, raised levels of aspiration, and were keen in criticism and encouragement. His musicianship brought acquaintance with the great all over Europe, including the Austrian emperor. Bobby Jones lived largely in a golfers' world, which developed his skills at the same time that he raised golfing standards and increased the popularity of the sport. His friendships have indeed been wide, including President Eisenhower.

5. As a result of many opportunities for real accomplishment, within his possibilities but of increasing challenge, the precocious musician or athlete has had the stimulation of many and increasingly strong success experiences—and his world acclaimed these successes. It is well recognized that frequent failure and continued frustration may debilitate personality and competency, just as a disease does. But the opposite also seems true, although it is not generally appreciated: frequent, much-admired successes increase effort, build up psychosomatic vigor, make attempts more vigorous, adequate, and better integrated, and build ability. The opinion is ventured that such "furtherance" is as important a phenomenon as frustration, and that systematic research regarding furtherance might well be as profitable as research on frustration has been.

At any age, development of any ability is fostered by a favorable immediate environment, expert instruction, frequent and progressive opportunities for the exercise of the ability, social facilitation, and frequent success experiences. Important advantages would seem to accrue from having these factors begin operation early. The physique may grow and adapt in congruence. As the young musician stretches out his hands and exercises needed muscles and coordinations, his skills may be not only learned but somewhat made part of his growth. This might be true, not for mechanical skills alone, but also for related integrations in the central nervous system, and for related percepts and concepts. So the precocious musicians played not only with skill but also with understanding, and they composed, notably and early. Possibly some integration of learning and growth might occur with abilities less closely related to a skill. Any ability, developing early, might benefit by having the great energies of childhood and youth devoted to it. Also, the child in the grip of a strong interest (as a hobby) seems often single-mindedly absorbed in it to an extent less common later, when problems of social status, economic responsibility, or the other sex may distract. If an interest is already well established when adolescence comes, the energies of that period may pour into it.

The thesis is that, in attempting to account for notable precocity in such fields as music and athletics, too much stress has been put on presumed extreme constitutional genius and too little on a concomitance of favorable factors, operating in the growth years. Instances of great athletic skill emerging from efforts to overcome a seemingly crippling handicap seem to emphasize the potency of these last factors. Presumably, the original physical potentials of these individuals were good, although not manifest, before the handicap struck; but the great potential of favoring circumstances seems especially evident. In this connection, Wechsler's argument[9] may well be recalled—that the range of human physical traits, as in height, strength, and quickness, is not really great, and that the range in mental capacities may be less extreme than is usually supposed. Rather, superior original capacity, *growing under a favorable concomitance of circumstances,* develops into genius.

So far, the discussion has dealt primarily with outstanding precocious skills, in athletics and music. May the youthful organism

[9] D. Wechsler, *Range of Human Capacities,* rev. ed., Baltimore: Williams and Wilkins, 1952.

not be capable of outstanding accomplishments more intellectual in nature? Here it should again be mentioned that notable musical performance would seem to involve keen musical understanding as well as dexterity (and outstanding athletic performance perhaps often involves more intelligence than is usually conceded). In youth, the famous precocious musicians not only performed but composed notably; and composing music is surely a highly intellectual activity.

But precocity has appeared in sundry other and clearly intellectual fields. John Stuart Mill began the study of Greek at 3. By the age of 8 he had read Xenophon, Herodotus, and Plato and had begun to study geometry and algebra. At 12 he began logic, reading Aristotle in the original. The next year he began the study of political economy; at 16 he was publishing controversial articles in that field.[10] When he was 6 years old, John Ruskin wrote verse. Macaulay compiled a "universal history" at the age of 7. Published poems of William Blake, Thomas Chatterton, and Alexander Pope go back to their twelfth years; poems of Robert Burns go back to his fourteenth year, and of Milton to his fifteenth year. Pascal wrote a treatise on acoustics when he was 12. Galileo made his famous observations of the swinging cathedral lamp when he was 17. Perkin discovered the first synthetic dye when he was 18.[11] Farnsworth, at 15, "evolved an electronic means of sending pictures through the air."[12] Recently, 11-year-old Italian Severino Guidi, 10-year-old Turkish Hasan Kaptan, and 11-year-old French Thierry Vaubourgoin have been mentioned as precocious painters.[13] Norbert Wiener has written his sensitive account of his own precocity: college entrance at 11, Harvard doctorate at 18.[14] As compared with music and athletics,[15] however, precocity seems more rare in art, literature, and science, and especially so in this country. Why?

[10] M. St. J. Packe, The Life of John Stuart Mill, New York: The Macmillan Co., 1954.
[11] H. C. Lehman, Age and Achievement, Princeton, N. J.: Princeton Univ. Press, 1953, pp. 198-219.
[12] Newsweek, March 28, 1949.
[13] Time, January 14, 1952; November 10, 1953; February 14, 1955.
[14] N. Wiener, Ex-prodigy, New York: Simon and Schuster, 1953.
[15] And the entertainment world in general; stars of the stage, screen, radio, and television have not been mentioned because physical attractiveness and luck in promotion, rather than ability, have often been of major importance. But the ablest seem usually precocious, as a result of those circumstances such as mentioned here.

INFLUENCES HAMPERING THE PRECOCIOUS

There is a general belief, fostered in this country by most child psychologists and "progressive" educators during the past 25 years, that intellectual precocity is somehow not quite healthy, is almost always a hazard to good social adjustment, and should be slowed down rather than facilitated. In the home, the early-reading precocious child causes anxiety, in spite of the usualness of such precocity in Terman's gifted group and in biographies of famous men.[16] The schools oppose entrance before the standard age of 6, in spite of the evidence, from some half-dozen experiments, that gifted tots admitted earlier have done well, both academically and adjustment-wise.[17] The general public tends to regard the intellectually gifted small child as a freak. In short, there is usually none of the initial encouragement in the family, early fostering, and favorable general social climate that got many musical and athletic prodigies off to a flying start.

As a result of mass education and indifference to the needs of the gifted, there is almost none of the individualized guidance and instruction for excellence that was mentioned as an important element in the rapid development of precocity in music and athletics. A good music teacher is usually especially interested in finding and training pupils who are gifted musically. The athletic coach tries to find and bring to peak performance the ablest young athletes in his school. But the usual public school teacher does not have the time, the attitude, or the methods to do much, if anything, for another young Macaulay or Farnsworth in his classes.

In contrast to possibilities of continuing intensive practice and rapid progress in music or athletics, opportunities often are entirely lacking for a youngster to indulge intensively and continuingly an aptitude in such a field as a science, advancing as he is capable. A boy precociously interested in chemistry may have to await schoolwork in that subject until the regular course in his high-school junior year. He must then start and progress with his classmates, and in his senior year must take other subjects (inten-

---

[16] C. M. Cox, *The Early Mental Traits of 300 Geniuses,* Stanford, Calif.: Stanford Univ. Press, 1926; L. M. Terman, *The Gifted Child Grows Up,* Stanford, Calif.: Stanford Univ. Press, 1947.
[17] S. L. Pressey, *Educational Acceleration: Appraisals and Basic Problems,* Columbus, Ohio: Ohio State Univ., 1949, p. 11.

sive work in one field is frowned upon as interfering with a broad program) and not "hang around" the chemistry laboratory.[18] Nor can the broadly gifted and precocious youngster advance in his total school program more rapidly than the average; acceleration is, in most schools, considered unwise.

Whereas the precocious young musician or athlete soon has an acceptance and a mounting status that is tremendously stimulating and educative for him, in musical or athletic groups—and these groups have status in school and community—the budding young scientist or scholar may be isolated or may associate only with a friend who is considered "odd" or may belong only to an anemic subject club of no prestige in the community.

In contrast to the early and continuing successes of the young athlete or musician, possibly mounting to international acclaim, the young scholar or scientist may have no opportunities to make good except in class assignments and may obtain no evidence of success other than good marks. The teacher (perhaps made uncomfortable by keen questions) may even criticize his intense interest, and the other youngsters may call him sissy or odd. For him there is frustration, *not* the furtherance of cumulative success.

Suppose that Mozart or Bobby Jones had not been allowed to begin his music or his golf until the other children did, or to practice more or progress faster, or had had only the instruction of a school class in music or physical education. Suppose that they had been kept from playing with older children or adults in the fear that they might become socially maladjusted, kept from associating much with other musicians or golfers because that would be narrowing and undemocratic, kept from public performances or tournaments because that would be exploiting the poor child! It surely may be questioned whether they would then have reached the preeminence they did. Abuses in the aforementioned directions are, of course, possible. But it is also an abuse to withhold opportunities

[18] Subjects that might arouse early interest often cannot be started in high school. Thus, a youngster may have no opportunity to study psychology until his junior year of college. But trial of group discussion of social adjustment in junior high school and secondary-school home-economics courses on "family life" have demonstrated the possibility of early beginning of a colloquial psychology. Children may be very shrewd in human relations. The opinion is ventured that precocity in psychology *should* be especially feasible. Such a youngster, entering adolescence with extensive relevant knowledge, might make distinctive contributions to knowledge of that period.

from precocious youngsters who are eager to advance and excel. The opinion is ventured that the last type of abuse is now, in this country, the more common one.

TOWARD MORE AND BETTER AMERICAN GENIUSES

The hypothesis thus is that a practicing genius is produced by giving a precocious able youngster early encouragement, intensive instruction, continuing opportunity as he advances, a congruent stimulating social life, and cumulative success experiences. In the instances given, however, the circumstances have all been so superior as to seem somewhat out of reach. Moreover, there was sometimes imbalance or exploitation. In the average college or school, what steps might be possible that would move with reasonable caution and good sense in the directions indicated here and perhaps somewhat benefit a great many youngsters as well as occasionally help toward the production of a "genius"? Two steps would seem feasible and of great possible fruitfulness.

The first proposal is that there should be, in a college or a school system, a person who might be given the somewhat colorless title of coordinator of special programs, lest the more precise label of personnel specialist for superior students cause them embarrassment and antagonize parents of students not selected or served by him. Such a person in a college should scan each entering student's record to find high-school valedictorians, science-fair winners, and others with evidence of superior ability. He should watch for such evidence especially among students in the freshman year. He might even follow reports on high-school science fairs and the like and recruit promising youngsters for his college in the manner of a football coach. (If other colleges object to this, maybe competition among colleges for the intellectually superior might be a good thing!) As he locates such cases he should seek them out, encourage them, and bring them to the attention of appropriate faculty members. He should try to help these students in any problems they have, find opportunities for them on campus, and perhaps arrange summer work or travel opportunities. He should make a special effort to bring congenial members of his group together and to foster stimulating companionship and morale. He should see to it that his program receives publicity and that his youngsters receive recognition. He should guide and further any plans they have for professional or graduate training and for careers.

In a secondary school or school superintendent's office, a person similarly designated to find and foster the most able students would try to keep the elementary schools alert to discover especially bright children there. As these move on to high school, he could watch for them. He would have the high-school teachers inform him of outstanding students in their classes and keep alert for other evidences of talent, as in hobbies. He would become acquainted with all such youngsters, encourage them, and bring them into contact with appropriate teachers and into appropriate subject clubs or other groups. Educative trips with other youngsters might be arranged and perhaps summer work that would be both financially and educationally profitable. A local business or professional man might be enlisted to sponsor an outstanding youngster who needed such support. Contacts might be readied with a college or university.

If such guidance or personnel specialists for the most able were generally available in colleges and high schools or public-school systems, it is believed that they could greatly increase the number of young people going into advanced training, select them better, and greatly improve the effectiveness of their education.[19] Such a position might be only half time, for a student counselor or assistant principal, but it should be seen as his distinctive opportunity. If in a college, he would work with the ablest students, the best teachers on the faculty, and the best professional and graduate schools. If in a secondary school, he would deal with the finest students and the community leaders most interested in young people. He would try cumulatively to build community interest in and opportunities for these ablest young people, as through the local papers and service clubs. He would have mutually profitable relationships with the best colleges and universities. At regional and national meetings, as of guidance associations, these personnel workers at all levels would meet with others doing like work. Slowly, they might change public attitudes to interest in the intel-

[19] Wolfle (op. cit., p. 251) has reported a study showing a substantial increase in the number of high-school students going to college as a result of a general guidance program. A recent account dramatizes possibilities of finding and furthering talent in even a small and isolated school (F. V. Rummell and C. M. Johnson, "Bill Lane's Students Win the Prizes," Reader's Digest, January 1955, p. 29).

lectually, as well as the athletically, able. Surely no position could be more finely rewarding.

It is not enough, however, to provide special student personnel or guidance service for superior students. *In proportion as they are very able and especially as they have special talents, special adaptations of the usual curriculums are likely to be desirable.* The able youngster not yet sure of his special interests may wish to explore very widely. Once he has found that interest he may, legitimately, wish to push it hard. Before long, his accomplishments may warrant his admission into courses ahead of his status. (The sophomore may desire some course not usually available before the junior year.) Soon he may be ready for an independent project under supervision of one of the ablest teachers, for an honors seminar, perhaps for a project off campus or work experience in the field of his interest—first attempts at real accomplishment in that field. There should be readily usable administrative machinery—it might be called an honors program—making it possible for an able student, perhaps under the guidance of a person as mentioned in the previous paragraphs, and under the general direction of a faculty committee, to have certain curricular freedoms and special opportunities to foster best his potentialities.[20]

It should be possible to adapt school and college programs to the needs of superior youngsters with regard to not only the nature of these programs but also their length. Occasionally a late start or an added year in school or college may be warranted. Far more often, an early start and rapid progress are desirable. Not only the occasional prodigy but most people of superior abilities show their superiority early and develop more rapidly than the average person.[21] Moreover, impressive evidence indicates that intellectual crea-

---

[20] A program of this general type was for some years in effect at Ohio State University, but unfortunately it was dropped at the beginning of World War II, primarily because of lack of any such personnel specialist as has been urged in the preceding paragraphs. Many of the undergraduates in this program did research or service projects worthy of publication (Pressey, "The New Program for the Degree with Distinction at Ohio State University," *School and Society,* 36, 280, 1932). The conventional honors program lacks the opportunities for work experience and for the research or service project (as distinct from a paper or library reading) that were found most distinctively valuable in the Ohio State University program.

[21] Terman, "The Discovery and Encouragement of Exceptional Talent," *Amer. Psychologist,* 9, 221, 1954 (pp. 41-57 in this volume). See also Terman, *The Gifted Child, op. cit.*

tivity reaches its peak relatively early in adult life.[22] The practically universal American educational policy, nevertheless, is the lockstep: every child must enter school at 6 (none more than a month or so earlier), progress a grade a year, and, if he seeks advanced training, continue his schooling often till around 30, which was the median age of receiving the doctorate in this country just before World War II. Now, military service may delay even more the completion of education. Yet numerous studies are practically unanimous in showing that able children can enter earlier and progress more rapidly than the average child, without harm and often with gain in regard to realized abilities and social adjustment.[23] Outcomes have been thus favorable in spite of most common use of the *worst* methods for "acceleration"—grade-skipping in school and a lengthened year in college. Better methods—admission to the first grade on the basis of readiness for school rather than chronological age, replacement of the first three grades by a "primary pool" out of which children would move early or late depending on when they finish primary work, rapid-progress sections doing three years' work in two in junior and senior high school, and credit by examination in college—should permit each youngster to move through educational programs at his own pace, without being conspicuous if his rate is not that of the average.

Not only are accelerates usually successful and happy in school, but they are more likely to complete collegiate and advanced training. At Ohio State University, 50 percent of the students entering when they were 16 years old graduated, compared with only 38 percent of the 18-year-old entrants, paired with them according to tested general ability at entrance and type of program. With selection for acceleration and guidance therein, outcomes should be even better. Of a group of students selected in their freshman year as capable of finishing a four-year program in less time and guided in so doing, 63 percent graduated. Further, accelerates seem more often successful in their careers than individuals proceeding through their education at the usual pace. From 1880 to 1900, 29 percent of those graduating from Amherst at 19 became nationally known, as compared with 12 percent of those graduating at 22.[24] Of

---

[22] See Lehman, *op. cit.*
[23] See Pressey, *op. cit.*, and Terman, "The Discovery and Encouragement of Exceptional Talent," *op. cit.*
[24] See Pressey, *op. cit.*

those in Terman's gifted group who graduated from high school under the age of 15 years and 6 months, 16 percent more graduated from college and 19 percent more took one or more years of graduate work than did those who finished high school when they were 16 and 6 months or older, although there was little difference between the two groups in general ability when they were tested in childhood. (The average IQs of the two groups at that time were 158 and 149, respectively). Moreover, twice as many of the first group (42 percent as compared with 19 percent) were very superior in respect to career.[25]

In short, simply to increase the number of bright American youngsters who "accelerate" should substantially increase the number obtaining technologic or other advanced training and make it easier for precocious genius to emerge. If it were possible for bright youngsters not only to move through school more rapidly but also in other ways to have their programs adjusted to their special needs, still more might be expected to complete such training, still more successfully, and with still more notable careers following. Moreover, they would finish their training and get into their productive careers sooner. And educational costs would probably be reduced! Thus it seems a reasonable estimate that every year there remain in the secondary schools around 300,000 students whom a reasonable program of acceleration would have graduated. Such a reduction in enrollment would involve substantial savings, which might more than provide for the suggested special counselors for the gifted.

To meet the needs for trained manpower mentioned at the beginning of this paper, greater efforts to interest bright students in collegiate and advanced training programs (as they are now), better guidance of students in those programs, and more scholarship or other financial aid, have been suggested. The suggestion is ventured here that special facilitated programs adapted to the needs of the gifted would be the best means of interesting them, that special guidance in such programs (as suggested here) would best keep these students in school, and that such facilitated and early-completed programs (often including paid work experience) would substantially reduce the need for financial aid to students. Finally, the proposed special measures should produce more "geniuses." To produce persons of notable accomplishment, educational efforts

[25] *Ibid.,* pp. 265-279.

should be directed straight toward that goal, in the light of all that can be found out about such persons and their upbringing. Simply to increase the number of students in physical education classes would probably *not* very much increase the number of athletic champions!

INTELLECTUAL RESOURCES

by Dael Wolfle

AMERICAN ASSOCIATION FOR THE ADVANCEMENT OF SCIENCE

The scientific and intellectual advances of a nation are generated by a comparatively small number of people. These few—the inventors, scientists, thinkers, and scholars who have given us the Declaration of Independence and atomic energy, railroads and radar, antibiotics and masterpieces of music and literature—have contributed to civilization out of all proportion to their numbers. In the United States we think immediately of such giants as Thomas Jefferson, Benjamin Franklin, Josiah Willard Gibbs, Thomas Hunt Morgan, Alexander Graham Bell, John Dewey, Mark Twain, and Walt Whitman. But the geniuses represent only a part of a nation's intellectual resources; for every genius there are hundreds of less eminent but highly competent men and women who also contribute significantly to the nation's intellectual progress.

The first step in appraising the intellectual resources of the United States, therefore, is to try to define just what group we are talking about. We cannot define it simply in terms of education, for our intellectual manpower certainly does not include all of the six million college graduates in the United States. Some of them have retired from work; some are in nonintellectual occupations; some, though they have obtained degrees, can hardly be classed as capable

[Reprinted from *Scientific American*, 185, 1951, 42-46, with the permission of Scientific American, Inc.]

of high-level mental work. Conversely, there are many people making important intellectual contributions who never went to college.

As a rough definition of our intellectual manpower let us say that it comprises all those who work primarily with their brains. We do not know how large this number is, because no exact census of them has ever been taken. Efforts are now being made to do so: the federal government, professional societies, and other agencies have been compiling rosters of specialists in the sciences, humanities, and various professions, and the 1950 Census made a number of new tabulations of scientific specialties.

It is estimated that we have about 400,000 engineers, 209,000 doctors, 200,000 college teachers, and 175,000 scientists. If we add the architects, editors, lawyers, social scientists, and persons in other high-level fields, the total number of brainworkers is perhaps a million and a half. Even if the actual number is twice that, we are still considering only 2 percent of the total population and 5 percent of the nation's labor force.

Individually the members of this group vary greatly in their intellectual contributions to society. But in general these are the people who have ideas, develop new inventions, processes, and products, manage the nation's social, intellectual, and administrative machinery, run its industry and commerce, and train others for these complex tasks. They are a growing resource. Through their work they have greatly increased the demand for people like themselves. Their scientific discoveries, inventions and social improvements have created new demands for engineers, scientists, social scientists, historians, scholars, and other men of ability and training who can manage our ever-more-complex society.

Our problem is: Where are we to find the resources to meet these additional demands? How many people have we who are capable of making creative contributions? How effectively are we discovering and utilizing our intellectual potential? Can we increase our intellectual manpower?

INTELLIGENCE IS NOT ENOUGH

To answer these questions we must have some reliable measure of intellectual ability. No one will pretend that this can be determined by a simple formula. Intelligence alone is not enough for effective intellectual work: to make creative contributions in a scientific or scholarly field one must also be endowed with interest in it, industry, persistence, strength of character, confidence, and some spark of originality.

Twenty-five years ago the American psychologist Catharine Cox Miles made an attempt to estimate the intelligence quotients of 300 of the most eminent men of history. Her estimates were based upon studies of their early writings, school progress, and other evidences of achievement in comparison with the records of average children. She concluded that the average IQ of these 300 geniuses was above 160, that few fell below 140, and that many were above 180. An IQ of 160 is so rare that theoretically only one person in a million ranks that high. But not everyone—in fact, scarcely anyone—who has an IQ of 160 goes down in history as a genius; the other traits also are necessary. There are 175 million people in the United States, but not 175 of the eminence of the group studied by Dr. Miles.

On the other hand, the psychologist Anne Roe recently studied 60 of the most eminent research scientists in the United States and found that they varied considerably in intelligence. What the 60 had in common was an intense driving interest in their chosen fields of science. They had become America's most eminent scientists despite the fact that they would not all make the very highest scores on an intelligence test. As for the little-understood gift of creative talent, it is apparently not restricted to geniuses; it exists in lesser amounts in many people—the people who develop short cuts, who put ingenious new ideas into the suggestion box, who think up improvements on old routines. No one knows for sure, but it is quite possible that creative talent is qualitatively the same sort of thing in such people as in geniuses, the only difference being that geniuses have more of it.

If intelligence is not a sufficient condition for creative intellectual work, at least it is a necessary one. Some minimum level of intelligence is necessary to master the basic concepts, problems, and techniques of a specialized field. The minimum level varies, of course, with the difficulty of the field. It turns out, for example, that people who go into work in the pure sciences score higher in intelligence tests, on the average, than those in applied fields; within the field of the basic sciences the physical scientists average a little higher than the biologists. Remember, however, that we are speaking only of averages; there are very high IQ's in all fields.

On the whole, we must depend upon intelligence tests, for want of a better measure, as the basis for estimating our potential intellectual resources. Such tests can measure a number of different kinds of ability, but for our general purpose a composite measure of academic aptitude, scored by the method used during World War II for the Army General Classification Test (AGCT), will suffice. The Army scale has an average score of 100 and a standard deviation of 20. These figures are quite arbitrary. They do not mean that the average man answered correctly exactly 100 of the test items. Rather, the raw score of the average man, regardless of what it actually was, was converted to a score of 100 points. Other raw scores were converted to arbitrary scores higher or lower than 100 so that the total distribution had a standard deviation of 20 points (so that 68 percent of the population would have scores between 80 and 120).

Now what do the AGCT scores show as to our intellectual potential and how much of that potential are we actually training for intellectual work? Suppose we take graduation from college as a standard of training for such workers. This is not a perfect criterion, because we need brains in many fields for which college is not always the best preparation, but colleges train most of the high-level specialists, and college graduation will serve as a rough measure of the extent to which we are exploiting our intellectual resources.

About 10 percent of the total population in each age group in the United States now graduates from college. The median score of these graduates on the AGCT is about 120; that is, half of them score 120 or higher. This means that the youths with an IQ of 120 or above who graduate from college represent 5 percent of the total population in an age group. But in the whole population 16 percent are at that level of intelligence or above. In other words, of those youths with intelligence equal to or better than that of the median college graduate, only about one in three graduates from college. Actually it would be better to take the score surpassed by three quarters of the college graduates, rather than the median score, as the measure of the ability to do college work. On the AGCT scale this score is 109. About 33 percent of the total population in an age group exceed this score, but less than a fourth of them go to college and receive a bachelor's degree.

The story is even less favorable when we examine what proportion of able people obtain the Ph.D. degree—today a requirement for many of our top-level intellectual occupations. During the 10 years from 1941 through 1950 American universities conferred an average of about 3300 Ph.D.'s a year. According to the best available information, the median score of Ph.D.'s on the AGCT is probably in the neighborhood of 134, and the score exceeded by 75 percent is approximately 123. About 12.5 percent of the total population scores above 123. Of this group, who possess the intelligence to earn a Ph.D., only about 1.5 percent actually do so. The proportion will probably increase during the next 10 years; perhaps the figure will be 2 percent instead of 1.5 percent. But even so only a fiftieth of the young men and women with AGCT scores over 123 will earn Ph.D.'s.

RAW MATERIAL IS AVAILABLE

This is not to imply that everyone with an AGCT score above 109 should graduate from college or that everyone with a score above 123 should get a Ph.D. Bright people are needed in some fields, for example, in business and the highly skilled crafts, where college training is not necessarily the most effective preparation, and the Ph.D. is not generally needed in such high-level fields as medicine, law, engineering, schoolteaching, business administration, or social work. Nonetheless, we have serious shortages of people in many specialties that do require college or Ph.D. training. Consequently we need to give serious attention to the large potential of intellectual resources that we fail to use to full capacity because of lack of the necessary education.

Clearly the raw material is available for training more engineers, more scientists, more people in other important fields. Just how many more we might realistically expect is hard to estimate. It is easy to see, however, how the numbers could be increased substantially; we need only look at the reasons why so many bright youngsters fail to go to college.

We could not add greatly to the number of potential intellectual workers by attempting to keep in school those who drop out before finishing high school; the great majority of these drop-outs are only of average or less than average ability. It is at the point of high-school graduation that the biggest single loss of bright students occurs. Only a third of the high-school graduates enter college, and of the two thirds who do not, a large proportion are above average in ability. The attrition among bright students continues in college, for half of the people who enter fail to graduate. Most of the dropouts, to be sure, are in the lower-ability brackets, but many are brilliant; even among that rare company who score above 150 on the AGCT more than 20 percent leave college before graduating.

There are two main reasons why bright students fail to go to college or quit before graduation if they do go: lack of interest and lack of money. Of these, lack of interest is the more common one. A great many able students forego college because their parents do not expect them to go, because they decide early on a vocation that does not require college, because they prefer to marry, or because their friends are not planning to go to college.

If the country wants to use the abilities of its ablest youngsters at the highest possible level, it must somehow encourage more of them to go on with their education. The first step, of course, is to identify these best brains. Fortunately this is not too difficult. The people who possess the talent for academic work and scholarship of a high order can be picked out at a fairly early age. Dr. Cox pointed out that the eminent people she studied gave evidence of their unusually high IQ's in early childhood. Voltaire wrote verses "from his cradle." Coleridge could read a chapter from the Bible at the age of 3. Mozart composed a minuet at 5. Goethe produced mature literary work at 8. Nowadays intelligence-test scores and school-achievement records make possible reliable early selection of the able children. Indeed, whether a youngster will be successful in college can be predicted about as well by tests given at the ninth-grade level as at the time of college admission.

The next step is to give active encouragement to those who show the greatest promise. In some cases it is necessary to offer financial help. At the highest levels of training considerable help is becoming available. The federal government, concerned about shortages of scientists and engineers, has started several new scholarship programs. The Atomic Energy Commission grants fellowships to graduate students in the sciences related to atomic developments. The Veterans Administration gives subsidies to college graduates interested in careers in clinical psychology. The new National Science Foundation plans to make a scholarship and fellowship program one of its chief activities. But I suspect that graduate fellowship programs will be less effective in increasing our intellectual manpower than their supporters hope. To qualify for a fellowship one must first finish college. If the goal is to enlarge the total pool of highly trained talents, money offered as scholarships to help bright youngsters start to college would probably be more effective than fellowships awarded to graduate students. There is no doubt that we need a great many more scholarships at the undergraduate level.

We have an even greater need, however, to improve our efforts to interest the brightest youngsters in pursuing an advanced education. In this task our schools frequently fall down. Despite the widespread school use of intelligence tests, too frequently the results are not used as a basis for encouraging the most promising. More school systems should follow the example of Iowa. Each Iowa child is given the Iowa Test of Educational Development at several points during his school career. The most promising are actively encouraged by their teachers to continue their education, and their parents are notified of their promise. The Iowa psychologist Leo Phearman found that 92 percent of the Iowa high-school seniors who scored in the top 2 percent on these tests, and 75 percent of those in the top 10 percent, continued their educational careers into college.

INTELLECTUAL RESOURCES ARE NOT EXPLOITED

Probably one of the reasons why so many bright students lack interest in going on to higher education is the poverty of stimulation in the school program to which they have been exposed. Elementary and secondary schools all over the country have gone in for "how-to-study" courses, remedial reading, sight-saving classes, opportunity rooms, and other commendable special provisions for the handicapped and the slow, but very few devote as much effort to special handling of their most brilliant students. One of the outstanding exceptions is the Bronx High School of Science in New York. This school each year selects a freshman class high in ability and eager for scientific careers. It then gives these students a high-school training and experience so effective that practically all of them graduate from high school and practically all of the graduates go on to college. A widely influential effort to encourage bright students is the annual Westinghouse Science Talent Search. The Jackson Memorial Laboratory in Maine each summer uses as research assistants a small selected group of high-school students who show interest and outstanding promise in biology. This approach—giving young students an opportunity to engage in research—seems to be an effective method of starting people on careers in science or scholarship.

The colleges themselves could do a good deal more to promote the development of superior students. One change that would cost little or nothing and would probably have good results would be to let the brightest students go ahead at their own pace. Youngsters of high IQs are capable of very rapid learning and early productive contributions. The Ohio psychologist Harvey Lehman, who has made a special study of this subject, cites many examples of great achievements by young thinkers. The grain binder was invented by John F. Appleby at the age of 18. Jane Austen finished *Pride and Prejudice* when she was 21. Louis Braille, blind since the age of 3, developed the Braille alphabet at 20. William Cullen Bryant wrote *Thanatopsis* at 18. Samuel Colt was 16 when he conceived the idea of the revolver. Sir Humphry Davy was 20 when he discovered the anesthetic properties of nitrous oxide gas. Galileo at 17 discovered the isochronism of the pendulum. Marconi was 21 when he transmitted the first radio signals. The first synthetic dye was discovered by William Henry Perkin at 18. Lord Kelvin had established a reputation in mathematical physics by the time he was 21 years old. And in general, according to Lehman's study, the great scientists and scholars who contributed the most in total creative output were the ones who started earliest.

We can find similar examples of early achievement in the current crop of youngsters in this country. An important new method for releasing archeological specimens from the limestone in which they are imbedded was developed just this year by a 21-year-old college student. An 18-year-old student at the University of Minnesota holds several patents on electronic equipment and serves as a consultant to a large electronic manufacturing company. One of the stellar contributors to the Los Alamos project during the war was a youth not old enough to vote.

No one knows how much is lost to science and creative scholarship by holding brilliant youngsters back to the pedestrian pace of the typical school and college. They can develop faster. As S. L. Pressey has effectively demonstrated at Ohio State University, they can do so without damage to health, without appreciable loss of opportunity to participate in extracurricular activities, without loss in quality of work and with the very positive benefit that a larger percentage of these accelerated students graduate from college than is true of equally bright but nonaccelerated students. They can start graduate work earlier and can begin contributing sooner to society and to their chosen fields of work.

From every standpoint it is clear that we are not exploiting the intellectual resources of the United States to anywhere near their full potential. We can have more engineers, more scientists, more doctors, more scholars and more specialists of all types if we need them. To obtain them, however, we must do better than we have done in the past to identify the brightest youngsters, encourage them to plan on higher education, offer them a chance to work in their chosen fields, give them financial assistance when necessary and give them the kind of education that will allow them to go ahead rapidly to take their places among America's intellectual leaders.

ARE WE SHORTCHANGING THE GIFTED?

by A. Harry Passow

COLUMBIA UNIVERSITY

The goals in educating gifted children are essentially the same as those for average students—to develop skills for daily living and to produce competent citizens. The gifted need to develop their special talents just as all youngsters need to develop whatever abilities they have. But when the gifted fail to mature their potential

[Reprinted from *School Executive*, 75, December 1955, 54-57, with the permission of *School Executive* and the author.]

strengths, the loss exceeds personal inadequacy or anguish—it robs society of the possibility of an outstanding contribution. No culture can afford to waste such precious human resources.

The leading question remains, how can we best cultivate giftedness within the structure of education for everyone? To increase our reservoir of talent and skilled manpower, we need more adequate identification and development of potential ability. The concept of equal educational opportunity must not be mistakenly translated into identical experiences for all.

The ideal of equal educational opportunity implies a recognition and acceptance of differences in both ability and needs among the children whom the public school serves. Only as we understand the reality of individual differences and how they should influence educational offerings are we able to infuse life into the dream of education for all.

Public schools have, since their beginning, been concerned with educating those children with outstanding ability and potential for superior achievement. Various kinds of administrative and instructional adaptations have been attempted to provide more adequately for the gifted youngster.

But what of the impediments to adequate educational consideration for our talented youth? Part of the answer lies in our cultural attitudes toward the gifted. At times, outstanding people have been viewed as hovering suspiciously near the borderline between insanity and genius. This sour view has not prevented us from using or enjoying the unusual contributions of the gifted. However, the clichés stuck firm until pioneering studies in psychology and psychometry put a brighter face on the truth about mental, physical, emotional, and social attributes of gifted children and adults.

Anthropologist Margaret Mead, in an analysis (*Journal of Teacher Education,* September 1954) of the superior child in our American culture, paints a rather grim picture of restraint of giftedness. Because any degree of superiority may cut one off from his group, we tend to level differences. We extol the success which caps hard work and perseverance; but we call it luck and even withhold recognition from the gifted person whose ability enables him to outshine his peers without straining.

Attitudes are not the same toward all talents nor at all age levels. In our culture the outstanding athlete may be welcomed and treated more sympathetically than the scholar; the child who is encouraged for his precocity in the early grades may be merely tolerated or even ridiculed in secondary school for the same behavior.

ARE SPECIAL PROVISIONS UNDEMOCRATIC?

Another set of obstacles to adequate provision for the gifted results from a misinterpretation of the democratic commitment of public education. The school is the agency which fills individual specialized needs of each child while meeting the social needs of democracy. This integrating function, however, is twisted by some schools into a reason for avoiding necessary special provisions for the gifted child. There are those who believe it is undemocratic to emphasize differences by making provisions for some which may not be available to all. They argue that special attention will tend to create an elite. They are afraid that to separate the gifted child from his peers may tip his social or emotional equilibrium.

Democracy is not the fruit of uniformity. Diversity within unity does not equal a single program in every classroom. The ideal is best achieved where arrangements include guidance and leadership to cultivate individual differences. Children do need opportunities to work and play together, to understand each other's strengths and limitations as part of their life experience. But they need equal opportunities for developing individual excellence. Democracy withers if potential growth is fettered by limited and limiting experiences.

Fortunately, Americans do not consider as undemocratic the extraordinary provisions made for exceptional children who are mentally, physically, socially, or emotionally handicapped. Schools have long recognized and met the need for special programs for these students. How odd, then, that many administrators fail to see that the gifted may *become* handicapped unless special provisions are made for them as well.

The thinking persists that talent will inevitably emerge and that no extra efforts need be devoted to identifying or developing these bents. Undoubtedly some gifted children do develop without any special efforts, but many others are stunted. Estimates by some of our manpower studies suggest that at least half of our most able youth do not develop anywhere near capacity.

How can the public schools better meet their responsibilities for educating gifted students? An adequate program of education for gifted children embodies identification, motivation, and development. Administrators and teachers, if they are to provide for individual aptitudes, must know what these are and how extensively they exist. Many of the same instruments and techniques used for studying children in general can be used to locate gifted pupils if constant vigilance is maintained.

School records, anecdotal materials, medical and psychological reports, case studies, leadership records, achievement data, home background information are all valuable sources of information. Tests of intelligence, special aptitude (academic and nonacademic), achievement, and other areas can prove useful.

Schools that already apply these instruments and procedures need only to reassess their results in order to know what else is needed to identify children with unusual potential. In some areas of endeavor, opportunities must be created for systematically testing and observing a child in a situation which will bring out his abilities. The unusual success in adult life of more than one thousand subjects in Lewis M. Terman's studies, published in 1947 by the Stanford University Press, attests to the ability to identify gifted children.

We know from past research that capacity alone is not enough to insure the development of giftedness. There must be both motivation and opportunity to use and develop these talents. Lack of motivation is a major reason why a large number of gifted children never go on for the advanced training essential to most professions. Differences in physical, emotional, and intellectual status of youngsters, as well as in their interests and the strength of their achievement motivation, will affect the development of their potential.

Some of these variations may be explained by home and family patterns, membership in ethnic or religious groups, peer-group relations, and home location. These are factors which, in most cases, are not within the control of the school. The school can, however, compensate for the effects of negative home and community experiences by instruction which enriches learning and offers challenge. Motivation can flower from a rich and flexible guidance program which helps superior children understand their own abilities in terms of their meaning for personal development and responsibilities to society.

Deterrents to achievement in terms of advanced training are

already well known. Schools have a responsibility beyond identifying those youngsters who are gifted and helping them make wise vocational and professional choices. Consider the child who comes from a home where there are no college aspirations or in which there are no concerns with professional preparation. Could not the school undertake early special counseling for the parents and their gifted child to point up the importance of advanced education?

Or, consider the promising child who lacks funds. Why could not the school and parents explore ways of securing financial assistance long before graduation? A school which is alert to the factors, including motivation, which affect post-high-school training can furnish special guidance early in the gifted child's career so that parents and the youngster are helped to understand his potential and are motivated toward taking necessary steps for its development.

GROUP STUDENTS ACCORDING TO ABILITY

While there are undoubtedly some situations which the school may not be able to modify, the quality of educational experiences is certainly within its province. Administratively, schools have acted in one or more ways to upgrade school life for the talented. The first method is grouping of students on the basis of special ability— that is, "segregation" or homogeneous grouping. The second approach is accelerating the progress of gifted students. The third, providing special opportunities and materials for talented children within the regular classroom—usually referred to as "enrichment."

Use of acceleration is urged in studies by Terman and Harvey C. Lehman which suggest that gifted students be enabled to complete formal schooling and engage in careers as early as possible, in view of our urgent manpower shortages. Ability grouping is found mainly in large cities where specialized high schools have been organized with a program designed for gifted students in a given talent area. Extracurricular activities may also improve the school life of the gifted.

Enrichment within the regular classroom is today the most widely supported and advertised of any of the administrative provisions, especially at the elementary level. It has been advocated on the basis that a flexible program within the heterogeneous group can stimulate the gifted child while keeping him with his social peers. Unlike special grouping, working with the gifted in the regular classroom requires relatively little extra expense and is possible even within small schools.

SPECIAL CLASSES SPEED PROGRESS

Various combinations of these administrative plans have been tested in public schools. Special progress classes in some systems allow for the completion of three years' work in two. In some elementary schools children are assigned for part of a day to their regular classroom and to a special enrichment class for the other part. College-level courses in some high schools have earned students admission with advanced standing to college, enabling them to complete their work in a shorter period of time or to take advanced work earlier.

Because these provisions acknowledge the special needs and particular abilities of the gifted, they help break the lockstep of identical experiences for all children. They emphasize the importance of flexibility in arranging for gifted children. Flexibility in time, class organization, instructional activities, materials, and requirements is practical in the public school.

We sometimes forget in our planning for gifted children that the range of individual differences is great, not only within a specific area of endowment, but from one talent area to another. No group of gifted children is homogeneous, any more than is any group of average children. These individual differences must be considered when administrators modify instructional programs which facilitate enriched experiences.

Schoolmen must ask the kinds of questions which will sharpen their insights into how each administrative provision can be used most effectively. Guide questions include: Where in the scope of the curriculum is acceleration most desirable? What bases provide for most satisfactory groupings? Which guidance procedures secure the best type of home-school cooperation from parents of gifted youngsters?

Enrichment for the gifted child is of particular concern to the public school because a curriculum which satisfies a large majority of children may not necessarily care for outstanding students. It is in instruction that offers experiences beyond grade expectations that individual emphasis of needs takes place.

For the gifted, good teaching procedures are those which enable the child to work independently as well as with others, to experiment with ideas and materials, to explore more widely in order to achieve greater mastery of content and skills, to experience numerous opportunities for creative expression.

Even when there is agreement that the public school has an obligation to develop individual capacities, many problems are manifest. What talents shall the school seek out to develop? Manpower studies emphasize the great need for scientists and engineers. Should the school focus its efforts in these directions or concern itself with a variety of aptitudes?

If there are indifferent or hostile attitudes in the community toward gifted children or toward specific talent areas, should school planners abandon their efforts? Leadership responsibility in the school and community must be assessed before curricular provisions for the gifted can be initiated and tested.

Inevitably, the budget enters our planning. Society must expect rewarding returns from the gifted child to warrant additional investment in his education.

There are problems of recognition, encouragement, and stimulation. How much of these does the child need to move him ahead? Does "well-adjusted" have the same meaning for gifted children as for those who are less able?

We know that the greatest loss in talent development is in the small school and it is there that a great deal of attention is needed. Should a well-balanced school program for the gifted child in small and large schools expect the talented musician to do well in mathematics and science as well?

To resolve these and other issues and problems takes time, hard thought, and intelligent experimentation. As with all effective educational programs, planning for the identification and nurture of gifted children demands the best possible contribution of many minds. Public schools can and have provided adequately for gifted children and others, particularly where their efforts have included community cooperation.

That there is a need for more adequate planning is unquestionable. A public-school system that has met the many challenges in educating so many children is certainly able to develop the flexibility and richness needed to meet the needs of the gifted children who will provide the intellectual, artistic, technological, and moral leadership of our nation.

2

IDENTIFYING

CHARACTERISTICS

⁓⚜⁓

THE DISCOVERY AND ENCOURAGEMENT OF EXCEPTIONAL TALENT

SOME CHARACTERISTICS OF CHILDREN DESIGNATED AS MENTALLY
RETARDED, AS PROBLEMS, AND AS GENIUSES BY TEACHERS

IDENTIFYING GIFTED CHILDREN

COUNSELLING PARENTS OF GIFTED CHILDREN

THE FOUR IQs

READING ABILITIES OF BRIGHT AND DULL CHILDREN
OF COMPARABLE MENTAL AGES

SOME SPECIAL-ABILITY TEST SCORES OF GIFTED CHILDREN

THE UPPER LIMIT OF ABILITY AMONG AMERICAN NEGROES

THE PRODUCTIVITY OF NATIONAL MERIT SCHOLARS
BY OCCUPATIONAL CLASS

THE MAINTENANCE OF INTELLECTUAL ABILITY IN GIFTED ADULTS

AGE AND ACHIEVEMENT

T HE PROBLEM of identifying gifted children has been one of the major obstacles in the path of those interested in "doing something for the gifted." The success of special programs is in large measure the result of their appropriateness for the selected groups. Some educators pay so little attention to identification that their efforts are wasted. This frequently occurs when educators, often new to the field, plan programs for students of extremely high ability and then find that such a population does not exist in their community. More frequently the problem is at the other extreme. The ability of students is often underestimated, even when the planners are in constant contact with them. Other workers spend so much time considering the problems of identification that they neglect plans for a constructive educational program.

The articles in this section were selected to help the reader understand the characteristics of the gifted and to gain some insight into the problems of identification. Specific examples of how gifted children are identified for special programs are found later in the sections describing these programs.

One of the reasons that identification of the gifted has been so difficult is that no one definition of giftedness has been universally accepted. It is important, therefore, to see how a particular author has defined giftedness. Some authors write about the individual who is superior in every conceivable characteristic; others write about those who enjoy specific talents. While individuals with general intellectual superiority make up most groups of "gifted" individuals, we are often in error trying to apply group statistics to any given individual. A major reason for our lack of knowledge about the gifted is our attempt to adhere too rigidly to a long list of characteristics of giftedness. The gifted as a group are certainly more homogeneous than the entire population and probably more homogeneous than the rest of the population, but within the gifted themselves there is great heterogeneity.

Using the average for children of the same sex and chronological age as a base, a composite list of the characteristics of gifted children follows:

1. Superior physique as demonstrated by earlier walking and talking; above-average height, weight, coordination, endurance, and general health.
2. Longer attention span.
3. Learns rapidly, easily, and with less repetition.
4. Learns to read sooner and continues to read at a consistently more advanced level.
5. More mature in the ability to express himself through the various communicative skills.
6. Reaches higher levels of attentiveness to his environment.
7. Asks more questions and really wants to know the causes and reasons for things.
8. Likes to study some subjects that are difficult because he enjoys the learning.
9. Spends time beyond the ordinary assignments or schedule on things that are of interest to him.
10. Knows about many things of which other children are unaware.
11. Is able to adapt learning to various situations somewhat unrelated in orientation.
12. Reasons out more problems since he recognizes relationships and comprehends meanings.
13. Analyzes quickly mechanical problems, puzzles, and trick questions.
14. Shows a high degree of originality and often uses good but unusual methods or ideas.
15. Possesses one or more special talents.
16. Is more adept in analyzing his own abilities, limitations, and problems.
17. Performs with more poise and can take charge of the situation.
18. Is not easily discouraged by failures.
19. Has more emotional stability.
20. Can judge the abilities of others.
21. Has diverse, spontaneous, and frequently self-directed interests.

While these 21 characteristics describe gifted children in general, they may not apply equally to all gifted children. There is no such thing as an accurate composite of a gifted child. Generally we expect gifted children as a group to have more positive and fewer negative characteristics, and they may acquire these characteristics both earlier and with more intensity. The intelligence of a child does not determine the degree to which he possesses these traits. Some individuals who are quite gifted may possess only a few of these characteristics. Such a list will not replace a good intelligence test for identifying a gifted child, but it will help identify him, or once he is identified, such a list might indicate areas where he is not fulfilling his potential.

Much success has been found by using only measured intelligence to define giftedness or intellectual talent. Even when this is the only criterion, the definitions vary widely in practice. Leta Hollingworth studied children with Stanford-Binet IQs above 180. The late Lewis Terman studied the top 1 percent of the population in his monumental longitudinal study in California. The gifted children in Cleveland's major work program represent about the top 5 percent. Now, following the lead of Robert Havighurst, major groups of educators are searching out the top 10 to 20 percent for special attention. We should expect to find some differences in the reports of Hollingworth and Havighurst because the populations they describe are different. In addition descriptive terms are not uniform.

A primary problem, then, in comparing the work of one author with another or with our own experience lies in definition and identification. The more similar the definition and methods of selection, the more valid will be the comparison.

Perhaps the best portrayal of the characteristics of the gifted was provided by the late Lewis Terman's classic thirty-year longitudinal study of 1500 gifted subjects, the results of which are summarized in "The Discovery and Encouragement of Exceptional Talent." Terman's study was the first extensive longitudinal study of gifted subjects. Since its beginning in May 1921 no other study of such a scope has provided such exhaustive evidence. (In 1951 Professor Donald E. Super began a Career Pattern Study, which will be another comprehensive longitudinal study, but comparable results will not be available until 1975.) It is possible, however, that Terman's group of 1500 subjects might not be representative of the top 1 percent of our population and that this sample might favor those with higher academic aptitudes and achievement. When the study started, it was not possible to screen the entire population with standardized tests. Terman used teacher nominations and age-grade placement for determining who should be given an individual intelligence test. Terman recognized the inadequacy of this method: "If one would identify the brightest child in a class of thirty to fifty pupils, it is better to consult the birth records in the class register than to ask the teacher's opinion." Yet he felt that he found at least 80 percent of the gifted in the school populations that were canvassed. It is generally believed that Terman's papers describing the characteristics of the gifted are perhaps the major contribution of the first half of the twentieth century to our understanding of the gifted. "The Discovery and Encouragement of Exceptional Talent" was presented on March 24, 1954, as the first Walter Van Dyke Bingham lecture and later appeared in the *American Psychologist.*

The second article, by W. Drayton Lewis, substantiates the belief that teacher's estimates are poor indications of the most intelligent pupils. In addition to revealing the teacher's problem of identifying the gifted, Lewis analyzes the characteristics of gifted, mentally retarded, and problem children as they were rated by teachers. Without extensive training one cannot identify intellectual capability without using intelligence tests. Supervisors in industry, armed-service personnel, and teachers all have equal difficulty. The correlation coefficient of teachers estimates with test data is about .50.

The general characteristics of a good program for identification are discussed by Robert DeHaan. This article draws heavily on DeHaan's experiences with Havighurst, Kough, and others in the Youth Development Project carried on in Quincy, Illinois, by the Committee on Human Development from the University of Chicago. In recent years, investigators have relied principally upon standardized tests. DeHaan and Kough developed a procedure for making "systematic observations" which will greatly facilitate the identification of students with special ability. DeHaan's article describes the main outline of a total program for the identification of gifted children, utilizing both standardized tests and the "systematic observation."

Some suggestions for the parents of gifted children are provided in the reading by Samuel R. Laycock. A lecturer and consultant on mental-health problems for the Canadian Mental Health Association and an emeritus professor of the University of Saskatchewan, Dr. Laycock set up and supervised Canada's second program of special classes for the gifted. In this article Dr. Laycock provides the basic assumptions necessary for counselors of parents of gifted children and enumerates three characteristics for a healthy personality and three needs that parents should impart to their gifted children. These suggestions form a framework for teachers and counselors to expand as they help parents to understand their children.

The more intangible factors affecting academic achievement, such as "inner quests, ideal qualities, and innate quirks," were examined by Edgar A. Doll, in a speech delivered to the Council for Exceptional Children. The material for this speech was drawn from Dr. Doll's rich experiences with the development of the Vineland Social Maturity Scale.

Some of the special abilities of the gifted are presented in articles by Emery P. Bliesmer and Frank T. Wilson. Dr. Bliesmer shows some of the differences found in the reading ability of bright and dull children with comparable mental ages. Using seven standardized tests, Dr. Wilson measured the artistic, musical, scientific, and mechanical talents of the highly gifted pupils in a special school and compared their scores with those of the norm groups. The general superiority of the gifted is shown in both studies.

Martin D. Jenkins has reported on the numbers of extremely intellectually capable American Negroes and their geographic distribution. His study suggests the impact of cultural and environmental considerations on intelligence. The influence of culture on "intelligence" is also implied in Horace Mann Bond's suggestive research on the home backgrounds of the first National Merit Scholarship winners.

The last two articles in this section pertain to the gifted adult. The maintenance, or perhaps the continued increase, of intellectual ability in the members of Terman's group will come as a surprise to many readers. This growth is not typical of the growth curves in many textbooks. Harvey C. Lehman's chapter from *Age and Achievement* has been included because so many authors and workers in the field refer to his monumental study of productivity. Dr. Lehman's personal interpretations should be particularly fruitful.

THE DISCOVERY AND ENCOURAGEMENT
OF EXCEPTIONAL TALENT

by Lewis M. Terman

My first introduction to the scientific problems posed by intellectual differences occurred well over a half-century ago when I was a senior in psychology at Indiana University and was asked to prepare two reports for a seminar, one on mental deficiency and one on genius. Up to that time, despite the fact that I had graduated from a normal college as a Bachelor of Pedagogy and had taught school for five years, I had never so much as heard of a mental test. The reading for those two reports opened up a new world to me, the world of Galton, Binet, and their contemporaries. The following year my MA thesis on leadership among children (10) was based in part on tests used by Binet in his studies of suggestibility.

Then I entered Clark University, where I spent considerable time during the first year in reading on mental tests and precocious children. Child prodigies, I soon learned, were at that time in bad repute because of the prevailing belief that they were usually psychotic or otherwise abnormal and almost sure to burn themselves out quickly or to develop postadolescent stupidity. "Early ripe, early rot" was a slogan frequently encountered. By the time I reached my last graduate year, I decided to find out for myself how precocious children differ from the mentally backward, and accordingly chose as my doctoral dissertation an experimental study of the intellectual processes of fourteen boys, seven of them picked as the brightest and seven as the dullest in a large city school (11). These subjects I put through a great variety of intelligence tests, some of them borrowed from Binet and others, many of them new. The tests were given individually and required a total of 40 or 50 hours for each subject. The experiment contributed little or nothing to science, but it contributed a lot to my future thinking. Besides "selling" me completely on the value of mental tests as a research

[Reprinted from the *American Psychologist,* June 1954, 221-230, with the permission of the American Psychological Association.]

method, it offered an ideal escape from the kinds of laboratory work which I disliked and in which I was more than ordinarily inept. (Edward Thorndike confessed to me once that *his* lack of mechanical skill was partly responsible for turning *him* to mental tests and to the kinds of experiments on learning that required no apparatus.)

However, it was not until I got to Stanford in 1910 that I was able to pick up with mental tests where I had left off at Clark University. By that time Binet's 1905 and 1908 scales had been published, and the first thing I undertook at Stanford was a tentative revision of his 1908 scale. This, after further revisions, was published in 1916. The standardization of the scale was based on tests of a thousand children whose IQs ranged from 60 to 145. The contrast in intellectual performance between the dullest and the brightest of a given age so intensified my earlier interest in the gifted that I decided to launch an ambitious study of such children at the earliest opportunity.

My dream was realized in the spring of 1921 when I obtained a generous grant from the Commonwealth Fund of New York City for the purpose of locating a thousand subjects of IQ 140 or higher. More than that number were selected by Stanford-Binet tests from the kindergarten through the eighth grade, and a group mental test given in 95 high schools provided nearly 400 additional subjects. The latter, plus those I had located before 1921, brought the number close to 1500. The average IQ was approximately 150, and 80 were 170 or higher (13).

The twofold purpose of the project was, first of all, to find what traits characterize children of high IQ, and secondly, to follow them for as many years as possible to see what kind of adults they might become. This meant that it was necessary to select a group representative of high-testing children in general. With the help of four field assistants, we canvassed a school population of nearly a quarter million in the urban and semi-urban areas of California. Two careful checks on the methods used showed that not more than 10 or 12 percent of the children who could have qualified for the group in the schools canvassed were missed. A sample of close to 90 percent insured that whatever traits were typical of these children would be typical of high-testing children in any comparable school population.

Time does not permit me to describe the physical measurements, medical examinations, achievement tests, character and interest tests, or the trait ratings and other supplementary information obtained from parents and teachers. Nor can I here describe the comparative data we obtained for control groups of unselected children. The more important results, however, can be stated briefly: children of IQ 140 or higher are, in general, appreciably superior to unselected children in physique, health, and social adjustment; markedly superior in moral attitudes as measured either by character tests or by trait ratings; and vastly superior in their mastery of school subjects as shown by a three-hour battery of achievement tests. In fact, the typical child of the group had mastered the school subjects to a point about two grades beyond the one in which he was enrolled, some of them three or four grades beyond. Moreover, his ability as evidenced by achievement in the different school subjects is so general as to refute completely the traditional belief that gifted children are usually one-sided. I take some pride in the fact that not one of the major conclusions we drew in the early 1920s regarding the traits that are typical of gifted children has been overthrown in the three decades since then.

Results of thirty years' follow-up of these subjects by field studies in 1927-1928, 1939-1940, and 1951-1952, and by mail follow-up at other dates, show that the incidence of mortality, ill health, insanity, and alcoholism is in each case below that for the generality of corresponding age, that the great majority are still well adjusted socially, and that the delinquency rate is but a fraction of what it is in the general population. Two forms of our difficult Concept Mastery Test, devised especially to reach into the stratosphere of adult intelligence, have been administered to all members of the group who could be visited by the field assistants, including some 950 tested in 1939-1940 and more than 1000 in 1951-1952. On both tests they scored on the average about as far above the generality of adults as they had scored above the generality of children when we selected them. Moreover, as Dr. Bayley and Mrs. Oden have shown, in the twelve-year interval between the two tests, 90 percent increased their intellectual stature as measured by this test. "Early ripe, early rot" simply does not hold for these subjects. So far, no one has developed postadolescent stupidity!

As for schooling, close to 90 percent entered college and 70 percent graduated. Of those graduating, 30 percent were awarded honors and about two thirds remained for graduate work. The educational record would have been still better but for the fact that a majority reached college age during the great depression. In their undergraduate years 40 percent of the men and 20 percent of the women earned half or more of their college expenses, and the total of undergraduate and graduate expenses earned amounted to $670,000, not counting stipends from scholarships and fellowships, which amounted to $350,000.

The cooperation of the subjects is indicated by the fact that we have been able to keep track of more than 98 percent of the original group, thanks to the rapport fostered by the incomparable field and office assistants I have had from the beginning of the study to the present. I dislike to think how differently things could have gone with helpers even a little less competent.

The achievement of the group to midlife is best illustrated by the case histories of the 800 men, since only a minority of the women have gone out for professional careers (15). By 1950, when the men had an average age of 40 years, they had published 67 books (46 in the fields of science, arts, and the humanities, and 21 books of fiction). They had published more than 1400 scientific, technical, and professional articles; over 200 short stories, novelettes, and plays; and 236 miscellaneous articles on a great variety of subjects. They had also authored more than 150 patents. The figures on publications do not include the hundreds of publications by journalists that classify as news stories, editorials, or newspaper columns; nor do they include the hundreds if not thousands of radio and television scripts.

The 800 men include 78 who have taken a Ph.D. degree or its equivalent, 48 with a medical degree, 85 with a law degree, 74 who are teaching or have taught in a four-year college or university, 51 who have done basic research in the physical sciences or engineering, and 104 who are engineers but have done only applied research or none. Of the scientists, 47 are listed in the 1949 edition of *American Men of Science*. Nearly all of these numbers are from 10 to 20 or 30 times as large as would be found for 800 men of corresponding age picked at random in the general population, and are sufficient answer to those who belittle the significance of IQ differences.

The follow-up of these gifted subjects has proved beyond question that tests of "general intelligence," given as early as six, eight, or ten years, tell a great deal about the ability to achieve either presently or 30 years hence. Such tests do not, however, enable us to predict what direction the achievement will take, and least of all do they tell us what personality factors or what accidents of fortune will affect the fruition of exceptional ability. Granting that both interest patterns and special aptitudes play important roles in the making of a gifted scientist, mathematician, mechanic, artist, poet, or musical composer, I am convinced that to achieve greatly in almost any field, the special talents have to be backed up by a lot of Spearman's g, by which is meant the kind of general intelligence that requires ability to form many sharply defined concepts, to manipulate them, and to perceive subtle relationships between them; in other words, the ability to engage in abstract thinking.

The study by Catharine Cox of the childhood traits of historical geniuses gives additional evidence regarding the role of general intelligence in exceptional achievement. That study was part of our original plan to investigate superior ability by two methods of approach: (a) by identifying and following living gifted subjects from childhood onward; and (b) by proceeding in the opposite direction and tracing the mature genius back to his childhood promise. With a second grant from the Commonwealth Fund, the latter approach got under way only a year later than the former and resulted in the magnum opus by Cox entitled *The Early Mental Traits of Three Hundred Geniuses* (1). Her subjects represented an unbiased selection from the top 510 in Cattell's objectively compiled list of the 1000 most eminent men of history. Cox and two able assistants then scanned some 3000 biographies in search of information that would throw light on the early mental development of these subjects. The information thus obtained filled more than 6000 typed pages. Next, three psychologists familiar with mental-age norms read the documentary evidence on all the subjects and estimated for each the IQ that presumably would be necessary to account for the intellectual behavior recorded for given chronological ages. Average of the three IQ estimates was used as the index of intelligence. In fact two IQs were estimated for each subject, one based on the evidence to age 17, and the other on evidence to the mid-twenties. The recorded evidence on development to age 17 varied from very little to an amount that yielded about as valid an IQ as a good intelligence test would give. Examples of the latter are Goethe, John Stuart Mill, and Francis Galton. It was the documentary information on Galton, which I summarized and published in 1917 (12), that decided me to prepare plans for the kind of study that was carried out by Cox. The average of estimated IQs for her 300 geniuses was 155, with many going as high as 175 and several as high as 200. Estimates below 120 occurred only when there was little biographical evidence about the early years.

It is easy to scoff at these post-mortem IQs, but as one of the three psychologists who examined the evidence and made the IQ ratings, I think the author's main conclusion is fully warranted; namely, that "the genius who achieves highest eminence is one whom intelligence tests would have identified as gifted in childhood."

Special attention was given the geniuses who had sometime or other been labeled as backward in childhood, and in every one of these cases the facts clearly contradicted the legend. One of them was Oliver Goldsmith, of whom his childhood teacher is said to have said "Never was so dull a boy." The fact is that little Oliver was writing clever verse at 7 years and at 8 was reading Ovid and Horace. Another was Sir Walter Scott, who at 7 not only read widely in poetry but was using correctly in his written prose such words as "melancholy" and "exotic." Other alleged childhood dullards included a number who disliked the usual diet of Latin and Greek but had a natural talent for science. Among these were the celebrated German chemist Justus von Liebig, the great English anatomist John Hunter, and the naturalist Alexander von Humboldt, whose name is scattered so widely over the maps of the world.

In the cases just cited one notes a tendency for the direction of later achievement to be foreshadowed by the interests and preoccupations of childhood. I have tried to determine how frequently this was true of the 100 subjects in Cox's group whose childhood was best documented. Very marked foreshadowing was noted in the case of more than half of the group, none at all in less than a fourth. Macaulay, for example, began his career as historian at the age of 6 with what he called a "Compendium of Universal History," filling a quire of paper before he lost interest in the project. Ben Franklin before the age of 17 had displayed nearly all the traits that characterized him in middle life: scientific curiosity, religious heterodoxy, wit and buffoonery, political and business shrewdness, and ability to write. At 11 Pascal was so interested in mathematics that his father thought it best to deprive him of books on this subject until he had first mastered Latin and Greek. Pascal secretly proceeded to construct a geometry of his own and covered the ground as far as the 32d proposition of Euclid. His father then relented. At 14 Leibnitz was writing on logic and philosophy and composing what he called "An Alphabet of Human Thought." He relates that at this age he took a walk one afternoon to consider whether he should accept the "doctrine of substantial forms."

Similar foreshadowing is disclosed by the case histories of my gifted subjects. A recent study of the scientists and nonscientists among our 800 gifted men (15) showed many highly significant differences between the early interests and social attitudes of those who became physical scientists and those who majored in the social sciences, law, or the humanities. Those in medical or biological sciences usually rated on such variables somewhere between the physical scientists and the nonscientists.

What I especially want to emphasize, however, is that both the evidence on early mental development of historical geniuses and that obtained by follow-up of gifted subjects selected in childhood by mental tests point to the conclusion that capacity to achieve far beyond the average can be detected early in life by a well-constructed ability test that is heavily weighted with the g factor. It remains to be seen how much the prediction of future achievement can be made more specific as to field by getting, in addition, measures of ability factors that are largely independent of g. It would seem that a 20-year follow-up of the thousands of school children who have been given Thurstone's test of seven "primary mental abilities" would help to provide the answer. At present the factor analysts don't agree on how many "primary" mental abilities there are, nor exactly on what they are. The experts in this field are divided into two schools. The British school, represented by Thomson, Vernon, and Burt, usually stop with the identification of at most three or four group factors in addition to g, while some representing the American school feed the scores of 40 or 50 kinds of tests into a hopper and manage to extract from them what they believe to be a dozen or fifteen separate factors. Members of the British school are as a rule very skeptical about the realities underlying the minor group factors. There are also American psychologists, highly skilled in psychometrics, who share this skepticism. It is to be hoped that further research will give us more information than we now have about the predictive value of the group factors. Until such information is available, the scores on group factors can contribute little to vocational guidance beyond what a good test of general intelligence will provide.

I have always stressed the importance of *early* discovery of exceptional abilities. Its importance is now highlighted by the facts Harvey Lehman has disclosed in his monumental studies of the relation between age and creative achievement (8). The striking thing about his age curves is how early in life the period of maximum creativity is reached. In nearly all fields of science, the best work is done between ages 25 and 35, and rarely later than 40. The peak productivity for works of lesser merit is usually reached 5 to 10 years later; this is true in some twenty fields of science, in philosophy, in most kinds of musical composition, in art, and in literature of many varieties. The lesson for us from Lehman's statistics is that the youth of high-achievement potential should be well trained for his life work before too many of his most creative years have been passed.

This raises the issue of educational acceleration for the gifted. It seems that the schools are more opposed to acceleration now than they were thirty years ago. The lockstep seems to have become more and more the fashion, notwithstanding the fact that practically everyone who has investigated the subject is against it. Of my gifted group, 29 percent managed to graduate from high school before the age of 16½ years (62 of these before 15½), but I doubt if so many would be allowed to do so now. The other 71 percent graduated between 16½ and 18½. We have compared the accelerated with the nonaccelerated on numerous case-history variables. The two groups differed very little in childhood IQ, their health records are equally good, and as adults they are equally well adjusted socially. More of the accelerates graduated from college, and on the average nearly a year and a half earlier than the nonaccelerates; they averaged higher in college grades and more often remained for graduate work. Moreover, the accelerates on the average married .7 of a year earlier, have a trifle lower divorce rate, and score just a little higher on a test of marital happiness (14). So far as college records of accelerates and nonaccelerates are concerned, our data closely parallel those obtained by the late Noel Keys (3) at the University of California and those by Pressey (9) and his associates at Ohio State University.

The Ford Fund for the Advancement of Education has awarded annually since 1951 some 400 college scholarships to gifted students who are not over 16½ years old, are a year or even two years short of high-school graduation, but show good evidence of ability to do college work. Three quarters of them are between 15½ and 16½ at the time of college entrance. A dozen colleges and universities accept these students and are keeping close track of their success. A summary of their records for the first year shows that they not only get higher grades than their classmates, who average about two years older, but that they are also equally well adjusted socially and participate in as many extracurricular activities (17). The main problem the boys have is in finding girls to date who are not too old for them! Some of them have started a campaign to remedy the situation by urging that more of these scholarships be awarded to girls.

The facts I have given do not mean that all gifted children should be rushed through school just as rapidly as possible. If that were done, a majority with an IQ of 140 could graduate from high school before the age of 15. I do believe, however, that such children should be promoted rapidly enough to permit college entrance by the age of 17 at latest, and that a majority would be better off to enter at 16. The exceptionally bright student who is kept with his age group finds little to challenge his intelligence and all too often develops habits of laziness that later wreck his college career. I could give you some choice examples of this in my gifted group. In the case of a college student who is preparing for a profession in science, medicine, law, or any field of advanced scholarship, graduation at 20 instead of the usual 22 means two years added to his professional career; or the two years saved could be used for additional training beyond the doctorate, if that were deemed preferable.

Learned and Wood (7) have shown by objective achievement tests in some forty Pennsylvania colleges how little correlation there is between the student's knowledge and the number of months or years of his college attendance. They found some beginning sophomores who had acquired more knowledge than some seniors near their graduation. They found similarly low correlations between the number of course units a student had in a given field and the amount he knew in that field. Some with only one year of Latin had learned more than others with three years. And, believe it or not, they even found boys just graduating from high school who had more knowledge of science than some college seniors who had majored in science and were about to begin teaching science in high schools! The sensible thing to do, it seems, would be to quit crediting the individual high school or the individual college and begin crediting the individual student. That, essentially, is what the Ford Fund scholarships are intended to encourage.

Instruments that permit the identification of gifted subjects are available in great variety and at nearly all levels from the primary grades to the graduate schools in universities. My rough guess is that at the present time tests of achievement in the school subjects are being given in this country to children below high school at a rate of perhaps ten or twelve million a year, and to high-school students another million or two. In addition, perhaps two million tests of intelligence are given annually in the elementary and high schools. The testing of college students began in a small way only 30 years ago; now almost every college in the country requires applicants for admission to take some kind of aptitude test. This is usually a test of general aptitude, but subject-matter tests and tests of special aptitudes are sometimes given to supplement the tests of general aptitude.

The testing movement has also spread rapidly in other countries, especially in Britain and the Commonwealth countries. Godfrey Thomson devised what is now called the Moray House test of intelligence in 1921 to aid in selecting the more gifted 11-year-olds in the primary schools for the privilege of free secondary education. This test has been revised and is given annually to about a half million scholarship candidates. The Moray House tests now include tests of English, arithmetic, and history. In 1932 the Scottish Council for Research in Education (18) arranged to give the Moray House test of intelligence (a group test) to all the 90,000 children in Scotland who were born in 1921, and actually tested some 87,000 of them. The Stanford-Binet tests have been translated and adapted for use in nearly all the countries of Europe and in several countries of Asia and Latin America. Behind the Iron Curtain, however, mental tests are now banned.

I have discussed only tests of intelligence and of school achievement. There is time to mention only a few of the many kinds of personality tests that have been developed during the last thirty-five years: personality inventories, projective techniques by the dozen, attitude scales by the hundred, interest tests, tests of psychotic and predelinquent tendencies, tests of leadership, marital aptitude, masculinity-femininity, and so on. The current output of research on personality tests probably equals or exceeds that on intelligence and achievement tests, and is even more exciting.

Along with the increasing use of tests, and perhaps largely as a result of it, there is a growing interest, both here and abroad, in improving educational methods for the gifted. Acceleration of a year or two or three, however desirable, is but a fraction of what is needed to keep the gifted child or youth working at his intellectual best. The method most often advocated is curriculum enrichment for the gifted without segregating them from the ordinary class. Under ideal conditions enrichment can accomplish much, but in these days of crowded schools, when so many teachers are overworked, underpaid, and inadequately trained, curriculum enrichment for a few gifted in a large mixed class cannot begin to solve the problem. The best survey of thought and action in this field of education is the book entitled *The Gifted Child,* written by many authors and published in 1951 (16). In planning for and sponsoring this book, The American Association for Gifted Children has rendered a great service to education.

But however efficient our tests may be in discovering exceptional talents, and whatever the schools may do to foster those discovered, it is the prevailing *Zeitgeist* that will decide, by the rewards it gives or withholds, what talents will come to flower. In Western Europe of the Middle Ages, the favored talents were those that served the Church by providing its priests, the architects of its cathedrals, and the painters of religious themes. A few centuries later the same countries had a renaissance that included science and literature as well as the arts. Although presumably there are as many potential composers of great music as there ever were, and as many potentially great artists as in the days of Leonardo da Vinci and Michaelangelo, I am reliably informed that in this country today it is almost impossible for a composer of *serious* music to earn his living except by teaching, and that the situation is much the same, though somewhat less critical, with respect to artists.

The talents most favored by the current *Zeitgeist* are those that can contribute to science and technology. If intelligence and achievement tests do not discover the potential scientist, there is a good chance that the annual Science Talent Search will, though not until the high-school years. Since Westinghouse inaugurated in 1942 this annual search for the high-school seniors most likely to become creative scientists, nearly 4000 boys and girls have been picked for honors by Science Service out of the many thousands who have competed. As a result, "Science Clubs of America" now number 15,000 with a third of a million members—a twentyfold increase in a dozen years (2). As our need for more and better scientists is real and urgent, one can rejoice at what the talent search and the science clubs are accomplishing. One may regret, however, that the spirit of the times is not equally favorable to the discovery and encouragement of potential poets, prose writers, artists, statesmen, and social leaders.

But in addition to the over-all climates that reflect the *Zeitgeist,* there are localized climates that favor or hinder the encouragement of given talents in particular colleges and universities. I have in mind especially two recent investigations of the differences among colleges in the later achievement of their graduates. One by Knapp and Goodrich (4) dealt with the undergraduate origin of 18,000 scientists who got the bachelor's degree between 1924 and 1934 and were listed in the 1944 edition of *American Men of Science.* The list of 18,000 was composed chiefly of men who had taken a Ph.D. degree, but included a few without a Ph.D. who were starred scientists. The IBM cards for these men were then sorted according to the college from which they obtained the bachelor's degree, and an index of productivity was computed for each college in terms of the proportion of its male graduates who were in the list of 18,000. Some of the results were surprising, not to say sensational. The institutions that were most productive of future scientists between 1924 and 1934 were not the great universities, but the small liberal arts colleges. Reed College topped the list with an index of 132 per thousand male graduates. The California Institute of Technology was second with an index of 70. Kalamazoo College was third with 66, Earlham fourth with 57, and Oberlin fifth with 56. Only a half-dozen of the great universities were in the top fifty with a productivity index of 25 or more.

The second study referred to was by Knapp and Greenbaum (5), who rated educational institutions according to the proportion of their graduates who received certain awards at the graduate level in the six-year period from 1946 to 1951. Three kinds of awards were considered: a Ph.D. degree, a graduate scholarship or fellowship paying at least $400 a year, or a prize at the graduate level won in open competition. The roster of awardees they compiled in-

THE DISCOVERY OF EXCEPTIONAL TALENT • 53

cluded 7000 students who had graduated from 377 colleges and universities. This study differs from the former in three respects: (a) it deals with recent graduates, who had not had time to become distinguished but who could be regarded as good bets for the future; (b) these good bets were classified according to whether the major field was science, social science, or the humanities; and (c) data were obtained for both sexes, though what I shall report here relates only to men. In this study the great universities make a better showing than in the other, but still only a dozen of them are in the top fifty institutions in the production of men who are good bets. In the top ten, the University of Chicago is third, Princeton is eighth, and Harvard is tenth; the other seven in order of rank are Swarthmore 1, Reed 2, Oberlin 4, Haverford 5, California Institute of Technology 6, Carleton 7, and Antioch 9. When the schools were listed separately for production of men who were good bets in science, social science, and the humanities, there were eight that rated in the top twenty on all three lists. These were Swarthmore, Reed, Chicago, Harvard, Oberlin, Antioch, Carleton, and Princeton.

The causes of these differences are not entirely clear. Scores on aptitude tests show that the intelligence of students in a given institution is by no means the sole factor, though it is an important one. Other important factors are the quality of the school's intellectual climate, the proportion of able and inspiring teachers on its faculty, and the amount of conscious effort that is made not only to discover but also to motivate the most highly gifted. The influence of motivation can hardly be exaggerated.

In this address I have twice alluded to the fact that achievement in school is influenced by many things other than the sum total of intellectual abilities. The same is true of success in life. In closing I will tell you briefly about an attempt we made a dozen years ago to identify some of the nonintellectual factors that have influenced life success among the men in my gifted group. Three judges, working independently, examined the records (to 1940) of the 730 men who were then 25 years old or older, and rated each on life success. The criterion of "success" was the extent to which a subject had made use of his superior intellectual ability, little weight being given to earned income. The 150 men rated highest for success and the 150 rated lowest were then compared on some 200 items of information obtained from childhood onward (14). How did the two groups differ?

During the elementary school years, the As and Cs (as we call them) were almost equally successful. The average grades were about the same, and average scores on achievement tests were only a trifle higher for the As. Early in high school the groups began to draw apart in scholarship, and by the end of high school the slump of the Cs was quite marked. The slump could not be blamed on extracurricular activities, for these were almost twice as common among the As. Nor was much of it due to difference in intelligence. Although the As tested on the average a little higher than the Cs both in 1922 and 1940, the average score made by the Cs in 1940 was high enough to permit brilliant college work, in fact was equaled by only 15 percent of our highly selected Stanford students. Of the As, 97 percent entered college and 90 percent graduated; of the Cs, 68 percent entered but only 37 percent graduated. Of those who graduated, 52 percent of the As but only 14 percent of the Cs graduated with honors. The As were also more accelerated in school; on the average they were six months younger on completing the eighth grade, ten months younger at high school graduation, and fifteen months younger at graduation from college.

The differences between the educational histories of the As and Cs reflect to some degree the differences in their family backgrounds. Half of the A fathers but only 15 percent of the C fathers were college graduates, and twice as many of A siblings as of C siblings graduated. The estimated number of books in the A homes was nearly 50 percent greater than in the C homes. As of 1928, when the average age of the subjects was about 16 years, more than twice as many of the C parents as of A parents had been divorced.

Interesting differences between the groups were found in the childhood data on emotional stability, social adjustments, and various traits of personality. Of the 25 traits on which each child was rated by parent and teacher in 1922 (18 years before the A and C groups were made up), the only trait on which the Cs averaged as high as the As was general health. The superiority of the As was especially marked in four volitional traits: prudence, self-confidence, perseverance, and desire to excel. The As also rated significantly higher in 1922 on leadership, popularity, and sensitiveness to approval or disapproval. By 1940 the difference between the groups in social adjustment and all-round mental stability had greatly increased and showed itself in many ways. By that time four fifths of the As had married, but only two thirds of the Cs, and the divorce rate for those who had married was twice as high for the Cs as for the As. Moreover, the As made better marriages; their wives on the average came from better homes, were better educated, and scored higher on intelligence tests.

But the most spectacular differences between the two groups came from three sets of ratings, made in 1940, on a dozen personality traits. Each man rated himself on all the traits, was rated on them by his wife if he had a wife, and by a parent if a parent was still living. Although the three sets of ratings were made independently, they agreed unanimously on the four traits in which the A and C groups differed most widely. These were "persistence in the accomplishment of ends," "integration toward goals, as contrasted with drifting," "self-confidence," and "freedom from inferiority feelings." For each trait three critical ratios were computed showing, respectively, the reliability of the A-C differences in average of self-ratings, ratings by wives, and ratings by parents. The average of the three critical ratios was 5.5 for perseverance, 5.6 for integration toward goals, 3.7 for self-confidence, and 3.1 for freedom from inferiority feelings. These closely parallel the traits that Cox found to be especially characteristic of the 100 leading geniuses in her group whom she rated on many aspects of personality; their three outstanding traits she defined as "persistence of motive and effort," "confidence in their abilities," and "strength or force of character."

There was one trait on which only the parents of our A and C men were asked to rate them; that trait was designated "common sense." As judged by parents, the As are again reliably superior, the A-C difference in average rating having a critical ratio of 3.9. We are still wondering what self-ratings by the subjects and ratings of them by their wives on common sense would have shown if we had been imprudent enough to ask for them!

Everything considered, there is nothing in which our A and C groups present a greater contrast than in drive to achieve and in all-round mental and social adjustment. Our data do not support the theory of Lange-Eichbaum (6) that great achievement usually stems from emotional tensions that border on the abnormal. In our gifted group, success is associated with stability rather than instability, with absence rather than with presence of disturbing conflicts— in short with well-balanced temperament and with freedom from excessive frustrations. The Lange-Eichbaum theory may explain a

Hitler, but hardly a Churchill; the junior senator from Wisconsin, possibly, but not a Jefferson or a Washington.

At any rate, we have seen that intellect and achievement are far from perfectly correlated. To identify the internal and external factors that help or hinder the fruition of exceptional talent, and to measure the extent of their influences, are surely among the major problems of our time. These problems are not new; their existence has been recognized by countless men from Plato to Francis Galton. What is new is the general awareness of them caused by the man-power shortage of scientists, engineers, moral leaders, statesmen, scholars, and teachers that the country must have if it is to survive in a threatened world. These problems are now being investigated on a scale never before approached, and by a new generation of workers in several related fields. Within a couple of decades vastly more should be known than we know today about our resources of potential genius, the environmental circumstances that favor its expression, the emotional compulsions that give it dynamic quality, and the personality distortions that can make it dangerous.

REFERENCES

1. Cox, Catharine C. *The Early Mental Traits of Three Hundred Geniuses.* Vol. II of *Genetic Studies of Genius,* L. M. Terman (ed.). Stanford: Stanford Univ. Press, 1926.
2. Davis, W. Cummunicating Science. *J. Atomic Scientists,* 1953, 337-340.
3. Keys, N. The Underage Student in High School and College. *Univ. Calif. Publ. Educ.,* 7, 1938, 145-272.
4. Knapp, R. H., and H. B. Goodrich. *Origins of American Scientists.* Chicago: Univ. Chicago Press, 1952.
5. Knapp, R. H., and J. J. Greenbaum. *The Younger American Scholar: His Collegiate Origins.* Chicago: Univ. Chicago Press, 1953.
6. Lange-Eichbaum, W. *The Problem of Genius.* New York: The Macmillan Co., 1932.
7. Learned, W. S., and B. D. Wood. The Student and His Knowledge. *Carnegie Found. Adv. Teaching Bull.,* 29, 1938.
8. Lehman, H. C. *Age and Achievement.* Princeton, N.J.: Princeton Univ. Press, 1953.
9. Pressey, S. L. *Educational Acceleration: Appraisals and Basic Problems.* Columbus: Ohio State Univ. Press, 1949.
10. Terman, L. M. A Preliminary Study in the Psychology and Pedagogy of Leadership. *Pedag. Sem.,* 11, 1904, 413-451.

11. ⸺ Genius and Stupidity: A Study of Some of the Intellectual Processes of Seven "Bright" and Seven "Dull" Boys. *Pedag. Sem.,* 13, 1906, 307-373.

12. ⸺ The Intelligence Quotient of Francis Galton in Childhood. *Amer. J. Psychol.,* 28, 1917, 209-215.

13. ⸺ (ed.) *et al. Mental and Physical Traits of a Thousand Gifted Children.* Vol. I of *Genetic Studies of Genius,* L. M. Terman (ed.). Stanford: Stanford Univ. Press, 1925.

14. ⸺ and M. H. Oden. *The Gifted Child Grows Up.* Vol. IV of *Genetic Studies of Genius,* L. M. Terman (ed.). Stanford: Stanford Univ. Press, 1947.

15. ⸺ Scientists and Nonscientists in a Group of 800 Gifted Men. *Psychol. Monogr.,* 68, 1954, in press.

16. Witty, P. (ed.). *The Gifted Child.* Boston: Heath, 1951.

17. *Bridging the Gap between School and College.* New York: The Fund for the Advancement of Education, 1953.

18. *The Intelligence of Scottish Children.* Scottish Council for Research in Education. London: Univ. London Press, 1933.

SOME CHARACTERISTICS OF CHILDREN DESIGNATED AS MENTALLY RETARDED, AS PROBLEMS, AND AS GENIUSES BY TEACHERS

by W. Drayton Lewis

SOUTHWESTERN LOUISIANA INSTITUTE

Teachers and specialists in child behavior are not always in agreement regarding children to be designated as problems, as retarded, and as geniuses. The data of this study present a picture of some factors which were influential in leading teachers to apply these designations to their pupils. The data here presented are of unusual value because they give the viewpoints of a representative cross section of elementary-school teachers of this country.

[Reprinted from the *Journal of Genetic Psychology,* 20, March 1947, 29-51, with the permission of The Journal Press and the author.]

The committee known as Coordinated Studies in Education, Incorporated,* secured data relative to elementary-school children from many widely separated localities. The data were gathered from 36 states, 310 communities, and 455 schools in the United States and include an elementary-school population slightly in excess of 45,000 found in grades 4 to 8, inclusive. Each child was given the Kuhlmann-Anderson Test, the Unit Scales of Attainment Battery Achievement Test, and the BPC Personal Inventory. They also were rated as to home and family background, father's occupation, economic status of the family, parental attitude toward child and home, and on the basis of 70 personality traits, 10 extracurricular activities, and 21 hobbies.

The following instructions were given to the teachers:

In the R column put a check mark for any child you class as extremely mentally retarded; in the G column check any child you rate as a genius; in the P column check any child you rate as a distinct problem.

It is important to note that no definitions were given of these three classifications. This means that the teachers were giving their judgments not only as to the children to be classified under the three headings but also as to what is a mentally retarded child, a genius, or a distinct problem.

This study deals with children whom teachers have selected as mentally retarded, geniuses, or as distinct problems. The writer believes that this gives the data unusual value since it makes possible the determination, to some degree, of the characteristics which ordinary classroom teachers believe differentiate these three groups of children. Norms also are available on unselected children from the same groups and these make possible a comparison of the teacher-selected groups with "average" children in the same grades and schools.

The teachers selected 3359 pupils, 2138 boys and 1221 girls, as retarded mentally. This is 7.3 percent of all the pupils, or 8.8 percent of the boys and 5.6 percent of the girls. The problem group is made up of 2041 children, 1567 boys and 474 girls, which is 4.4 percent of all the children, or 6.5 percent of the boys and 2.1 percent of

* The writer wishes to acknowledge his indebtedness to the Advisory Committee of Coordinated Studies in Education, Incorporated. He also acknowledges his indebtedness to Dr. William McGehee and Dr. Ruth Moncreiff who first worked up the data on retarded and problem children.

the girls. The teachers selected very few children as geniuses—the group includes only 341 children, 158 boys and 183 girls. Thus, only 0.74 percent of all children were selected as geniuses, 0.65 percent of the boys and 0.83 percent of the girls.

Sex differences are evident in these selections. A superior adjustment of the girls to the school situation, or, inversely, an inferior adjustment of the boys is indicated. Of the retarded group 63 percent are boys, 37 percent are girls. The boys appear to even greater disadvantage in the problem group: 77 percent are boys and only 23 percent girls. Thus, 3.3 times as many boys as girls are designated as problems. This is probably very close to the average of other studies, although in some the differences are as great as four or five to one. These sex differences indicate that boys do not find that the present elementary school setup meets their needs. Several explanations might be offered: the curriculum may be better adapted to the girls, the boys may be handicapped by a slower rate of mental development, the preponderance of women teachers may be unfavorable to the boys, girls may be less aggressive and more inclined to conform to the school situation, boys may have been conditioned by adults against school, and, accordingly, not expect to be happy in school.

The differences are not so unfavorable to the boys of the genius group, composed of 46.5 percent boys and 53.5 percent girls. This is the most favorable consideration the boys receive but even so the percentages are lower than those reported in other studies. Terman and Burks (7, p. 778) have summarized the finding of studies relative to the sex distribution of gifted children and, in each case, more boys than girls are found. Witty's study showed a ratio of 104 boys to 100 girls, Goddard's 109 boys to 100 girls but, in other studies, the ratios are from 121 to 100 to 135 to 100 for elementary-school pupils. The writer (2, pp. 12-13), dealing with the same population of elementary-school pupils which is involved in this study, found that superior girls outnumbered superior boys 144.5 to 100. It must be recognized that these differences may be to some degree a function of the measuring instrument employed, the Kuhlmann-Anderson Test. It is necessary to recognize, I believe, that intelligence tests do not give reliable measures of sex differences (5, pp. 305-306).

Table 1 shows that each group is composed of a rather wide distribution of mental ability. Even though the teachers were instructed to check those who were "extremely mentally retarded," it is apparent that many are designated as retarded who are shown not to be so by the standardized test. McGehee (3, pp. 5-6) has shown that only 52 percent of this group fall within the lowest 10 percent in intelligence. That is, 48 percent of this teacher-designated group can scarcely be regarded as mentally retarded and certainly not as "extremely mentally retarded." It is to be noted that some of these retarded children are average or, in exceptional cases, even superior in ability as indicated by the test.

The genius group shows an equal range of mental ability: 57 percent of this group fall within the upper 10 percent in mental ability, that is, attained intelligence quotients higher than the

TABLE 1

The Percentage Distribution of the Intelligence Quotients of Normative, Retarded, Problem, and Genius Children

IQ Range	Norm	Retarded	Problem	Genius
120 and above	5.4	.2	2.3	39.7
110-119	19.2	.7	6.3	33.2
90-109	55.7	25.3	42.9	22.2
80-89	13.9	37.2	27.0	2.9
70-79	4.6	25.5	15.3	1.4
Below 70	1.2	11.6	6.2	.6

lower limits of the upper 10 percent (2, p. 15). Thus, 43 percent of the group designated as geniuses are not of superior mental ability as measured by the standardized intelligence test. There are at least three possible interpretations of this: (1) the teachers did not interpret the term, genius, as applying solely to superior mental ability; (2) teachers may have been very poor judges of the mental capacities of their pupils (1, pp. 46-47); (3) the test scores may have underrated many of the children because of any one of a number of things that influence test results, namely, emotional disturbances, illness, and the like. These data appear to offer some grounds for concluding that teachers fail at times to judge correctly the potential learning capacity of their pupils. This does not necessarily imply a lack of ability on the part of the teachers. Their judgments must be based very largely on the pupil's classroom achievements which may or may not correlate closely with measured ability.

Low intelligence, it is evident, is only one factor in problem behavior. Only 48 percent fall in which might be called the dull and retarded groups, that is, have intelligence quotients below 90. Over half of this group, 51.5 percent, have at least average ability or better. A few fall definitely in the superior group.

Both the retarded and problem groups are retarded relative to chronological age. They are, as a group, older than the average child in this study. The retardation of the mentally retarded group is approximately twice that of the problem group. In other words, the average retardation of the problem group for both boys and girls is 0.75 years whereas the retardation of the retarded group averages 1.55 years for the boys and 1.45 for the girls. The genius group is accelerated to some degree since the boys of this group average 0.4 years and the girls 0.26 years younger than the average for their grades.

PERSONALITY CHARACTERISTICS

Teachers were asked to rate their pupils on 70 personality traits. These ratings were to be made before any tests were given in order that the ratings would not be influenced by test results. The following instructions were given.

There are two columns just beneath this. In the one to the right there are 70 personality traits or general characteristics. Study these points carefully and in the large blank column put the numbers of the traits or characteristics which are *most* descriptive of each child in your estimation. You can pick out at least five of these for almost any child; you probably should not pick out more than 10 or 12. Be sure to rate each child; and be sure that all characteristics noted for each child are outstandingly descriptive of him.

The 70 traits were rated by 50 mental hygienists and composite evaluations were obtained, ratings from 1 to 5 being assigned. A rating of 5 indicates that the trait is regarded as having definite hygienic value, a rating of 1 as being definitely undesirable or very harmful to the mental health of the child. The purpose of this phase of the study is to investigate the personality traits which are most frequently assigned to each of the three groups of children—genius, problem, and mentally retarded.

The traits listed in Table 2 are those considered by mental hygienists as being those of the 70 traits having the most definite hygienic value. It is noteworthy that in every instance the genius group is assigned the trait more frequently than the normative group and that both the retarded and problem groups are assigned the traits less frequently than the normative group. The genius

TABLE 2

The Percentage of Normative, Genius, Retarded, and Problem Children Assigned Traits Which Are Rated by Mental Hygienists as Having Definite Hygienic Value

Trait	Norm	Genius	Retarded	Problem
		BOYS		
Dependable	31.1	60.8	10.5	6.3
Friendly	32.5	47.1	13.9	12.0
Happy	37.8	49.6	22.6	16.7
Honest	32.5	42.8	17.9	10.8
Likes jokes	19.4	30.4	10.2	11.9
Original	10.0	45.8	1.4	4.9
Self-controlled	6.9	9.2	2.3	.9
Self-reliant	8.0	21.1	1.3	2.6
		GIRLS		
Dependable	42.2	73.0	16.3	9.6
Friendly	36.4	58.6	12.4	11.5
Happy	43.4	53.8	24.6	16.5
Honest	37.0	51.2	22.0	13.4
Likes jokes	12.6	17.6	6.4	6.3
Original	10.9	47.6	.7	3.8
Self-controlled	9.1	11.2	3.4	2.0
Self-reliant	10.0	21.3	1.1	2.1

group is, in no instance, assigned a given trait less than twice as frequently as either the retarded or problem group. The traits on which the teachers rated the groups as differing the least are *happy, friendly,* and *honest.* The greatest differences are found on the traits *dependable, original,* and *self-reliant.* Again, the problem group is assigned these eight most desirable traits less frequently than the retarded group, with two exceptions. These two exceptions are *original* and *self-reliant.* All of these differences are large enough to be statistically reliable except when the retarded and problem groups are compared on *friendliness* and *likes jokes* and

the genius and normative groups are compared on *self-control.*
Table 3 presents ratings of the various groups on traits which
were given a ranking of four by mental hygienists, indicating that
the traits have some hygienic value but not as much as some others.
A perusal of the table reveals that the genius group is again accred-

TABLE 3

*The Percentage of Normative, Genius, Retarded, and Problem
Children Assigned Traits Which Are Rated as Having Some
Hygienic Value But Not as Much as Some Others*

Trait	Norm	Genius	Retarded	Problem
		BOYS		
Adventuresome	14.2	29.8	5.9	15.0
Ambitious	21.7	66.1	4.5	6.3
Artistic	7.3	29.1	4.2	4.0
Energetic	24.4	31.6	14.8	19.8
Generous	17.0	24.2	10.4	6.7
Investigative	11.7	44.0	2.0	4.3
Leader	7.2	31.0	1.3	3.6
Persistent	12.4	16.1	6.1	3.1
Polite	32.2	34.6	20.3	10.2
Precocious	3.4	38.4	.2	2.1
Systematic	3.1	13.6	.6	.9
		GIRLS		
Adventuresome	8.1	28.5	1.7	8.0
Ambitious	33.9	75.6	5.4	9.9
Artistic	15.6	41.1	5.8	6.8
Energetic	21.2	32.0	10.4	14.6
Generous	21.8	32.0	15.2	10.9
Investigative	7.5	22.4	.9	3.7
Leader	9.9	38.4	1.7	4.2
Persistent	15.3	25.2	7.0	7.1
Polite	44.1	38.4	32.0	19.2
Precocious	4.3	34.2	.2	3.5
Systematic	6.1	10.4	1.7	1.9

ited with possessing these desirable traits to a greater degree than
any of the other three groups. The children of the genius group are
rated as possessing these traits at least twice as frequently as the retarded and problem children with the exception of *energetic,* where
the ratio drops to 1.6 to 1.

The children who were selected as geniuses are assigned six

of these traits from 7 to 15 times as frequently as the other two groups. The distinctive characteristics of the genius group are *ambitious, artistic, investigative, leader, precocious,* and *systematic*. All the differences are statistically reliable, as far as the genius group is concerned when compared with the other groups, except for *physically energetic, generous,* and *persistent* in the case of the boys, and *polite* in the case of the girls.

The problem group compares much more favorably with the retarded group on the traits rated 4 than it does on the most desirable traits. They are rated as manifesting seven of these traits more frequently than the retarded group. These traits are *adventuresome, ambitious, artistic, energetic physically, investigative, leader,* and *precocious*. The differences between the retarded and the problem groups are mathematically reliable except in the case of *artistic* and *systematic* for both boys and girls, and *persistent* for girls. There is no definite clue here as to why these children were selected as problems.

The retarded group rates inferior to both the normative and the genius groups on every one of these traits and the differences are large enough to be statistically reliable. The same is true of the problem group except on the trait *adventuresome*.

Nine traits were rated by the mental hygienists as having no particular significance. The distribution of these traits is significant in revealing what teachers have in mind when they designate certain children as problems. Two of these traits are rated as being particularly characteristic of genius children but the differences are small and not reliable. These traits are *sympathetic* and *tidy,* traits which will probably attract favorable attention from teachers. These traits are assigned relatively infrequently to the problem group.

The relative great frequency with which the problem groups are checked as *disturbing class* gives an important clue to why they are listed as problems. Other traits in this group which are assigned more frequently to problem children are *domineering—but not cruel, sex-conscious, talkative, uses tobacco, whispering, writes notes*. These differences are statistically reliable in all cases when comparisons are made with the normative group. The same is true when the four groups are compared on *disturbing class* and *talkative, verbose* for both boys and girls, *domineering,* excepting the genius group, and *tidy* in the case of the girls. These are all traits which are apt to antagonize the teacher and turn her against the child.

We see here the difference in the attitudes of teachers and mental hygienists toward problem children. Mental hygienists rate these traits as being of no particular significance, yet the fact that the teachers assign certain of them to problem children with so much greater frequency indicates that teachers believe that the traits are sufficiently important to designate certain children as problems.

The differences between the retarded and normative groups are not so striking. Both boys and girls of the retarded group are rated as *disturbing class* more and as being more *sex-conscious*. The differences are statistically reliable for both boys and girls, on the latter trait, and for the boys on the first-named trait. The retarded boys *use tobacco* more. This difference is also reliable. The retarded girls are significantly less *domineering* and both boys and girls are significantly less *sympathetic* and *tidy* than the average.

Equally significant differences are found when the groups are compared relative to those traits rated as undesirable or harmful by mental hygienists. A number of these traits are accredited to the genius group, as compared with the normative group, so much less frequently as to give statistically reliable differences. These traits, in the case of both boys and girls, are *daydreaming, disobedient, dull, immature, inattentive in class, irregular in school attendance, lack of interest in work, lazy, "quitter," "sissy or tomboy,"* and *suggestible,* in the case of boys only, *cute* or *"cocky," rude, self-conscious, slovenly* or *dirty,* and in the case of the girls only, *sickly.* It is to be noted that these are traits the absence of which tends to make for successful school adjustment. The only traits with which they are accredited more frequently than the normative group are *impatient with others, overcritical of others,* and *selfish,* but these differences are not great enough to yield statistical reliability.

Traits which appear to be definitely characteristic of the retarded group, that is, they are assigned to this group with sufficiently greater frequency to provide statistically reliable differences, are *daydreaming, dull and mentally sluggish, lack of interest in work, lazy, nervous* or *restless,* and *slovenly* or *dirty.* There are, in addition, other traits which are assigned to the retarded group with sufficiently greater frequency than to any other group except the problem group to give statistically significant differences. These traits are *cheating, destructive, disobedient, immature, inattentive in class, irregular in school attendance, lying, quarrelsome, "quitter," stubborn,* and *tardiness.*

Traits in this group which distinguish the problem group from the normative and genius groups, since the differences are statistically reliable, are, for both boys and girls, *cheating, cute* or *"cocky," destructive, disobedient, impetuous in own actions, impatient with others, lying, nervous or restless, overcritical of others, pouting* or *resentful, profane, quarrelsome, rude* or *defiant, selfish, stubborn, temper tantrums,* and, for the boys only, *"sissy,"* and *stealing.* It is to be noted that, almost without exception, these are traits which would tend to bring the child into conflict with the teacher. It seems evident that here, in part at least, we have a major reason for the selection of these children as problems.

Five traits—*cruel, bully type; dishonest* or *unreliable; oversensitive about self; unhappy, depressed, moody; will not work or play with others*—were rated 1 by the mental hygienists. This means that they were considered as being definitely or unequivocally undesirable or very harmful to the mental health of the child. The teachers did not assign these traits to very many children, the highest percentages in the normative group being *cruel* or *bully type,* 11.2 percent for boys, and *oversensitive about self* to about 10 percent of both boys and girls. These traits were assigned to the genius group relatively infrequently and the only statistically reliable difference is on the trait, *oversensitive about self,* which is less characteristic of this group than of any other.

These traits are more characteristic of the retarded group than of either the normative or genius group. Differences are statistically reliable on the following traits: *unhappy* or *depressed,* and *will not work or play with others,* both boys and girls; *dishonest,* boys; and *oversensitive about self,* girls.

Two traits are characteristic of the problem group, *cruel, bully type,* and *dishonest* or *unreliable.* These traits were assigned to them more than twice as often as to any other group and the differences are reliable. They also are credited with the traits, *unhappy, depressed* and *will not work or play with others* with a mathematically reliable greater frequency than the normative group.

Table 4* reveals positive factors which operated in the selection of the three groups. Every trait found in the list of the 10 most fre-

* Tables 4, 5, 6, and 7 have been omitted in reprinting.

quently assigned to the genius group is rated by the mental hygienists as having definite hygienic value, with one exception. This exception is *tidy*, for girls, and would no doubt be rated very high by teachers, if not by mental hygienists. Five of the traits assigned most frequently to the boys of the genius group are rated 5 and the other five are rated 4 and, for the girls, five traits are rated 5, four traits 4, and one trait 3. Thus, five of the eight traits rated 5 compose half of the 10 traits assigned most frequently to the genius group.

The ratings of traits assigned most often to the normative group do not differ materially from those of the traits assigned with greatest frequency to genius children. Teachers, however, find the children designated as geniuses to possess the desirable traits to a greater degree than average children. Eight traits, for boys, and six traits, for girls, are assigned more frequently to genius children than any trait is assigned to the normative group. Two traits, *ambitious* and *dependable*, are assigned to over 70 percent of the girls and to over 60 percent of the boys. Three traits are particularly characteristic of the genius group—*ambitious, dependable,* and *original. Investigative* and *precocious* are significant for the boys and *leadership* for the girls.

Dullness, as might be expected, is the most distinctive characteristic of the retarded children, slightly less than 70 percent being so designated. This is the most important distinction which the teachers made between the problem and retarded children, although the problems are definitely those who are classroom disturbers, as indicated by the 10 traits most often used to describe them.

The traits most characteristic of the retarded group are, on the whole, not so undesirable as those characterizing the problem children. Four of the traits most frequently assigned to retarded boys and girls are rated as having some hygienic value while five are rated as being harmful. Two only of the traits most frequently assigned to problem children are rated as having hygienic value, whereas eight of the 10 are rated as being harmful. Six of the traits most frequently assigned to retarded boys, and five out of the 10, for girls, would probably be annoying to the teacher. On the other hand, nine out of 10, and perhaps all 10, of the traits most frequently assigned to problem boys and nine of the 11, for girls, would undoubtedly be a source of annoyance for most teachers. It appears that problem children, from the teachers' viewpoint, are children who are classroom disturbers, children who do not fit into the classroom decorum, who do not successfully adjust themselves to the classroom situation.

The ratings of traits assigned with the least frequency to the four selected groups are enlightening. None of the traits which are least characteristic of the genius and normative groups are rated as having definite hygienic value. The situation is different with the retarded and problem group. Seven of the traits assigned with least frequency to retarded boys are rated beneficial and, for the girls, four are rated beneficial. Of the traits assigned with least frequency to the problem group, for the boys, six are rated beneficial and, for the girls, seven out of 12 are rated beneficial. This is the reverse of the picture presented relative to the 10 traits assigned with least frequency to the genius and normative groups.

Traits which the teachers do not find to be characteristic of either the retarded or problem groups are *precocious, self-reliant, leadership, systematic, self-control, originality,* and *investigative ness.* The problem boys are found to be lacking in *persistence.*

Probably the most significant fact about the personality characterization of the teachers is the very definite picture they give of children they check as geniuses. Some traits are credited to well over half of the children and to 75 percent in one case. It is evident that this is a group with very outstanding personalities since no such trait distributions are to be found relative to the other groups. One might expect an equally definite characterization of the problem group. The highest percentage, however, for any trait with the problem group is 43 percent. This may not mean that they are not as distinctive personalities as the genius children, since it may be merely an expression of the reluctance of teachers to use the undesirable traits. Either undesirable traits are not found in children to the degree that desirable traits are or a child has to manifest an undesirable trait to a far greater degree than a desirable trait before the teacher will assign the trait to him. This may be the reason genius children appear to have much more distinctive personalities than problem children.

The traits which teachers, as indicated by their ratings, consider as most characteristic of genius, in order of the frequency of assignment, are *ambitious, dependable, original, precocious, artistic, leader, investigative, adventuresome,* and *self-reliant.*

It is difficult to find any trait which clearly distinguishes the retarded group from the problem group unless it is the trait *dull.*

Traits which tend to distinguish the retarded and problems from the genius and normative groups are *daydreaming, dull, inattention in class, lack of interest in work, oversensitive about self, "quitter," sleepy* or *apathetic* or *lazy, unhappy* or *moody* or *depressed, will not work or play with others.*

There are a number of traits which distinguish the problem group from the other three groups in the opinion of the teacher: *disturbs class, talkative* or *verbose, cheating, cruel* or *bully type, cute* or *"cocky," dishonest, disobedient, destructive, immature, impetuous in own actions, lying, nervous* or *restless, overcritical of others, pouting* or *resentful, profane, quarrelsome, rude* or *defiant, selfish, stubborn,* and *suspicious type.* This emphasizes that problem children, as far as teachers are concerned, are children who are active, aggressive, and generally maladjusted to the classroom situation.

The fact that teachers do not have the same conception of problem children as mental hygienists is emphasized by the tendency of teachers to characterize problem children by the traits just listed and by their failure to use, except in relatively rare cases, such traits as *self-conscious, suggestible, suspicious, temper tantrums, too easily frightened, oversensitive about self, unhappy* or *moody* or *depressed, will not work or play with others.* That is, they fail to see as problem behavior the withdrawing and egocentric type of behavior which mental hygienists emphasize.*

EDUCATIONAL ACHIEVEMENT

A factor which might be expected to enter into the selection of two of the groups under consideration in this study, that is, the retarded and genius groups, is educational achievement. This type of achievement was measured by the standardized battery known as Unit Scales of Attainment. This battery is composed of 11 individual subject-matter tests but only four of these were selected for detailed analysis, reading, geography, arithmetic problems, and language usage. It was assumed that these four would give a cross section of the scholastic achievement of the pupils involved. The raw scores on the achievement tests were converted into C-scores

---

* Sections entitled Personal Inventory Scores and Interests have been omitted in reprinting.—EDITOR'S NOTE.

according to directions given in the manual which accompanies these tests, and the C-scores were used in making all comparisons in respect to academic achievement.

Comparisons of median mental ages reveal no particular retardation, certainly no "extreme mental retardation," on the part of the retarded group. As a matter of fact, their median mental ages exceed those of the lower 10 percent at every grade level and for both sexes. These differences in median mental ages run from .26 to .69 years, for an average of .44 years, for the boys, and from .15 to .53 years, for an average of .30 years, for the girls. They are retarded in comparison with the normative group, the differences running from 0.88 to 1.18 years, for the boys, and from 1.17 to 1.38 years, for the girls. Comparisons between the lower 10 percent and the retarded group on median mental ages are more significant for determining whether they are retarded as far as mental development is concerned. On this score, it appears that the teachers were not particularly efficient in their selection of retarded children.

Retardation might mean retardation in school achievement. In fact, it would seem that it would have to mean this since teachers, without benefit of standardized intelligence tests, would have no other criterion of retardation. There is little difference in the median achievement scores of the lower 10 percent and the retarded group, although the scores of the latter group tend to be slightly above those of the former. While the retarded group is decidedly below the normative group in achievement, their retardation as compared with those who are really mentally retarded, the lower 10 percent, is not striking.

A comparison of achievement relative to mental ability was attempted. The quartile deviation of the median mental ages and the quartile deviation of the median achievement test scores were determined. These were compared to determine whether the median achievement scores exceed or fall below the quartile deviations of the median mental ages. It is assumed that, if a group is working up to capacity, the quartile deviation of the median achievement score will equal that of the median mental age. When the quartile deviation of the median achievement score is greater than that of the median mental age, it is assumed that the group is working superior to capacity, if the deviation is negative, and working below capacity, if the deviation is positive.

When the achievement of the retarded group is looked at from this point of view, it is found that, while the retarded group is achieving above expectation, its acceleration relative to ability is less than that of the lower 10 percent. The picture is not clear-cut and the over-all picture is not one of great retardation, particularly when they are compared with the lowest group in measured mental ability. It must be held in mind that the picture is intended to be one of extreme mental retardation.

The problem group appears to be achieving about what would be expected of them in terms of measured ability, so that it would appear that they are not problems as far as achievement is concerned. This is in line with the findings of most studies.

Educational achievement appears to be a factor in the selection of the genius group. Their median mental age is slightly below that of the upper 10 percent, their average chronological age is below that of the other three groups, yet their median achievement-test scores tend to exceed those of the upper 10 percent as well as those of the other groups. They are achieving more in terms of ability than the upper 10 percent of this population. This suggests that the academic achievement of these children played a part in their selection.

FAMILY BACKGROUND OF THE SELECTED GROUPS

Home conditions play a role in the adjustment of the child. Some information is available relative to the homes from which the various selected groups under consideration in this study come. The data deal only with factors which are relatively tangible and, consequently, most susceptible of measurement. It must be realized that such things are not crucial to the adjustment of the child and are only important in so far as they are closely related to the more crucial factors such as attitudes which are intangible and, as yet, very difficult to measure.

The occupations of the fathers were classified according to the Terman-Taussig classification (6, p. 64). This classification lists the occupations under five headings: (1) professional, (2) semiprofessional, or business, (3) skilled labor, (4) semiskilled or slightly skilled labor, and (5) common labor. The comparisons in Table 8 do not disclose any factors which might enter into the selection of the various groups. The distributions of the fathers' occupations differ, at the most, only slightly from what would be expected. The genius group differs only slightly from the upper 10 percent. They may be slightly above expectation, but the differences are too small to be significant. The retarded group differs only slightly from the lower 10 percent and this difference, while not significant, is in the direction to be expected since their median IQ is slightly higher than that of the lower 10 percent. The problem group tends more toward the higher classifications than the lower 10 percent, but less so than the normative group. This is in line with the median IQs of these groups.

A socioeconomic rating schedule was used which took into account the father's occupation, the presence of a telephone, automobile, radio, regular servant, or newspaper in the home, and the room-

TABLE 8

The Percentage of the Fathers of the Normative and Selected Groups, Together with Those of the Upper and Lower 10 Percent Who Are Engaged in Each Type of Occupation

Occupational classification	Norm	Upper 10 percent	Genius	Lower 10 percent	Retarded	Problem
1	4.3	10.3	10.3	.6	.9	2.9
2	21.6	35.9	37.2	10.9	12.6	15.4
3	41.9	37.4	36.1	41.6	44.4	46.0
4	12.9	10.3	9.1	15.6	14.3	17.5
5	19.2	5.9	7.3	28.9	28.1	18.2
CASES	12,390	4,289	341	3,697	2,743	1,492

per-person ratio. The median scores of the groups on this basis are: normative, 6.5; genius, 8.3; retarded, 4.9; and problems, 6.1—the range being 0 to 18. These merely substantiate the findings noted above relative to the father's occupation.

Much has been made, on occasion, of the importance of the birth order of the child, particularly as regards problem behavior. The findings of this study are mostly negative. The birth order of the problem children is not significant since they tend to follow expectations relative to the average mental ability of the group. McGehee (3, p. 93) has pointed out that children of low intelligence tend to come from larger families, and Lewis (2, p. 76) has pointed out that superior children tend to come from smaller families. It is to be expected that genius children tend to fall in lower birth orders since they come from smaller families. There do tend to be more only children in the problem group than would be expected, but the differences are so slight that there is no justification, on the basis of this data, for holding that only children tend to be problem children. There appears to be nothing in the data relative to the family background of the selected groups which would reveal reasons for their selection.

CONCLUSIONS

The fundamental purpose of this study has been to determine the distinction which elementary-school teachers tend to make between those of their pupils whom they believe to be either extremely retarded mentally, problems, or geniuses. The BPC Personal Inventory and factors in the home background such as fathers' occupations, socioeconomic status, and birth order in family, do not reveal any factors which functioned in the selection of the three groups.

The teachers selected 7 percent of their pupils as being "extremely retarded mentally." The fact that it is not easy for teachers to select those of their pupils who are in this class is revealed by the results of the Kuhlmann-Anderson Tests which showed their median IQ to be slightly over 90.

The picture obtained of this group is largely negative. The desirable traits appear to be less characteristic of them than of any group. This is very definitely true when comparison is made with the normative and genius groups. In general, the teachers find them lacking the positive characteristics of the genius group and normative group, and lacking to an appreciable degree the aggressive traits which express themselves in overt, undesirable behavior that characterize the problem group. They have few interests, particularly those that are intellectual and academic in nature.

The teachers' conception of problem children is quite different. They selected 4.4 percent of their pupils as problems, the boys outnumbering the girls three to one. They represent a wide range of mental ability and are not educational problems, at least not in terms of scores obtained on achievement tests. The teachers find them lacking in desirable personality traits except for certain traits which suggest aggressive personalities. The traits, however, which are found to be most characteristic of this group are undesirable traits which would prove very annoying to the teacher. It is quite evident that the teachers' conception of a problem child is one who upsets the classroom routine, who is aggressive and disturbing. The evidence indicates that the genius group was selected because of their ability to adjust to the classroom situation, because of their interests which tend to be intellectual and academic, because of their highly desirable personalities and their academic achievement. Teachers evidently believe that the term genius should be applied only to very exceptional children since they selected only .74 percent of their pupils as geniuses.

REFERENCES

1. Hollingworth, L. S. *Gifted Children.* New York: The Macmillan Co., 1927.
2. Lewis, W. D. A Study of Superior Children in the Elementary School. *Peabody Coll. Contrib. Educ.,* 266, 1940.
3. McGehee, W. A Study of Retarded Children in the Elementary School. *Peabody Coll. Contrib. Educ.,* 246, 1939.
4. Moncreiff, R. A Study of Factors Relating to Problematic Behavior in Elementary School Children. *Peabody Coll. Contrib. Educ.,* 294, 1939.
5. Scheinfeld, A. *Women and Men.* New York: Harcourt, Brace, 1943.
6. Terman, L. M. *Genetic Studies of Genius.* Vol. I. Stanford, Calif.: Stanford Univ. Press, 1925.
7. Terman, L. M., and B. S. Burks. The Gifted Child. In C. Murchison (ed.), *A Handbook of Child Psychology.* Worcester, Mass.: Clark Univ. Press, 1933.

IDENTIFYING GIFTED CHILDREN

by Robert F. DeHaan

HOPE COLLEGE

Suppose a teacher is casually observing the children passing by in the hallway on their way to their classrooms. Approximately one out

[Reprinted from *School Review,* 65, 1957, 41-48, with the permission of the University of Chicago Press and the author.]

of ten of the children passing before his gaze has sufficient mental ability to be designated as "gifted" and in need of special educational opportunities to develop his ability; another one out of the ten has artistic ability that warrants the provision of special educational programs; still another one out of ten has unusual musical ability; and similar ratios of the children have dramatic talent, creative writing ability, mechanical skills. Many children have two or three talents that place them in the upper 10 percent of their age group. By the time five hundred children have passed by the teacher, he will have looked at approximately one hundred who can be considered gifted in at least one important way.

The teacher would not be able, by casual observation only, to distinguish the gifted pupils from the others. The gifted are not staggering under a towering load of books. Neither are they blundering along the fringes of the group trying unsuccessfully to "get in" with other children, as is sometimes supposed to be true of them. On the contrary, they are quite as carefree and as well adjusted as any children in the hallway; hence the need for inaugurating methods of identifying them.

Identification consists in the process of screening children by means of standardized test procedures and/or observational methods and selecting the superior children for educational programs designed particularly for them. The purpose of the procedure is to enable educators to decide whether special educational provisions should be made for a given child and, if so, what kind of special opportunities should be provided. The purpose is not to tie on the child a tag that will stay with him the rest of his life, for better or for worse. Neither is identification a goal in itself. It is a means to the goal of getting each gifted child into the educational program most suited to develop his capacities and his whole person.

Procedures for identifying gifted children should be functional, systematic, and inclusive. The identification procedures should be geared into the over-all testing program of the school. All the children should be tested at regular intervals with a wide range of tests so that numerous kinds of abilities can be found. Without this kind of identification program, it is likely that a considerable number of able children will be overlooked.

Additional benefits accrue to the school system that employs systematic, inclusive identification procedures. Since many of the screening devices used to discover gifted children are inherently stimulating to all children, they enhance the instructional program in the classroom. For example, teachers and children so enjoy some of the fine-arts tests that they want to continue them long after the testing period is concluded. The procedures of identification help to tailor the educational program to fit the particular combination of abilities of each gifted child by providing indispensable information about him. Almost invariably, a good identification program stimulates teachers and administrators to do something for the children they have identified.

A good identification program should discover other characteristics of gifted children besides their aptitudes and capacities. The *interests* of gifted children are important in a program for these children. "Interests" are any activities in which the child prefers to engage when given a free choice. These interests often point to activities which will motivate a pupil, and they can sometimes be used as a springboard to extend his participation into other activities.

Another important kind of information to have about gifted children is their academic achievement, the level at which they are successfully performing on specific learning tasks.

Other factors, such as *motivation, personality,* and *social* factors, can and should be tested and observed in order to round out the picture of a given child and to provide important leads for his educational program. In this connection it is important to assess such personality factors as the amount of withdrawal or aggression in a child's behavior. If the child is extreme in either of these behaviors, his aptitudes may never show through enough to be recognized and appreciated. Social factors, too, are important. Some children from lower social and economic groups and from certain racial groups may be so deprived of cultural stimulation in their homes and neighborhoods that their potential aptitudes are present only to the most observant eyes.

Two general approaches can be used to identify gifted children: standardized tests and systematic observations. Some abilities are best identified by use of objective tests; others can better be discovered through observations; and still others need an approach combining both methods. Some educators prefer one approach over the other, but, in general, best results are obtained from a maximum use of both. An example of the intensive use of both approaches is found in the Youth Development Project carried on in Quincy, Illinois.[1]

Of the many kinds of standardized tests now available, one of the most familiar is the standardized group intelligence test. Tests of this type are particularly valuable for the first rough screening. It is important to administer these tests fairly regularly in the school career of a given child. Some school systems give group intelligence tests every two or three years. Additional information about the intellectual level of a child can be gained by use of individual intelligence tests. The individual test usually gives a more reliable measure of intelligence than does a group test, and hence increases the confidence in the accuracy of the identification procedures. Some schools routinely examine all candidates for special classes for the gifted with an individual intelligence test.

Tests of specialized abilities will supply a fuller understanding of an individual pupil or will select pupils for certain specialized courses. There are standardized tests of such skills as clerical ability, mechanical aptitude, and some kinds of motor aptitudes. There usefulness is much more limited in the education of gifted children than the tests of intellectual abilities.

Many kinds of interest inventories are available for use in an identification program. Some inventories inquire directly into the child's interests. Others are more indirect, using incomplete sentences which the child completes. Still other interest inventories ask the child to list his activities both in school and out of school. Vocational interests are of great importance, for adolescent boys in particular, and vocational-interest inventories can be used to discover those interests.

Achievement tests are probably the most commonly used of any kind of educational test. In addition to measuring achievement in reading, spelling, arithmetic, language, and science, they may be used to discover academic disabilities of gifted children and to point the way for remedial work or special emphasis in teaching.

Since personality factors are often taken into account in selecting pupils, personality tests are important in an identification program. These tests also yield supplementary data which can be used

---

[1] Paul H. Bowman and others, *Studying Children and Training Counselors in a Community Program*, Supplementary Educational Monographs, No. 78, Chicago: Univ. Chicago Press, 1953, Chs. 3-5.

in counseling and guiding children in planning their educational program.

Abilities in the fine arts can best be identified by a method which combines some features of standardized tests and some aspects of personal observations. This method consists in obtaining a "work sample," which is rated for excellence by a panel of expert judges. Such a method probably provides the best procedure available for screening youngsters with aptitudes in the fine arts—graphic arts, music, writing, dramatics, dancing, and mechanics.

The "work-sample" method has been developed primarily in the pilot schools participating in the gifted-child program in Portland, Oregon. Procedures are used to discover children with abilities in art, creative writing, music, dramatics, physical aptitudes, and mechanical skills. The intent of the procedures is to identify the most talented pupils (the upper 10 percent) in each of the fine arts.

The procedure for screening children with creative writing ability will illustrate how such procedures are used in the other fine arts as well. The creative writing exercises are designed for fifth- and sixth-grade classes. Five such exercises are given, one each week for a period of five weeks. Each exercise is completed in one school period. Discussions and comments are avoided once the class has begun to work on the exercises. The exercises are (1) developing expressive sentences, (2) developing a paragraph from a stimulus sentence, (3) writing a story from descriptive phrases, (4) describing a real-life experience, and (5) writing an imaginative composition.

The written products are rated by the classroom teachers on a five-point scale according to criteria previously given them. Teachers are asked to look for creative thought and expression rather than excellence in the mechanics of writing. They are told that the number of creatively gifted children in a classroom may vary from one to seven or eight but that, as a general rule, there will be from one to three. The papers are judged on the following criteria: originality of ideas, depth of understanding of emotional situation, choice of expressive words, conciseness of expression, developmental logic present in sentences, good paragraph development (when appropriate), well-planned plot (when appropriate), maintenance of a point of view.

Talents in other fine arts and in practical skills such as mechanics can be identified by this basic method of having a group of experts judge the products of the children. The product must be obtained from the children under as standardized conditions as possible. The experts can work singly or as a panel. It is important that they be given training in what to look for and objective criteria by which to judge the level of performance of each child.

In addition to the standardized tests of intelligence and the semistandardized tests in the fine arts described above, observation is an important method for identifying able children. The role of human observation and judgment in screening and selecting is a major one. Almost every program of identification includes teacher observations and judgments among the procedures.[2]

Teachers' observations and judgments are particularly appropriate for identifying children's talents that are expressed rather consistently but not necessarily intensively. Examples of such talents are leadership and friendship, which can be observed in children every day. Most teachers, however, can readily observe a wide variety of talents as children engage in the many kinds of educational experiences provided in the classroom. Teacher judgments can also be used to identify talents of types for which good tests are not available and to corroborate and correct the evidence obtained from the results of standardized tests.

For the most effective use of teachers' observations as talent-identifying procedures, teachers should be provided with behavioral descriptions of children's characteristics that are valid clues to the talent for which they are looking. More reliable results are obtained when a teacher observes many specific behaviors related to a given talent than when he makes a global, over-all judgment about a child's abilities. The latter method covers up many specifics that, if noted, help make the teacher's judgment reliable. Some school systems have set up guides for teachers to follow in making observations, which present descriptions of behavioral characteristics for all important varieties of talent as well as for scientific and intellectual abilities.[3] A modified forced-choice instrument called the Behavior Description Chart was used in Quincy, Illinois, to aid the

[2] Robert J. Havighurst, Eugene Stivers, and Robert F. DeHaan, *A Survey of the Education of Gifted Children*, Supplementary Educational Monographs, No. 83, Chicago: Univ. Chicago Press, 1955.
[3] A detailed guide to teacher observations is found in Jack Kough and Robert F. DeHaan, *Identifying Children with Special Needs*, Teachers' Guidance Handbook, Vol. I, Chicago: Science Research Associates, 1955.

teachers in identifying ability in social leadership.[4] The instrument presented eighteen groups of five items in each group, and the teacher was asked to mark the item among the five which was *most like* and the one which was *least like* the child under consideration.

Given this kind of guidance and training in observing, teachers may become adept in recognizing and identifying children with unusual abilities of many kinds. One of the important bonus benefits obtained from teachers' observations is that observation tends to make the teachers more sensitive to individual differences in children and more aware of giftedness.

Another source of systematic data for screening purposes is children's observations of one another. Because of their contacts in situations quite removed from the classroom, children can provide information that is ordinarily unavailable to the teacher. These observations by youngsters can best be obtained by familiar sociometric devices. Children can be asked to identify almost any talent or aptitude that a teacher wishes to discover, from intellectual ability to mechanical aptitude to social leadership. The teacher needs only to present the children with descriptions of behaviors which it is possible for them to observe and behaviors which are truly symptomatic of the talents he wishes to identify.

Probably no one knows as much about a given child as do his parents. However, parents' knowledge is often unsystematized and unevaluated. Parents rarely have any way to judge the quality of the ability of their children and hence may be likely to make large errors. Nevertheless, the information that parents have about their children supplies valuable supplementary data to corroborate the results of tests and teachers' observations or to provide decisive information in some borderline cases where tests and observations are inconclusive. Information from parents can be obtained through conferences or by means of questionnaires.

Screening is an ongoing process that is never completely finished. Even if the identification procedures used in elementary schools are adequate, efforts to identify gifted children should be continued in the secondary schools. It may happen, for instance, that a pupil needs the combination of physical and social maturation, interesting high-school curriculum, and masterful teaching to motivate him to put forth his best efforts in a given endeavor. This combination of circumstances may be missing from the lives of a

[4] Bowman, *op. cit.,* pp. 24-32.

significant number of pupils until they reach high school or even college. It is important for high-school teachers and guidance counselors to use the information that was obtained in the elementary school. Data gathered in an identification program should not be allowed to gather dust.

The names of all the children selected as gifted should be drawn together on a master roster. This represents the group for whom special provisions are to be made. An individual card should be set up for each selected child, summarizing the test results and the special provisions made for him. The card should follow the child throughout his school career. Test information can be used judiciously for guidance of the child, his teachers, and parents.

This article has described the main outlines of a total program for identification of gifted children. If such a program is inaugurated in a school, the teacher standing in a hallway watching the children pass by will be able to recognize the one in ten who has intellectual ability. The teacher will know the pattern of the able child's ability, his interests, and his personality characteristics. The teacher will also be able to point out other talented children and to give some account of their aptitudes, their interests, their achievement. Such identification of gifted children and knowledge about them are indispensable if teachers are to provide the kinds of special programs needed to develop the capabilities of gifted children to the fullest extent.

COUNSELLING PARENTS OF GIFTED CHILDREN

by Samuel R. Laycock

UNIVERSITY OF SASKATCHEWAN

There is increasing evidence that the old idea that gifted children are bound to develop their capacities, in spite of an unfavorable en-

[Reprinted from *Exceptional Children*, 23, December 1956, 108-110, 134, with the permission of the Council for Exceptional Children and the author. A reprint of this article is available from the CEC.]

vironment and a lack of opportunity, isn't true. On the contrary, if these children are to find the satisfactions which come from a full development of their potentialities they need the fullest understanding and the widest possible guidance on the part of their parents and teachers. Then, too, in the present state of world unrest, a nation that neglects the development of its potential leaders is playing fast and loose with its own survival. It needs the contributions of its gifted individuals both for development and defense.

Since parents necessarily play the most significant role in the guidance of gifted children, teachers, counselors, administrators, and other educators are now studying the problem of how best to counsel the parents of gifted youngsters so that the latter may achieve the best possible realization of their abilities.

BASIC ASSUMPTIONS

Those who counsel the parents of the gifted need to proceed on certain basic assumptions.

1. *The gifted child is, first of all, a child.* Parents often need help in seeing their exceptional youngster as, first of all, a child with a child's problems of development as he advances through the various stages from infancy to maturity. Cases are on record (as John Stuart Mill) where gifted individuals were allowed to have no childhood and where emphasis on the child's intellectual development completely obscured his social and emotional growth. Sometimes this results from the parental expectation that their child who is very advanced intellectually for his age will also be equally advanced socially and emotionally. Parents may, therefore, expect too great a degree of mature behavior from their gifted child or shoulder him with responsibilities for which he is not ready. Such parents need help in seeing their child's growth in its totality—emotional, social, and physical as well as intellectual. They need to know that their gifted youngster, in his growing up, is faced with the developmental tasks of all children—in early, middle, and late childhood and in adolescence—and that he may be exceptional only in his intellectual growth or special talent.

2. *The gifted child is a unique individual rooted in a certain family, community, and culture.* Gifted children cannot be stereotyped. While certain general principles apply to their guidance,

each child differs from his gifted fellows. He is unique in his innate characteristics and in the way he interacts with his own family circle, with his community, and with the culture of his own nation and of the contemporary world.

3. *The gifted child, like all children, has four sets of teachers*— home teachers, playmate teachers, school teachers, and community teachers (church, Sunday school, Scouts, movies, radio, television, recreational facilities, and the standards held by the adults of the community). Since a child develops in terms of *all* the influences that play upon him, each of these sets of teachers share in all phases of his development—intellectual, social, emotional, and so forth. For the child's best development there must be close cooperation between his different sets of teachers—certainly between his home, school, and community teachers.

4. *Parents of gifted children are human beings with emotional problems of their own and need a good measure of self-understanding.* Parents of bright youngsters may, like any parent, suffer from feelings of insecurity and inadequacy or they may possess deep-seated feelings of hostility and resentment. They need help not only in understanding why their children act as they do, but also in understanding why they themselves react to their children the way they do. Otherwise they may exploit their gifted child, resent him, be jealous of him, or overdominate or overprotect him.

OBJECTIVES FOR THE GIFTED CHILD

Parents often need help in envisaging what they want for their gifted child. Their objective may be best expressed in an old objective of mental health—to help their child to grow up in such a way that he gives his best to the world and knows the deep satisfaction of a life richly and fully lived. Parents need to know that the two aspects of the above statement are almost inseparably linked. Few gifted individuals will find their richest possible satisfactions in life if they are not realizing their potentialities. Few, too, will realize their potentialities unless their emotional and social development is reasonably mature and satisfying.

The National Association for Mental Health lists three characteristics for a healthy personality which might well serve as objectives for parents in the guidance of the gifted—to feel comfortable about oneself, to feel right towards others, and to be able to meet the demands of life in accordance with one's abilities.

Certainly the gifted child must find satisfaction for his basic psychological needs for affection, belonging, independence, achievement, recognition, and self-esteem if he is to make his maximum contribution to society and be happy in so doing.

WHAT THE GIFTED CHILD NEEDS FROM PARENTS

Gifted children need three things from parents: (1) acceptance, (2) understanding, and (3) guidance.

ACCEPTANCE IS IMPORTANT

Parents must, first of all, accept their child as a *gifted child*. As a *child* he needs to be accepted for his own sake as a loved and treasured human being—not because he brings his parents prestige by his achievements. Tender loving care is at least as important in the case of gifted children as in the case of all children. Feeling secure in affection of his parents will enable the gifted child to better handle his emotions of fear, rage, guilt, and love, to accept his own shortcomings, to have self-respect, and to fare forth to meet the problems of life. Expecting too much of the gifted child, exploiting his abilities or overdominating, or rejecting him will damage him in the same way as any child may be damaged by a sense of insecurity and inadequacy.

The parents also need to accept their gifted child as *gifted*. Otherwise they will not be able to guide him intelligently. While many parents overrate their child's ability, it is also true that parents often do not realize that their child has exceptional potentialities. They should be helped to appreciate signs of brightness. They should know that, *on the average*, the gifted youngster is likely to walk early, to talk early, and to learn to read early (often well before five years of age). Other signs of exceptional ability are intellectual curiosity, superior insight into problems, and superior ability in generalizing, reasoning, and dealing with abstractions. The gifted child learns readily and easily, has a good memory and listens to, understands, and carries out directions readily. He has a longer interest span and many interests as well as a longer attention span in listening to a story or in carrying out a project of his own. If he gets a good chance in school, he is likely to outdistance his fellow pupils. In addition to the child of high general intelligence there are, of course, children whose gifts lie in specific directions—art, music, dramatics, leadership, and so forth.

Whatever the nature of the child's high abilities, parents need to accept their child for what he is and endeavor to help him to realize his highest potentialities. There is no more justification for parents refusing to accept their child as gifted than for their refusal to accept their child who is mentally retarded, deaf, blind, or orthopedically handicapped.

Parents need to help the gifted child to accept himself. Usually he is well aware that he achieves in a superior fashion to his age mates. Trying to make him believe he is mediocre is frustrating and discouraging. Rather, as in the case of all children, normal and exceptional, the gifted child should be encouraged to recognize and accept, in realistic fashion, his assets and his limitations. At the same time he needs help from his parents in recognizing the various strong points of others and the dignity of human personality in all individuals. Long ago, Leta Hollingworth remarked that the gifted child needs to learn "to suffer fools gladly"—not bitterly, cynically, or despairingly, but gladly. He needs help in learning to respect others who differ from him and to be modest about his own abilities.

Parents need to help their gifted child to win acceptance from others without sacrificing his own individuality or ruining his special gifts through an enforced conformity which spells mediocrity. There is danger that parents will overemphasize conformity and teach the child to play down his special gifts so that he may be "popular" with the gang or crowd. In the case of other exceptional children, parents and teachers help these youngsters to learn how to make friends and to be accepted by others in spite of being blind, deaf, orthopedically handicapped, or mentally retarded. Is it too much to expect that the gifted child can find reasonable acceptance in spite of being different? Surely democracy does not mean an attempt to secure a dead level of mediocre conformity. Rather, it should mean the chance for every individual to use his unique gifts in the service of all. The gifted child does, however, need help from his parents in learning, as other children have to learn, the principles of good human relationships—principles based on a genuine respect and liking for others.

In our society which overemphasizes athletic prowess, the gifted child who is not athletically inclined should not be forced into athletics but rather helped to find other ways of mingling happily with his fellows whether this be through the medium of library clubs, science clubs, art clubs, music clubs, dramatics, hobby clubs. Certainly attempts to force all children, gifted or not, into extroverted glad-handedness can be a devastating experience for many youngsters. Reasonable individuality should be encouraged.

UNDERSTANDING IS VITAL

Parents can best help their gifted child if they understand the characteristics and evidences of giftedness as set forth earlier in this article. They need to understand, too, some of the problems that are often the lot of the gifted—problems of loneliness, of concern over destiny and death, of their intellectual development being out of step with their emotional and social development, of frustration in school work that is so beneath them as to be boring and futile, and of teachers who do not understand them or who resent them. Those who counsel parents of the gifted need to help them to become aware of the above and of other difficulties which their child is likely to face.

GUIDANCE IS A RESPONSIBILITY

In addition to guiding their child's social adjustment to others, parents have a heavy responsibility in guiding their child's intellectual development. This involves the guidance of his education, both formal and informal.

As far as the gifted child's education in school is concerned, this is frequently, in our society, a frustrating and damaging experience. The general public, who are coming to interpret equality of opportunity for handicapped youngsters as giving these children an equal chance to develop in accordance with their own needs and abilities, are, as yet, largely unwilling to apply this principle to the gifted. They claim that this would be undemocratic and would lead to class distinctions. As a result vast numbers of gifted children are faced with school work far beneath their ability—work that is utterly boring and frustrating and destroys effective habits of study and of thinking.

In an attempt to improve the education of the gifted, some educators are experimenting with acceleration, enrichment, and special groupings of gifted pupils on a part-time or full-time basis. Parents of gifted children need to be made familiar with the problems which each of these methods involves. A reading of *A Survey of the Education of Gifted Children,* by Havighurst and others (University of Chicago Press) would give parents an idea of the different ways which are currently being tried to meet the needs of gifted children. Before such techniques and methods are introduced into any school system, administrators and teachers should attempt to obtain public understanding and support. In any event, success of such efforts is apt to depend on close cooperation with the parents of the gifted youngsters.

Unfortunately, due to the attitudes of the general public, and prevalence of large classes in the schools, many parents can do little to improve the quality of the education their gifted child receives in school. They can, however, do a great deal to foster their child's informal education outside the school. This means an early encouragement of the child's reading; seeing that the child has easy access to a wide variety of books, magazines, and pamphlets; providing the child with as wide an experience as possible by visits to construction projects, zoos, museums, art galleries, and civic centers; taking the child on trips; and providing for his attending concerts, lectures, exhibitions, and other activities. Without in any way forcing the child, his parents can foster his expressed interest in music, art, dramatics, creative writing, collections, and hobbies. These things are not the sole preserve of the rich. There is an abundance of free and inexpensive material available (see *The Wonderful World of Children,* by Peter Cardozo, Bantam Books). Indeed many a gifted child has, in the past, been stimulated by catalogs of department stores, advertising material in magazines, and free material from travel bureaus, industrial firms, and departments of government.

If gifted children are to explore their interests on a wide front, they need the sympathetic encouragement and interest of their parents. The latter must be willing to take time to listen, to discuss, and to stimulate. They can also see that their youngster has the opportunity for contact with important people in the field of his major interest.

In one other area, parents have a significant part to play in the guidance of their gifted children. That is in the field of vocational choice. Here parents can give active help to their child in assisting him to discover his assets and limitations—physical, mental, and social—and to match these with the requirements of different vocations. Whatever the gifted child's choice of a vocation may be, it is important that it not be that of a routine job but rather one in which his capacity for seeing relationships will be utilized to a maximum degree. It should also be a vocation that will provide for his continued intellectual development throughout life.

In conclusion, just as teachers and other educators have become increasingly aware of the importance and difficulty of counseling parents of handicapped children, so they must become equally aware of the need for counseling the parents of gifted children. Only with a high degree of parental acceptance, understanding, and guidance are gifted children likely to have that equal chance for the development of their potentialities which is the goal for all children in a democratic society.

THE FOUR IQs*

by Edgar A. Doll

BELLINGHAM, WASHINGTON, PUBLIC SCHOOLS

The IQ is now used as if it were a household word which the users understand as well as mph and degrees Fahrenheit—as if it were an absolute—that given a high IQ there should, if the schools were adequate to their job, be high achievement. And, conversely, that

---

* The abstract (prepared by T. H. W. Martin, Inspector of Special Education, Toronto, Canada) is of an address delivered at the Southwestern Regional Conference of the International Council for Exceptional Children, Phoenix, Arizona. The author is indebted to Paul Yaffe's brief note in the *Baltimore Bulletin of Education*, 33, March 1956, pp. 9-11, on the significance of "inner quest." This cue induced the present dynamic philosophy. The reader should not permit the whimsical alliteration, nor the setting of special education, to obscure the seriousness of this homely formulation and its timely import.

[Reprinted from *Exceptional Children*, 24, October 1957, 56-58, with the permission of the Council for Exceptional Children and the author. A reprint of this article is available from CEC.]

given a low IQ, there is little hope for success. These are fallacies. There are in reality four IQs which must be recognized as factors in achievement. These are:

1. *The Intelligence Quotient,* which is a measure of intellectual potential, a measure of brightness—not of capacity or maturity level.
2. *The Inner Quest,* which is the individual's answer to "What am I?" and "What am I living for?" It is made up of aspirations and values, not always in the conscious mind. It is a strong lever for education.
3. *The Ideal Qualities,* which are the traits of personality which evaluate and maintain a balance between the Inner Quest and the Intelligence Quotient.
4. *The Innate Quirks,* which are the obstacles which lie between us and the fulfillment desired by our Inner Quest, made possible by our Intelligence, to the extent determined by our Innate Qualities. Some of these quirks are in the person; some are environmental.

The Intelligence Quotient is a relative measure, indicating where the candidate stands among his age-peers in the performance called for by the test which has been chosen. These tests, generally, call for (1) rational comprehension of a situation and (2) an effective response. In Dr. Doll's opinion, many of the tests are heavily weighted towards the academic, requiring the verbal comprehension and response prized in education. For making the most of one's self, other measures of rational comprehension and response are needed. For example,

1. Of and to *social situations*—the intelligence which enables us to get along with other people. This is most certainly a factor in success or failure in school as well as in the world outside;
2. Of and to *things*—like machinery, for example.

These two factors of intelligence should not be relegated to separate fields and degraded, as many educationists do. Nor should verbal intelligence be made a prerequisite for opportunity.

Intelligence-test results depend upon many variables: what test, who administers, when, where, why. Implicit assumptions are that the child hears (or reads) and understands, that there is no emotional interference with either comprehension or response, that there is no malingering, that there is no handicap. Dr. Doll pointed out that in testing situations, severe impairments are obvious, and usually compensated for, but that mild impairments which are not observed can handicap a candidate considerably.

It is a fallacy that the tests actually measure true intelligence. The candidate's performance is measured, but it is always the minima. We can get not better than his best, but often get far less. What we do get might often better be termed Expressive Intellectual Performance—not intelligence. Something more is needed to determine potential.

Hence, says Dr. Doll, the assumption that there is a 1:1 relationship between intelligence and learning is based upon a fallacy. Relatively large numbers of the intellectually gifted are underachievers in school and out. The reasons for this underachievement *may* be found by making a study of the other three IQs.

THE INNER QUEST

The Inner Quest produces "drive." Whence it derives, no one knows. Some suspect the adrenals; some blame thyroid deficiency. We do know that it is highly variable, both from person to person and within the same personality. We do know that it is sometimes more than we can stand, as parents or teachers; that it can be smothered by an overenthusiastic parent or teacher as effectively as by one who is indifferent. It is as elusive as an instinct when we attempt to locate its origin, and quite as powerful. Water is for swimming to one who is born "goose," but not to one who is born "chicken." To require swimming for both is as great a folly as to prohibit it for both. With this example, Dr. Doll asked us to consider the effects upon achievement produced by a blocking of the Inner Quest through the demands of conformity in curricula. He pointed out that neither the duck nor the chicken *knows* its attitude towards water, it only *feels* the rightness or wrongness. He then cited the case of a child whose infancy was spent in one of Hitler's concentration camps. The child had no conscious memory of the terrors—no words about the shattering experiences, "but his nervous system remembers!"

Children need assistance in developing their self-concepts— their Inner Quests—discovering whether they are duck or chicken, or rabbit or squirrel, in their nature, and all who deal with children must appreciate the power, differences, and the variabilities of Inner Quests.

THE IDEAL QUALITIES

Observe Miss B. leaving her apartment at eight in the morning, tastefully but rather plainly dressed, her expression interested, but rather prim and quite virtuous, on her way to be a teacher. The ideal qualities are evident; there will be interest, work, and no nonsense in her class.

Observe Miss B. leaving her apartment at eight in the evening, on her way to be a "date." Are the same qualities now ideal? If she goes out prim, plain, and in no mood for nonsense, she might better stay home and put her feet up, for she will be on them in the classroom for another forty years.

Dr. Doll then cited his own case. To a teacher whose pupil he is examining as a psychologist, he appears as a source of help and a fount of wisdom. But when, on parent's night, he goes to the school where his children attend, he is "just another parent, to whom incompetence is imputed as a matter of course!"

The Ideal Qualities which maintain a productive balance between Intellectual Capacity and Inner Quest are those which enable the individual to achieve peace of mind. They protect the ego and the sense of dignity and worth. They enable one to achieve enough acceptance to satisfy the gregarious drive. They provide a sense of status, neither overestimating nor undervaluing either the capacity or the quest.

In school we recognize this need for status and acceptance when the reactions of a child are dramatically evident. We cannot teach the sick child, the unruly child, the unhappy child, or the disturbed child. They have no peace of mind, no inner quietude which will permit learning. When there are no dramatic evidences, we tend to think that all is well when we may well be faced by a lack of balance, soon to erupt in a dramatic scene. Dr. Doll urged that teachers, being more mature, go more than half-way to bring about that sense of tranquility which comes from status. Without this inner quietude there can be no concentrated effort at learning.

In some areas of our curriculum, Dr. Doll thinks we tend to be hidebound ritualists, especially in subjects like arithmetic. There, he believes, we often let the "training" aspect of the work inhibit "the spontaneous learning which should characterize the school of performance."

THE INNATE QUIRKS

These are the handicaps and the obstacles which stand between us and the goal set by our Inner Quest, within our Intellectual Capacity, kept in balance by our Ideal Qualities. Some of these obstacles are in the person; some, in the environment. Dr. Doll pointedly reminded us that the teacher is part of the environment.

In general, Dr. Doll thought that we tend to pressure pupils toward the typical; that we are so concerned with scholastic achievement that we are, in effect, punishing the handicapped child for his handicap; that we are so concerned with our planned program of progress for the class as a whole we punish the gifted child for his giftedness.

Quirks may be points of view, attitudes, values, or prejudices. They may be common to our family, our social group, or our community, or we may be mavericks in these respects.

Quirks may be in our physical environment. Barren or lush, it is a factor which must be considered and compensated for. We must not, as teachers, think of environment as only that of the home. The street, the playground, the community, and the general social climate are all important factors making for success or failure. Above all, let us consider the environment of the school and the classroom. Is it lush or barren? in space? in numbers? in staff? in equipment? in services?

These then are the four IQs—Intelligence Quotient, which is not an absolute; Inner Quest, which is the most potent factor in achievement; Ideal Qualities, which maintain balance; Innate Quirks, of which we all have our share. Educators, then, should not glibly compare achievement and intelligence quotient. Each individual's progress is the product of a great array of factors, often hard to identify, and often still more difficult to influence.

This does not mean we must adopt a laissez-faire attitude to achievement. Rather, it emphasizes the need for continuous and greatly expanded research which will, in time, enable us to act with more assurance than we now can do.

READING ABILITIES OF BRIGHT AND DULL
CHILDREN OF COMPARABLE MENTAL AGE *

by Emery P. Bliesmer

UNIVERSITY OF VIRGINIA

In a recent study by Kolstoe (2), the usefulness of mental age as a unit of measurement was investigated by comparing the mental abilities of bright and dull children of similar mental ages. In general, his results revealed only minor differences in the traits measured. The present investigation is a companion study which involved essentially the same samples of bright and dull children as those employed by Kolstoe. Its purpose was to determine the extent to which children of equal mental age but markedly different in chronological age and IQ tend to be alike with respect to achievement in reading. This was done by comparing bright and dull children with approximately equal estimated true mental ages with respect to each of several abilities involved in reading comprehension. The criterion for "dull" was an estimated true Stanford-Binet IQ of 84 or below; the one for "bright" was an estimated true Stanford-Binet IQ of 116 or above. Thus the minimum separation between the two groups was approximately two standard deviation units along the IQ continuum. Estimates of the true IQs and MAs were obtained by applying the standard formula for correction for regression to the obtained IQs and MAs, with the reliability coefficients used in the formula being those reported by Terman and Merrill for various IQ levels.†

Results of the extensive investigations of Lewis (3) and of McGehee (4), earlier studies by Almack and Almack (1) and by Van

---

* This article is based on the writer's Ph.D. dissertation. The work was done at the State University of Iowa under the codirection of Professors A. N. Hieronymus and J. B. Stroud.
† L. M. Terman and M. A. Merrill, *Measuring Intelligence*, Boston: Houghton Mifflin, 1937, p. 46.

[Reprinted from the *Journal of Educational Psychology*, 45, October 1954, 321-331, with the permission of Warwick and York, Publishers, and the author.]

Wagenen (8), and a later study by Thomas (6) suggest that, in general, bright children achieve below, and dull children achieve above, levels consistent with their indicated mental ages. One might expect, therefore, that a direct comparison of the achievement of bright and dull children with approximately the same mental ages would show results favoring the latter. The fact that the older, low IQ children have been in school longer and have been exposed to instruction in certain specific reading skills not taught in the lower grades would also lend support to such an hypothesis. On the other hand, most of the investigations of the relationship between brightness and over- and underachievement have failed to take into consideration regression effects resulting from lack of reliability in the mental-age measures, which would account for some of the observed differences. Ceiling and floor effects, and procedures used in extrapolating age and grade scales on standard reading tests, may also be responsible for finding very little overachievement among high IQ groups and underachievement among groups of low IQ pupils. Thus, assuming equal variability of reading-age scores and mental-age scores, it is virtually impossible for a pupil at or near the 99th percentile on an intelligence test to "overachieve" or a pupil near the first percentile to "underachieve."

In a study by Ramaseshan (5), ninth-grade pupils of similar mental ages (Chicago Tests of Primary Mental Abilities) were grouped according to chronological age. Children with similar mental ages but different chronological ages (and, consequently, differing IQs) were compared on the subtests of the Iowa Tests of Educational Development (ITED). Her bright group was found to excel on all of the subtests of the ITED, but differences were statistically significant for only three of these subtests. Of some pertinence to the purposes of the writer's study is the fact that no significant differences were found on the three subtests measuring the ability to read and interpret material in specific content areas.

Unsicker (7) equated groups according to mental age by matching groups of bright third- and fourth-grade pupils with groups of dull seventh- and eighth-grade pupils, first on the basis of Kuhlmann-Anderson Intelligence Test scores, then on the basis of California Tests of Mental Maturity results. When the groups matched on the basis of Kuhlmann-Anderson MAs were compared with respect to reading comprehension scores earned on the Iowa Tests of Basic Skills, Unsicker found significant differences favoring the bright group. Differences between the groups matched on the basis of California MAs were not significant.

In addition to the fact that different criterion tests were employed, the present study differs from most of those in which the problem has been investigated previously in that estimated true scores were used in the matching procedure, individually administered intelligence tests rather than group tests were employed, and the criterion tests were of an appropriate level of difficulty so that ceiling and floor effects did not operate to bias the means.

PROCEDURE

METHOD OF SAMPLING

In order to measure a wide range of comprehension abilities, it was decided to employ test materials which are appropriate at the fourth- to fifth-grade level of reading ability. Considering the IQ criteria for "bright" and "dull" (lower and upper IQ limits of 116 and 84, respectively), and studying the overlap of MAs at various CAs for these bright and dull criteria, it was decided to use a mental-age range of from ten years, seven months, through twelve years, six months, and to restrict the bright group to children with CAs of ten years or less and the dull group to children with CAs of fourteen years or above.

Children in the dull group were selected from regular eighth- and ninth-grade classes and some special education classes in two junior high schools, and children in the bright group from regular third- and fourth-grade classes in three elementary schools, in the public-school system of a large Iowa city. For identification of pupils likely to meet sample specifications, the cumulative record folder of each child in the two junior high schools and in third and fourth grades in the three elementary schools was studied. A list was made of all the junior high pupils who were fourteen years of age or older and for whom IQs of 90 or below had been obtained with group intelligence tests which had been administered by the schools in previous years. In the elementary schools, a list was made of all third- and fourth-grade pupils who were ten years of age or younger and for whom IQs of 110 or above had been obtained with group intelligence tests in previous years.

From the list of pupils indicated as likely to meet specifications for the dull group, pupils were selected randomly and the Revised Stanford-Binet Scale, Form L, was administered until there were obtained twenty-nine pupils who met the following specifications:

1. Estimated true IQs of 84 or below.

2. Estimated true MAs of from ten years, seven months, through twelve years, six months.

From the list of third- and fourth-grade pupils indicated as likely to meet sample specifications for the bright group, pupils were selected randomly and the Revised Stanford-Binet Scale, Form L, was administered until there was obtained a sample of pupils meeting the following specifications:

1. Estimated true IQs of 116 or above.

2. Estimated true MAs of from ten years, seven months, through twelve years, six months.

TABLE 1

Characteristics of the Samples

	Groups	
	Bright	*Dull*
Range of CAs	8-7 through 9-10	14-2 through 16-3
Mean CA	9-2.5	15-5.4
Range of MAs (est. true)	10-8 through 12-6	10-8 through 12-6
Mean MA	11-3.2	11-3.0
Range of IQs (est. true)	116 through 138	72 through 84
Mean IQ	126.5	79.5

3. As many bright children in each of four six-month mental-age intervals or levels (which constituted the two-year range indicated in the preceding specification) as there were dull children in that interval.

In the process of obtaining enough bright cases in each level to match the number of dull cases in that level, extra cases were obtained for some of the levels. For purposes of statistical analysis, extra cases in each level were later discarded randomly. The final sample contained twenty-eight children in each group, dull and bright, one case originally selected for the dull group having been lost because of incomplete data. In the dull group, there were fifteen boys and thirteen girls; thirteen in Grade 8, six in Grade 9, and nine in special classes. The bright group was composed of sixteen boys and twelve girls; fifteen in Grade 3 and thirteen in Grade 4. A summary of information relative to the dull and bright groups in the sample is presented in Table 1.

SELECTION OF COMPREHENSION ABILITIES INVESTIGATED

A survey of the professional literature, teachers' manuals accompanying series of readers, standardized tests, and reported results of factorial studies was made for suggestions of specific abilities involved in reading comprehension. Consideration was also given to availability of measuring instruments for these specific abilities, the possibilities of adapting available instruments to the purposes of this study, and the purported importance of given abilities. This resulted in the selection of the following abilities for inclusion in this investigation:

1. Word recognition (the ability to recognize given words "on sight").

2. Word meaning (the ability to understand or recognize the particular meaning of a word as it is used in context).

3. Memory for factual details (the ability to recall specific facts which have been definitely stated in a selection).

4. Location or recognition of factual details (the ability to locate or recognize specific factual details which are explicitly stated in a given selection).

5. Perception of relationships among definitely stated ideas (the ability to recognize or to formulate an idea which is not explicitly stated in a selection but which is contained in the selection when two or more definitely stated ideas are considered together).

6. Recognition of main ideas (the ability to recognize the central thought or main idea of an entire selection, a paragraph, or a specific part of a paragraph).

7. Drawing inferences and conclusions (the ability to recognize, or to formulate, an idea which is not stated in a selection but which is dependent upon the combination of an idea [or ideas] which is [arc] definitely stated in a selection and one which is outside the selection and within the informational or experiential background of the individual).

In addition to these abilities, measures of reading rate and listening comprehension were also obtained. Reading-rate scores were secured not only because comparisons between the groups were of some interest in themselves, but also because marked differences in rate could be responsible for differences in comprehension abilities, even though the tests were untimed. The measures of listening comprehension were obtained in order to determine whether differences in general comprehension ability exist when unencumbered by possible difficulties with mechanical skills in reading.

CRITERION TESTS USED

Eighty words from the Flashed Word Recognition and Word Analysis Test of the Durrell Analysis of Reading Difficulty and twenty more difficult words from various forms (Q through T) of Part II (Vocabulary) of the Reading Comprehension Test, Advanced Battery, of the Iowa Tests of Basic Skills were included in the word-recognition test. These one hundred words were arranged in lists of twenty each and were presented tachistoscopically for a duration of approximately one second. Only results obtained with the last four lists (eighty words) were included in the analysis of results.

The word-meaning test was a multiple-response test consisting of a representative sample of fifty items chosen from various forms (Q through T) of Part II (Vocabulary) of the Reading Comprehension Test, Elementary and Advanced Batteries, of the Iowa Tests of Basic Skills.

A test of comprehension abilities was made up of nine reading selections and one hundred and thirty items which were adapted from the Reading Comprehension Test of the Elementary and Advanced Batteries of the Iowa Tests of Basic Skills, Forms L through T. Five subtest scores, each based on from twenty-five to twenty-seven items, were obtained as measures of these five specific abilities: memory for factual details, location or recognition of factual details, perception of relationships among definitely stated ideas, recognition of main ideas, and drawing inferences and conclusions. The reading selections were chosen on the basis of relative difficulty, apparent interest value, and the extent to which items accompanying selections represented the specific abilities named above. To obtain subtests of approximately equal length and difficulty, a number of original items were eliminated and additional ones were constructed when necessary.

A listening-comprehension test was constructed in a manner similar to that for the test of comprehension abilities, except that items for location or recognition of factual details were not included. The test consisted of four reading selections and forty-two items. The test booklets contained only the questions related to the selections. The selections and the test items were read aloud to the subjects by the examiner; and subjects marked their chosen responses to each question after it and its answer choices had been read.

The reading-rate test consisted of a selection of approximately fifteen hundred words of fourth- to fifth-grade level of difficulty. Subjects were instructed to read the selection once "at the same speed as you usually read." They were told before they began that there would be questions about the material read. A short comprehension test, consisting mainly of items measuring memory for details, followed the reading of the selection. The rate score was a complement of the number of complete ten-second intervals which had elapsed during the reading of the selection.

All of the criterion tests were administered by the writer during an eight-day testing period. All were administered as group tests, without time limits, with the exception of the word-recognition test, which was administered to each subject individually. All test items, except those for the word-recognition test, were of the four-choice multiple-response type. Except for the reading-rate test rate scores, all scores used in the analyses of results represented the number of items answered correctly.

ANALYSIS OF RESULTS

An analysis of variance design, "group-by-levels," was employed in the analysis of results.* The bright and dull children represent the "groups," and the intervals of six months in the two-year mental age range used in the study constitute the "levels." A schematic presentation of the groups-by-levels design as it applies to this study is shown below.

MA level	MA (est'd true)	Criterion scores	
		Bright group	Dull group
I	12-1 to 12-6	$N = 7$	$N = 7$
II	11-7 to 12-0	$N = 9$	$N = 9$
III	11-1 to 11-6	$N = 7$	$N = 7$
IV	10-7 to 11-0	$N = 5$	$N = 5$

In the case of each ability investigated, the null hypothesis was tested: that the means of the populations of which the dull and bright groups were representative samples were the same. To test this hypothesis, the ratio of the mean square for groups to the mean square for within cells was employed. This ratio yields a value which

* E. F. Lindquist, *Design and Analysis of Experiments in Psychology and Education,* Boston: Houghton Mifflin Co., 1952.

is distributed as F, provided that the hypothesis is true and that certain conditions are met. A five percent coefficient of risk, selected in advance of the analysis, was employed in rejecting the null hypothesis.

RESULTS

A summary of the obtained results is presented in Table 2. The table includes the mean and standard deviations for each group, the differences between the means, and the F values obtained in the tests of the significance of the differences between the means of the bright and dull groups. Positive differences favor the bright group.

Obtained differences between the mean scores of the two groups favored the bright group with respect to all the abilities except word meaning. In the case of this one exception, the difference was not only nonsignificant, but also less than one raw-score unit. The analyses of variance yielded significant differences with respect to the following five abilities: location or recognition of factual details, recognition of main ideas, drawing inferences and conclusions, total comprehension abilities, and listening comprehension. While not significant at the required level, differences between the mean scores for memory for factual details and for perception of relationships among definitely stated ideas were substantial, and further investigation with respect to these two abilities seems warranted. Differences with respect to word recognition, word meaning, and reading rate were not significant.

The test of listening comprehension was included in anticipation of the possible event that the group which was found significantly poorer on most of the abilities would be found to be significantly better with respect to listening comprehension. Then such results might have been interpreted in terms of possible difficulty with mechanical skills in reading rather than in terms of differences in intellectual abilities or specific comprehension abilities. However, the bright group, which excelled on nearly all of the abilities, also excelled significantly on the listening-comprehension test. Similarly, if a significantly higher rate had been found for the group also found to be significantly poorer with respect to most of the abilities, the poorer showing might have been attributed, in part, to tendencies to read carelessly and too hastily. However, no significant rate difference was found between the two groups and analysis of the reading-rate-comprehension check indicated that the two groups had read the reading-rate selection with comparable degrees of understanding. These findings with respect to reading rate and listening comprehension tend to further indicate that superiority in reading comprehension involves superiority in intellectual functions rather than in the more mechanical skills.

TABLE 2

Summary of Results: Mean Scores for Each Group, Differences between Means, and F Values, for Each Ability

Ability	Bright		Dull		Differences $(M_B\text{-}M_D)$	F^*
	Mean	SD	Mean	SD		
Word recognition	58.6	11.8	56.2	13.0	+ 2.4	0.499
Word meaning	30.4	6.1	30.8	6.1	— 0.4	0.076
Memory for factual details	17.4	4.0	15.1	4.8	+ 2.3	3.678
Location or recognition of factual details	15.8	3.6	12.7	3.3	+ 3.1	10.126†
Perception of relationships among definitely stated ideas	15.4	3.6	14.0	3.6	+ 1.4	2.058
Recognition of main ideas	16.3	4.1	13.9	3.9	+ 2.4	5.319†
Drawing inferences and conclusions	14.9	3.1	12.9	3.7	+ 2.0	4.628†
Total-comprehension abilities	79.8	15.1	68.4	16.7	+ 11.4	7.922†
Listening comprehension	30.6	3.6	23.6	4.7	+ 7.0	47.574†
Reading rate (rate score)	61.6	17.9	55.4	15.9	+ 6.2	1.602
Reading rate (comprehension score)	10.7	2.4	9.8	3.4	+ 0.9	1.444

* For each F value, df $= 1, 48$; $F_{05} = 4.04$.
† Significant at 5-percent level.

Tests for interaction between groups and levels were also made. No significant interaction effects were found for any of the abilities tested, thus satisfying one of the necessary conditions or underlying assumptions involved in the particular design of the study.

Inspection of the frequency distributions for the various abilities involved in this study revealed that, in general, obtained scores did not closely approach the maximum possible at the upper end of the distribution or the "chance" scores at the lower end. Thus, neither ceiling nor floor effects operated to bias the results.

CONCLUSIONS

In the strictest sense, the sample studied may be regarded as a representative sample only of hypothetical populations that show the same relative distribution of MAs, IQs, and CAs as the groups in the sample itself; and generalizations based upon obtained results should be restricted to these hypothetical populations. However, since no significant interaction effects between groups and levels were found, restrictions upon extending generalizations to real populations may be lifted to a considerable extent. Therefore, generalizing to a population of dull and bright children with widely differing IQs but approximately equal MAs within the MA ranges found in this study and with reference to the various comprehension abilities as defined operationally, the following conclusions seem warranted:

1. Bright children are significantly superior to dull children of comparable mental ages with respect to total reading comprehension and the following specific abilities: locating or recognizing factual details, recognizing main ideas, and drawing inferences and conclusions.

2. It seems probable that bright children are also superior to dull children of comparable mental ages with respect to memory for factual details and perception of relationships among definitely stated ideas.

3. Bright children are superior to dull children of comparable mental ages with respect to listening comprehension.

4. Reading rates of bright and dull children of comparable mental ages appear to be approximately the same when comparable degrees of understanding of material read are attained, with a wide range in rate being found in both groups.

5. Bright and dull children tend to be alike with respect to ability in word recognition and word meaning. Bright children are significantly superior to dull children of comparable mental ages with respect to the relatively more complex, and intellectual, comprehension abilities.

6. It would seem that levels of expectation with respect to the more complex comprehension abilities should not be as high for dull children as for bright children of comparable mental ages.

REFERENCES

1. Almack, John C., and James L. Almack. "Gifted Pupils in the High School." *School and Society,* 14, September 24, 1921, 227-228.
2. Kolstoe, Oliver P. "A Comparison of Mental Abilities of Bright and Dull Children of Comparable Mental Ages." *J. Educ. Psychol.,* 45, March 1954, 161-168.
3. Lewis, W. Drayton. *A Study of Superior Children in the Elementary School.* George Peabody College Contributions to Education, No. 266, George Peabody College for Teachers, Nashville, Tenn., 1940.
4. McGehee, William A. *A Study of Retarded Children in the Elementary School.* George Peabody College Contributions to Education, No. 246, Nashville, Tenn.: George Peabody College for Teachers, 1939.
5. Ramaseshan, Rukmini S. "A Note on the Validity of the Mental Age Concept." *J. Educ. Psychol.,* 41, January 1950, 56-58.
6. Thomas, G. I. "A Study of Reading Achievement in Terms of Mental Ability." *Elem. School J.,* 47, September 1946, 28-33.
7. Unsicker, Willard D. *A Psychological Study of Bright and Dull Children with Comparable Mental Ages,* unpublished doctoral dissertation, Iowa City: State Univ. Iowa, 1950.
8. Van Wagenen, M. J. "A Comparison of the Mental Ability and School Achievement of the Bright and Dull Pupils in the Sixth Grade of a Large School System." *J. Educ. Psychol.,* 16, March 1925, 186-192.

SOME SPECIAL-ABILITY TEST SCORES
OF GIFTED CHILDREN

by Frank T. Wilson

HUNTER COLLEGE

The pupils of the Hunter College Elementary School have, for the past ten years, been admitted on the basis of IQ scores in the upper 1 percent of their age groups. The average IQ for the 1947-1948 year, according to the entering Binets of the children in the year of their admittance, was about 151.

[Reprinted from the *Journal of Genetic Psychology*, 82, March 1953, 59-68, with the permission of The Journal Press and the author.]

It was of interest to know something of their abilities in special areas and therefore, in so far as it was practicable within rather severe limitation of research possibilities, a variety of special abilities was measured by standardized instruments. The testing was limited to 11-year-old groups and took place during various years from 1947 to 1950.

The age range of the Hunter College Elementary School pupils is from 3 to 11 years. "Promotion" is chronological and enrichment in a regimen of informal and interest-motivated activities is the underlying approach to meeting their growth needs.

Findings from tests in five special-ability areas given to children during their last year in the school are reported here. Validity of administration was high. Directions were carefully followed with ease and clarity, and the response by the children was excellent in terms of effort and interest. They characteristically were cooperative, accepted the tests as challenges, exhibited poise, and worked with unhurried care and dispatch. Only occasionally did any individual show any resistance or lack of seriousness.

In connection with some of the analyses of these findings use has been made of results of the Wechsler-Bellevue Scale I (8), which was given to the children within a year of the time the special-ability tests were administered. The Wechsler provides both a verbal and a performance IQ as well as a full-scale score, which adds some interest to the study. As shown elsewhere, the Wechsler clearly taps other abilities as well as some of the same that enter into the Binet scores, on which the children were admitted to the school, or they do so in different proportions, since they characteristically ran 20-25 points lower than the Binets and since correlation of the Binet and Wechsler-Bellevue scores has been found to be .49±.04 for 153 cases of these children.

ART

The Meier Art Judgment Test was given to 89 children. This test is based upon "the general assumption that esthetic judgment is one of the most important, if not the most important, single factor in artistic competence" (5, p. 4). The task set the subject is to choose, between two almost identical versions, the better one, so keyed because therein an artistic "principle functions to make for a greater esthetic value." The alternate version presents the same picture except that in it the functioning of the principle has been impaired. The answer sheet on which the subject marks his judgment informs him "regarding what aspect of the composition change has affected some principle, but the principle is not named." "The subject is to respond to the separate versions as to a whole." "Materials have been devised on the basis of works of established merit." All are in black and white only.

The test was given to 40 boys and 49 girls of the sixth grade.

Very similar median scores for boys and girls were recorded, but a considerably wider variability among the boys. Norms are not given in the manual for Grade 6. Norms for 1445 junior-high-school pupils, grades seven, eight, and nine, are provided, however, and are about 88.3 for the median score and 95.5 for the upper quartile of scores. The upper quartile score for the Hunter grade-six children, obtained by adding one quartile deviation, 8.86, to the median score of the group, 85.0, is 93.86.

This level in the norms is considered critical in that, the manual says, "Individuals falling into this range should, other things being equal, find almost certain success in an art career." A large proportion of the upper quartile of these sixth-grade children fell within the range of the upper quartile of the junior-high-school pupils on whom the norms were established. That fact seems to support the conclusion that there was a strong trend toward superior art-judgment ability in this group of sixth-grade children.

MUSIC

DRAKE MUSICAL MEMORY TEST

The Drake Musical Memory Test was devised to measure *"capacity* for musical achievement" (2, p. 2). "Discovery of innate talent is the chief aim" of the test according to the author. It is made up of 12 series of two-bar melodies, increasing in difficulty and in span of memory, which are played on the piano. In each series the first melody is repeated one or more times with slight changes in either key, time, or notes, or is played without change. The pupils indicate for each repetition what change is made, or if it is the same. The score is the number of errors made.

Form A was given to several 11-year-old groups, a total of 144 children being tested.

Compared with the norms both the boys and the girls scored in the average age group of 22 years "based on 1979 cases from the third grade through college," for Form A. By percentile rank for average 11-year-olds the group average is at the 87.5 percentile for boys and the girls 11-13 years of age, averaging 12 years old.

In order to indicate whether or not general intelligence contributed markedly to this superior rating of musical memory ability, correlation coefficients of Wechsler-Bellevue I IQs and Drake Memory Test error scores were computed. Small negative coefficients resulted. Since the scores of the music test are error scores, the relationship is an inverse one by definition. The table* needs to be inversely interpreted, therefore, to express the relationships between the music abilities discriminated by the test and mental abilities measured by the Wechsler test. So interpreted, the relationships are in the main quite small in degree, and somewhat varied in respect to parts of the test and to sex differences. The relatively low figures for both the number of cases and the size of the coefficients probably means that the differences obtained were of uncertain significance.

KWALWASSER-RUCH TEST OF MUSICAL ACCOMPLISHMENT
FOR GRADES 4-12

This test "is designed to measure the achievement of pupils in the typical public-school music course" (3, p. 1), validated against "specifications adopted by the Music Supervisors' National Conference," 1921. Thus the content was not especially suited to use in this school where enrichment and adaptability of experiences are major principles determining young children's activities. The median scored by 45 children on this test of formal music knowledge, was 92.5, 3.5 points below that of the norm for Grade 6.

Variability was quite large, reflecting what was known to be true regarding learnings from private music lessons taken by many of the children. Boys seemed less accomplished on the whole than girls, although a boy made the highest score in the group.

SCIENCE

The elementary form of the Calvert Science Information Test was given to three 11-year-old groups in the spring of 1947. This test

* Tables 1-9 have been omitted in reprinting.—EDITOR'S NOTE.

was standardized for use in grades four-six, but it was entirely inadequate to measure these children, since 59 of the 72 who took it scored above the top grade equivalent of 8.5+.

Accordingly, in the spring of 1949 Form A of the Ruch-Popenoe General Science Test, "primarily for grades eight and nine" was given to 19 boys and 23 girls of two 11-year-old groups. The test was "designed primarily to measure the accomplishment of pupils in general and elementary science courses in either the eighth or ninth grade" (6, p. 1).

The general reaction of the children to this test was unusual. Most of them were completely at a loss in regard to many of the exercises and omitted a great many altogether. There seemed to be an emotional element best described as frustration for many of the children who squirmed, groaned, and mumbled about their situation. However, they made scores on both parts of the test and the medians for boys and for the total group of boys and girls were not far below the norms for the children who had had one semester of science in grade eight or nine. This is all the more significant in view of the fact that no special teacher of science has been provided in the school and what work the children had was under the direction of their regular classroom teacher with no special materials. The findings bear out opinions that gifted children tend to be especially interested in science and acquire unusual understanding in that area.

There were 41 cases for whom W-B scores were available. A rho correlation of .45 indicates that general mental ability had a fair degree of relationship to the science abilities, but probably did not have a marked effect on scores.

MECHANICAL ABILITY

The Stenquist Mechanical Aptitude Test II was given to 76 eleven-year-olds; 37 of the group were children in a special class of gifted children in a New York City public school whose IQ scores were similar in range and median to those of the HCES children. The Stenquist scores were also similar to those of the Hunter pupils and so in order to have a larger sampling for purposes of comparing sexes the two groups were combined.

An eight-point difference in medians between the sexes was found—a finding consistent with a well-substantiated fact that boys tend to surpass girls in achievement in mechanical ability. The variability was also greater for the boys. However, one girl scored at the interval next to the highest interval reached by the boys, and one boy scored at the interval just above that of the lowest girl.

The median score for each sex was much above the Stenquist norm for 1087 children reported in 1922. The manual is not clear as to the sex of the standardization group as the words "children," "pupils," and "boys" are used in various connections. The score of one of the illustrative cases, a 14-year-old boy, was interpreted as being "exceeded by 97 percent of boys of *his own age*" (7, p. 17). If the norms are for boys only, then the 47 girls of this study presumably surpass the abilities of girls in general, even more than is shown by the comparison in the table.

The percentile positions and T-scores used in the Stenquist norms show, of course, similar evidence of superiority of these pupils, the boys scoring at the 91 percentile and the girls at the 77 percentile of the standardization group, equivalent to about $+1.2$ SD and $+.5$ SD, respectively, of the distribution of sources of that group.

In order to see what relationship to general intelligence might be indicated correlations of the 39 HCES children and W-B scores were computed for the total Stenquist score and three component parts of it. All coefficients are fairly high, but even within the limits of their PE's would indicate considerable, but far from major, overlap of abilities. Stenquist reported a Pearson r of $.21\pm.04$, and that of 275 seventh- and eighth-grade boys in a New York City school who "were above-average in general abstract intelligence, 52 percent were also above-average in general mechanical aptitude." The standardization group was, presumably, more nearly representative of seventh- and eighth-grade boys than the group herein reported.

The Detroit Mechanical Aptitude Examination, Form A, was also given to a group of 22 HCES boys and girls. The median score was 160.6, $Q\pm15$, total range 109 to 202. According to Baker's Table 1, this is in the upper 8 percent of scores for 11-year-old children, which includes scores 149-337. He suggests that A and B scores, according to "approximately 200 Detroit counselors and teachers," indicate promise as "artist, civil engineer, dentist, laboratory teacher, osteopath, shop teacher, and surgeon" (1, p. 15)—an interesting selection, and names of occupations numerously represented in the parental vocations of parents of the HCES children.

The Revised Minnesota Paper Form Board Tests were given to

20 children in January 1948. The 1948 manual says that the tests appear "to measure the ability to perceive spatial relationships" (4, p. 2). "Scores have predictive value for achievement in mechanical fields and shopwork. . . ." The test is designed for use in high schools, colleges, and for industrial purposes. Although for this reason it was very difficult for 11-year-old children, it was administered to a small group of 11-year-old pupils of the school to see what these gifted children could do with it.

Considerable variability for both the boys and the girls was found, the range for both running from 16-55. A girl made the highest score and a boy the lowest one, although the boys' median was some six points above that of the girls. The norm on the group nearest these children in age was for boys and girls in grades nine and ten who scored a median of 39. Compared with that older group the Hunter children scored a median of 30.4, equivalent to the 28th percentile for the nine and tenth graders.

SUMMARY

Gifted 11-year-old children who had spent most of their school life in the Hunter College Elementary School for young gifted children showed, in general, superiority in abilities in art judgment, music memory, science, and mechanical abilities, as measured by seven different standardized tests. The degree of superiority was most marked, apparently, in music memory, and least in music accomplishment as measured by the 1921 Kwalwasser-Ruch test.

The distribution of scores approached more closely to the normal curve in all of these measures, than did the IQ scores on which the children had been admitted to the school. Variability in the measures was also very marked.

Correlations of scores on these tests with recent Wechsler-Bellevue IQ scores of the children were from near zero to moderate in degree.

The findings corroborate other reports of trends toward excellence in abilities of various kinds among gifted children together with relatively unimpressive correlations with IQ. They also indicate pronounced individual variability among young gifted children in terms of their various individual abilities and in comparison with one another.

REFERENCES

1. Baker, H. J., P. H. Voelker, and A. C. Crockett. *Detroit Mechanical Aptitudes Examination, Form A* (Manual). Bloomington, Ill.: Public School Publishing, 1928-1939.
2. Drake, R. M. "Musical Memory Test, Forms A and B." *A Test of Musical Talent* (Manual). Bloomington, Ill.: Public School Publishing, 1934.
3. Kwalwasser, J., and G. M. Ruch. *Kwalwasser-Ruch Test of Musical Accomplishment for Grades IV-XII* (Manual). Iowa City: State Univ. Iowa, 1942.
4. Likert, R., and W. H. Quasha. *The Revised Minnesota Paper Form Board Test* (Manual). New York: Psychological Corporation, 1948.
5. Meier, N. C. *The Meier Art Test: I. Art Judgment* (Manual). Iowa City: State Univ. Iowa, 1942.
6. Ruch, G. M., and H. F. Popenoe. *Ruch-Popenoe General Science Test* (Manual). New York: World Book, 1926.
7. Stenquist, J. L. *Stenquist Mechanical Aptitude Tests* (Manual). New York: World Book, 1922.
8. Wechsler, D. *The Measurement of Adult Intelligence.* Third Ed. Baltimore: Williams and Wilkins, 1944.

THE UPPER LIMIT OF ABILITY AMONG AMERICAN NEGROES

by Martin D. Jenkins

MORGAN STATE COLLEGE

More than three decades of psychometric investigation among American Negroes has yielded a rich fund of information concerning this population group. Perhaps the most generally known finding, and certainly the most emphasized, is that when "comparable" groups of whites and Negroes are tested, the Negro group is almost invariably

[Reprinted from *Scientific Monthly,* 66, May 1948, 399-401, with the permission of the American Association for the Advancement of Science and the author.]

inferior to the white in psychometric intelligence (intelligence as measured by psychological tests). Preoccupation with the significance of the low *average* performance of Negro groups has served to divert attention from an equally important phenomenon—the variability of the group, and especially the upper limit reached by its really superior members.

The question of the upper limit of ability among Negroes has both theoretical and practical significance. Psychologists generally attribute the low-average performance of Negro groups on intelligence tests to cultural factors. It is well known that Negroes generally experience an inferior environment; and there is certainly no question but that an inferior environment tends to depress the psychometric intelligence. There are, however, many Negro children who are nurtured in an environment that is equal or superior to that of the average white child. Thus, we may hypothesize that *if race in itself is not a limiting factor in intelligence, then, among Negroes whose total environment compares favorably with that of the average American white, there should be found a "normal" proportion of very superior cases, and the upper limit of ability should coincide with that of the white population.* This hypothesis is especially attractive from a negative aspect; thus, if very superior individuals are not to be found in the Negro population, the environmental explanation would clearly be inadequate to account for the phenomenon. The existence of such individuals, on the other hand, would afford additional evidence, but not absolute proof, of course, of the validity of the environmental explanation of "racial differences" in psychometric intelligence.

The practical significance of the question is apparent. If Negroes are to be found at the highest levels of psychometric intelligence, then we may anticipate that members of this racial group have the ability to participate in the culture at the highest level. In these days of reconsideration of the role of the dark races throughout the world, this question has more than mere national significance.

Analysis of the literature relating to the intelligence-test performance of Negro children reveals that a considerable number of these children have been found within the range that reaches the best 1 percent of white children (IQ 130 and above) and at the level of "gifted" children (IQ 140 and above). There are at least sixteen published studies that give an account of Negro children possessing IQs above 130; twelve of these report cases above IQ 140. These investigations were made by different psychologists in various localities and under varying conditions; moreover, the IQs were derived by a number of different tests. Further, the populations studied were located almost exclusively in Northern urban communities. Consequently, one may not justifiably generalize, from a composite of these studies, concerning the incidence of Negro deviates. It is of significance, however, that of the 22,301 subjects included in the thirteen studies for which Ns are reported, 0.3 percent scored at IQ 140 and above, and fully 1 percent scored at IQ 130 and above. These percentages are similar to those obtained from a "normal" IQ distribution of American school children.

Of especial significance are the cases of very bright children of Binet IQ 160 and above. It may be estimated that fewer than 0.1 percent of school children are to be found at or above this level. As the IQ rises above 160, the frequency of occurrence, of course, decreases. Statistically, cases at or above IQ 180 should occur about once in a million times, although they actually occur with somewhat greater frequency. In his classic California study of the gifted, Terman found only 15 children testing as high as IQ 180; and Hollingworth reports: "In twenty-three years seeking in New York City and the local metropolitan area I have found only twelve children who test at or above 180 IQ (S-B)." It is apparent then, that children who test upwards of Binet IQ 160 are extreme deviates in psychometric intelligence and representative of the very brightest children in America.

I have assembled from various scores the case records of 18 Negro children who test above IQ 160 on the Stanford-Binet examination. Seven of these cases test above IQ 170, four above IQ 180, and one at IQ 200. Two of these cases were tested initially by me; the other 16 were reported by psychologists in university centers and public-school systems. Analysis of the case records indicates that these children, during the early years of their development, at least, manifest the same characteristics as do other very high IQ children: originality of expression, creative ability, and surpassing performance in school subjects. Some of these children, but not all, are greatly accelerated in school progress. Two, for example, had completed their high-school course and were regularly enrolled university students at age thirteen; both of these subjects were elected to Phi Beta Kappa and earned the baccalaureate degree at age sixteen.

It is of some significance that all these children were found in

Northern or border-state cities (New York, Chicago, Washington, and Cincinnati). No Southern Negro child, so far as I have been able to ascertain, has been identified as testing at or above Binet IQ 160. It is certain that among the 80 percent of the total Negro population that lives in the Southern states, children with potentiality for such development exist. Whether the fact that no children with this development have been discovered is due to lack of environmental opportunity and stimulation, or merely lack of identification, is not surely known.

I am not attempting here to show that approximately as many Negro children as white are to be found at the higher levels of psychometric intelligence. There appears little doubt that the number of very bright Negro children is relatively smaller than the number of bright white children in the total American population. Nevertheless, it is apparent that children of very superior psychometric intelligence may be found in many Negro populations, and that the upper limit of the range attained by the extreme deviates is higher than is generally believed.

The performance of extreme deviates at the college and adult levels has not yet been extensively studied. Such evidence as is available, however, indicates that at maturity, as in childhood, some Negroes are to be found at the highest level of psychometric intelligence. In a recent unpublished study conducted at Harvard University, it was found that of approximately 3500 Negro freshmen entering the College of Liberal Arts over a period of seven years, 101 scored in the upper decile, and 8 in the upper centile (national norms) on the American Council on Education Psychological Examination. In a more extensive study, the National Survey of Higher Education of Negroes, there were, among 3684 students in twenty-seven Negro institutions of higher education located chiefly in the Southern states, 23 cases in the upper decile and 4 in the upper centile on the ACE Psychological Examination. It is of some significance that in the same study 12 upper decile cases are reported among the 105 Negro students in two Northern universities (almost half as many as were found altogether among the 3684 students in the twenty-seven Negro colleges). This contrast is in accord with the general but undocumented opinion that among Negro college students there are proportionately fewer extreme deviates in psychometric intelligence in the Southern segregated colleges than in the Northern nonsegregated institutions.

The Army General Classification Test data assembled during World War II have not yet become fully available. One may predict with a fair degree of confidence, however, that these data will reveal some Negro cases at the very highest levels of performance.* In view of the fact, however, that the Negro selectees were predominantly from communities that provide inadequate provision for the educational and cultural development of Negroes, we may expect that a very small proportion of the total population will be found at the higher levels of performance. Subgroups which have had a normal cultural opportunity should, in accordance with our hypothesis, yield an appreciable proportion of superior deviates.

The findings of the studies cited in this article support the hypothesis formulated at the outset. In some population groups there is to be found a "normal" proportion of Negro subjects of very superior psychometric intelligence, and the extreme deviates reach the upper limits attained by white subjects. Although the incidence of superior cases is much lower among Negroes than whites, a phenomenon which might well be accounted for by differential environmental factors, we may conclude that race per se (at least as it is represented in the American Negro) is not a limiting factor in psychometric intelligence.

The abstract mental tests that contribute to psychometric intelligence do not measure the factors of personality and motivation that largely determine success in life. The findings of studies of gifted children, especially those of Terman, Hollingworth, and Witty, indicate that the highly gifted child usually fulfills his early promise. But not aways. Failure among the gifted is also frequent.

The data of this article bring into sharp focus the limitations that our society places on the development of the highly gifted Negro. These superior deviates are nurtured in a culture in which racial inferiority of the Negro is a basic assumption. Consequently, they will typically experience throughout their lives educational, social, and occupational restrictions that must inevitably affect mo-

* Although these data never became generally available, there is no reason to doubt the author's statement. A recent review of the literature pertaining to the full range of intelligence appears in William M. McCord and Nicholas J. Demerath III, "Negro versus White Intelligence: A Continuing Controversy," *Harvard Educational Review*, spring 1958, pp. 120-135. In their own study, McCord and Demerath used the Kuhlmann-Anderson group test and the Stanford-Binet with 612 Northern, urban boys and "found no significant difference in intelligence between Negroes and whites" (p. 134).—EDITOR'S NOTE.

tivation and achievement. The unanswered question relative to the influence of this factor on the adult achievement of superior Negroes is a problem for future investigators to solve.

THE PRODUCTIVITY OF NATIONAL MERIT SCHOLARS BY OCCUPATIONAL CLASS

by Horace Mann Bond

ATLANTA UNIVERSITY

The 1956 *Report* (1) of the National Merit Scholarship Corporation includes a table (p. 18) that gives the "Occupations of fathers as reported by scholars." When the occupations listed by scholars are grouped according to the major occupational categories of the United States Census, it is possible to work out a ratio between scholars and numbers of workers, called here an "Index of Productivity of National Merit Scholars by Occupational Class." Table 1 is the result.

A further breakdown of suboccupational groups yields even more striking suggestions as to the factors involved in the productivity by occupational classes of National Merit Scholars. The five highest subgroups in productivity were:

	Numbers	*Scholars produced*	*Index*
Librarians	6,390	2	3195
College presidents, professors, and instructors	96,030	28	3429
Architects	22,830	5	4566
Lawyers and judges	165,300	34	4861
Clergymen	112,679 *	13	8667

* Corrected by subtracting Catholic clergy from U. S. Census totals.

[Reprinted from *School and Society*, 85, September 28, 1957, 267-268, with permission of *School and Society* and the author.]

TABLE 1

The Productivity of National Merit Scholars by Various Basic Occupational Classes, 1956

Major U. S. Census occupational groups ranked in order of their proportionate productivity of National Merit Scholars	The Number of male workers in these classes, 1950 Census	The Number of scholars who reported this group for father's occupation, 1956	The Index of "productivity" of scholars by occupational class (how many workers required to produce one scholar)
I. Professional, technical, and kindred workers	2,965,350	234	12,672
II. Managers, officials, and proprietors	4,272,510	115	37,153
III. Sales workers	2,639,490	34	77,632
IV. Clerical and kindred workers	2,670,870	28	95,380
V. Craftsmen, foremen, and kindred workers	7,846,290	56	140,112
VI. Operatives and kindred workers	8,470,740	27	313,731
VII. Service workers	2,563,890*	7	366,270
VIII. Farmers and farm managers, farm laborers, and foremen	6,234,300*	16	389,643
IX. Laborers, except farm and mine	3,581,370	1	3,581,370
Total, Male workers, 1950	42,068,820	518	81,213

* Lack of specification in the reports of occupation of scholars' fathers has led us here to combine, in "service workers," the two separate classifications used by the census, "private household workers" and "service workers except private," and the two Census categories for farm workers, "farmers and farm managers" and "farm laborers and foremen."

Thus, an American child, whose father is a librarian, has 1120 times the chance to win a National Merit Scholarship as a child whose parent is a laborer. The odds against a child, whose father is in one of the farming occupations, to win a National Merit Scholarship in competition with a child of one of the professional occupations is 30-1. While 168,000 physicians produced 26 scholars, 972,300 carpenters produced seven, 516,360 machinists produced three, 289,-140 plumbers produced two, and 1,376,910 truckers produced three.

Some will argue, of course, that the spread of "aptitude" represented by these distributions is a fairly accurate index to the distribution of "native intelligence" in occupational classes. The author prefers a contrary explanation.

The National Merit Scholarships were awarded—as, indeed, they *had* to be awarded—on the basis of competitive tests (after state quotas had been established). These "aptitude" tests accurately measure the degree of facility in the manipulation of verbal and mathematical symbols by the student. Children in whose homes such symbols are now a part of the occupational stock-in-trade of parents (homes where such facility probably has characterized family operations for several generations) almost invariably will surpass children —testwise—from homes not so privileged.

A number of questions remain unanswered. Have we, in the "young" United States, already developed a class system that is almost as fixed and immutable as that long established in Western European social hierarchies? Is our vaunted social mobility a phantom? If there is "talent" in the occupationally underprivileged, what educational processes and institutions are best calculated to liberate it: scholarship schemes or the provision of the widest possible opportunity for higher education accessible to the masses? And how may we devise instruments to look below the surface of deficiencies in verbal facility induced by familial and environmental circumstances?

Even those most deeply committed to "intelligence" and other "aptitude" tests as the best existing instruments for evaluating academic promise may agree that the odds of 1120 to one, now faced by a laborer's child in competition with a librarian's for National Merit Scholarships, scarcely reflect the absolute in human capacities among American laborers. What, if anything, can the American educational system do about it?

REFERENCE

1. Stalnaker, J. M. *Annual Report for the Year Ending June 30, 1956.* Evanston, Ill.: National Merit Scholarship Corp.

THE MAINTENANCE OF INTELLECTUAL ABILITY IN GIFTED ADULTS*

by Nancy Bayley

NATIONAL INSTITUTE OF MENTAL HEALTH

and Melita H. Oden

STANFORD UNIVERSITY

Although numerous studies have shown a tendency for adults to exhibit decreasing intellectual abilities (as measured in test scores) with age, the amount of decrement has been found to vary with the nature of the measuring instrument. In fact, several investigators have found slight but consistent increases up to about 60 years of age in scores earned on tests of vocabulary or word knowledge. These increases have been found to occur in populations of above average ability and education, and in tests that do not put a premium on speed of performance. The increases do not seem to hold for tests that require fast reactions, or for persons of low intelligence.

In a recent summary of research on changes in intellectual function with advancing age, Shock (5) has pointed out that several researchers give evidence of significant changes in mental organization with age; that very few studies have been made in which the same subjects have been retested after a lapse of time; and that most of the tests used are inadequate to differentiate changing abilities at the upper levels of intelligence. Several studies published since

* Figures, tables, and portions of the text have been omitted.—EDITOR'S NOTE.

[Reprinted from the *Journal of Gerontology*, 10, January 1955, 91-107, with permission of the Gerontological Society, Inc., and the authors.]

Shock's summary give important information bearing on the relation between age and score in adults. Owens (4) retested 127 college men on the Army Alpha after a lapse of 31 years. Corsini and Fassett (2), in a study of Wechsler-Bellevue scores, controlled sampling differences related to age by using a "forced sample" of 1072 prison inmates whose ages ranged from 15 to 75 years. Berkowitz (1) reported on Wechsler-Bellevue scores of 1233 veterans ranging in age from 20 to 84 years. All three of these studies indicate that many intellectual functions do not decline with age and that such abilities as information and word knowledge even show continuous improvement well into the later adult years.

THE SAMPLE AND TESTS

The data we are offering here are relevant to some of these questions which are raised by Shock and other investigators. We are comparing retest scores earned approximately twelve years apart by a group of intellectually superior adults on a highly different test. The subjects in this investigation are from the Stanford Study of the Gifted, a research program which was undertaken by L. M. Terman of Stanford University more than thirty years ago. In 1921-1922 a group of 1528 intellectually gifted children ranging in age from 3 to 19 years (average 11.5 years) was selected by means of intelligence tests. The younger subjects, who were chiefly in elementary school and comprised about two thirds of the total group, were located by the 1916 Stanford-Binet test. Their IQs ranged from 140 to 200 with a mean IQ of 151. A group of high-school students who earned scores within the top 1 percent for their age norms on the Terman Group Test comprised most of the older members of the sample (6). These gifted subjects have been followed continuously since 1921 to the present time by means of field-worker interviews, questionnaires, tests, and personal correspondence. Information is available on the later careers of 98 percent of the 1434 members of the original group who were still living in 1950.

When in 1939 Terman planned to test these people as adults, there was no test available which could be administered in a brief period and which had sufficient top to differentiate at a very high level. He found it necessary, therefore, to devise a new test. This test, called Concept Mastery, Form A, is composed of two subtests:

I, Synonyms and Antonyms, and II, Analogies. The test is given with no time limit, but ordinarily takes about 40 minutes to complete. Terman and Oden characterize the test as follows:

> Both the synonym-antonym test and the analogies test are of the type commonly designated as "verbal." They are not as exclusively linguistic, however, as they appear to be. It is possible to devise verbal tests which measure not only vocabulary but a wide variety of information. In the selection of items, an effort was made to tap as many fields as possible by the use of concepts related to physical and biological science, medicine, mathematics, geography, history, logic, literature, psychology, art, religion, music, sports, et cetera. It was relatively easy to secure variety of this kind in the analogy items, but more difficult in the synonym-antonym items. The test has been named the Concept Mastery test because it deals chiefly with abstract ideas. Abstractions are the shorthand of the higher thought processes, and a subject's ability to function at the upper intellectual levels is determined largely by the number and variety of concepts at his command and on his ability to see relationships between them (6).

Terman and Oden (6) have estimated, by comparison with a college sample who were given both the Stanford-Binet and the Concept Mastery, A, tests, that in the 1939-1940 testing the gifted subjects earned scores that average 2.5 standard deviations above the general population. This regression of about one half a standard deviation from the original testing is in line with statistical expectations. The younger subjects scored lowest on the Concept Mastery. This fact was attributed to their youth at the time of selection and the consequent greater likelihood of regressive changes in relative scores during growth.

For use in the most recent testing of these subjects, in 1950-1952, Terman and Oden devised an alternate form of the Concept Mastery. Tests of reliability and validity of Form B show it to be as good as, and probably superior in many ways, to Form A.

In order to secure equivalent scores for Forms A and B we have given both forms, either in immediate succession or at one-week intervals, to 148 college undergraduates and other adults. Form A was given first to half of the subjects and Form B first to the other half. This sample was composed of 108 Stanford undergraduates and 40 graduate students and faculty members at the University of California. After correction for practice effects, the transformation by "line of equivalents" was made and a conversion table of Form B to B(E) scores was set up. For this sample of 148 the r between the two forms is .94.

There were 954 gifted subjects who took Form A of the Concept Mastery Test in 1939-1940 and 1004 who took Form B in 1950-1952, and of these 768 took both Form A and Form B. Their average age at the earlier testing was 29.5 years, with an SD of 3.7 years; at the later testing they averaged approximately 41.5 years. We have additional data on the husbands and wives of these subjects: 527 spouses took the test in 1939-1940 and 677 spouses took it in 1950-1952. Of these, 335 took both forms. The average age of the spouses in 1950-1952 is 41.2 years; SD, 3.3 years. Their test scores in 1939-1940 averaged the same as a group of college graduates who took the test: that is, about 1.6 SD above the average for the general population. Our report is thus based on scores made by 1103 twice-tested adults who are, with few exceptions, above average in intelligence.

In this paper all of the test-retest comparisons are between the 1939-1940 scores on Form A and 1950-1952 scores for the same individuals (unless otherwise indicated) on Form B(E). Some of these comparisons are made for both the subjects of the study and their spouses; other comparisons have been limited to the original gifted group, for whom we have more complete information.

RESULTS

The test-retest correlations for the 12-year interval are generally high. The r is .88 for 422 gifted study men, and also .88 for 346 gifted study women; it is .92 for 144 husbands, and also .92 for 191 wives. Such difference as there is between the correlations for the gifted study subjects and their spouses can be accounted for by the greater variability in scores of the spouses who comprise a sample that is less highly selected in this respect.

The scores at the later testing, when the subjects are approximately 12 years older, are consistently higher than for the first testing. The increases in scores amount to about half an SD and are highly significant, the level of confidence being better than .001 for both the men and the women.

Comparison with those who were tested only once indicates that the twice-tested groups are typical of the total sample. The mean score on Form A for the 422 gifted study men in the twice-tested sample is 98.65 and for the 95 who took only Form A the mean is 98.18. The Form B(E) scores are 114.90 for the twice-tested, and 116.98 for those who took only Form B. Similarly, for the women, the mean A score for the twice-tested sample of 346 is 94.88, and for those who took only Form A it is 89.98. The B(E) scores average 110.45 and 105.42, respectively. The greatest difference is 5 points, or about one sixth of the SD of any one group. Whatever is operating to produce higher scores at the later testing seems to be generally effective, and the failure of subjects to take the tests twice seems to have been unrelated to their ability.

When other investigators have made comparisons of age changes in scores on synonym-antonym and analogies tests they have found a greater difference between the two types of function at the older ages. This difference usually takes the form of a greater decrement with age in the analogies scores. Jones and Conrad (3), for example, using the Army Alpha test, found that the analogies scores drop off more rapidly with age. Owens's (4) twice-tested college men improved .145 SD on the analogies subtest and .549 SD on the synonym-antonym test. We should expect, therefore, that the synonym-antonym scores earned by our subjects will increase more than the analogies. All increments, in both subtests, are highly significant for all four groups of subjects. Although the synonym-antonym scores increase on the average about half an SD, the analogies scores improve by about one third an SD. This latter is more than twice the increment that Owens found for an interval two and a half times as long in the Army Alpha analogies. Although they are called by the same name, the two tests may not be closely similar. Possibly the content of the analogies test used here is heavily weighted with the same kind of verbal knowledge that is measured in the synonym-antonym.

In general, we may conclude that the trend toward increase in retest scores is a function of the entire Concept Mastery test. The average gains are a little larger for the synonym-antonym, and for the groups who originally tested higher. Nevertheless, the gains are highly significant for both sexes and for both gifted subjects and spouses. It may be noted here, also, that for the gifted study subjects the SDs are consistently smaller at the second testing, while the reverse is true for the spouses.

With the fact established that the scores of these adults increase on their retests, we turn now to an attempt to discover factors that may be related to the change. Of course not all of the people gained in scores. A few, only about 9 percent, actually lost more than 5 points: in one or two instances the loss was as great as 25 to 30 points, or about 1 SD of the population here studied. Large gains, however, were frequent. There were 97 instances (9 percent) of gains of 35 points or more, and there was one gain of 62 points, or about 2 SDs. This would be the equivalent of about 27 IQ points (6).

It has seemed reasonable to expect that the change in score, the tendency to gain or to lose in ability during these adult years, could be due to the nature of the persons' activities as reflected in such things as occupational level or amount of education. Or the changes could be related to general health or emotional adjustment, or to changes in motivation in taking the test itself. Or it could be related to age; perhaps the losses were more frequent among the older subjects. There is the further possibility that changes are a function of the initial score, either regression from extremes, or a tendency for greater gains to occur at certain levels of ability.

When we eliminate the three men who were nearest the ceiling on Form A and who, in the equating of the two forms, were forced to lose a few points on the retest Form B(E), there remains some evidence of regression in the scores of both the men and the women in the gifted study. However, among the spouses regression is less evident, and a fair number of low-scoring spouses do not regress upward toward the mean but score even lower on the second test. Also, with few exceptions, gains of 35 points or more occur among those whose Form A scores range between 35 and 100, and tend not to be at the lowest extreme of the scale. At the upper extreme large gains are impossible, and a few high scorers crowd the ceiling of the test. This ceiling, whether it is in the test itself, or at the real upper limit of the subjects' ability, serves to reduce the variability of retest scores in the high-scoring groups. Regression, it seems, accounts for only a part of the changes in scores from the first to the second test.

Although there was general high motivation among the people taking the tests, there were probably some whose motivation changed on the retest. We have no way of identifying these individuals. Such changes could very well occur, perhaps for different reasons, at all levels of ability.

At the first testing occupational classification* in the case of men was definitely related to Concept Mastery score, but at the second testing, although there is still a relation between scores and occupational class, the differences between classes are greatly reduced. The lower the occupational group, the greater the gain in scores. The reduction in class differences is reflected in the critical ratios. For example, the CR between mean scores of the men in Group I compared with Groups III, IV, V, and VI combined is 9.5 on Form A and 5.8 on Form B(E). Of course, the higher scores earned in occupational group I are so much nearer the test ceiling that for many of these men there was no possibility of large gains.

The women in this study for the most part have not been interested in careers, which may explain why their occupational classifications show less differentiation on the basis of Concept Mastery. The largest class, housewives who are not gainfully employed, seems to be representative of the total group. At the first testing no occupational class earned scores significantly different from any other class. At the later testing, however, the women in the "other professions" group forged ahead to earn the highest average score. The B(E) scores of this group are significantly higher than those earned by the housewives and by those in office and business occupations, the two lowest-scoring classes. The women in college teaching and research, who in 1940 tested highest, made practically no gain, while the other four groups gained approximately equal amounts.

Some interesting things come out of the comparison of A and B(E) scores of professional men when they are grouped according to type of profession. In 1939-1940 the engineers made the lowest scores, and these were significantly below scores made by university teachers. In 1950-1952 the engineers have made large gains and are at the average of the total professional group. Their place as lowest scorers has been taken by those who teach below the university level. The difference between the two groups of teachers is significant at the .03 level of confidence at the first testing and at the .05 level at the second test.

In general the tendency has been for the scores of all occupational groups to improve, the lower-scoring ones most, so that here again we find smaller differences between groups than were present

* The classification used is as follows: I, professional; II, semiprofessional and higher business; III, clerical, retail business, and skilled trades; IV, agricultural; V, minor clerical, minor business, and semiskilled; and VI, slightly skilled.

in 1940. This trend, too, may be attributed in part to ceilings on B(E) scores limiting the gains of those who originally scored very high.

The *educational level* achieved by subjects of the gifted study correlates positively with their intelligence test scores. In this respect our data are in agreement with the usual findings. In order to maintain a constant sample, we have grouped subjects according to their education in 1950-1952. Only a few who had not quite completed their schooling in 1939-1940 would have been classified differently at that time. The gains in score occur in all educational levels, but seem to be somewhat greater for those with less education. This tendency is more evident for the men than for the women. To the extent that it occurs, it is in accord with the general tendency already noted for those groups scoring low at the first testing to gain most on the retest. It is contrary, in this instance, to Owens's finding of greater gains in Army Alpha and particularly, the analogies subtest, among his subjects with over five years of college (4). Differences in method of selecting the samples may account for this discrepancy.

Mental health and general adjustment were rated on a three-point scale by Terman and Oden on the 1940 data (6) from all available information about each subject of the gifted group. Using the same method and criteria, the ratings were made again on the 1952 data. Most subjects are classed as normal or as having "satisfactory adjustment." Category III includes only those with serious maladjustment, in some instances including a history of hospitalization. The relations of these ratings to Concept Mastery scores were made. In this comparison the data for Form A are as published in Volume IV (6), while the data for Form B(E) are for the twice-tested sample.

There is, for both sexes, a tendency for the more seriously maladjusted individuals to earn higher scores. The differences are greater for the men and for the 1940 data. Those whose adjustment was classified as satisfactory made greater gains, and again the differences between classes are reduced at the later testing. However, large gains in scores occur in all three classes.

Self-ratings of physical health were not significantly related to the Concept Mastery scores at either testing, and so are obviously not significant determiners in the intellectual functioning of these adults.

In the light of earlier findings, that intelligence test scores of adults decrease with age, perhaps age is the crucial factor to be considered here. The one thing that these 1103 people have in common is that between the two testings they grew about twelve years older. Because the year of birth of the gifted subjects ranged from 1903 to 1920, it has been possible to subdivide the samples into several age groups. We can thus study the trends of scores for groups ranging from their early twenties at the first test to their late forties at the second test. The impressive thing that comes out of this division into age groups is that all groups show similar and significant tendencies to increase in scores over the twelve-year interval. There is, perhaps, a slight tendency for the increments to become smaller with successively older age-groups. This tendency is more evident for the analogies than for the synonym-antonym subtest.

Although there seem to be sampling differences in the abilities of the different groups, it also becomes evident that the lower scores of the younger subjects are in part a function of their age at the time of testing. This is true, in particular, for the young gifted men, who at the second testing did as well as the older men did at the same age. The younger women and the older men in the gifted groups seem, at these testings, to be in general somewhat less able than the rest of the gifted subjects. However, it should be noted that these groups are composed of comparatively few cases.

The age groups of the spouses show greater variability. This may be accounted for by the facts that they were not selected for intelligence test scores in the first place and that the number in any one age group is often very small. The spouses's highest scores seem to occur in the early and middle-age ranges for the men and in the middle ranges for the women. But for any one age group there is the same tendency for scores to improve from the first to the second testing.

DISCUSSION

The material presented here is in disagreement with many of the results of earlier studies of intelligence in adults. The apparent disagreements, however, may be due to the fact that much of this material is of a kind that has not been secured before. Our subjects are well motivated and highly intelligent. The test used was designed to differentiate abilities at the upper levels. Finally, the tests have been repeated on the same subjects after an interval of time that is long enough to allow for significant changes to take place. Our material does not, however, cover the later ages at which real senescent decrements in intellectual functioning are to be expected. Furthermore, our material is not concerned with measures of speed, either in physical action or intellectual processes. The Concept Mastery test, rather, calls for knowledge of symbols and abstractions, and the ability to use these in relation to each other.

The implications to be drawn from our data are that this kind of knowledge and ability improves in superior adults, at least between the ages of 20 and 50. This improvement occurs about equally for all levels of education. It occurs in all levels of occupation represented, but to a greater extent among the middle occupational classes than in the higher classes. Also, within the professional class, the engineers and chemists, whose training was relatively specific and narrow, evidently broaden their abilities with time, so that on this general type of verbal test their scores attain equality with those of the other professions. This broadening tendency may operate generally among intelligent adults in our culture. Such a factor could serve to account for the reduction of class differences in scores at the second testing.

It should be noted that this leveling tendency occurs for subclasses within the groups of already high-scoring gifted study subjects. When we compare the four main groups, the higher-scoring groups show the greater gains on the retest. The rank order, both of mean scores and of gains in scores is: gifted-study men, gifted-study women, husbands, and wives. The general tendency for greater increase in test scores to occur in the more highly intelligent persons is curtailed at the upper extremes of the test by a ceiling. It is impossible to say on the basis of these data whether these individuals would have gained in score on a test with more top, or whether they had already reached their upper limit.

The results of this study tend to be in agreement with those of Owens (4), who also retested the same subjects after a lapse of years. Thus the phenomenon of adult gains seems to be general and not a peculiarity of this test or this sample.

Intellectual changes after 50 should be investigated by similar means. It seems likely that there will be great individual differences in the age at onset of senescent decline.

SUMMARY

A test designed to measure superior intelligence was administered twice, about twelve years apart, to 1103 adults. Of these, 768 were selected as children by Terman, for inclusion in the Stanford Study of Gifted Children. The other 335 are spouses of subjects in the Terman study.

There was a highly significant increase in scores at the second testing, both by the subjects of the gifted study and by their husbands and wives. The order of mean scores, from highest to lowest, was the same as that of gains on the retests, i.e., gifted men, gifted women, husbands, and wives. The increases occurred in all occupational and educational levels represented, at all levels of ability tested, except where the test ceiling prevented, at all ages from 20 to 50 years. The gains were found in both the synonym-antonym and the analogies halves of the test, but were somewhat larger in the former.

Variability of scores was less for the gifted-study subjects and decreased at the second testing and with increasing age. Within these groups occupational, educational, and mental-health class differences were reduced at the second testing. Variability of the spouses' scores was greater and increased on the retest.

The retests of this large group of superior adults give strong evidence that intelligence of the type tested by the Concept Mastery scale continues to increase at least through 50 years of age.

REFERENCES

1. Berkowitz, B. The Wechsler-Bellevue Performance of White Males Past Age 50. *J. Gerontol.* 8, 1953, 76-80.
2. Corsini, R. J., and K. K. Fassett. Intelligence and Aging. *J. Genet. Psychol.* 83, 1953, 249-264.
3. Jones, H. E., and H. S. Conrad. The Growth and Decline of Intelligence. *Genet. Psychol. Mono.* 13, 1933, 223-298.
4. Owens, W. A. Age and Mental Abilities: A Longitudinal Study. *Genet. Psychol. Mono.* 48, 1953, 3-54.
5. Shock, N. W. Gerontology. *Ann. Rev. Psychol.* 2, 1951, 353-370.
6. Terman, L. M., and M. H. Oden. *The Gifted Child Grows Up.* Vol. IV, in *Genetic Studies of Genius.* Stanford, Calif.: Stanford Univ. Press, 1947.

AGE AND ACHIEVEMENT

by Harvey C. Lehman

OHIO UNIVERSITY

By means of statistical distributions and graphs the preceding chapters show the ages (1) at which outstanding thinkers have most frequently made (or first published) their momentous creative contributions, (2) at which leaders have most often attained important positions of leadership, and (3) at which high-salaried workers in several areas have most commonly received large annual incomes. A few data for professional athletes are included to show their similarity to the other findings.

The creative thinkers and the leaders whose lives were studied are mostly deceased persons. Because adequate data were not available for deceased recipients of large annual incomes and deceased athletes, living persons who fall in these two categories were studied. For all groups investigated proper statistical allowance was made for the fact that young men are more numerous than older ones.

Because dates of first publication rather than dates of actual achievement were usually available, the only thing that can be asserted with certainty is the fact that, as regards their most profound insights, our creative workers attained their highest average rate of productivity *not later than* certain specified age levels.

The most notable creative works of scientists and mathematicians were identified by experts in the various specialized fields of endeavor. For such fields as oil painting, education, philosophy, and literature, a consensus of the experts was obtained by a study of their published writings. In each field listed below the maximum average rate of highly superior production was found to occur not later than during the specified range of ages. For example, item 1 of this list, chemistry, 26-30, is to be interpreted as follows: in proportion to the number of chemists that were alive at each successive

[Reprinted from Chapter 20, "Summary and Interpretation," of *Age and Achievement*, Princeton, N. J.: Princeton University Press, 1953, with the permission of the American Philosophical Society and the author.]

age level, very superior contributions to the field of chemistry were made at the greatest average rate when the chemists were not more than 26-30. The remaining items here and those in the tabular lists that follow are to be interpreted in similar manner.

Physical sciences, mathematics, and inventions

1. Chemistry, 26-30
2. Mathematics, 30-34
3. Physics, 30-34
4. Electronics, 30-34
5. Practical inventions, 30-34
6. Surgical techniques, 30-39
7. Geology, 35-39
8. Astronomy, 35-39

Biological sciences

9. Botany, 30-34
10. Classical descriptions of Disease, 30-34
11. Genetics, 30-39
12. Entomology, 30-39
13. Psychology, 30-39
14. Bacteriology, 35-39
15. Physiology, 35-39
16. Pathology, 35-39
17. Medical discoveries, 35-39

In this, and in succeeding tabulations, very precise cross comparisons should not be attempted because the maximum ages vary somewhat both with the era during which the workers were born and also with the quality of the output under consideration, and it was not possible to equate all these different kinds of contributions upon both these bases.

For most types of superior music, the maximum average rate of good production is likely to occur in the thirties. Here are the maxima.

Music

18. Instrumental selections, 25-29
19. Vocal solos, 30-34
20. Symphonies, 30-34
21. Chamber music, 35-39
22. Orchestral music, 35-39

23. Grand opera, 35-39
24. Cantatas, 40-44
25. Light opera and musical comedy, 40-44

For the study of literary creativity, fifty well-known histories of English literature were canvassed. The works most often cited by the fifty literary historians were assumed to be superior to those cited infrequently. Best-liked short stories were identified similarly by use of 102 source books, and "best books" were ascertained by study of a collation of fifty "best-book" lists. As is revealed by the following tabulation, literary works that are good and permanently great are produced at the highest average rate by persons who are not over 45 years old. It is clear also that most types of poetry show maxima 10 to 15 years earlier than most prose writings other than short stories.

Literature

26. German composers of noteworthy lyrics and ballads, 22-26
27. Odes, 24-28
28. Elegies, 25-29
29. Pastoral poetry, 25-29
30. Narrative poetry, 25-29
31. Sonnets, 26-31
32. Lyric poetry, 26-31
33. Satiric poetry, 30-34
34. Short stories, 30-34
35. Religious poetry (hymns), 32-36
36. Comedies, 32-36
37. Tragedies, 34-38
38. "Most influential books," 35-39
39. Hymns by women, 36-38
40. Novels, 40-44
41. "Best books," 40-44
42. Best sellers, 40-44
43. Miscellaneous prose writings, 41-45

An examination of 50 histories of philosophy, 49 histories of education, and 20 books dealing with the history of economics and political science provided the following maxima.

44. Logic, 35-39
45. Ethics, 35-39
46. Aesthetics, 35-39
47. "General" philosophy, 35-39
48. Social philosophy, 36-44
49. Metaphysics, 40-44
50. Contributions to educational theory and practice, 35-39
51. Contributions to economics and political science, 30-39

Although the maximum average rate of output of the most important philosophical books occurred at 35-39, the total range for best production extended from 22-80, and for mere quantity of output—good, bad, and indifferent—the production rate was almost constant from 30-70.

In the body of this book mean ages, median ages, and modal ages are all set forth, but here in this summary, in order to save space, only modal ages are listed. Sixty books which contain lists of so-called "master paintings," one book on American sculpture, and one book on modern architecture yielded the following maxima.

Art and architecture

52. Oil paintings, 32-36
53. American sculpture, 35-39
54. Modern architecture, 40-44
55. Oil paintings by contemporary artists, 40-44

Chapter 12* shows that a very large proportion of the most re-nowned men of science and the humanities did their first important work before 25, and that in general the earlier starters contributed better work and were more prolific than were the slow starters. In Chapters 12 and 13 more than one hundred examples of outstanding creative achievements by youths not over 21 are briefly described. To avoid giving the false impression that *only* the young can do great things (Goethe's remark to Eckermann), Chapter 14 cites numerous outstanding accomplishments at advanced ages.

For most types of creative work the following generalizations have been derived. Within any given field of creative endeavor: (1) the maximum production rate for output of highest quality usually occurs at an earlier age than the maximum rate for less distinguished works by the same individuals; (2) the rate of good production usually does not change much in the middle years and the decline, when it comes, is gradual at all the older ages—much more gradual than its onset in the late teens or early twenties; (3) production of highest quality tends to fall off not only at an earlier age but also at a more rapid rate than does output of lesser merit; and because the statistical distributions of age for the highest quality of work are skewed toward the older age levels, both the mean and the median ages are higher than the modal values.

The first item in the following list of high-salaried workers shows that, when taken in relation to the total population alive at successive age levels, leading movie actors attain their greatest box-office popularity not later than 30-34.

High-salaried workers

56. Movie actors who are "best money-makers," 30-34
57. Movie actresses who are "best money-makers," 23-27
58. "Best" movie directors, 35-39
59. Receivers of "earned" annual incomes of $50,000 or more, 60-64
60. Outstanding commercial and industrial leaders, 65-69
61. Receivers of annual incomes of $1,000,000 or more, 80-89

Item 62 in the following tabulation shows that, in proportion to the number of men who were still alive at each successive age level, presidents of American colleges and universities have served

* Chapter numbers in this paragraph refer to other chapters in *Age and Achievement*.—EDITOR'S NOTE.

most often at 50-54. The other items in this tabulation are to be interpreted similarly.

Public office

62. Presidents of American colleges and universities, 50-54
63. Presidents of the U.S. prior to Truman, 55-59
64. U.S. ambassadors to foreign countries from 1875 to 1900, 60-64
65. U.S. Senators in 1925, 60-64

66. Men in charge of the U.S. Army from 1925 to 1945, 60-64
67. Justices of the U.S. Supreme Court from 1900 to 1925, 70-74
68. Speakers of the U.S. House of Representatives from 1900 to 1940, 70-74
69. Popes, 82-92

An analysis of age data for the most highly successful athletes reveals that their modal ages differ less from the norms for intellectual proficiency than is commonly supposed. The following comparisons are illustrative.

Sports

70. Professional football players, 22-26
71. Professional prizefighters, 25-26
72. Professional ice-hockey players, 26
73. Professional baseball players, 27-28
74. Professional tennis players, 25-29
75. Automobile racers, 26-30

76. Leading contestants at chess, 29-33
77. Professional golfers, 31-36
78. Breakers of world billiards records, 31-36
79. Winners at rifle and pistol shooting, 31-36
80. Winners of important bowling championships, 31-36

To find out whether, with the passage of time, there has been any significant change in the modal ages at which important creative contributions have been made, data were isolated for noted achievers in such various fields as literature, practical invention, philosophy, geology, medicine, and the like. Two statistical distributions were then made for the workers in each field, one for those born prior to 1775, the other for those born between 1775 and 1850. In almost every instance the more recent workers exhibited their outstanding creative ingenuity at younger ages than did the workers of the earlier era.

In contrast with this age change for creative thinkers, the more recently born 50 percent of most kind of leaders were found to be significantly *older* than were their predecessors who held the same nominal positions—both in the United States and also in certain other countries. Thus, for each of the following groups of non-American leaders, the more recently born 50 percent functioned at somewhat older ages than the earlier-born 50 percent: the popes of the Roman Catholic church, the prime ministers of England, the archbishops of Canterbury, and hereditary rulers all over the world. The more recent leaders also were more nearly the same ages than were their predecessors.

When seven groups of earlier-born athletic champions were compared with seven groups of those more recently born, the field of sport being kept constant in each comparison, the later born were found to be older than the earlier born. The changes that have taken place in the modal ages of creative thinkers, leaders, and athletes all evidence the fact that these modal ages are not due solely to genetic factors. Whether the modal ages will continue to change and whether they can be subjected to some kind of human control are quite different questions.

A mere increase in man's longevity should not change greatly the modal ages at which man exhibits his greatest creative proficiency since, both for long-lived and for short-lived groups, the modal age occurs in the thirties.

POSSIBLE CAUSES FOR THE EARLY MAXIMA IN CREATIVITY

At present we are in no position to explain these curves of creativity that rise rapidly in early maturity and then decline slowly after attaining an earlier maximum. Undoubtedly multiple causation operates in these complex behaviors and no discovered contributing condition is likely to be of itself a sufficient or necessary cause. Nevertheless, it is profitable here to list sixteen of the factors which have been suggested as contributing to these representative functions with their early maxima, for such factors indicate possible lines for further research. Here is the list.

(1) A decline occurs prior to 40 in physical vigor, energy, and resistance to fatigue. This decline is probably far more important than such normal age changes as may occur in adult intelligence prior to outright senility.

(2) A diminution in sensory capacity and motor precision also takes place with advance in age. For example, impaired vision and hearing handicap the older individual in many cumulative ways, and writing by hand also becomes more difficult with advance in age.

(3) Serious illness, poor health, and various bodily infirmities more often influence adversely the production rates of older than of younger age groups.

(4) Glandular changes continue throughout life. It is conceivable that hormone research may some day reveal a partial explanation for the changes and especially for the early maxima.

(5) In some instances unhappy marriages and maladjustment in the sex life, growing worse with advance in age, may have interfered with creative work.

(6) The older age groups, more often than the younger, may have become indifferent toward creativity because of the death of a child, a mate, or some other dear one.

(7) As compared with younger persons, older ones are apt to be more preoccupied with the practical concerns of life, with earning a living, and with getting ahead.

(8) Less favorable conditions for concentrated work sometimes come with success, promotion, enhanced prestige, and responsibility.

(9) In some cases the youthful worker's primary ambition may not have been to discover the unknown or to create something new but to get renown. Having acquired prestige and recognition, such workers may try less hard for achievement.

(10) Too easy, too great, or too early fame may conceivably breed complacency and induce one to rest on his previously won laurels before he has done his best possible creative work.

(11) Some older persons may have become apathetic because they have experienced more often the deadening effect of non-recognition and of destructive criticism.

(12) As a result of negative transfer, the old generally are more inflexible than the young. This inflexibility may be a handicap to creative thinking, even though it is dependent on erudition.

(13) Perhaps in part because of the foregoing factors, some older persons experience a decrease in motivation which leads to a weaker intellectual curiosity and interest.

(14) Younger persons tend to have had a better formal education than their elders, they have grown to maturity in a more

stimulating social and cultural milieu, and they have had less time to forget what they have learned.

(15) In some few cases outright psychosis has clouded what was previously a brilliant mind. Psychoses occur more often in the latter half of the normal life span.

(16) In other extreme cases, the individual's normal productive powers may have been sapped by alcohol, narcotics, and other kinds of dissipation. Here, as elsewhere, it is difficult to separate cause from effect.

POSSIBLE CAUSES FOR THE OLDER AGES OF LEADERS

The factors that make for the older ages of leaders are also multiple, complex, and variable. The mere age of a country or of a people is not the determining factor. For example, from 1907 to 1939 only 7 percent of the service of Chinese cabinet members was rendered by men of 60 or above, whereas, for England, France, and the United States, the corresponding percentages were 41, 39, and 32 respectively. It is true also that from 1871 to 1918 the chancellors of the German empire had a median age more than ten years older than the median age of the German chancellors who served from 1918 to 1945. This latter age difference could not be due to greater longevity on the part of the German people during the *earlier* era. Data set forth in Chapters 11 and 17 of this book for some fifty other groups of leaders suggest that when a new group is being formed or when social unrest and dissatisfaction develop in a long-established organization, relatively youthful leaders are likely to emerge.

Consider next the possible contributory factors that cause leadership to occur usually at elderly ages. Examples of such factors are the following:

(1) Normally, for most kinds of leaders, the attainment of their leadership depends largely upon what the leader's potential followers think of him and his prospective leadership, a relationship that is probably less usual for the creative thinker even though the latter must act more or less in harmony with his *Zeitgeist*.

(2) Social institutions, like the church and the state, tend to be conservative; they are engaged primarily in the perpetuation of

themselves and the existing cultural pattern. The leader is the instrument through which they act. Since older persons tend to be conservative more often than younger ones, the older are usually regarded as safer and saner leaders.

(3) For most kinds of leaders the recognition received, the prestige attained, and the honor achieved are likely to be far greater than for those who do creative work. Thus, other things equal, members of the older age groups are likely to be more strongly motivated in seeking and exercising various kinds of leadership than they are in pursuing creative work.

(4) The function of the leader differs from that of the creative thinker. Strictly speaking, leadership is less a personal attribute than a social relationship. An example of this is the fact that for many persons the leader serves as a father substitute, an important function which is, nevertheless, only one contributing factor, for there have been many young leaders.

(5) Nominal leaders have sometimes remained in office for years after they become incapacitated by illness or by other bodily infirmities for the routine performance of their duties. Thus, and especially at the uppermost age levels, some years of nominal leadership may represent merely the ages at which certain individuals have drawn their salaries. Needless to say, my creativity data are not vitiated by any analogous factor.

Upon the basis of all these statistics what is one to conclude? Whatever the causes of growth and decline, it remains clear that the genius does not function equally well throughout the years of adulthood. Superior creativity rises relatively rapidly to a maximum which occurs usually in the thirties and then falls off slowly. Almost as soon as he becomes fully mature, man is confronted with a gerontic paradox that may be expressed in terms of positive and negative transfer. Old people probably have more transfer, both positive and negative, than do young ones. As a result of positive transfer the old usually possess greater wisdom and erudition. These are invaluable assets. But when a situation requires a new way of looking at things, the acquisition of new techniques or even new vocabularies, the old seem stereotyped and rigid. To learn the new they often have to unlearn the old and that is twice as hard as learning without unlearning. But when a situation requires a store of past knowledge then the old find their advantage over the young.

Possibly every human behavior has its period of prime. No

behavior can develop before the groundwork for it has been prepared, but in general it appears that the conditions essential for creativity and originality, which can be displayed in private achievement, come earlier than those social skills which contribute to leadership and eminence and which inevitably must wait, not upon the insight of the leader himself, but upon the insight of society about him.

3

GENERAL
PROVISIONS

THE READINGS in this section provide an overview of the proposals and provisions for the education of the gifted in the public schools of the United States. There are several administrative provisions to be considered. For example, the gifted child can be retained in the same grade as his chronological peers or he can progress through the public school at a more rapid pace than his age mates. The later procedure is usually referred to as acceleration. However, acceleration includes all of the ways in which an individual can complete formal schooling in less than the average amount of time and *not* merely "grade skipping," one of the poorest means of acceleration (see Section 6). The fact that the students are grouped by chronological age or some other method does not rule out acceleration. Students *can* be accelerated in any operative plan.

The gifted child can always be grouped with representatives of his chronological age mates or he can be instructed either part or all of the day with students who are more similar to him in intelligence, achievement, emotional stability, social maturity, physical development, and/or interests than are his chronological-age mates. A more complete consideration of special grouping appears in Sections 4 and 5.

There is considerable sentiment in favor of providing for the gifted in regular classes instead of grouping them on a basis other than chronological age or accelerating them. Educators with these sentiments hold that in a classroom with 20 to 30 students a flexible program with a good teacher will allow (1) children to develop to the limit of their ability, (2) children of varying ability to be given the opportunity to work and play together and to benefit from contact with a variety of aptitudes, (3) the less talented students to be stimulated by the presence of the more highly endowed, and (4) the school situation to reflect life more faithfully. The greatest difficulty seems to be in finding a "good" teacher for every 25 students in school today.

Although in many situations special help in regular class is the only feasible provision for the gifted, there are certain drawbacks to

140

this method in practice. Even when teachers can provide challenging assignments for the gifted, they rarely have the time to guide these efforts because of the demands of the less able students. The educational problems presented by a group with greatly varying ability in the average large class, whether in academic or non-academic work, make it unlikely that the teacher will be able to devote enough time to help the better students fulfill their potential either academically or socially.

Recent surveys of teachers and administrators indicate that most educators favor "enrichment" as a means of providing for gifted children. It seems inaccurate, however, to refer to the available provisions for the gifted as special classes, acceleration, and enrichment. Every child should have an enriched school environment regardless of his administrative classification. As we provide for individual differences, we enrich the curriculum for that child. There can be no acceleration without enrichment, and the major reason for the existence of the special class is to facilitate enrichment.

Some authors refer to enrichment in depth instead of acceleration. These same authors then add "in breadth" when they mean providing more educational experiences at the same level of difficulty. One might think of the knowledge one possesses as having the shape of a column. Then enrichment in depth would be extending the length of the column while enrichment in breadth would be extending the circumference of the column. The distinction between the two is easier to talk about than to practice. A given program may appear to enrich one way or the other, but actually the two have a tendency to merge. In a good program, enrichment in depth must build on a broad base and in a program enriching in breadth students just naturally probe more difficult levels. Schematically, then, we see a cone instead of a column and the question becomes, "How broad must the base be at any one time for optimum development?"

In most instances special classes for the gifted have been considered because traditional provisions have left something to be desired. To support their view, proponents of special classes have presented long lists of reasons, only some of which are backed up by research. Some of the reasons follow.

1. When students are grouped intellectually, the range of IQs may not be greatly reduced, but it will be for most students. With

students of high ability teachers can provide a program of greater depth and/or breadth. Basic material can be covered more quickly and the teacher can devote more time and attention to enriching activities.

2. Other teachers will have more time for their students, since the range of IQ differences in their class is narrower.

3. Instead of being required continually to stimulate others, intellectually capable students can stimulate, and be stimulated by, their intellectual peers.

4. If the gifted were the leaders in the regular class, they will have more competition in the special class. The leadership role which they vacate in the regular class will be open for others who would not have the opportunity otherwise.

5. Increased competition will tend to reduce "smugness" when students find that many others are just as capable as they are. Average students will derive greater satisfactions from the regular class because they will not always be outdistanced and outclassed.

6. The selected competition faced by the special- and regular-class students is a more realistic portrayal of the competition they will face as adults.

The opponents of ability grouping outside the walls of a classroom turn these statements to support grouping only by chronological age. Whatever the arrangement of classes may be, conscientious educators must decide how they can promote the best teaching (or perhaps the most academic learning), the best adjustment, the most satisfied parents, and the most efficient expenditure of funds.

As communities seek to improve their schools, they must seek answers to the questions suggested by the six statements above. How much duplication of teaching exists in special and regular classes? In a special class what use is actually made of the time saved from routine drill? Can the gifted be adequately stimulated by classmates of lesser ability? Does the slower pace of their average classmates impede the progress of the highly endowed?

While most people agree that educators should provide each pupil with learning experiences that will help him grow to the best of his ability, the administrative arrangements for providing these learning experiences are still hotly and emotionally debated in many localities. To help clarify their position the members of the Educational Policies Commission of the National Education Association took a definite stand in 1956. The EPC went on record[1] as favoring:

1. Curriculum enrichment at all levels.
2. Acceleration in the upper-elementary and high-school levels for the socially mature.
3. Extensive use of cocurricular activities to develop high standards of performance.
4. Some ability grouping to facilitate both enrichment and acceleration, yet provision for some experiences in ungrouped classes.

The introductory article of this section by Anne Hoppock was chosen to emphasize the democratic principles involved in helping each child discover and develop his unique gifts by providing him with experiences which have meaning and use for him. The article is taken from a publication recognized as the source of the philosophy of the Association for Childhood Education International. In the second article Lewis Terman and Melita Oden identify the "Major Issues in the Education of Gifted Children." Of the many unresolved issues in the education of gifted children, Terman and Oden chose five for brief discussion in a symposium. The problems centering around democracy, the lockstep, identification, feasible educational opportunities, and the need for guidance are still unresolved, and they emerge whenever provisions for the gifted are discussed.

Educational objectives should be concisely stated in understandable terms so that teaching will be directed toward certain goals. Donald Kincaid's excellent report on the educational objectives for the gifted in California elementary schools is presented here because of its timeliness for schools throughout the country. Similar surveys of objectives could profitably be made in other states to determine the consensuses of opinion among school people and thereby chart a course for the better education of all children.

In the next two articles the social psychologist and sociologist Robert Havighurst describes the community features and conditions that play such an important role in settling the issues and converting objectives into specific statements of behavioral outcomes for each system.

The firsthand reports by Earl McWilliams of his tour of over

---

[1] Educational Policies Commission, *Manpower and Education*, Washington, D.C.: National Education Association, 1956, pp. 104-105.

eighty schools reveal what is actually being done for the gifted at the junior- and senior-high-school level. Dr. A. Harry Passow explains the adequacy of the provisions of the comprehensive high schools and suggests some specific curricular arrangements that would benefit the gifted. The concluding article by Dr. Herbert Klausmeier, a specialist in human learning at the University of Wisconsin, starts with the crucial question, "What kinds of individuals would we like gifted and talented children to be as a result of our educational efforts?" He concludes with nine general proposals for developing moral values and social competence as well as intellectual achievement.

SOME GUIDELINES FOR ACTION

by Anne S. Hoppock

NEW JERSEY STATE DEPARTMENT OF EDUCATION

All children have undiscovered potentialities. Their gifts differ in degree and kind, but creativeness is present in some degree in every child. Democracy's assignment to teachers is clear. It is to help each child discover and develop his unique gifts.

Our public tax-supported schools are designed for all of the children of all of the people. Every parent has a right to expect that the school will value his child and help him to become his best self.

By seeking the undiscovered resources which lie within every child, we best assure the identification of very able children. Regardless of claims which are sometimes made, we are not now able to identify in childhood those who will make remarkable contributions in adulthood. Many unpredictable factors, such as motivation and physical and emotional status, influence achievement. The only sure way to locate the human resources of remarkable talent is to focus study and guidance upon each child.

How do teachers discover where a child's strengths lie, what his compelling motivations are? Particularly effective are organized, intensive programs of child study in which teachers become expert in learning to know their children intimately. However, there are available to all teachers some simple tools for studying the strengths and needs of the children in their classrooms. For example, teachers can:

Observe child behavior at work, at play, alone, and with other children;

Talk individually with children in informal situations;

Learn from children about other children (a child is often aware of another child's talents not revealed in the classroom);

Talk with parents about a child's persisting interests, what he chooses to do and does well at home;

[Reprinted from *All Children Have Gifts*, Washington, D. C.: Association for Childhood Educational International, 1957, pp. 6-9, with the permission of the Association and the author.]

Share information about children in staff conferences;

Discuss with children their reactions to stories, books, films, group experiences;

Use sociograms and other techniques for studying relationships;

Use interest inventories;

Study cumulative folders with their anecdotal records, summaries of tests, samples of work, and other data;

Confer with child guidance personnel regarding ways of discovering, assessing, and encouraging the talents of each child.

Perhaps the most effective way to find the creative potentialities of children is to put them in an environment which encourages them to behave creatively. Children reveal their abilities as they participate in creative writing, dramatizing, dancing, painting, working with clay and tools, singing, playing instruments, composing, solving real problems, exploring widely in books, seeking many sources of information, experimenting, evaluating. As children assume the responsibilities of citizenship in the school community, they manifest abilities in leadership, creativeness in human relations, and willingness to give of self to the common welfare.

MANY KINDS OF ABILITIES NEEDED IN A MODERN SOCIETY

As teachers of growing children, let us keep our perspective in gift-valuing. A wide variety of talent is apparent in the classroom. Nan is the only one who voted for Bill to be student council representative. She privately and shyly reveals that it is because she knew no one else would vote for him and that would be "very hard on him." At eight years, she has unusual ability to project herself into the feelings of others. Joel can compose soft and exciting and humorous mood music as background for the puppet show. Nora's dialogue for the funny puppet shows a fine sense of comedy. Ted has just come back from the kindergarten where he helped the little block builders rig up a movable bridge that will let the boats go through. The boys in his room follow Ted's lead; his love for fun and adventure is so balanced by good sense and kindness that he tends to keep the boys' behavior within acceptable bounds. Charles has been absorbed for days in an individual study of the cause of a coming eclipse of the sun and is now ready to report and demonstrate. Yesterday when the teacher was called away by an emergency, Frances helped the children carry out the day's plan "almost as good as a real teacher." All of these abilities are important to the good living which goes on in this little community of children. Valued and nurtured, they will result in worthy contributions in adult living.

The cold war and rapid technological progress are major facts of our time. Therefore, abilities required to keep our nation in the forefront of science are highly valued. But for every person who discovers or invents, many people with a great variety of skills are needed to convert the inventor's idea into production and use.

Scientific ability and the technical skills needed in utilizing it are not our only urgent needs. Our continued survival and living other than on the brink of catastrophe may now depend more upon social than scientific achievement. The world has been made so small by machines that methods of securing world order are imperative. Man is becoming aware that social controls must be found to keep the remarkable products of his inventiveness from destroying him. Self-interest dictates unselfishness; if our children are to be fed in peace, children in a far corner of the world must be kept from starving. We must live by our own Bill of Rights in order to keep the trust of faraway peoples striving for human rights. Wisdom, social inventiveness, moral courage, and ethical standards of high order are needed if we are to survive the convulsions of this phase of the industrial revolution and find life worth living. These social and spiritual qualities are needed not only by those in high places but by people in every community in the land.

CREATIVENESS IN ARTS

The times call, too, for the development of gifts in the arts and other forms of creative and re-creative activities. One by-product of automation is the steadily increasing amount of leisure which many people have. Our children need to learn creative, productive ways to use this precious gift of time. How important that their lives not be eroded by idleness, that they not become a generation of spectators, consumers only of the creative products of the few!

The implications for the elementary school are clear. Our democracy needs personalities of many kinds to give it balance and richness. *We need the abilities of all citizens to fulfill the practical and spiritual requirements of our century. The curriculum of the elementary school must therefore be broad based.* We must make it possible for each child to find and demonstrate his abilities and to be valued for his contributions. In this way, he learns what he has to give to society; he learns the confidence and the desire to give it.

IT TAKES TIME TO GROW

An ingredient in the development of children's potentialities is time to grow. Children in the elementary schools are still children. Their bodies are still growing. They are still in the process of learning who they are and how to live in the world. They need time to move leisurely through the orderly processes of growing up. Our first concern must be that they grow well. Forced feeding defeats its purpose. Indeed, the best hope that a child will be a productive adult lies in providing him with experiences which have meaning and use for him now.

STATE FOR THE CHILDREN, NOT CHILDREN FOR THE STATE

Childhood is not just a time of preparation for adulthood. It is part of a person's life, important in itself. In this country, we believe that children have a right to be children. They are not the possessions of the state, to be hurried into adulthood for the greater power and glory of the state.

MAJOR ISSUES IN THE EDUCATION
OF GIFTED CHILDREN

by Lewis M. Terman and Melita H. Oden

STANFORD UNIVERSITY

Of the many unresolved issues in the education of gifted children, we have chosen five for brief discussion in this symposium. These

[Reprinted from the *Journal of Teacher Education*, 5, September 1954, 230-232, with the permission of the *Journal* and Melita H. Oden.]

are: (1) democracy and the IQ, (2) the educational lockstep, (3) early identification of the gifted, (4) educational opportunities that are feasible, and (5) needed guidance and counseling.

DEMOCRACY AND THE IQ

This is a very old issue, but it was the late Professor Bagley who first brought it to the fore and who did more than anyone else to prejudice the minds of educators against offering any kind of special opportunities for the gifted. He wrote with particular scorn of training the gifted for leadership, and proposed instead that the important thing was to teach the average people when and where to tell their would-be leaders to get off. To argue, as Bagley did, that all children should have the same kind of school training, at least through the grades, seems to us no less absurd than to argue that all children should have the same kind of medical treatment. Yet the Bagley point of view not only survives; it is in fact fairly widespread, thought it is losing ground.

THE EDUCATIONAL LOCKSTEP

This refers to the belief that for the sake of normal social adjustment the gifted child should be kept with others of his own age, and that only such opportunities should be provided for him as are possible under this limitation. The doctrine is based on the belief that the social maladjustment caused by acceleration outweighs any of its advantages. The truth is that the evidence from every serious investigation of the problem shows this view to be largely false. Our data show there is a marked tendency for children of very superior IQ to be more mature both socially and physically than children of average ability. This is not to say that every child should complete high school and college as early as his IQ would permit. The gifted child who is already maladjusted or exceptionally immature socially should be allowed little acceleration or none, but the facts obtained in the thirty-year follow-up of our large gifted group prove conclusively that children of 135 IQ or higher who are accelerated one, two, or even three years are usually more successful in later life than equally bright children who are held in the lockstep. If you don't believe it, see Chapter 20 in *The Gifted Child Grows Up*.* Acceleration is especially desirable for those who plan to enter a profession that calls for years of graduate study. Other advantages are that the accelerated find their school work more challenging and that earlier graduation enables them to marry earlier (which, on the average, they do).

EARLY IDENTIFICATION OF THE GIFTED

Thirty years ago if you wanted to know who was the brightest child in a classroom, your best single chance of finding out was not to ask the teacher but to take the name of the youngest child in the room. But in these days when tests of intelligence and school achievement are so easily available, one might suppose that nearly all of the gifted would be identified at an early age. Such is not the case. There are still millions of children who leave school without ever having had any kind of standardized test. Even where tests are used, their results are so frequently misinterpreted that some of the gifted are likely to be overlooked. One reason why early identification is important is that acceleration by grade skipping is most feasible in the lower grades. Another reason is that the earlier the gifted child is identified the better his later education can be planned for.

EDUCATIONAL OPPORTUNITIES THAT ARE FEASIBLE

Under current conditions of teacher shortage and overcrowded classrooms, about the only kinds of special opportunity that are readily feasible for the gifted are three: (1) segregation in special classes; (2) parallel classes for fast, medium, and slow learners, and (3) acceleration.

The pros and cons of segregation have long been debated. Our belief is that segregated classes at their best are very good indeed, but that they are rarely at their best. Parallel classes are a great help, but they are possible only in the larger schools. Acceleration, on the other hand, is always possible and in the majority of cases is desirable whatever other special provision may be made. As for

* Vol. 4 of *Genetic Studies of Genius,* Stanford, Calif.: Stanford Univ. Press, 1947.—EDITOR'S NOTE.

the curriculm enrichment that is so often praised as the ideal solution for the gifted, it is indeed fine in theory but it is very difficult in practice. Under the conditions that presently prevail it can hardly be regarded as a panacea. We believe, nevertheless, that teachers should be alerted to the desirability of special assignments for the gifted in their classes and that they should be instructed by school supervisors and principals in the kinds of enrichment that are possible.

NEEDED GUIDANCE AND COUNSELLING

In 1953 the National Manpower Council, composed of twenty nationally eminent persons, reported after extensive investigation that 40 percent of the young men and women in the United States who are potentially good college material either do not enter college or, if they enter, do not continue to graduation. What causes are responsible for this appalling wastage of brainpower at a time when there is an acute shortage of well-trained minds in nearly every field of science, teaching, scholarship, and business?

There are doubtless many causes, but we believe that two of the most important are: (1) frequent failure to identify the gifted and (2) when they *are* identified, failure to provide the kind of counseling service that is so badly needed in high schools and colleges. Of the more than 1450 members of our gifted group (all of them in the top 1 percent in general intelligence), nearly 15 percent did not enter college and 30 percent did not graduate. It is true that the schooling of some was cut short by the great depression, which began shortly before or shortly after most of them reached college age. We are quite certain, however, that many more of them would have gone to college if there had been adequate counseling service in the high schools they attended. As a matter of fact there was little or none at all in most of the schools. The result was that nearly two hundred did not enter college and more than four hundred did not graduate. The situation has improved in the last twenty years, especially in the educationally more progressive cities, but we are reliably informed that in both amount and quality the counseling available in most high schools is far below what is needed.

Counseling at the high-school level is not only necessary to insure that more of the brighter students will get the amount of training they should have, but also to insure that each will get the kind of training best adapted to prepare him for later specialization. This means *vocational* counseling, not for the purpose of encouraging the student to choose once and for all the occupation he will enter, but rather to discover the broad general fields where his abilities and interests lie. One of the most valuable single tools for this purpose is Strong's Vocational Interest Test, especially the form designed for men. This test reveals more clearly and accurately than any other what the student's patterns of interest are like; for example, whether they resemble most closely the interest patterns of successful men in the physical sciences, engineering, medicine, law, architecture, journalism, or some of the thirty other occupations for which the test can be scored. The thing that counts is not so much the score in a particular occupation but rather the patterns of interest that are disclosed. To interpret the great variety of patterns that are found calls for skill and experience, but when properly used the test is so valuable that every boy should be given a chance to take it before the end of his senior year. If the Strong test had been available and could have been taken by all the men in our gifted group when they were in high school, at least 10 to 20 percent might have made a better choice of career.

OBJECTIVES OF EDUCATION FOR GIFTED CHILDREN IN CALIFORNIA ELEMENTARY SCHOOLS

by Donald Kincaid

LOS ANGELES CITY SCHOOLS

STATEMENT OF THE PROBLEM

It was the purpose of this study to make an analysis and evaluation of the objectives of education for gifted children in California ele-

[Reprinted from *Los Angeles City School Districts Research Report* #2, April 1956, with the permission of the author.]

mentary schools. Answers were sought to the following questions:

1. Are there objectives of education which have particular importance for gifted elementary school children?

2. Do representative groups such as supervisors, principals, teachers, guidance directors, parents of gifted children, and gifted high-school students differ in their evaluation of the importance of objectives of education for gifted children?

3. Have objectives of education been formulated by those California elementary school districts which have special programs for gifted children?

SPECIFIC OBJECTIVES OF EDUCATION FOR GIFTED CHILDREN

The principal instrument used in this study was a list of objectives of education which could be rated in terms of their relative importance for gifted children in California elementary schools. A total of 119 specific objectives were formulated and classified in the twelve major areas of citizenship, character and human relations, basic skills, health and safety, understanding of environment, vocational competence, consumer effectiveness, successful family life, use of leisure time, appreciation of beauty, effective thinking, and world understanding.

THE EVALUATION OF OBJECTIVES OF EDUCATION
FOR GIFTED CHILDREN

Six representative groups evaluated the relative importance of the 119 specific objectives of education for gifted children. These groups included a statewide sampling of elementary-school principals, teachers, and supervisors; the guidance directors of Los Angeles County; parents of gifted children; and gifted high-school students.

A brief check list also was completed by each of the six groups of raters. This check list was designed to obtain the point of view of the rater to the attainment of objectives of education for gifted children and the degree to which certain instructional plans should be utilized in the education of gifted children. Critical ratios were calculated among the six groups of raters for each objective and for the check-list questions to determine significant differences among their ratings.

SURVEY OF CALIFORNIA ELEMENTARY-SCHOOL DISTRICTS

A brief questionnaire was sent to 635 California elementary-school districts to determine present policy and practice with respect to objectives of education for gifted children. Two items on the questionnaire related to the point of view of the district regarding objectives of education for gifted children and the degree to which certain instructional plans were utilized in special programs for gifted children in the district. These two items corresponded to the two questions of the check list which was completed by the six representative groups and so made possible statistical comparisons between the responses of the groups of raters and actual practice in elementary schools. Districts which had special programs for gifted children also listed the objectives of these programs and afforded an important basis of comparison with the objectives which rated as having more importance for gifted children by supervisors, principals, teachers, guidance directors, parents, and students. Special programs for gifted children were reported by thirty-nine California elementary-school districts.

FINDINGS

REGARDING OBJECTIVES OF EDUCATION FOR GIFTED CHILDREN

A summary of the findings regarding those objectives which were rated as having more importance for gifted children is presented in the following section. The twelve major areas of objectives are discussed in their order of relative importance for gifted children as determined by the responses of the six groups of raters.

Effective Thinking. Objectives in the general area of effective thinking were rated by all groups as having more importance for gifted children than the objectives in any other area. The objectives in this area related to recognizing a problem, seeing parts in relation to the whole, gathering facts, using sources of information, weighing evidence, checking conclusions, thinking objectively, and creative thinking. More objectives also were reported by California elementary-school districts in the area of effective thinking than for other major areas.

Basic Skills. The general area of basic skills was rated second in importance for gifted children by the six representative groups. The objectives in this area which involved the application of basic skills such as writing clearly, reading, checking information with facts, listening intelligently, understanding the meaning behind number relationships, understanding the language of arithmetic and methods of checking computed results, were rated as having more importance for gifted children. The area of basic skills was fourth in importance in California elementary-school districts having special programs for gifted children.

Citizenship. The third most important area was that of citizenship. All groups of raters were in close agreement regarding objectives in this area and rated objectives which referred to group action, civic affairs, and application of knowledge as having more importance for gifted children. Citizenship was the second most important area in special programs for gifted children in California elementary schools, but involved a more limited concept of citizenship than that agreed upon by the six groups of raters.

Understanding of Environment. Understanding of environment was the general area rated fourth in importance by six groups of raters. Objectives which pertained to relationships between environment and other factors such as customs of the people, social institutions, and scientific development and an understanding of science and atomic energy were rated as having more importance for gifted children. No objectives in the area of understanding of environment were reported by California elementary-school districts having special programs for gifted children.

Appreciation of Beauty. The area rated fifth in importance by the six groups was appreciation of beauty. Objectives which concerned the discovery of special talents in the arts, the understanding of peoples through their arts, the acquiring of an understanding of art and music, and participation in community cultural activities were rated as having more importance for gifted children. Only one school district, of the thirty-nine districts having special programs, for gifted children, reported an objective in the area of appreciation of beauty.

World Understanding. The area of world understanding was rated sixth in importance. The objectives which were rated as having more importance for gifted children pertained to the understanding and correcting of world problems. No objectives in this general area of world understanding were reported by elementary-school districts having special programs of education for gifted children.

Character and Human Relations. The area rated seventh in

importance for gifted children was that of character and human relations. Objectives in the area of character and human relations related to accepting responsibility, service to others, understanding the differences among people, practicing courtesy and kindness to others, and developing a philosophy of life. There were no clear-cut differences between those objectives which were rated as having more importance for gifted children and those which were rated as having about the same importance for all children. The area of character and human relations was third in importance among the thirty-nine California elementary-school districts having special programs for gifted children.

Vocational Competence. Vocational competence was rated eighth in importance by the six groups. Although there was general agreement that most objectives in this area had about the same importance for all children, all groups rated the objective which involved a vocational choice based on self-appraisal and occupational opportunity as having more importance for gifted children. The area of vocational competence was fifth in importance in California elementary-school districts having special programs for gifted children.

OTHER OBJECTIVES

Other objectives include use of leisure time, health and safety, successful family life, and consumer effectiveness. On the basis of the reactions of the six groups of raters and the objectives reported by California elementary-school districts, it was apparent that objectives in the general areas of use of leisure time, health and safety, successful family life, and consumer effectiveness had about the same importance for all children.

OBJECTIVES RATED AS HAVING MORE IMPORTANCE FOR GIFTED CHILDREN

The specific objectives of education which were rated as having more importance for gifted elementary-school pupils by all groups —supervisors, principals, teachers, guidance directors, parents of gifted pupils, and gifted high-school pupils—were as follows:

Citizenship

Accepts responsibility in group undertakings and in civic affairs. Applies his knowledge of such subjects as history, to the understanding and solution of community, state, national, and world problems.

Develops ability to detect and analyze propaganda in public affairs.

Basic Skills
Checks information with facts.

Searches for the meaning behind the number or the numerical relationships he uses.

Understands methods of checking computed results and uses these methods in checking problems.

Understanding of Environment
Recognizes the possibilities of improving environment through scientific and industrial development.

Realizes the powerful social and economic implications of atomic energy.

Acquires a store of knowledge and understanding concerning science.

Effective Thinking
Recognizes a problem and defines it clearly.

Thinks in terms of the whole and sees parts in relationship to the whole.

Gathers and studies facts about a problem, distinguishing between fact, opinion, and propaganda.

Learns to use sources of information effectively.

Weighs evidence, makes inferences, and draws conclusions.

Checks his conclusions for accuracy, modifying his thinking as the evidence indicates.

Detects within himself and tries to overcome such things as subjectivity, rationalization, projection, and prejudice, which inhibit effective thinking.

Does creative thinking, such as using the imagination, uniting the thinking of a group to form a new concept.

World Understanding
Realizes that education is a powerful force in alleviating misunderstandings, tensions, and persecutions arising out of variations in peoples and their cultures.

ATTAINMENT OF OBJECTIVES OF EDUCATION BY GIFTED CHILDREN

There was agreement by a majority of the supervisors, principals, teachers, guidance directors, parents, and students that:

1. In general, the objectives of education for gifted children do not differ materially from those for all children.
2. In general, the gifted child should attain most objectives of education at an earlier age than other children.
3. In general, gifted children should attain most objectives of education to a greater degree than other children.

A majority of the 39 California elementary-school districts also reported that objectives of education did not differ materially from those for all children and that gifted children attain most objectives of education to a greater degree than other children; however, only 40 percent of the districts reported that gifted children attained most objectives of education at an earlier age than other children.

ENRICHMENT IN REGULAR CLASSES

The majority of all groups of raters believed that enrichment in regular classes should be utilized for gifted children. The school people, however, rated enrichment in regular classes as relatively more important for gifted children than did parents and students. All of the thirty-nine elementary school districts, with special programs for gifted children, utilized enrichment in regular classes to some degree, with one half of the districts utilizing much enrichment.

ENRICHMENT THROUGH SPECIAL CLASSES

The majority of supervisors, principals, teachers, and guidance directors believed that enrichment through special classes should not be utilized for gifted children although a majority of parents and students reacted favorably to this plan. Only about one fifth of the California elementary-school districts having special programs for gifted children utilized enrichment through special classes.

ENRICHMENT THROUGH SPECIAL-INTEREST GROUPS

A large majority of the six groups of raters believed that enrichment through special interest groups should be utilized for gifted children. Only a slight majority of the special programs for gifted children in California elementary-schools utilized enrichment through special-interest groups.

PROVISION FOR ACCELERATION

A marked majority of principals and a large majority of students believed that provision should be made for acceleration of gifted children. Teachers, guidance directors, and parents favored some acceleration, but the majority of supervisors reacted adversely to acceleration. A majority of the thirty-nine California elementary-school districts having special programs for gifted children utilized acceleration to about the same degree as recommended by teachers, guidance directors, and parents.

SUMMARY OF FINDINGS FOR EACH GROUP OF RATERS

Considerable agreement was found among the six groups of raters regarding the objectives rated as having more importance for gifted children and in their point of view toward the attainment of objectives of education by gifted children and the instructional plan which should be utilized for gifted children. Some marked differences of opinion also were found, however, among the six groups of raters. The summary of findings for supervisors, principals, teachers, guidance directors, parents, and students follows:

Supervisors. Supervisors rated fewer objectives as having more importance for gifted children than any other group of raters. The point of view of supervisors toward the attainment of objectives of education by gifted children differed consistently and often significantly from the ratings of the other five groups, with the supervisors tending to rate objectives as having about the same importance for all children.

Principals. Principals were, in general, between the two extremes in their point of view toward the importance of objectives of education for gifted children. In the case of only one of the 119 objectives was there a significant difference in the ratings between principals and teachers.

Teachers. Teachers were, in general, between the two extremes in their point of view toward the importance of objectives of education for gifted children. Fewer significant differences in ratings were found between teachers and other groups than between any other pairs of raters.

Guidance Directors. Guidance directors, more than any other group, rated objectives in the general areas of effective thinking and understanding of environment as having more importance for gifted children. Guidance directors rated more objectives as having more importance for gifted children than any other school group.

Parents. Parents, more than any other group, rated objectives as having relatively more importance for gifted children which were in the general areas of character and human relations, vocational competence, successful family life, and use of leisure time.

Students. Students rated more objectives as having more importance for gifted children than any of the other five groups. Students rated the general areas of basic skills, understanding of environment, and world understanding as having more importance for gifted children than did other groups. Students rated objectives in the general areas of effective thinking, successful family life, and the use of leisure time as having relatively more importance for gifted children than did the supervisors.

CONCLUSIONS

Some of the major conclusions which were derived from an analysis of the findings were:

1. Since the most important areas of objectives in rank order of importance for gifted children were effective thinking, basic skills, citizenship, understanding of environment, appreciation of beauty, world understanding, character and human relations, and vocational competence, it may be concluded that in planning a special program for gifted children consideration should be given to objectives in the above areas in the order in which they are listed.

2. Since objectives in the general areas of use of leisure time, health and safety, successful family life, and consumer effectiveness were rated by all groups as having about the same importance for all children, it may be concluded that these areas should not have special attention in planning a program for gifted children.

3. Those objectives which were rated as having more importance for gifted children were, in general, those which were more difficult of attainment and which involved the ability to generalize and to apply knowledge.

4. The objectives which all groups rated as having more importance for gifted children provide a basis for common understanding among the groups. Consideration of these areas of agree-

ment may provide a basis for increased agreement in areas in which there are disagreement such as the most effective instructional plan to provide for gifted children.

5. The fact that enrichment through special interest groups was the only instructional plan which was regarded highly by all groups would indicate that this is a plan for making special provision for gifted children which would be less controversial than other plans.

6. Some acceleration seems advisable for gifted children although supervisors reacted adversely to this plan. The fact that principals were highly favorable to acceleration might be an indication of the relative administrative ease of making provision for acceleration without necessity of making additional budget provisions.

7. The responses of supervisors differed consistently and often significantly from the responses of the other five groups. The facts that supervisors rated fewer objectives of education as having more importance for gifted children than any of the other five groups and rated enrichment in the regular classroom as the best instructional plan for gifted children probably were a result of the emphasis by supervisors on the importance of objectives of education for all children rather than their particular importance for gifted children.

8. The fact that guidance directors rated objectives in the general areas of effective thinking and understanding of environment as having relatively more importance for gifted children than other groups may have been related to the specialized training and experience of guidance directors. Knowledge of occupational information relating to manpower shortages coupled with a specialized knowledge of the characteristics and needs of gifted children may have resulted in more discrimination in the ratings in these areas by the guidance directors.

9. The fact that parents of gifted children stressed the importance of objectives which related to the adjustment of the child at home, at school, and on the job more than other groups may have been the result of the more direct and personal concern and interest by parents in their children's adjustment than a result of the giftedness of children.

10. The fact that objectives of education were not reported by 14 of the 39 districts having special programs of education for gifted children and the fact that less than one-third of the 39 districts reported objectives in even the most important areas such as effective

thinking, citizenship, and basic skills would indicate that many districts have not formulated objectives of education for gifted children.

11. The fact that 22 of the 39 districts, as evidenced through mimeographed or printed materials, had given serious study to a statement of the objectives of the special program of education would indicate that objectives of education have been formulated or are being formulated by a majority of districts having special programs for gifted children.

12. It may be concluded that additional attention should be given by most districts to the formulation of objectives of education for gifted children and that additional attention should be given by all districts to stating the objectives of education for gifted children in more specific terms so that evaluative procedures can be planned.

RECOMMENDATIONS

In view of the findings of this study and the conclusions which were based on these findings certain recommendations are indicated as follows:

1. The areas in which there are agreements among school people, parents, and students should be the basis for future planning for gifted children. It is possible that common understandings and agreements on the part of all people who are concerned with the education of gifted children will provide a foundation for a better understanding in areas where there are differences.

2. Additional attention should be given by school districts to making provisions for gifted children by enrichment through special-interest groups. This instructional plan may afford some of the advantages of enrichment in regular classes as well as enrichment through special classes without some of the disadvantages which are found with either one separately.

3. It is recommended that parents and students be invited by school workers to participate in the educational planning for gifted children. The areas of agreement point to the possibility of initiating discussions with common understandings and the areas of disagreement point to the need for increased communication between school people and parents and students.

4. Any program for gifted children, as well as for any group of children, should be based first on the objectives for such a program. These objectives should be stated as specifically as possible. By statting objectives in behavioral terms, the teacher and principal are better able to plan educational experiences which will lead to attainment of these objectives.

5. Evaluative procedures should be discussed and planned as objectives are formulated and instructional procedures are implemented.

6. The objectives of education which were rated as having more importance for gifted children should provide the basis for development of instructional materials for use by the classroom teacher for the enrichment of instruction for gifted children.

CONDITIONS FAVORABLE AND DETRIMENTAL TO THE DEVELOPMENT OF TALENT

by Robert J. Havighurst

UNIVERSITY OF CHICAGO

How many of the gifted children found in the schools will realize their potentialities and become distinguished persons, contributing in an outstanding way to the welfare of their society and gaining for themselves the satisfactions of excellent performance? Under present conditions, certainly less than half of them will do so.

Even this, however, is not a bad situation when compared with what other societies have done for their gifted children. Probably no other society has done as well as the United States in this respect. Even Athens at the height of her creativity in the fifth century, B.C., or Florence in the Renaissance, or England in the sixteenth century, reached these peaks without having utilized the latent talent of the great mass of the people, who were submerged in slavery or grinding

[Reprinted from *School Review*, 65, March 1957, 20-26, with the permission of the University of Chicago Press and the author.]

poverty. It is only when the facts of the development of talent in present-day America are compared with what might be and what the democratic ideal suggests they ought to be that the record looks inadequate.

Americans generally believe in the unique value of the individual and in the desirability of his developing his abilities, whatever they are, along socially valuable directions. The development of ability requires education, and Americans have great faith in the power of education to bring out the latent excellence of a person.

Then, too, there is the American discovery that the poor and downtrodden produce many children who have remarkable talents. It is understood that these talents cannot flourish in a nonsupportive family or a barren community environment. As people have come to recognize the importance of the environment in developing talent, the attitude has gained ground that society should seek to discover and to help the talented but underprivileged child or youth.

These positive attitudes toward the use of education to develop gifted children are balanced by some negative attitudes. There has been the belief that "talent will out" in the American environment; that, if it is real talent, it will be irrepressible; that it will follow a natural course of development; that it should not be rewarded until it has fully proved its worth in competition. Coupled with this has been the Puritan attitude that nothing good should come easily, that a person should work slavishly, especially while young. He should sell newspapers on cold street corners, memorize long lists of spelling words, work all the problems in the geometry book, wait tables in the fraternity house, wash beakers in the chemistry laboratory. To complicate the situation further, Americans tend to distrust the talented person who is somewhat "queer." If a child has a remarkable aptitude in mathematics, or music, or poetry, especially if he does well in these areas without apparent effort, he is regarded as psychologically abnormal, with the unfavorable nuances that are part of abnormality in American thought. As a result of these attitudes, there is an American tendency to discourage the development of special gifts in children and to encourage them to become "well-rounded" superior persons rather than somewhat eccentric geniuses.

This emphasis upon social and emotional adjustment has been buttressed by a corresponding emphasis in society as a whole on security and conformity at the expense of freedom. Children and adults are taught the virtues of cooperation, of being a smooth-working part of a team, or group, or corporation. In this situation an outstanding individual success may cut one off from the group, and this may be such a severe threat to a student that he will deliberately do less than his best, "reduce output," so as not to get better marks than most of his fellows. The aloneness of creative achievement cannot always compete with the need to be a part of the group.

Under these circumstances, despite the relatively large educational opportunities in America, a great deal of talent remains undiscovered, undeveloped, and unrewarded. By any ordinary definition of talent, at least half of the talent of American youth suffers this fate. Thus it seems that the gifted child is favored by the abstract American ideals of opportunity and of the desirability of developing the individual to his maximum but that specific attitudes penalize him. In school and community the gifted child may be treated in ways which make him content with a performance and a developmental level definitely under his capacity or which may even discourage his attempts at spontaneity and individual excellence.

With the public's ambivalent attitudes toward gifted children, the American school system also operates both to encourage and to discourage the development of talent. By offering educational opportunity at the secondary-school and college levels to a higher proportion of youth than does any other country, the American schools act to discover and develop talent, especially of the intellectual variety. On the other hand, the fact that the schools are nonselective means, in effect, that the average high-school student body consists mainly of boys and girls with ability just average or slightly above or below average. The proportion of gifted youth can hardly exceed 25 percent in the ordinary comprehensive high school. (This estimate is based on the assumption that the top 20 percent of the population may be regarded as gifted intellectually, artistically, or socially. Since a few of the slower pupils drop out of high school, the proportion of gifted in the high school will be somewhat greater than it is in the general population.)

Thus the gifted youth are likely to be outnumbered in the high school and college classes as well as in the elementary school. Unless the teaching is remarkably skillful and clearly directed toward stimulating gifted students, such students tend, when outnumbered, to adopt the learning pace and the attitudes toward learning of their average age-mates. This is particularly likely to happen in America where the pressure of the peer group to conform to peer standards is greater and more effective than it is in any other country that has been studied in this connection.

While conditions in the schools are ambiguous with respect to the development of talent, there is no such ambiguity about the demand for talent in the adult world. The American economy is desperately short of highly trained minds. This pressing, immediate need has been well publicized in recent years. What is less well understood is the present crisis in world civilization as a whole. Civilization is rapidly approaching the point in its development where it must achieve new levels in the utilization of the resources of the world or forever fail to develop them. The burden of making such advance in controlling and developing the environment falls largely on the shoulders of the gifted.

Social conditions may favor or discourage the development of gifted people. In exploring the influence of such conditions, it is necessary to distinguish between the production of highly specialized talent, such as artists or musicians, and the production of superior persons with adequate training to do work that requires a high level of skill and knowledge but does not necessarily require creativity.

Conditions favoring the appearance of productive genius may not be the same as conditions favoring the appearance in large numbers of superior craftsmen of the mind and the market place. One such condition has already been mentioned: the demand for well-trained superior people. Another condition is economic prosperity. With economic prosperity there is money that can be spent by parents and by philanthropy on the training of young people. There is also money to spend on art, music, literature, and the theater and thus to support the work of people in the arts. Less tangible, but certainly important in the making of an environment favorable to the development of gifted children, is the belief that everyone should attempt to achieve in relation to his capacity. "From each according to his ability" is a generally accepted American attitude.

In general, because the economic situation is favorable and because the attitudinal climate is at least partially favorable, children with superior potential abilities are in a relatively good position to receive help in developing their potential abilities into real existing abilities. The society expects education to give this help. It is as clear a mandate from society as any of the schools are likely to receive.

If only about half of the ablest 20 percent of gifted children actually develop their abilities to a point where they make an important contribution to society, who are the other half, and why do they not develop their talents more fully? The general answer to this question is that those with undeveloped talent are persons whose environments have been least favorable to the production of high-level ability.

Girls, and children from families of low socioeconomic status, form the two large groups of persons with potentially high ability whose environment has not provided stimulation for the development of talent. Children from low-status families fail to develop their abilities because of lack of opportunity and stimulation—a lack commencing in their earliest years. Their families do not encourage them to read, to learn music, to draw pictures, to develop scientific hobbies, or to do any of the things that can bring budding talent into flower. Many of them live on subsistence farms, where the family simply struggles to survive. Lack of stimulation is, in general, characteristic of low socioeconomic families, but there are exceptions in which a working-class family does as well by a gifted child as does a family with more means. When the child of a lower-status family reaches high school, he often feels a pressure to get out and earn money, and he seldom gets the kind of financial support, from home or through scholarship aid, which will carry him through college or a program of special training.

The true importance of the factor of socioeconomic background has not always been recognized because until quite recent decades the notion has prevailed in Europe and America that high ability was to be found almost entirely in the upper classes and was inherited according to simple laws of heredity. The modern view is that a large amount of potential ability remains underdeveloped because of lack of environmental stimulation and that most of this underdeveloped ability is to be found in people of lower socioeconomic status and in women of all social levels.

Women as a group do not develop their abilities to as high a degree as men because society does not expect them to do so. Girls, however, show fully as much talent as boys do. In fact, girls excel boys in achievement tests and in artistic, musical, and writing ability. They hold their own with boys in social leadership up into the high school years. In adolescence the pressures of society make them want to adopt feminine rather than masculine roles. The feminine roles stress tenderness, tranquility, submissiveness, in contrast to the ambitiousness, productivity, and aggressiveness which are stressed in the masculine roles.

Even though the twentieth century gives women a wider variety of acceptable roles than did the nineteenth, the social pressures still operate to suppress the high-level development of talent in most women in favor of motherhood, homemaking, and emotional support of a husband. Thus, although there are excellent women novelists and poets and singers, among women there are no musical composers of note; no orchestra conductors; few famous performers on musical instruments; relatively few college presidents, artists, lawyers, doctors, or scientists.

Most of the children of both sexes who exhibit giftedness come from middle-class homes, although the majority of all children enrolled in the schools come from working-class homes. These facts are illustrated by the results of a program of discovery of talent in the seventh grade in the public schools of Quincy, Illinois. Fifteen schools were ranked on the basis of the average socioeconomic status of the children attending them. The school in the high-status neighborhood enrolled a relatively high proportion of the children who, at the age of twelve or thirteen, showed a high-level ability, while the school in the slum neighborhood enrolled almost no gifted children. Still, a considerable number of boys and girls showing talent at this age came from working-class and lower-middle-class families (1). It is in this group that lack of financial ability and lack of family expectation will operate most heavily to prevent the development of latent talent through education or special training.

From another part of the country there is further evidence of the effect of low socioeconomic status in suppressing the development of talent. Boys in the second and third years of public high schools of the Boston metropolitan area were studied. The highest 20 percent in intellectual ability were asked whether they expected to go to college (3). Those whose fathers had high-status occupations generally expected to go to college, while boys whose fathers had low-status occupations generally did not expect to go to college.

Estimates of the educational progress of the ablest youth in the population of the entire country show that most children of upper- and upper-middle-class families go to college if they are in the upper quarter of the population in intellectual ability. On the other hand, while 45 percent of the ablest quarter of youth come from homes of manual workers, less than one fourth of this group graduate from college (2). While the factors of environmental stimulation and of financial ability both operate to reduce the numbers of able youth who develop their abilities through higher education, there has been great progress in the past fifty years in recognizing the potentialities of these youth and in giving them educational opportunities. Compared to the nineteenth century, the present century is more favorable to the discovery and development of talent in children of lower socioeconomic status and also in girls.

REFERENCES

1. Bowman, Paul H., and others. *Mobilizing Community Resources for Youth*, Supplementary Educational Monographs, No. 85. Chicago: Univ. Chicago Press, 1956, pp. 20-21.
2. Havighurst, Robert J., and Bernice Neugarten. *Society and Education*, New York: Allyn and Bacon, 1957, Ch. X.
3. Kahl, Joseph A. Educational and Occupational Aspirations of "Common Man" Boys. *Harvard Educational Review*, 23, Summer 1953, 186-203.

COMMUNITY FACTORS IN THE EDUCATION
OF GIFTED CHILDREN *

by Robert J. Havighurst

UNIVERSITY OF CHICAGO

The current rise of interest in gifted children has caused a number of school systems to create programs more or less explicitly aimed at serving talented youth. These programs vary from one community

* This article is taken from *A Survey of Education for Gifted Children* by Robert J. Havighurst, Eugene Stivers, and Robert F. DeHaan, Supplementary Monographs, No. 83, Chicago: Univ. Chicago Press, 1955.

[Reprinted from *School Review*, 63, September 1955, 324-329, with the permission of the University of Chicago Press and the author.]

to another, and their nature depends on certain community factors. A survey of what is being done for gifted children in about forty cities or schools has led the writer to formulate a theory of the relation between the type of program and the type of community which creates and supports the program. This theory will be reported and illustrated in this article.

PROGRAM POSSIBILITIES FOR A COMMUNITY

There are three general procedures whereby a school can stimulate gifted children and help them to develop their abilities. *Enrichment* is primarily a teaching procedure, while *special grouping* and *acceleration* are administrative devices.

Every school which claims to have a good program for gifted youth uses enrichment procedures. These practices may be carried on in the regular classroom where the gifted children are a minority of the group, or enrichment may be practiced together with a special grouping of gifted children.

There are two basic alternatives open to a school system. The first, which we shall call *simple enrichment,* attempts to make schoolwork more interesting and valuable to a gifted child without taking him out of his age group or out of a regular classroom of children with varied abilities. The second, which we shall call *special-group enrichment,* places the gifted child in special groups of children of like ability and often provides for acceleration of his passage through school. [An elaboration of the three general procedures has been omitted.]

COMMUNITY FACTORS AFFECTING PROGRAM CHOICE

In the course of studying the programs for gifted children in large and small cities and in private schools, the writer noticed that the big cities seemed most likely to have special grouping for gifted children, while small cities and private schools were more likely to use simple enrichment. Medium-sized cities were divided, some having special groups and others using simple enrichment, while still others were uncertain about the type of plan they might adopt.

Community factors might cause these differences in the following ways. The larger cities have tens of thousands of school children and thousands of teachers and thus are in a position to make good use of specialization. Special groups of many kinds, with specialist teachers, can be set up efficiently and economically.

The larger cities generally have large classes—sometimes with forty or more children in the average elementary-school classroom. Teachers of such large classes find it difficult to work out enrichment procedures for individual pupils. In these circumstances it is natural to set up special classes of smaller size for gifted children and for any other groups which deserve special treatment. Special treatment for special groups is more likely to be acceptable to the public in a large city than in a smaller city because people in a large city expect variety and specialization in city services.

Furthermore, the people of a large city tend to be anonymous to one another and, therefore, not much interested in what class the neighbor's child is in or whether the neighbor's child gets into a school group which is taught differently from the group their own child is in. Special classes in the schools are not as highly "visible" to parents in a large city as in a smaller city. Those whose children are not in the special classes may be ignorant of the existence of a special program which could in a smaller city be construed by some people as showing favoritism toward some families.

New York City has gone further than any other in providing special groups for gifted children. Other cities in the survey which have also done a great deal in this direction are Birmingham, Los Angeles, Indianapolis, Baltimore, Detroit, Cleveland, and Pittsburgh.

In contrast to the larger cities, the schools of upper-middle-class suburbs of cities and the private schools seem least likely to have the special-group type of program. These communities or schools might be called "favored." The communities are fairly homogeneous as to socioeconomic status, and they send 80-90 percent of their high-school graduates to college. They may spend twice as much money per pupil on their schools as does the average community. Their schools have relatively small classes, are extremely well equipped, and have relatively well-trained teachers. The average intelligence quotient of children in such communities is a great deal higher than that in the average community, and there is a tendency, encouraged by the parents in this type of community, to attempt to treat all children as though they were at least headed for college, if not actually gifted.

The Malvern School in Shaker Heights, a suburb of Cleveland, belongs in this category of schools. It relies on enrichment in the regular classroom, as do the elementary schools of Winnetka (Illinois), Bronxville (New York), and similar communities.

Closely related to the favored-community schools are the "good" private schools. They draw their pupils from upper-middle-class homes, and the average intelligence quotient in such schools is likely to be 120 or above. These schools also tend to rely upon enrichment without special grouping. This is true of Fieldston (New York City), Francis Parker (Chicago), and the University of Chicago and Ohio State University laboratory schools. While there are usually a number of small special groups in such schools, these are interest groups, clubs, and activity groups rather than talent groups.

In general, it seems safe to say that the favored communities and the private schools serving upper-middle and upper-class families tend to avoid special grouping as far as possible and to count on small classes, well-trained teachers, well-equipped schools, and special-interest projects and activities both for gifted and average children.

In addition to the facts that such schools and communities spend more money on schooling and that they have relatively more bright children, there is a psychological factor which operates to prevent special grouping. Parents of children in these schools generally want their children to have all possible educational advantages, and they are alert to make sure that this happens. They pay for expensive schools, and they want the best for their children. Therefore they would protest if they thought that the school was giving other people's children more help than their own children were getting.

For this reason the school administration would not dare announce that there was a special group for gifted children, which received special attention. However, it is considered desirable to set up special-interest groups, because "everyone knows that children have special interests." In such a school there are many special-interest groups, and few children are left out of them. An example is seen in University City, an upper-middle-class suburb of St. Louis, where gifted children meet once or twice a week in special groups, which are treated as special-interest groups.

Although opposed to special grouping of gifted children, this type of community or school can accept a program of acceleration just as a large city can, but for different reasons. This community expects either that acceleration should be for everybody (as at the University of Chicago Laboratory School) or that it should come at the end of the high school, when youth are likely to leave the community and secure their acceleration without ostentation.

The large average type of community, which includes all large cities, is most likely to use special-group enrichment if it pays any special attention to its gifted youth. The medium and the small favored community is least likely to use special-group enrichment. The small average-type community is also unlikely to use special-group enrichment for two reasons. This community is a rural village or a town under five thousand in population. Its schools are too small to permit economical special grouping, and its teachers generally are not equipped to give specialized help in the arts, creative writing, and the like. Furthermore, in such a community, "everybody knows everybody," and parents are likely to resent anything that they might construe as special favors for some children.

A most interesting case is provided by the medium-sized average-type city, which varies from 5000 to 100,000 in population and is not a satellite of a large city. Since this type of community is between the small and the large, its program for gifted children can hardly be predicted. For instance, Allentown (Pennsylvania) and Brockton (Massachusetts) employ special grouping, while Cedar Rapids (Iowa) and Quincy (Illinois) lean toward enrichment within the regular classroom. Berkeley (California) offers special interest groups in music and art at the elementary-school level but does not use special groups based on mental ability until Grade 7. In this kind of community, special grouping is generally more popular in the high school than in the elementary school, for the reason that students's programs are differentiated according to their aims and interests in high school, thus providing special groups which can easily be supplemented by classes for gifted youth. A number of favored communities have special grouping in the high school but not in the elementary school. Examples are New Trier Township High School (Winnetka, Illinois), Evanston (Illinois) High School, Sewanhaka High School (Floral Park, New York), and the George School (Pennsylvania), a private school.

A few larger cities offer programs for gifted children with

minimum use of special-group enrichment in the elementary schools. Examples are Portland (Oregon) and San Diego (California). Perhaps it is significant that these are Pacific Coast cities, which have something of the favored-community ideology as well as good school facilities.

THE INFLUENCE OF LEADERSHIP

While there are systematic community influences such as we have described, it is also true that powerful or persuasive individuals in the community can create programs that do not fit the general pattern. The superintendent of schools may determine whether there is to be special grouping or not, particularly in the medium-sized community where the forces for and against special grouping are closely balanced. A strong principal may create in his school a program which is quite different from the trend in a city. A committee of citizens might successfully put its weight on the side for or against special grouping, especially in an undecided middle-sized community.

CONCLUSION

The nature of the school program for gifted children thus depends in a fairly predictable fashion on the following factors:

1. Size, complexity, and wealth of the community, which affect (a) expenditure per pupil, (b) class size, (c) possibilities for specialized assignments to teachers, and (d) possibilities for special schools and classes.

2. Social structure and social values of the community, which determine (a) whether people will tolerate a variety of school programs for various socioeconomic and various interest groups and (b) whether special emphasis is put on programs for one or another group of children, that is, the slow learners, the crippled, the gifted, and so forth.

3. Leadership in the community (lay or professional) which determines (a) whether the community will lead or follow the procession in setting up a program for gifted children and (b) what kind of program shall be adopted in communities where the other forces working for or against special grouping are fairly evenly balanced.

ENRICHMENT PRACTICES FOR GIFTED JUNIOR
HIGH SCHOOL PUPILS

by Earl M. McWilliams

WEST JEFFERSON HILLS PUBLIC SCHOOLS (PENN.)

Educators who have studied the problem of the identification of intellectually gifted youth have, in general, reached conclusions that are in common agreement, and it is possible to devise identification procedures that are acceptable universally.[1] Once gifted pupils have been identified, however, we find a wide disparity in both theory and practice as to the means by which these pupils shall be given the opportunity to develop to the utmost of their abilities. A survey of school programs for the gifted reveals that local school systems in all parts of the country have developed provisions in accordance with their educational philosophies and the needs of the communities they serve, with a resultant variety of practices with respect to segregation and acceleration for these pupils.

Enrichment of the educational experience of gifted pupils is recognized by every school as a necessity if their needs are to be adequately met, whether there is segregation of any degree or acceleration to any extent. The practices described in this article were observed in junior high schools from coast to coast, and their application can be made within the program of junior high schools regardless of the school staff's position on segregation or acceleration.[2] The possibilities for contributing vitally to the education of the gifted are limited only by the imagination and resources of the school and community, and each of the provisions mentioned below is an example of successful practice in a given school. The areas discussed are special classes, enrichment in the regular classroom, extraclass

[1] Jack W. Birch, and Earl M. McWilliams, *Challenging Gifted Children,* Bloomington, Ill.: Public School Publishing, 1955.
[2] Earl M. McWilliams, "The Gifted Pupil in the High School," *The Bull. of the NASSP,* 39, May 1955, 1-9.

[Reprinted from *The Bulletin,* 40, September 1956, 72-81, with the permission of the National Association of Secondary-School Principals and the author.]

activities, function of the library, and the use of community resources.

SPECIAL CLASSES

When there are enough children of high ability and evident interest in one area of the curriculum within a junior high school, it is common practice to organize a special class for these pupils. Where such classes are organized for particular subjects, the members thereof are usually scattered throughout the other subject classes to assure that the student body retains democratic heterogeneity. The term "partial segregation" is often used to describe a plan that puts gifted pupils into special classes for part of their schedule.

The most common type of special class for gifted pupils in grades seven and eight is one in a foreign language. Cities which encourage such opportunities include: Indianapolis, Indiana; Portland, Oregon; Pittsburg, Kansas; Scarsdale, New York; Lafayette Parish, Louisiana; Pittsburgh, Pennsylvania; and New York City. A lay-professional committee that studied the curriculum of the Bloomfield, New Jersey, Junior High School recommended that foreign language study should begin in the seventh grade.[3] Latin is part of the eighth-grade program at the Latin School in Boston, Massachusetts, and is offered to eighth-grade pupils at Byers Junior High School in Denver, Colorado. A world language class at the Hudde Junior High School (No. 240) in Brooklyn, New York, gives gifted seventh-grade pupils an orientation in five foreign languages and their corresponding cultures. A general language class at the Pasteur Junior High School in Los Angeles, California, provides a background of history, word study, grammar, and language appreciation for eighth-grade pupils of high ability who will take French or Latin later.

In the study of English, special classes in the junior high school are organized most often on the basis of test scores or past achievement, and the number of such classes is great. However, some schools organize special English classes of groups of pupils with common interests and abilities in specific areas of the broad field of language arts. An Honors English class at Halsey Junior High School (No.

[3] Curriculum Development Committee, *Curriculum Plan for Bloomfield Junior High School*, Bloomfield, N. J.: Bloomfield Junior High School, 1952, pp. 39-40.

157) in Forest Hills, New York, spends most of the time on creative writing. Pasteur Junior High School, Los Angeles, has a creative writing class, as does the Nichols School at Evanston, Illinois. At Roosevelt Junior High School in Fond du Lac, Wisconsin, there is a dramatics class which meets at the same time as the regular English classes and draws pupils from them for three weeks at a time to work on plays. These pupils are selected by tryouts in the English classes. In the junior high schools of the Lafayette Parish, Louisiana, there are two special sessions a week for gifted pupils, in which the approach to improving oral and writing skills is based upon a study of semantics.

Special classes for those talented in science or mathematics are not found in junior high schools with any frequency comparable to those in the language arts. The prevailing pattern in those schools with homogeneous grouping is to provide enrichment within the top classes or acceleration within the subject itself. Schools with heterogeneous classes provide individual enrichment, to be described later in this article.

Providing special classes for the gifted in music and art has been common procedure in junior high schools for many years. Such groups as the Choral Music class for selected girls at the Mark Twain Junior High School in Modesto, California, and the Special Art group at the Creston School in Portland, Oregon, are examples of the kind of fine opportunities made available to pupils gifted in these areas.

Typing is offered as an elective to gifted children in junior high schools or elementary schools in many places. The Madison District Schools at Phoenix, Arizona, have found this a worthwhile activity.

While many schools with core-type programs maintain heterogeneous grouping, the New Yosemite Junior High School in Fresno, California, established differentiated core classes, with pupils assigned to the various levels on the basis of several factors indicative of ability.[4]

ENRICHMENT WITHIN REGULAR CLASSROOMS

Since giftedness occurs in only a small percentage of our pupil population, the chances that the average junior high school will

[4] Joseph C. Deaton, Sr., "A Core-organized School in Action," *Calif. J. of Second. Educ.* 27, March 1952, 133-138.

have enough gifted pupils to form special classes are not very great. Therefore, a much more common problem is that of enrichment for one or a few gifted pupils in the regular classroom of an average school. The following examples show what some schools are doing to meet the needs of such pupils.

Classes in the language arts offer a myriad of opportunities for providing activities that will develop ability in both oral and written expression, as well as appreciation of literature. Pupil participation in such activities as debate, oratory, dramatics, elocution recitals, and creative writing has been a traditional part of the program of American schools since the early days. Not all of these activities are to be found in all schools today, but each can be found flourishing somewhere in every section of the nation.

Provisions for encouraging creative writing are common, and examples of the high quality of writing by pupils can be found in *Forest Trails,* a literary magazine by English pupils at Halsey Junior High School (No. 157) at Forest Hills, New York, and in *The Latin School Register* of the Boston Latin School. Classes which are characterized by worthwhile creative activities within the regular English class program are to be found at the Roland Park Junior High School in Baltimore, Maryland; the Roosevelt Junior High School in Fond du Lac, Wisconsin; and in several schools in Portland, Oregon. The material used in the closing-day exercises of the Lincoln Junior High School at Kenosha, Wisconsin, is written by gifted pupils. A strong interest in poetry writing is encouraged by participation in a "Browning Poetry Contest" at Rogers Junior High School in Long Beach, California. This activity at Rogers continues from year to year. The Gifted Child Project at Portland, Oregon, issued a mimeographed bulletin of suggestions for incorporating creative dramatics into the activities of a regular classroom. Essay writing by the gifted is encouraged in the Modesto, California, schools as a means of aiding children to learn to organize and present ideas in writing.

English classes at the Byers Junior High School in Denver, Colorado, are outstanding in the use of pupil imagination in presenting material to the group. This school does many of the things which are so effective in elementary classrooms to make both materials and rooms attractive and interest-catching, but the teachers at Byers recognize the relative maturity of their pupils and do not allow such activities to be regarded as "kid stuff" or to interfere with the progress of learning. An eighth-grade class studying folklore collected and put into notebooks material from the literature of all cultures, illustrating categories of folklore such as: exaggeration, mechanical devices, animals, and natural wonders. A seventh-grade class developed a deep interest in the medieval period through reading, so they decided to organize their class as a round table. Bulletins were issued as royal edicts. Class members moved through three stages—serf, squire, and knight or lady—as they completed the work assignments of the class. A shield designed by members of the class was on the wall, and a motto was adopted. An illuminated chart of the class-written "Standards of Knighthood" contained one that would have given King Arthur a surprise: "A knight is a good student. He tries hard in all subjects and can never get a 'D'."

In an eighth-grade English class at Simis School in Phoenix, Arizona, the writing of a newspaper evolved out of the work in language. After the paper had been produced, gifted members of the class conceived the idea of making a filmstrip to show how such a paper is made. They took their own pictures and wrote the captions for the filmstrip.

Oral and written reports give an opportunity for the gifted pupil to develop individual interests and express his ideas and findings. Introducing such reports into a class for discussion can be most helpful to the teenager. Pupil-written biographies are used effectively in many English classes, as well as social studies.

Some gifted children are weak in grammar, while others are ahead of the average in their classes. A teacher at Western Hills High School in Cincinnati, Ohio, allows gifted pupils who have a good mastery of grammar to teach the class when this phase of the work is scheduled. Pupils can progress at their own speed when provided with individual assignments and individual progress records like those at the Skokie Junior High School in Winnetka, Illinois.

Social studies classes offer innumerable opportunities for enrichment, both for individual pupils and for groups. Class planning can be very effective in this subject field, and there are many examples of excellent teacher-pupil cooperation in planning units to be studied. Sometimes this takes place in classes where unit topics are assigned and then the class plans how to study the topic, as at the Roland Park Junior High School in Baltimore, Maryland. Here the gifted have an opportunity to develop leadership in group thinking.

Special reports of individuals and groups are invaluable devices for enrichment here, as in language arts. Two bright pupils in a ninth-grade civics class at Hawthorne Junior High School in Wauwatosa, Wisconsin presented to the class and then led a discussion on the results of an inquiry they had made, through reading and interviews, into the nature of the soul and mind of the human being. This had been prompted by reading about Plato and his ideas.

Role playing is a stimulating experience to imaginative pupils and lends itself to use in the social studies. At the Lakewood Junior High School in Long Beach, California, a Latin American Conference gives pupils an opportunity to engage in role playing, and the gifted have opportunities for intensive research in preparation for their part in the conference.

Some social studies classes write their own books. At the Cedar City Junior High School in Cedar City, Utah, a class studying Utah history wrote their own textbook, which was presented to the school library when the class had finished using it. Another class of seventh-grade pupils at Cedar City collected pioneer stories from their families and put these tales into a booklet which was mimeographed. Such activities offer the gifted opportunities to serve as editors and organizers, as well as writers. An eighth-grade class in American history at Waukegan Road School in Northbrook, Illinois, wrote a history book, with responsibility for the various sections taken by class committees. A gifted boy wrote chapter introductions. A class in Long Beach, California, which was studying the Civil War, wrote two newspapers of the period of the war, one representing the northern viewpoint and one the southern.

Although the majority of junior high schools have arrived at the conclusion that acceleration of subject matter is the best way to provide for the gifted in the skill subject of mathematics, there are many enrichment possibilities in this field.[5] Such activities can help the gifted to develop their interests in mathematical topics and in the broad applications of the subject matter. The faculty of the Garrison Junior High School in Baltimore, Maryland, made a study of the gifted in their mathematics classes and prepared a bulletin of their recommendations.[6]

[5] Earl M. McWilliams and Kenneth E. Brown, *The Superior Pupil in Junior High School Mathematics,* United States Department of Health, Education, and Welfare, Bulletin 1955, No. 4, Washington, D. C.: U. S. Government Printing Office.
[6] Mathematics Department, *Dealing with the Superior Student in Mathematics.* Baltimore, Md.: Garrison Junior High School, 1951.

Our gifted children live in a world where every day brings forth some exciting new development in the field of science, and the teachers of this subject have found that they can enrich the schoolroom experiences by capitalizing upon the science hobbies and reading which the pupils are enjoying outside the school. In countless science classrooms, individual and group projects are demonstrating pupils' interests and their intensive work on scientific topics to a degree that proves how worthwhile it is to provide such activities within the school program.[7] The procurement of suitable materials is a troublesome problem in science, and to keep up to date on such topics as atomic power, teachers often use pamphlets issued by leading industrial and research organizations. Often these materials are written especially for pupils.

Because most of the attention in discussions of providing for the gifted centers upon the mentally gifted, much excellent work that is going forward in the field of industrial arts and home economics goes unnoticed. A significant effort is being made in Portland, Oregon, to identify those who are gifted mechanically and to provide the best possible education for them. In several New York City junior high schools, gifted boys and girls are scheduled for coeducational home economics and industrial-arts classes.

An example of the kind of industrial-arts class which serves mechanically gifted pupils and at the same time provides valuable experiences for otherwise gifted pupils is to be found at the Hyattsville Junior High School in Hyattsville, Maryland. The shop class is organized on the same plan as the personnel organization of an industrial plant. There is a class foreman and assistant foreman, with duties of shop management and control of both personnel and matériel. The activities of the class are under the following departments: safety and health, equipment, materials and supplies, maintenance, records, and clean-up. The setup is flexible, so that newly elected foremen may rearrange and reorganize to suit their plans. Foremen are elected for two-week periods and may be re-elected. One advantage of this plan is that boys who may not be mechanically inclined can have the experience of learning about industrial organization and discovering the possibilities for those whose giftedness is in other directions to find places for themselves in personnel work, management of production, accounting, drafting, and design.

[7] Morris Meister, "What Provisions for the Education of Gifted Students?", *The Bull. NASSP*, 35, April 1951, 30-38.

The fine arts, well taught, are enrichment classes per se, and in most junior high schools a tradition of individual work for creative giftedness is to be found. Capable teachers in all subjects are alert to the possibilities of enrichment by using the fine arts in every classroom. An outstanding art program, which serves all subject areas in a multitude of ways and still provides adequately for creative individual production, is the one at Mosholu Parkway Junior High School (No. 80) in The Bronx, New York City. Interesting work in "free" art projection by gifted pupils has been done in the art classes at Lee Junior High School in Baltimore, Maryland.

To turn from specific subject areas, there are some general principles of enrichment which apply to all classroom situations. Critical thinking is one aim of education of the gifted, and many teachers plan lessons or whole units with this objective in mind. A test to evaluate critical thinking of junior-high-school pupils has been devised at the University of Oregon.[8] Another trait which is essential to help the gifted child cultivate is the ability to listen critically. Reference to the need for this recurs often in discussion of gifted pupils. Some schools help these pupils to develop a sense of responsibility for management of affairs by assigning to them such duties as planning and arranging classroom and school bulletin-board displays, clerical duties in classes or offices, helping other pupils who are having difficulties with their lessons, and assuming control of a classroom when a teacher is called away.

To aid the classroom teacher there are available many fine audio-visual materials. Several schools appoint gifted pupils to positions as operators and caretakers of films and projectors, with the intention of thus enriching their experience in many directions. The filmstrip is a good enrichment device for an individual pupil, for it can be used in a corner of a classroom without interrupting other activities. The educational television station in Pittsburgh, Pennsylvania, is experimenting with enrichment programs for the regular classrooms.

Since the range of reading ability varies so widely in the average class, teachers must have on hand materials to suit all ability levels. For the advanced reader, this often means books and magazines written for senior high-school pupils or adults.

[8] M. T. Macy and Hugh B. Wood, "Test of Critical Thinking," *Curriculum Bulletin No. 99*, Eugene, Ore.: School of Education, University of Oregon, December 18, 1951.

ENRICHMENT THROUGH EXTRACLASS ACTIVITIES

Junior high schools throughout the nation provide for individual differences through extraclass activities. Here the early adolescent pupil can explore areas of human activity not touched upon in his classroom and develop his particular abilities and interests. For the gifted it is an area of great potential value for enrichment.

Student-council organizations enable pupils to develop social leadership. These councils all across the country are grappling with the same type of problems, and it is encouraging to witness the democratic manner in which most of these organizations operate. The school government at Skokie School in Winnetka, Illinois, is outstanding both in the degree to which it really governs the life of the school and in the unique structure of the school society of which it is a part. This school program offers a unique experience to its pupils, who live in a school environment which closely approximates our complex, highly organized society, with a multitude of opportunities for gifted leadership to operate. The representative government of Skokie levies a graduated income tax on the citizens of the school and a corporation tax. The latter is an assessment on the earnings of the school operations, which engage in various enterprises such as beekeeping, raising of pets, bank and credit union, manufacture of ink and face cream, consumers cooperative, a mutual insurance company (for dish breakage in the cafeteria), raising shrubs and trees, and a closed-shop dishwashers's union.[9]

Several junior high schools have outstanding programs that provide exploratory experiences for all pupils, and the gifted should be encouraged to sample a variety of extraclass activities. The Exploratory Hour is part of the daily program at the Junior High School in Cedar City, Utah. Pupils elect an activity each semester, and only those gifted in music are encouraged to choose the same activity for more than one semester. The groups organized in a typical semester are: student council, wild life, journalism, photography, square dancing, glee club, band, lapidary club, store and bank, dramatics, reading, agriculture, and aviation.[10] This list varies from year to year as pupil interests and needs change.

[9] Donald G. Cawalti, "Laying the Groundwork for Effective Economic Citizenship," *Educational Leadership*, 5, October 1947, 29-34.
[10] Lorin C. Miles, "The Adolescent Explorer Finds What He Needs," *NEA J.*, 43, December 1953, 557-558.

The Major Interest Workshops at the Hudde Junior High School (No. 240) in Brooklyn, New York, give pupils an opportunity to explore in depth a given field of activities in the seventh and eighth grades. Here, too, the list of workshops changes from semester to semester but may include these areas of interest: vocal music, instrumental music, dramatics, creative writing, journalism, art, science, French, Spanish, typing, and dancing. The pupils at Hudde who are enrolled in the workshops often find their interest to be transitory, as well as sometimes discovering deep interest and ability in an explored area.

At the Central School in Glencoe, Illinois, there is a Special Needs Period which meets four times a week. This is an exploratory program for the most part, but some pupils who have deficiencies in school learning areas are scheduled for remedial work at this time. The pupils elect new activities every nine weeks.

An attribute to human adjustment that is essential in the life of every growing child is his social competence. Schools must recognize the achievement of this to be one of the primary aims of their planning, especially at the junior-high-school level, where the "storm and stress" of adolescence begin to affect youth. A national organization which is concerned with the welfare of gifted youth rates social adjustment as a vital outcome of provisions for these youth.[11] Extraclass activities, by their very nature, are rich in potentiality for development of social competence in individual pupils. One of the most successful plans for helping pupils in this respect is the Human Relations Course of the Madison Schools in Phoenix, Arizona.[12] This program is based upon learning to live by the Golden Rule. Through the years of its history, much of the planning has been by gifted pupils.

Pupils in a science class at Walnut Hills High School in Cincinnati, Ohio, decided that some of the special reports given in their class would be interesting to other pupils in the school. They drew up a list of these reports and offered to present them as part of the home-room programs for any group interested. The idea caught on, and the original plan has been expanded into a speakers' bureau

[11] Pauline Brooks Williamson, "The American Association for Gifted Children: Objectives and Growth," *Understanding the Child,* 22, October 1953, 121-124.
[12] Loula Grace Erdman, "Three R's and a Fourth," *National Parent-Teacher,* 48, May 1954, 4-7.

called "Programs, Incorporated" which offers talks and demonstrations on a wide array of subjects.

THE FUNCTION OF THE LIBRARY

The school librarian can be one of the most influential teachers of the gifted. Within the library is the collected wisdom and inspiration of our civilization, and to help a pupil explore this storehouse is a privilege rich with exciting possibilities. The librarians of the Newark Public Schools, conscious of their obligations to the gifted, have made a study of how to serve them best.[13]

At the University School in Columbus, Ohio, the library does outstanding work in serving the pupils in this core-type program. The library is a resource center open to individuals and groups all through the school day. Records are kept of the free reading of pupils, and the librarian has frequent conferences with individuals about their reading program. This type of assistance assures that they will have encouragement and guidance in achieving both breadth and depth in their reading.

A definite attempt to encourage gifted pupils to read on an adult level was successful at the Harman Junior High School in Hazleton, Pennsylvania.[14] School librarians everywhere report that they are constantly alert to discover books and periodicals that meet the demands of pupils with advanced reading ability. As a supplementary source of books, some schools organize local chapters of the Teen Age Book Club, sponsored by *Scholastic Magazine,* which offers paper-bound books of high quality to its members.

At the Boise School in Portland, Oregon, a survey of independent reading at home was made among the pupils. Field trips to the nearest city library were then arranged for pupils with above-average reading ability who did not have reading opportunities at home.

The Cincinnati schools have circulating collections of books which are being considered for purchase as auxiliary reading material. Gifted pupils in the various schools are asked to read these

[13] Newark School Librarians Association, *The Librarian and the Gifted Child.* Newark, N. J.: Public Schools, 1953.
[14] Margaret Gregory and William J. McLaughlin, "Advance Reading for the Bright Child," *The Clearing House,* 26, December 1951, 203-205.

books and evaluate them. This gives them an opportunity to render service and, at the same time, to widen their reading horizon.

USE OF COMMUNITY RESOURCES

Junior high schools in many places have lay representation on committees that plan and evaluate programs for gifted pupils. These schools have found that not only do they benefit from the balancing effect of nonprofessional viewpoints in discussions, but also there is a decided improvement in public relations and support for innovations.[15] Portland, Oregon; Modesto, California, and San Diego, California, all include citizens on policy-making committees and in evaluation studies.

Another facet of school-community resources for the gifted is that of using the community as a laboratory for learning experiences. Field trips have become an accepted part of the American school scene, and teachers of the gifted find that these pupils benefit immeasurably from excursions into the community, especially if they are motivated to regard the visits as research projects.

Studies of city government give student leaders an opportunity to become acquainted with the machinery of practical political activities. Seventh-grade pupils at Gaskill Junior High School in Niagara Falls, New York, interviewed city officials and reported back to their classmates. At the Central School in Glencoe, Illinois, pupils from the sixth, seventh, and eighth grades make an annual study of their village government and then give the student body and a local service club their observations and criticisms.

Talented youth can often find opportunities to participate in programs outside the schools. The Phoenix Symphony Youth Orchestra at Phoenix, Arizona, accepts capable young musicians of junior-high-school age. Junior-high-school pupils in Pittsburgh, Pennsylvania, work with their drama teachers in a summer workshop program at the University of Pittsburgh. The program is sponsored by the Speech Department of the university and the local Children's Civic Theater Society. In many communities, museums and libraries sponsor activities for youth interested in science, art, and reading.

[15] Merle R. Sumption, "Let the Community Plan the Program for Educating Gifted Children," *Exceptional Children,* 20, October 1953, 26-27.

Interest in gifted students is growing rapidly in American education. The literature of our profession is containing more and more articles and books on the subject. While it would be foolish for any school to slavishly copy the provisions made by another school, there is much help to be derived from knowing what has been successful elsewhere. Probably one of the most helpful things school administrators could do for their faculties would be to assemble for their use a comprehensive collection of materials on the education of the gifted.

THE COMPREHENSIVE HIGH SCHOOL
AND GIFTED YOUTH

by A. Harry Passow

COLUMBIA UNIVERSITY

Recent manpower studies, as well as criticisms of our educational programs, tend to depict the secondary school as a wasteland for young talent. As the demands for great numbers of trained specialists reach a peak and the great reappraisal of American education continues, more and more individuals and groups will scrutinize the provisions made for promising youth.

This current period of educational soul searching raises many familiar issues and problems. However, the setting, perspective, and pressures are altered. For many years, the concern was whether high schools were up to "the weighty task of giving life to the great ideal of educational opportunity for the varied children of a heterogeneous people." [1] More recent anxieties about the nature of the secondary-school program have been linked to the question of national survival. As a consequence, education of gifted youth is no

[1] Educational Policies Commission, *Public Education and the Future of America*, Washington, D. C.: National Education Association, 1955, p. 24.

[Reprinted from the *Teachers College Record*, 58, December 1956, 144-152, with the permission of the *Record* and the author.]

longer a matter of concern for the school alone but occupies the attention of governmental and lay groups of all kinds as well.

At various times and from various quarters the school has been accused of neglecting or providing inadequately for one group or another—the slow, the average, the gifted, the academic, the nonacademic. If the comprehensive high school does not furnish instruction appropriate for the optimum development of the gifted, then it certainly cannot claim to be fulfilling its obligations to all youth.

In assessing the responsibilities of the secondary school for the gifted, one must dispose first of the question, Who is to be considered gifted? When the major function of the secondary school was to prepare its students for college, it was the child of academic ability who was considered gifted. The school's concern was with youngsters who learned rapidly what was taught in the traditional classrooms. With the development of intelligence tests, the child who scored high on these instruments was included in the gifted group.

In more recent years, writers have advocated a broadened definition of giftedness to include a variety of talents, both academic and nonacademic. Witty, for example, has urged that any child be considered gifted "whose performance, in a potentially valuable line of human activity, is consistently remarkable." [2] Manpower studies tend to classify as gifted those individuals with the ability (usually based on high intelligence) to fill positions that require specialized advanced training. Artistic and social talents have only recently been considered in connection with this problem, and because of the lack of knowledge about the nature of such talents, criteria in these areas are even less definitive.

Although there is no single, widely accepted definition of *gifted* or *talented,* the trend is toward a more inclusive interpretation—one which is in harmony with the broad role of the comprehensive school. In practice, the greatest emphasis is still on the intellectually able; and most current programs for identifying gifted children include high intelligence as a criterion for selection. Because criticisms of educational programs and findings relative to shortages in manpower focus on the intellectually and scholastically able, this analysis will be limited to the academic areas.

[2] Paul Witty, "What Is Special About Special Education? The Gifted Child," *Exceptional Children,* 19, April 1953, 255.

FITTING EDUCATION TO ALL YOUTH

Unique in modern American education is the underlying concept that free and equal educational opportunities should be available for all youth through the secondary level. Instead of being rigidly selective, as in many European countries, the American high school has become more and more inclusive. Fifty years ago only one of every ten young people of high-school age was in school. By 1951-1952, some 77.3 percent of youth between fourteen and seventeen years of age were enrolled in secondary schools; and it is quite likely that the figure is now over 80 percent.[3]

The effort to provide secondary-level education for all American youth has entailed more buildings, larger staffs, extended school years, longer compulsory attendance periods, and increased budgets. But the most significant modification, of course, has been the changing role of the secondary school. In addition to their clear function of preparing students for college, the high schools began to accept diverse responsibilities for the general and special education of all students, two thirds of whom even now are not college-bound.

It was the Commission on the Reorganization of Secondary Education which defined this new role—with the publication in 1918 of *Cardinal Principles of Secondary Education*. This influential report also gave impetus and support to the comprehensive high school as the unified organization in which all youth could have equal opportunities—youth of "all races, creeds, nationalities, intelligences, talents, and all levels of wealth and social status." [4] This integrating function, Cremin has pointed out, was particularly important in a culture increasingly marked by diverse immigrant populations, industrialization, and growth of urban centers.[5]

The degree of success with which the comprehensive high school has provided appropriately for youth with great differences in abilities, interests, aspirations, and experiential backgrounds has

[3] U. S. Office of Education, *Biennial Study of Education in the United States, 1950-1952, Statistical Summary of Education, 1951-1952*, Washington, D. C.: U.S. Government Printing Office, 1955, p. 21.
[4] Franklin J. Keller, *The Comprehensive High School*, New York: Harper, 1955, pp. 31-32.
[5] Lawrence A. Cremin, "The Problem of Curriculum Making: An Historical Perspective," in *What Shall the High Schools Teach?*, Washington, D. C.: Association for Supervision and Curriculum Development, NEA, 1956, pp. 6-26.

provoked criticism and praise. How to develop such a school as a "means for creating social unity without crushing individuality and for developing individual diversity without cultivating social cleavages"[6] is a problem that has troubled both theorists and practitioners.

Although the comprehensive high school is the typical secondary-education institution, there is no typical comprehensive high school. Schools vary in size, physical plant, teaching staff, course offerings, budget, administrative structure, curriculum organization, and community resources. In many instances, schools called comprehensive are, in reality, academic high schools. The common element is found in the purpose of the comprehensive high school, which, as Keller puts it, "has as its broadest objective the teaching of all varieties of skill, all kinds of knowledge to all kinds of youth bent upon socially profitable lives. To each one it seeks to give the courses for which he seems best fitted."[7]

For the most part, where there is a single high school in the community, this is either a comprehensive school or an academic one in the process of diversifying its program to provide for noncollege-bound youth. It is in these kinds of secondary schools that the gifted are, and in all probability will continue to be, found and educated.

CRITICISM OF COMPREHENSIVE HIGH SCHOOLS' PROVISIONS

The competence of the all-inclusive secondary school to provide adequately for gifted youth has been challenged almost since its birth. For example, contrasting education in the United States with that in Europe, Learned wrote:

The schools are nonselective and undifferentiated with respect to the quality of the pupil. A low average level of operation is the result. . . . Intellectual prince and intellectual pauper make their selections and are grouped promiscuously side by side. They keep step together from four to six years, one doing his poor maximum and the other his fair minimum on material suited to neither but determined by the weaker pupil. Each doubt-

[6] Will French, "The Role of the American High School," *Bull. Nat. Assoc. Secondary School Principals,* 39, February 1955, 9.
[7] Keller, *op. cit.,* p. 32.

less "gets something," as the phrase goes, but the capable mind is bored and contracts lazy and wasteful habits, while the other is depressed by continual failure with things too hard instead of encouraged by clear success at his own level.[8]

In 1939, Kandel warned:

The danger that confronts this country is not that it is providing equality of educational opportunities; the danger lies in the cult of mediocrity. No country has a stronger tradition of faith in education than the United States; in no country is there more information available on differences of ability than in the United States; and yet with all the faith and with all the knowledge less is being done than elsewhere to give the best education to those who might do the most with it. A fallacious interpretation of democracy has tended to reduce equality of opportunity to identity of education. . . .[9]

The major charges against the comprehensive high school's provisions for the intellectually gifted may be summarized as follows:

1. The secondary schools fail to get many of the brightest youth to go on to college and advanced training. The Commission on Human Resources and Advanced Training reported that "fewer than half of the upper 25 percent of all high school graduates ever earn college degrees; only six out of ten of the top 5 percent do." [10]

A dynamic society which emphasizes science and technology and a system of democratic values which encourages social and cultural change necessarily put a high premium on trained intelligence. A college degree has become a prerequisite for work in most areas requiring special talent or intelligence. Without such advanced training, it is difficult or impossible, in our present society, for youth to become producing members of the culture in such fields. Our way of life requires the services of many trained specialists; yet the storehouses of talent seem always partly empty. Therefore, it is argued, if half of our most intellectually able youngsters do not go on for advanced training, their talents are wasted.

[8] William S. Learned, *The Quality of the Educational Process in the United States and Europe,* New York: The Carnegie Foundation for the Advancement of Teaching, 1927, p. 5.
[9] I. L. Kandel, "Leadership and Education in Other Times and Other Lands," *Teachers Coll. Rec.,* 40, April 1939, 573.
[10] Dael Wolfle, *America's Resources of Specialized Talent,* New York: Harper, 1954, p. 269.

2. Guidance and educational procedures fall short in motivating able youth, judged according to two criteria: first, the number of gifted youth who are working up to capacity, and, second, the number who will go to college. The lack of desire for college training is second only to inadequate finances as a reason for bypassing college.[11] This lack of motivation is attributed to the school by many critics who challenge both its ability to develop programs which lead youth to want higher education and its resources for counseling to increase college-going among able youth.

3. The educational process in American schools lacks the quality found in European education and, as a consequence, gifted youth suffer, American secondary schools are accused of failing to provide intellectual rigor and sustained scholarship. James B. Conant observes:

For the European youth who starts at age 10 or 11 in his long journey towards the university, and of whom about half will become in fact university students, the instruction is far more rigorous, the work far harder than we can imagine here in the United States—harder in terms of hours put in, harder in terms of subjects studied, and more rigorous in terms of accomplishments demanded. One might well say of this small group that, when they enter a university, they have two or three times as much knowledge and acquired skills as the best college entrants in the United States.[12]

4. The comprehensive high-school program is watered down, fragmentized, and incohesive. Critics have charged that standards have been lowered or abandoned, rigorous examinations eliminated, intellectual mediocrity accepted. Comparisons have been made of school offerings in the early part of the century with those of today to show that courses have been "thinned" to make them palatable to a large number of students who are neither academically oriented nor college-bound—all at the expense of the gifted.

In the matter of course offerings alone, the range has increased during the last forty years to a point where it is estimated that "American high schools are now offering somewhere in the neigh-

[11] Robert J. Havighurst and Robert R. Rodgers, "The Role of Motivation in Attendance at Post-High School Educational Institutions," in Byron S. Hollinshead, *Who Should Go to College?*, New York: Columbia Univ. Press, 1952, pp. 161-162.
[12] James B. Conant, "Text of Address at the National Citizens Commission for Public Schools Annual Dinner," *Better Schools*, 1, January 19, 1956, 7.

borhood of 500 discernibly different courses." [13] Critics have argued that solid geometry and safety education, history and homemaking, should not have the same weight because they do not have the same quality. While not always arguing for a rigid hierarchy of subjects, these critics see some offerings as *more nearly equal* than others, particularly for some students. The elimination of required sequences for college entrance and the multiplying list of electives, critics maintain, have robbed school programs of cohesion, continuity, and depth. The European student, we are reminded, pursues courses years longer than his American counterpart does, and consequently attains far greater intellectual mastery.

In the end, the charge is this: by draining educational programs of depth and challenge, by equating education with training, by emphasizing quantity rather than quality, by teaching to what has been characterized as "the colorless mean," the comprehensive high school has neglected the gifted student. It has failed to meet its special obligation to this segment of American youth.

ADEQUACY OF COMPREHENSIVE HIGH SCHOOLS' PROVISIONS

It is important to remember, first of all, that in a nation whose schools are locally controlled, practices are so varied as to void most blanket criticisms except as a starting point for thoughtful and thorough examination of school programs. Has the high school really shunted its gifted youth into the common pile? Is it really neglecting talent in its effort to do all things for all youth? The discussion which follows refutes these criticisms.

1. The holding power of today's secondary school is very high, particularly with respect to the intellectually able. Most academically gifted youth enter and are graduated from high school. The "loss" is in the fact that half of our most able youth do not go on to college. Proportionately and in gross numbers, the college-going group is greater than ever before. In 1900, one youth out of every sixty graduated from college; today one out of every eight earns a

---

[13] Kenneth Hovet, "What are the High Schools Teaching?" in *What Shall the High Schools Teach?*, Washington, D. C.: Association for Supervision and Curriculum Development, NEA, 1956, p. 75.

college degree.[14] Of the top 2 percent of high-school graduates, two thirds earn college degrees. By creating a situation in which a larger proportion of our youth enter and complete secondary school, we have made it possible for larger numbers to secure advanced training.

As Professor Harold Clark of Teachers College, Columbia, has pointed out, no real study has been made of what part the 50 percent of our most able youth who do not go on to college play in our culture. We know that they cannot enter certain specialized professions, but we have no authoritative report on what kinds of important contributions they make to the general welfare or what kinds of specialized training they secure outside of our established institutions of higher education. Some industries, for example, have established their own employee education programs which match in size, purpose, and program those of many of our colleges and universities.

2. Factors affecting motivation for college-going are numerous, many having nothing to do with the school. Socioeconomic class, ethnic origin, sex, geographic residence, cultural pressures, and family relationships are some of the factors which influence individual motivations and aspirations. By providing appropriate educational experiences, improving counseling procedures, tapping financial resources for able youth, and creating positive attitudes toward scholarship and learning, schools in some communities have helped direct ever more young people toward college. The proportion of high-school graduates who go on to college ranges from practically none to more than 90 percent for different schools.

3. The quality of the educational process can be judged only in terms of how well this process attains accepted goals. As Learned put it, "in European schools the whole body of human knowledge and of scholarly achievement is conceived as constituting the supreme achievement of the race, to be preserved, increased, and handed on to posterity as its most precious possession." [15] Conceding European superiority in certain areas, supporters of our secondary school programs maintain that gifted American youth excel in effective citizenship, group membership, ethical values, and similar traits which our culture seeks. Disagreeing on what constitutes a cultivated, well-rounded individual, we tend to balk at comparing

[14] Wolfle, *op. cit.*, p. 24.
[15] Learned, *op. cit.*, p. 7.

the academic accomplishments of our own youth with those of the less than 10 percent of European youth who are selected for special training. It is true, however, that our youth do not have the "immemorial reverence for learning" that Learned ascribed to European youth.

4. High schools have attempted to modify their offerings to serve the present heterogeneous student population. Some former subjects (for example, Greek) were dropped, others (say, mathematics) were modified, and still others (such as driver training) were added. The continued stress of high schools on academic preparation, however, led to such movements as Life Adjustment Education, which were intended to prepare for jobs those students who were not college-bound. In some instances courses were watered down, but in others the basic nature of offerings was altered to achieve new purposes. In general, able youth were guided into the "harder" subjects but here they also found some less able students enrolled. Breathing life into their ideal of providing for individual differences has proved more difficult than theorists once believed—but not impossible.

SPECIAL CURRICULAR ARRANGEMENTS

Scope and sequence problems have always plagued curriculum planners. Some educators feel that continuity comes from particular course sequences pursued over a period of years; others believe that integration is a by-product of building a hierarchy of skills, concepts, and relationships and argue that *how* something is studied is as important as *what* is studied. For the gifted, academic disciplines provide better vehicles for continuity than some of the "practical" subjects. But the quantity of knowledge or its difficulty is only a partial guide in the selection of learning experiences for the gifted; how much this experience will increase meanings and appreciations is also important.

Among the modifications in instructional or administrative procedures or both which have been made by secondary schools to differentiate educational experiences for gifted youth are the following:

1. Acceleration of individuals and groups of gifted youth— that is, reducing the time spent in secondary school or in a course or sequence; increasing the learning tempo; or providing desired

learning experiences at a younger age or an earlier stage than is usual.

2. Grouping students on the basis of ability, aptitude, interest, or motivation in order to facilitate desired kinds of learning—establishing advanced or honors classes; separating students for special experiences regularly or periodically.

3. Personalized instruction of gifted students in the regular classroom, permitting deeper and more extensive study; providing different materials and activities; or modifying requirements and time schedules.

Schools have added courses and made it possible for gifted students to carry heavier or different loads. They have modified teaching methods to emphasize experiences particularly appropriate to gifted youth. Despite more than a half century of research, none of these "packaged solutions" has proved conclusive. None has provided a single dramatic answer, although the proponents of each have suggested that it might. Any examination of the advantages and disadvantages of specific program modifications must be made in terms of their possible contribution to recognized individual goals for gifted youth.

The size and nature of a community, its wealth and resources, its values and leadership affect the kinds of modifications possible in that situation. What the large city system, with a sizable number of gifted youth and several high schools, can undertake may be out of the question for suburban and rural communities. The talent loss may well be greatest in rural areas. It has been advocated by some that smaller communities pool their resources to set up one special high school to serve the gifted youth from several localities.[16] Such cooperation is already functioning for vocational education. On a more limited scale, one rural area brought gifted youth from six different schools to a special seminar one afternoon per week. Small schools need to explore ways of increasing their resources and flexibility. There are at least four possibilities: teacher guidance of independent study in advanced areas; correspondence courses and self-teaching materials; community specialists invited to share their skills and resources with students; small classes as the backdrop for individualizing instruction.

[16] I. L. Kandel, "Some Unresolved Issues in American Education," *The Educational Forum,* 20, March 1956, 266-278.

LIBERALIZING EDUCATION OF THE GIFTED

Should gifted youth be developed or educated differently from other students? The Educational Policies Commission has recommended:

First, because they are human beings, citizens, consumers, and prospective parents, they need a good general education, not unlike what is needed by all their fellow students, to equip them to deal competently with themselves, their environment, and their fellow man. Second, and in addition, because they are the potential leaders in the professions, in business, and in other fields in a contracted world at an advanced stage of technological development, they need a wide acquaintance with the record of human experience, familiarity with foreign cultures and languages and basic training in the tools and concepts of modern science.[17]

In addition, gifted children need to cultivate their abilities to think searchingly and critically, to build meanings and concepts, to see relationships between past, present, and future learnings. They need training in how to learn and how to discipline their intelligence in the interest of scholarship. The distinctive characteristic of the intellectually gifted youth is his fertile, creative mind; the optimum development of this creative intellect is another specific objective. The extent to which the school can and will develop other socially valuable talents depends on its resources and the efforts it is willing to make; but it must accept responsibility for building this common core of experience and developing the unique intellectual abilities of its gifted youth.

The school has accepted varying degrees of responsibility for the intellectual, social, aesthetic, physical, and moral development of its youth. For some of these areas the school has a major responsibility, for others an incidental concern. Only as the school defines and clarifies its responsibilities in the development of youth as cultural consumers and producers can it evolve meaningful educational programs. What are the specific goals of secondary education for the gifted, the objectives beyond those of the high school for all youth? The secondary school owes it to society and gifted youth to

---

[17] Educational Policies Commission, *Education of the Gifted,* Washington, D. C.: National Education Association, 1950, pp. 86-87.

develop: (1) a pool of highly able, liberally educated youth from which society can draw now and in the future; (2) youth who can become highest level consumers of the cultural heritage; (3) youth with the understandings to insure optimum social change along with the highest ethical standards of leadership.

To attain these goals, educational programs for gifted youth should stress the acquisition of ideas, meanings, insights, and relationships; the building of concepts and understandings; the opportunity for creating; stimulation of the intellect and respect for healthy curiosity. Gifted youth need these kinds of experiences if they are to accumulate the broad liberal base which is essential for any area of specialization. They need fundamental skills and processes, the knowledge and resources with which to think independently, and opportunities for developing skills. Because the humanities, the sciences, and the arts offer breadth, depth, and emphasis on meanings, they are probably more appropriate and essential in the education of gifted youth than other subjects. Similarly, methods which stress research, independent thinking, and wide understanding are more appropriate than rote learning. Talented youth can certainly use practical and functional courses too, but these should round out, not supplant, the vital liberal learnings. In summary, a program for gifted youth should stress that which they are able to do best: think, understand, create, initiate, relate, and synthesize.

The daily press and professional journals alike clamor about shortages of scientists and engineers. Scholarships are more numerous, and special programs and recruitment efforts and studies are more vigorous in these areas than in any other. Yet equally great shortages hamper the humanities, social sciences, and other specialized fields. Manpower needs are great and fluctuating. Not too long ago we were worried about an *oversupply* of engineers and urged youth to train for other professions. Manpower studies which fasten on numbers alone, when examining supply and demand, miss the important dimension of quality. Perhaps our most frightening shortages are not in the general supply of scientists but in those rare persons with imagination, creativity, motivation, competence, and education who can contribute something fresh and basic to our understanding of man's relations with man.

The talent a society produces is often talent that the society is willing to pay for or feels that it needs. But a changing society such as ours, needs and will continue to need as much trained talent as it can produce. The role of the secondary school, then, is not to force youth to specialize in one area or another but rather to build a sound liberal foundation which will support the development of specialized competency at the higher education level. To undergird liberal learning, the comprehensive high school must: (1) Re-examine its curriculum, not in terms of adding a course or a requirement but rather with a view toward developing an over-all framework which will emphasize concepts, understandings and appreciations, skills and knowledge—all of which contribute to a liberal education; (2) restudy its teaching procedures, content, and materials so that these are based on what is known about the nature and needs of gifted youth; (3) develop flexibility in programming, teaching assignments, use of school resources, and requirements to make room for differentiated experiences; (4) involve other community resources in extending the range and depth of learning experiences.

Some individuals and groups challenge the ability of the comprehensive high school to provide equally well for all youth. They score the neglect of the gifted. Some, in near panic about vaunted successes of the schools of the USSR in training engineers and scientists, call for abandoning the comprehensive school or modifying it drastically. The quality of our educational process must be examined in terms of *American* values and goals; the competence of comprehensive high schools must be judged on the basis of what *we* want and not on the basis of what the Russians want or do.

The comprehensive high school is an expression of values which our American culture holds dear. Democracy's schools have an obligation to educate responsible leaders and intelligent followers. To fill this role, they must necessarily adapt experiences to different individuals. So long as this democracy selects youth for special programs or provisions on the basis of ability and not class, color, religion, or ethnic origin; so long as it does not contribute to the self-perpetuation of a single group; and so long as it is open to public scrutiny and censure, it need not fear that its concern for the gifted will give rise to an elite. With imaginative planning, comprehensive schools, more than any other agency in the land, can develop socially precious gifts with certainty of a good yield—but they must use more creative approaches than they have to date.

❦

THE GIFTED: WHAT WILL THEY BECOME?

by Herbert J. Klausmeier

UNIVERSITY OF WISCONSIN

Test all four- and five-year-old children. Allow the potential high-achievers to start the first grade a year earlier than most children and two years earlier than the slow developers.

Identify the potentially gifted children in the first grade and put them together in a separate class or separate school for special instruction thereafter.

Follow the European pattern of identifying the university-bound children at age ten to twelve and set up special schools and instruction for them.

Accelerate the gifted so that they may enter college at age sixteen.

Make sure that every gifted child has at least four years of high-school mathematics, or science, or Latin, or whatever else the promoting individual or group desires most.

Do away with general education in high school and go back to the liberal arts; increasing numbers of high-school graduates are going to college; the gifted need a liberal education.

How shall the public, tax-supported schools, responsible for providing good education to all children of all parents, respond to the many current pressures to identify and make special arrangements for gifted children? The most important question to be answered by the schools, by parents interested in education of gifted children, and by those organized groups who wish the public schools to get more gifted students ready to meet certain college or career

[Reprinted from the *Phi Delta Kappan,* 12, December 1956, 112-116, with the permission of Phi Delta Kappa and the author.]

requirements is: What kinds of individuals would we like gifted and talented children to be as a result of our educational efforts? This broad question needs further defining in the areas of intellectual achievements, social competence, and moral values.

INTELLECTUAL ACHIEVEMENTS

(1) Do we want the gifted high-school graduate to be very highly specialized in one or two areas such as mathematics, science, English, art, foreign languages, and business education? (2) Do we want a nonspecialized individual with some competence in several subject-matter areas and in several expressive areas? For example, do we want the gifted graduate to have two years of work in several areas such as mathematics, science, language, English, and social studies and also some experiences in music, art, dramatics, homemaking, business education, agriculture, shop? (3) Do we desire the gifted graduate to have quite high specialization in one or even two areas and also competence in several others?

SOCIAL COMPETENCE

(1) Do we want the gifted high-school graduate to avoid others so that he may use his talents exclusively in individual efforts? (2) Do we want the gifted student to be skilled only in working and living with others of similarly high achievement? (3) Do we want the gifted person to find satisfactions in independent work and in communicating and living with others of many levels of competence and many areas of interest?

MORAL VALUES

(1) Do we wish the gifted person to be unconcerned with the effects of his efforts on self and others? For example, do we want a person so strongly motivated for high achievement that he ruins his own health in the process or is unconcerned with producing a "monster" product or idea that destroys the happiness or endangers the welfare of others? (2) Should the gifted high-school graduate use his talents for personal gain only, taking advantage of those of lesser abilities to achieve economic, social, or political mastery over them? (3) Do we desire the gifted youth to use his talents in caring for his own needs and to be concerned with improving conditions for effective living for himself and others?

PROPOSALS

The writer proposes that we should strive to identify and develop individuals who, upon high-school graduation, will have rather high specialization in at least one area in which their particular talents lie, will find satisfactions in living with others of varying talents and interests, and will use their talents to improve conditions for themselves and others. None of the practices listed in the opening paragraphs will reach this goal for all the potential high-achievers in all schools, and some will prevent his fulfillment. The nine proposals which follow are applicable to many situations, are in line with achieving the stated goal, and pertain to education from kindergarten through high school.

1. Develop a systematic, continuous program for the identification and development of any talent any child may possess.

Only the amateur proposes that he can reliably identify in the elementary grades every child who will make an outstanding contribution to society as an adult. Psychologists and educators, working together with high-school students, recognize that many factors which they cannot control lead to one student with a Stanford-Binet IQ of 115 and high motivation achieving at a higher level than another with an IQ of 140 and low motivation or an emotional problem. The best minds in our universities have not yet found an efficient way of predicting which entering Ph.D. candidates will complete the requirements and which will fail—much less of predicting who will contribute significantly and who will not after the degree is awarded.

Faced with an increasing demand for creative, gifted individuals, the schools must make certain that they do not eliminate future high-achieving adults from specially provided school programs. Instead of limiting the special provisions to the 1 percent with Stanford-Binet IQs above 140, or the 2 percent with IQs above 132, or even the 16 percent with IQs above 116, we would do well to provide every child with the opportunity to express himself creatively. As part of the process of identification and development of talent, especially in the first nine years of school, we probably need much more emphasis on instruction in the expressive areas —music, art, dance, creative writing, dramatics—and in various areas of organized knowledge such as science and literature, so that reasonable opportunities are present to ascertain the areas in which the child's talents may lie (or may be developed) and so that the child and his parents may become aware of it. Were this done on a more widespread basis, many above-average but not outstanding students would possibly find an area of interest which could be developed to a very high level prior to high-school graduation. And those few towering intellects of genius proportion could advance in this environment as rapidly and as broadly as their curiosity and energy impel them.

The number of individuals who achieve high in any society at a given time is determined not only by what is in the individuals, but also by society's opportunities and demands for high achievement. The experiences of World War II demonstrated that many young men and women of varying talents, when presented with the opportunity and the demand to achieve, responded well. Apparently the Russians are now providing more opportunities and are developing more talented individuals. Much research yet remains to be completed before children who have the potentiality for making significant contributions to society as adults can be identified without error. Much research needs to be done to determine how our society can increase the opportunities for creative significant contributions. While this research is in progress, upgrading the quality of education for all children, and especially those with academic or other talents, is the most reasonable way for making sure that the really gifted are adequately provided for and that the best in all children is developed to meet society's demands.

2. *Admit all children to kindergarten or first grade at about the same chronological age, giving all of them opportunity to profit from such attendance, and making certain that as much attention is given to identifying and providing for the potential high achievers as to the physically handicapped, mentally retarded, slow learners, and average children.*

Even if we could reliably identify the future high-achieving adults among the present four-, five-, and six-year-old children (which we cannot), the practice of admitting some to first grade at five, others at six, and still others at age seven, would likely lead to widespread dissatisfactions among children and parents. For within a family of several children we might have one entering first grade at age five while another waits until age seven. And among neighboring families the same entrance ages might occur.

Only in very large cities and other communities where parents care little about the education of children residing in their close vicinity is it possible to have differential entrance ages to the first grade without incurring parental disapproval of the policy. Even where the policy is practiced, we should recognize that many slower-maturing six- and even seven-year-olds may eventually achieve higher than some of the faster-maturing five-year-olds.

3. *Place children, throughout the elementary grades, in classes which have both a range and variety of talents, and group within the class or individualize instruction within the class to meet the needs of all.*

Some segregating of the potential high-achievers in the intermediate grades for some portion of the instruction—such as in reading, arithmetic, music, art, dramatics, student council, and library work—may prove beneficial. Some sectioning into special classes for part of the instruction in those larger schools where only one or two outstanding pupils in each class we found might also prove beneficial, but segregating the potential high-achievers for all instruction into a special class or a special elementary school deprives these children during the formative years of learning how to understand and live pleasantly with those of lower talents. While it is possible in poorly taught classes for the fast learner to develop snobbishness and feelings of superiority, it is also possible in the well-taught, heterogeneous class group for the gifted child to develop his creative powers and at the same time learn wholesome attitudes and communication skills in living with the less talented.

4. *Accelerate during the intermediate grades and junior high school through double promotions only those potential high achievers whose physical, social, and emotional development is in harmony with their intellectual development.*

While positive correlations are found between age and such factors as height, weight, carpal development, and social and emotional development, the correlations are so low as to be practically useless when applied to individual cases. Many of our actually and potentially talented intermediate-grade and junior-high-school students are near the average in each of the areas listed. Accelerating these would be unwise except in poor schools which cannot enrich the curriculum offerings or otherwise adequately meet the intellectual needs of the high achievers.

5. *Encourage the potential high achievers in the high school to complete the usual requirements for four years in three years, or increase the number of subject-matter areas and emphasize depth of understanding and skills in the areas which the gifted pursue.*

The latter procedure could lead to the granting of college credits upon admission to college. If we were assured that society would make higher education possible for every high-achieving graduate, rather than force thousands of them, because of financial need, to go into careers in which their talents are not challenged and developed, we would now be preparing more fast-maturing high-school students for college entrance in three years. The principle of having the gifted student complete the usual requirements for four years in three could also be applied to college education. Many gifted young adults are pursuing identical courses and at the same rate as those less gifted whose best efforts are required to make sufficiently high marks to remain in college.

Thus, if we generally favor acceleration of the gifted students, ample opportunity is present for acceleration at the senior-high-school and college levels with little if any need for it in those elementary and junior high schools which have material resources and adequately prepared teachers to provide for the gifted children. Assuredly, the closer the individual is to full physical maturity and the closer he is to becoming intellectually, economically, and socially independent, the more reliably can his potential achievements be appraised and the more responsibility can and should be assumed for making his own decisions concerning his career and speed of reaching it.

6. *Continue to emphasize general education for effective citizenship for all youth of high-school age; and as the size and resources of the high school allow, offer various curriculum patterns which provide for a degree of specialization for the academically gifted and for those with talents in such areas as visual art, music, dramatics, creative writing, applied arts, and other career areas.*

Specialization of instruction in high school necessarily involves some grouping of children according to areas of interest and must be done to meet the possible career goals of the gifted. Classes are needed, however, in social studies, core, or other areas in which children of all performance levels learn the attitudes and skills needed for living effectively with others of various abilities and interests. As the general high school in the larger community and the vocational high school in the larger city have assumed responsibility for preparing some less gifted students for gainful employment immediately following graduation, so should we make certain that potential high achievers are provided with opportunities to get the most from their education, including some specialization toward a career which will involve college education.

7. *Re-examine the requirements placed upon the high-school graduate for being admitted to the various careers attainable through college education.*

It is possible that denying college students admission to programs of higher education leading to certain careers may actually be keeping many potential high achievers from entering these careers. While some youth know the career they wish to pursue as early as age thirteen or fourteen, others are very uncertain even as college freshmen and sophomores. These latter individuals frequently decide upon a challenging career only to find that because of "lacks" in their high-school preparation they cannot enter the necessary program. In some cases, their only opportunity is to get the required courses through evening high-school work, correspondence, or transfer to another college. It is tempting for the gifted student not to do any of these but to make a career selection to which he can be admitted "as is."

8. *Utilize community resources fully.*

Many schools and classrooms are more crowded today than they were five years ago, and we have not secured nearly enough talented and gifted persons to pursue teaching as a career. It is not uncommon to find a teacher attempting to provide instruction in English each day to as many as 180 adolescents in five separate classes. The nonathletes in high school often get their physical exercise (it really cannot be called physical education) in groups as large as 100. Parents are still expected to pay for the private music, art, and dance lessons the child needs to develop his talents—the school lacks space, time, and teachers. We yet find many persons trying to teach adolescents mathematics and science who themselves have poor backgrounds in the areas. Instruction in foreign languages is often offered by persons who cannot speak the language well. The principal cause of this educational neglect of the talented and gifted children lies squarely within our total society, which persistently refuses to provide adequate support for education at all levels—kindergarten through higher education. We apparently are committed to defend ourselves with military might developed and maintained through high individual federal income taxes, while defying the localities and states to find sufficient remaining tax resources to provide good education for children and youth. This condition has existed for many years and probably will continue. Therefore, parents and school people may well look toward every available resource in the community to aid in the education of the gifted and talented. Community recreation programs which offer crafts; YMCA and YWCA programs in which are, science, and physical talents may be developed; the museum, art gallery, music hall, and science exhibit which may spark a dormant interest; some special commercial television programs for children and youth; some educational television programs; the retired professional or business man with an interest in his field and in children; the various special-interest groups which develop in school and carry on out-of-school activities; the education programs for children and youth carried on by the college or university in the fine arts, languages, and the like—any of these which may exist within the community are useful in the identification and development of talent. Children, teachers, and parents should be aware of them and utilize them. Efficient utilization will mean many hours of work for a teacher or other school person in addition to his regular duties; the rewards—intellectual, moral, and social—are worth such effort.

9. *Inform society fully of the loss of the gifted which is occurring at present after high-school graduation.*

Many gifted youth do not have the money to continue higher education; many go into occupations before or after high-school graduation in which their talent is lost, with no attempt made by employers to identify or develop them; many young men enter military service and do not then or later develop their potentialities fully; many academically gifted young adults find the first two years of college work so unchallenging that they leave. The loss of the gifted is probably much higher after than during the twelve years of elementary and high school.

Careful attention directed toward identifying the motivations which society generally provides for the gifted should also prove fruitful. Who is awarded recognition and economic gains, as revealed by our mass media of communication—newspapers, popular magazines, television, and radio? Millions of youth and young adults observe prowess in athletics, the ability to make large audiences chuckle or guffaw, and managerial knack receiving the ovations from all sides. Relatively little incentive is provided for our children and youth to apply their potentialities in other areas where creativeness is desperately needed, such as in government, the fine arts, the professions, industry, and organized labor. Only occasionally is a Dr. Jonas Salk lionized; the man-of-the-year is usually selected from management. The brilliant discoverer of Vitamin D is relatively unknown to the typical high-school student, but everyone knows the first- and even the third-string quarterback. The creator of an expressive dance is obscure, while the physically attractive and sometimes intelligent Miss Mainstreet receives wide publicity and is well paid to advertise some wonder product on the television screen; the poet's audience is counted in hundreds while the rock-and-roll singer reaches the millions.

SUMMARY

In summary, it must be said that there is no one best way to identify, motivate, and provide for the gifted child. We do not want all gifted children to be alike; we need many kinds of gifted individuals and we need to develop any useful talent that any child may possess. The better way of providing for the gifted depends in part upon the nature of the individual child, his family, the school he attends, and the community in which he resides. None of the varying solutions practiced in New York City, or Cleveland, or Portland, or in the private schools may work well in a smaller city, in suburbia, or in the rural public school. Educational solutions for the gifted are complex, involving many persons rather than a few. But any proposed solution needs the careful consideration of the persons with the most responsibility for the gifted—parents and school people—and should generally start with attempting to answer the question: "What kinds of individuals would we like the gifted children to be as a result of our educational efforts?"

4

CLASSIC ELEMENTARY- SCHOOL PROGRAMS

HUNTER COLLEGE ELEMENTARY SCHOOL

THE COLFAX PLAN

SPECIAL CLASSES FOR GIFTED CHILDREN IN CLEVELAND

GIFTED CHILDREN IN AN ENRICHED PROGRAM

CLASSROOM SEGREGATION has become a highly emotionally charged issue. Various authors have suggested dropping the term altogether to facilitate discussion, but whatever words are used we must consider the problem. From the time school populations outgrew the one-room schoolhouse, there has been some segregation. Even in a one-room school, the single teacher segregated her students within the room according to their academic progress. Today pupils are segregated into rooms one way or another. Location of the pupil's home and the date of his birth are the most common means of segregation, but these methods have been selected for convenience and because they have been used with some success.

When segregation based on ability has been suggested to improve academic instruction, many people fear that the arrangement will have detrimental effects on the students. They are afraid that a differentiated instructional program will prevent some children from receiving their fair share of instruction, will create an elite class, will keep the gifted from learning to understand others, will not speed up the emergence of talent, or will not significantly help because educators do not know enough about the new provisions. Educators favoring some form of segregation on intellectual lines answer each of these charges with statements showing the other side of the coin. If we want each child to receive the instruction from which he can profit optimally, instruction must be planned to meet the needs and readiness of each individual. Snobbishness and communicative skills are learned, and good teaching in any setting will bring about desirable responses. We have learned that our present system is not fully developing available talent and that talent needs to be nurtured if it is to emerge. Continued delay in taking action until "everything" is known often leads to complete paralysis. Though there is much about the development of talent that is not understood, there is a great deal that is known.

Chronological age does not provide a perfect basis for grouping students for instruction; nor does IQ or even a combination of the two methods. Many authors feel that there is nothing undemocratic about classes or class sessions for selected children as long as the selection is based upon ability and no one is excluded because of race, or social or economic status. Perhaps one drawback to current plans is the assumption that all the objectives and means of reaching them for gifted children are equally applicable to all gifted children. As gifted children differ one from another, so will the most desirable educational program differ in some degree for each individual. When one differs too greatly from a group, he will not profit as much from the instruction for the group as will the others. Even though a community's plan of education for gifted children is successful, it may not be desirable to force all gifted children into that program.

Of the many programs for intellectually superior children, four have emerged as classic elementary-school plans for enrichment in breadth with varying degrees of segregation. They are the Hunter College Elementary School in New York City, the major work classes throughout Cleveland, the Colfax Elementary School in Pittsburgh, and the enrichment sessions in University City, Missouri (a St. Louis suburb).

From these plans other schools have devised their base of operation and have come up with an exact replica or a hybrid program. One such hybrid is found in most Lincoln, Nebraska, elementary schools. There a teacher meets daily with academically talented fourth graders for an hour and a half to provide instruction in the language arts and general enrichment. After the fourth grade, she meets selected fifth graders, then sixth graders. The Lincoln plan is a cross between the Colfax and University City plans. St. Louis has an administrative arrangement like the major work classes, but has more formalized instruction and includes only grades four through eight.

The four classic programs are summarized in the accompanying table. Insight into how the programs originated and evolved is provided by the author's descriptions of the programs. It would be well to study the table again after reading the more elaborate descriptions of the programs.

An editor's summary of the Hunter program follows.

HUNTER COLLEGE ELEMENTARY SCHOOL

The Hunter school was a traditional laboratory school functioning for a teachers college, but in 1941, breaking with tradition, only children of superior mental ability were enrolled. The change was made so that future teachers might have a good opportunity to work with children of superior ability. Enrollment in the elementary school is limited to 450 children, ages 3 to 11, whose IQ on the Stanford-Binet places them in the top 1 percent of the total population. Throughout Hunter the pupils are classified by chronological age rather than by grade. There is one regular classroom teacher for each class and two or three classes at each age level. These teachers meet the New York City requirements including a Master's degree, and, in addition to managing the classroom, they supervise student teachers. Special teachers are provided for German and French, music, art, health, workshop, and audio-visual assistance. Many of the facilities of the college are also available to the pupils.

Parents are active in support of the school; they have furnished much of the science equipment and have provided the major source of revenue for the library. A volunteer parent committee meets once a week in the library to mount maps and pictures, mend valuable volumes, catalogue new pamphlets and books, arrange bulletin-board displays, and consult with other committees. After-school activities, initiated and supervised by parents, include dancing classes, horseback-riding groups, ceramics, judo classes, swimming, science, Brownies, and Cub, Boy, and Girl Scouts. Many other parents volunteer their special services when needed.

Freedom to study independently and pupil participation in the formulation of unit topics or study themes characterize the instructional procedures at Hunter. Study units are worked out in group conferences and each day's work is an outgrowth of the preceding day's activities. The children are encouraged to participate in discussions and to develop attitudes of tolerance toward different opinions expressed by others.

The school has set up a number of goals for the curriculum, including sound mental and physical health, learning to become economically competent, developing skills in social relations, and understanding the role of world citizenship. The entire school program is planned to promote good mental hygiene. Problems that are too complex for teachers to handle are referred to specialists, in some cases the college educational clinic or faculty members who specialize in child guidance or behavior problems. Considerable use is made of objective tests for measuring achievement and personal

Characteristic	Hunter	Plan Major Work	Colfax	University City
Population (drawn from)	Widely scattered homes in Manhattan	Regular Cleveland school districts	Colfax school district in Pittsburgh, Pa.	Regular elementary school districts (8) in St. Louis suburb
Socioeconomic background	Complete range but middle income	Complete range but predominantly upper-middle class	Complete range but predominantly upper-middle class	Predominantly upper range
Degree of segregation	Complete curricular and co-curricular segregation in separate building	Segregated classes in regular elementary schools and MW pupils participate in regular gym classes, club periods, orchestra, crafts, and student council	Segregated half day (4 periods) in academic "workshop" and not segregated half day in home room for other work	Segregated for "enrichment" classes which meet only twice a week for 40 or 50 minutes
Intelligence level	Top 1% of population with median SB IQ of 150 plus	Top 5% of population with mean SB IQ of 130.2	Top 2-3% of population with all above SB IQ of 130	Top 10% of school but top 1% of population; 85% have SB IQs above 150
Grade levels	Classes for each CA 3-11 (or nursery through grade 6)	Grades 1, 2, and 3 together and grades 4, 5, and 6 together but the more classes in a school the smaller the age span	Junior workshop grades 2 and 3, intermediate workshop grades 4 to 5.5, senior workshop grades 5.5 through 6	Classes for each grade, 2 through 6
Size of classes	15 to 28 of the same CA	35 from 1 to 3 grades	31 to 36 from 1½ to 2 grades	8 to 10 from 1 grade
Basis of referral for individual intelligence test	Parents	Group intelligence test and teacher recommendation	Group achievement tests and teacher recommendation	Previous achievement, group intelligence tests, and teacher recommendation
Teachers	One academic and many special and student	Major work, art, music, and French	Workshop and home room	Regular and enrichment
Parent participation	Extensive	Interest of women's City Club pushed development of program	No more than usual	No more than usual
Continuation of program	Hunter College Junior and Senior High School for Girls	Planned program for both boys and girls in certain junior and senior high schools	Continuation of program	Continuation of program

traits (see Wilson, pp. 103-110). The cumulative-record system is quite comprehensive. Reporting to the parents is done chiefly through individual conferences, although written reports are also used to inform them of pupil progress in terms of school objectives.

The school follows the Course of Study for New York schools as a minimum curriculum, but enrichment takes many forms. The responsibility for class procedure rests largely with the classroom teacher. Much learning is achieved through direct experience and emphasis is on the unified approach to subject matter by the development of basic themes for study.

The physical features of the building are quite desirable for a school in a large city. The school is housed in several floors of a wing of the college, a building completed in 1940. Two private elevators bring the children directly from the lobby to their own floors.

There are 22 classrooms, all quite well equipped with built in cloakrooms, cabinets, and movable furniture of modern design. The greatest drawback is that the rooms are inadequate in size for an informal program for the 25 to 28 pupils in each class beyond the nursery.

Several thousand books on the library shelves vary from picture books for the youngest children to professional books for teachers and student teachers. The facilities of the college are of great help to the teachers.

THE COLFAX PLAN

by Hedwig Pregler

COLFAX SCHOOL

The democratic philosophy of providing each child with an equal opportunity has frequently been obscured by false conceptions of both opportunity and equality. That which is an opportunity for an average child may be a burden to a slow-learning child. That which challenges the mentally superior child would be considered an imposition by the average. Equality lies in providing opportunity in accordance with the ability of each group, not in providing the same program for all. Today the emphasis is shifting more and more from a uniform education of the group to a child developmental program that centers its interest on the child and his needs, rather than on the curriculum.

There is no best way to provide for mentally superior children. Every administrator, teacher, or parent who sincerely tries to meet the needs of the gifted child in his care will contribute something to a better program that will eventually evolve. Each must, however, be willing to evaluate that which he contributes, be willing to have it evaluated by others, and to add to the program the good that has been found, discarding that which, by his own experience, he has found worthless. It is in this spirit that this description of the Colfax School plan is presented.

EARLY ATTEMPTS

Colfax School in Pittsburgh, Pennsylvania, is an elementary school with kindergarten and grades one through six. At present it

[Reprinted from *Exceptional Children,* 20, February 1954, 198-201, 222, with the permission of the Council for Exceptional Children and the author.]

has an enrollment of over a thousand children. When the program for mentally superior children was started there were less than 700. Both situations had advantages. With low pupil enrollment there was more space to spread out. Larger numbers of children mean that more groups are possible.

Children are classified on the basis of chronological age. The policy of no acceleration and no retardation makes it necessary to provide for those children who are at the extremes of the learning ability curve. Provision was easily made for the slow learners and for those who for various other reasons needed extra help to keep up with their classes.

The first attempt to enrich the program of the accelerated children was made by grouping together, for two hours a week, those children who had achieved at least two years above grade level on a standardized test in the fifth and sixth grade. During this time they were to work together on a special project. One such project was called measuring time through the ages.

This attempt to group children with high achievement for learning soon proved to have various limitations. First, selection based solely on academic achievement without regard to mental capacity was not wise. Pressure was unintentionally exerted on children who were already using all of their capacity. Second, permitting these children to meet twice a week caused a scheduling problem for teachers who dismissed them from their classes. Some teachers permitted them to leave and not make up the work missed, assuming that they were chosen because they already had achieved in the content subjects. These teachers used this time to drill the remainder of the class. This technique proved most beneficial. Other teachers insisted that if these children were bright enough to be chosen to do extra work, they were bright enough to do both assignments. Here again the point of view differed. There were those who helped the children make up missed work while others believed that they should be able to "dig" for themselves, and therefore refused to wait until the entire class was present or to repeat the lesson taught. This sounds as though the teachers were antagonistic toward the program and that those who were interested were striving against great odds. This was not the case. Teachers were feeling their way. Each interpreted the philosophy of grouping for learning as he understood it and did his best. The third difficulty lay in the fact that the children in this enrichment class were responsible for their academic work to both the regular academic teacher and the enrichment teacher. Being gifted, these children were most capable of thinking up excuses. They used one class as an excuse to get out of work for the other. It soon became evident that, for these various reasons, the plan would not work.

The next year, it was decided to use the same two periods in the schedule, but to interrupt the entire school program in grades four to six with a club program. Children were given two choices and then were assigned as nearly as possible to the club of their choice—that is, all children except the ones who had been selected by tests for the enrichment class. What had been entirely overlooked was the fact that the children in the enrichment class wanted to join the clubs too.

THE PROGRAM TAKES SHAPE

At this point the whole program was re-evaluated. During this period the librarian offered to do some guidance with these children, who now were selected not only by their achievement but also on the basis of Stanford-Binet test results. This period of guidance was most valuable because it met the real need that these children have for such help and it gave them an opportunity to talk to someone who cared.

Out of this came the idea of the workshop for mentally superior children. In order to avoid the difficulties encountered before, time for the workshop was built into the schedule and the enrichment teacher became the academic teacher of the group. These children were assigned to her and she became responsible for the entire academic program. The group, made up of two grade levels, meets at the same time as do the other academic groups. This schedule is still being followed, although there now are three workshop teachers with three workshop groups on full time academic schedule. The primary and intermediate workshops were opened when it was found that many of these children, by the time they had reached their fourth year in school, had acquired poor work habits. It was deemed wiser to try to find them and test them in kindergarten and in the first school year, and start them in the workshop.

A teacher who was to devote her full time to the workshop had to be capable, interested in working with these children, not afraid of hard work, willing to experiment; she should not look upon the children with awe, but should respect their abilities and yet see them as children with children's limitations, endowed with superior intelligence but lacking in maturity and wisdom. Furthermore, she had to be on the staff at Colfax School since no additional teacher could be hired. The teacher selected was largely responsible for the impetus the program received during the five years that she guided the senior workshop. The second teacher, selected a year later, was asked to work with the younger children and soon developed her own techniques of classroom management.

The three workshops have the same number of children as the regular classes in Colfax. Each room has no more equipment than any other room, except for a typewriter and a microscope.

The Colfax plan is based on the belief that grouping for learning is advantageous for all children. Grouping for teaching of reading is advocated so that those pupils who are able may read together and move on. It also gives those who need more drill an equal opportunity which may mean more time and also allows them to work at a pace more suitable to their needs. The same grouping takes place at Colfax School on a larger scale: the mentally superior children are grouped together for a part of each day to read, to discuss, to work, to plan, and to execute together at any pace they may set for themselves.

Half of the day is devoted to the workshop. The children spend the other half with their chronological age groups, with whom they report to a homeroom for art, music, physical education, and other cultural experiences. Then, just as some might leave the class for orchestra or band one period a day, these children leave for the workshop four periods a day. Thus they owe their allegiance to and feel themselves a part of their homeroom where their social and community activities are centered. This places them in the proper relationship to the society in which they find themselves. Many mentally superior children find it necessary to hide their ability in order to be popular in the social group. Grouping for learning makes this unnecessary. In the workshop the mentally superior child can give and take many mental lickings without stigma because of his ability.

The courses of study in Pittsburgh are particularly adapted for use in workshop classes, since they have been carefully devised to meet the needs of all children. Many suggestions made for enrichment can be utilized, and activities that need cooperative planning can be carried out since the prescribed course of study is covered in less time than is regularly required. Time saved by these children will more likely be used to advantage in the climate of like minds in such a workshop group.

Enrichment should broaden the base of the education of the mentally superior child not only by adding greater knowledge but by developing a high level of mental skills. An ill-planned program of "enrichment" may become mere busy work, or advanced work which the average can do at a later time. Mentally superior children should develop skills beyond the level of ability of the average at any age. Their knowledge of subject matter should be broadened through coping with tasks that will challenge their mental powers.

In the workshop the range of subjects taught has been increased by adding Spanish and typing. More detailed analysis is made within the content subjects and the topics outlined in the course of study are explored more intensely. Related matter, for which the average child has neither the time nor the inclination, is studied avidly.

BOTH GROUP AND INDIVIDUAL ACTIVITIES PROVIDED

Both individual and group projects, especially of creative and research types, are used. Such group projects increase opportunity for cooperative enterprises and for a wide sharing of interests and purposes. In the workshop the boys and girls have an opportunity to think, plan, and work in groups for the completion of a common task. The self-direction that individual research necessitates is the training that these children need. It is essential that they have freedom in order to learn to assume responsibility. Training children how to do research is an essential part of the workshop program.

Sharing research projects with the group also develops the child's ability to compare, organize, analyze, and express his ideas in language, whether written or oral, that his classmates will understand. This experience ends in a group discussion or evaluation of the work done.

Grouping for learning provides the teacher with an opportunity to use those techniques that have been found most adequate for teaching mentally superior children. Democratic procedures give the teacher the proper relative position in the class. She, too, becomes one who would learn. The problem approach gives the students an opportunity to develop initiative and the ability to accomplish without direct teacher aid. It is fascinating to watch six- and seven-year-old children decide on a project, define the problem, suggest means whereby they might solve it, and then proceed to a solution. This may take weeks of independent work. Careful supervision is necessary lest they base their conclusions on false premises. The teacher's place as a director or guide is of increasing importance as the children move on from year to year. However, she must, whenever possible, remain in the background until she is needed.

First-grade children in the workshop are fascinated by the laboratory or experimental approach. They are encouraged to conduct many varied experiments either to prove a truth or to "see what it will do."

Though the curriculum provides for enrichment of the learning process and in the training of the child in proper attitudes, it is hoped that these are but a means whereby his real asset is developed. He must learn to think quickly, analytically, logically, critically, and reflectively. He must know how to find facts and how to evaluate opinion. He must be able to express the results of his thinking so that society will understand. This is the training that workshop experiences provide for the children.

Thus the Colfax plan through its workshop provides mentally superior children with three essential experiences: group activities both with their social and mental peers; individual activities through projects; and the drill in mental skills. Since there is no one way to provide for gifted children, the workshop is one attempt to cull out of the various programs, experiments, and studies that have preceded it those techniques, methods, and ideas that meet the needs of the children at Colfax School.

SPECIAL CLASSES FOR GIFTED CHILDREN IN CLEVELAND

by Walter B. Barbe

UNIVERSITY OF CHATTANOOGA

and Dorothy Norris

BOARD OF EDUCATION, CLEVELAND, OHIO

While little or no attention has been given to the special educational needs of gifted children in many parts of the country, Cleveland has for thirty years been working on a program for children with superior ability. The most important characteristic of this plan, the major work program, is enrichment. The gifted children, grouped together in classes, are not pushed through subject matter at a more rapid rate, but are allowed to delve more deeply into material and find out more about the subject matter taught at the same grade level than the average child would be able to do.

The program is, of course, concerned with the development of knowledges and skills in the subject areas, but it has other less tangible aims as well. Some of these are:

1. Increasing the range of knowledge and skills for the students.

2. Developing alertness.

3. Developing initiative and creative power.

4. Developing critical thinking.

5. Developing power to work independently, to plan, to execute, and to judge.

6. Developing increased ability to share in an undertaking.

7. Developing leadership (4).

ORGANIZATION OF THE MAJOR WORK PROGRAM

There are major work classes in 20 different elementary schools, three junior high schools, and three senior high schools. In

[Reprinted from *Exceptional Children,* 21, November 1954, 55-58, with the permission of the Council for Exceptional Children and the authors.]

221

some of the elementary schools in Cleveland there are several major work classes, while in others there is none. Children who are eligible for major work from schools in which there are no classes usually transfer to a school having such a class. In the three junior high schools and the three senior high schools there is ordinarily one major work class at each half grade. When there are enough students to warrant more than one class, another class is organized.

Each elementary-school major work class includes three grades. The earliest level at which this combination begins is the second half of the first grade. The combination of the three grades varies, but second, third, and fourth, or fourth, fifth, and sixth are the usual combinations. At the high-school level there is only one grade in each class, but the student frequently takes subjects of his choice with the general high-school group rather than the special group. An effort is made to keep the size of major work classes to a minimum, but because of heavy elementary-school enrollment, there are often up to 35 pupils in a class.

In no instance is any child accelerated or double-promoted in the Cleveland schools. Those who grasp materials rapidly enough to progress at a faster rate are candidates for the major work classes.

Every child in the Cleveland public schools is given a group of intelligence tests soon after entering school. From this test a PLR (Probably Learning Rate) is derived. Those children who receive a PLR which indicates that they might possibly be major work candidates are given the Stanford-Binet individual intelligence test. If the test indicates an IQ of 125 or above, the child is recommended for the major work program.

The school then informs the parents of the child's superior ability. With their permission he will be enrolled in a major work class. This may occur in any grade from the first through the twelfth, but usually happens around the third. Probably 75 percent of the major-work-class students are identified by the time they reach the third grade. Parents in Cleveland are well aware of, and interested in, major work classes. They rarely fail to give consent for their children to enter into the program.

Elementary-school teachers for major work classes are chosen from those in Cleveland's regular classrooms. A teacher who has two years of experience with the highest rating from her supervisors may be considered for the assignment. Not all teachers want a major work class, nor are all teachers who are rated "excellent" in the regular classroom situation successful as major work teachers. One of the reasons "excellent" teachers have sometimes been unsuccessful in the major work situation has been because they were more traditional in their thinking and were unable to adjust to the unregimented methods in the classes for the gifted. Those who are interested in teaching and able to teach a major work class are chosen. They confer regularly on problems and methods of teaching procedure. The program is characterized by superior teaching.

SUBJECT MATTER

The content in actual subject matter treated both in elementary and high schools in major work classes is only slightly different from that of regular classes. In elementary school, as indicated elsewhere, the children learn French as well as the usual elementary subjects. High-school students make the ordinary high-school subject-matter choices except that gifted children more often choose college preparatory work than the average.

There are some special provisions for the major work classes in junior and senior high school but they are less formalized and not as easily described as those at the elementary-school level. The gifted students continue to be grouped together in home rooms and frequently, but not invariably, to the same classes. The gifted young people share many subject classes with the general school population and their program differs from the regular program only as each individual subject teacher may choose to vary it for a class with superior intellectual ability.

THE PROCEDURES

The greatest differences between the major work plan and the ordinary classroom plan lie in the elementary-school procedures. It is these procedures which are described at length here.

Visitors to elementary-school major work classes often remark on these facts.

1. The children do not hold up their hands before speaking.

2. The pupils solve disciplinary problems.

3. The pupils decide when to continue to another unit of work.

4. The group leader is responsible for seeing that everyone participates.

5. Pupils present well-prepared talks.

6. Talks and group reports are evaluated by the pupils.

7. The study of French begins in the primary grades.

8. Each pupil is eager to learn.

To many teachers none of these facts seem unusual. They could correctly be labeled as "elements of modern education." It is the degree to which they are carried out and their effectiveness that is outstanding.

Major work children are taught immediately upon entering the class that when they have something to say to the class, all they have to do is speak as they would in ordinary conversation. Of course the child needs to learn certain rules to govern him in making his contribution. He must not interrupt when someone else is speaking, nor should he monopolize the conversation when he has the floor. If two or more children begin to speak at the same time, the child who has spoken more recently yields to the other.

The teacher is usually not the leader but is an active participant in conducting the class. A child known as the group leader or president is usually in charge during the presentation of a unit or any type of material. He is responsible for maintaining discipline— that is, for seeing that the ordinary rules of courtesy are respected. In their enthusiasm these children, like others, are sometimes carried away by what they are doing and forget the rights of others in the class. The teacher may enter in, but more frequently the leader will reprimand the pupil. The leader always has the backing of the teacher. If he is wrong, he will be told so privately, but the decision at the time is made by the leader.

Sometimes the best-prepared lesson will not end exactly when it should. Either it will drag out so that it becomes boring, or it is cut too short and the points are not crystallized. In the ordinary class, the teacher must decide when a unit should end. In the major work class, since the pupils are in the best position to know when they have really learned the material, the responsibility for ending the study and discussion lies with the leader and the group. This means that all students must learn early to be objective about the value of a discussion to the whole group.

The group leader is also responsible for seeing that all children participate in the discussion. If, at the end of a unit, certain pupils have not contributed and others were allowed to monopolize the conversation, the group leader's grade is lowered. Since group leaders change several times daily and each child realizes that he will soon be a leader and must depend upon the class for cooperation, the children are usually careful to see that everyone who should speak does.

These children do research even at the primary level, presenting their material to the class in the form of talks. Each child is responsible for presenting a research talk about 20 minutes long once a semester. He is not assigned a topic or a date—both of these are entirely up to him. He marks the date when he wants to present his talk on the calendar in the front of the room, and on that date the chairman presents him to the class. Sometimes the "catchy" title entered on the calendar does not describe the subject, and the talk is a surprise to the entire class.

Often several months are spent in preparation of these talks. Five-minute talks are frequently assigned during the semester, but the 20-minute talk is a standing assignment that every child must meet. The ability of even the youngest child to organize his thoughts, collect information, and present the material to the class in an interesting manner is a goal early achieved and one which most adults never attain.

At the end of each unit of study or talk, the chairman of the group or the president of the class begins discussion by calling the meeting to order. Following *Robert's Rules of Order* carefully (the parliamentarian will delight in discovering infractions in the rules) nominations are made as to the quality of the work.

Discussions follow which point out strengths and weaknesses of the work and what was learned from it. If a child does not know why he dislikes something, he does not speak. It is the responsibility of the chairman to see that the criticism is always constructive. The teacher's opinions are sometimes given and considered. Then the chairman integrates the material presented in discussion and someone calls for a vote. In this way group reports are evaluated and the children receive grades.

The "extra" subject in major work classes is French conversation. It was made a part of the curriculum because of the enthusiasm and ability of young children for a foreign language. Both German and Spanish have been tried but have not had the acceptance that French has received. For approximately 30 minutes each day elementary children are taught French—half of the class at a time leaving for the special room where the French teacher is waiting. Dramatizations and games, every possible device is used to increase the spoken vocabulary. For instance, in presenting a dramatization of *The Three Bears,* the pupils and the teacher ad-lib at length. They change the script as it suits their own purposes, and no two presentations are the same. The delight with which the children greet this activity suggests that it might have even wider application in the schools.

No French grammar is taught in the elementary schools, for it is believed that at this age the acquisition of a vocabulary is more natural. Each French teacher teaches at four or five different elementary schools. Her salary is the only item in which the program for the gifted is more expensive than that of the average child in the public school.

MASTERY OF SUBJECT MATTER

"Do these children learn the subject matter so essential in the early primary grades?" is the question some strangers ask. Achievement tests indicate that they are more than adequately mastering the material at their grade level and are, in addition, being stimulated to greater participation.

AN EFFECTIVE PROGRAM FOR THE GIFTED

The procedures used in major work classes are not greatly different from those found in any good classroom. The extent to which many of the procedures can be carried out is, of course, greater for the children have greater abilities. The purpose of the major work program is to provide a situation in which the children actively participate in every learning situation to the limit of their ability. The effectiveness of the program is reflected not only in the children's classroom achievement in school, but in what they have achieved and the adjustments they have made in later life (1).

The Educational Policies Commission summarizes its findings in *Education of the Gifted* in the statement that "most effective educational programs for the gifted will combine a good general education with various special provisions designed to meet their special needs" (2, p. 66). Acceleration is sometimes the only provision which poor, small schools think they can provide. In school systems too small to support a special teacher for the gifted or to supply enough pupils for a special class, the National Society for the Study of Education recommends the employment of a special supervising teacher of the gifted. One such teacher can serve and advise a fairly large district.

In cities of a hundred thousand or more, it is possible to establish special classes for the gifted of sufficient size at each grade or age level (3, p. 55). Enrichment, as a general policy, is to be recommended for all gifted students at all levels (2, p. 55).

REFERENCES

1. Barbe, Walter B. *A Follow-up Study of the Graduates of Special Classes for Gifted Children.* Unpublished doctoral dissertation, Northwestern University, 1953.
2. Educational Policies Commission. *Education of the Gifted.* Washington, D.C.: National Education Association, 1950.
3. Sumption, Merle R., Dorothy Norris, and Lewis M. Terman. "Special Education for the Gifted," edited by Samuel Kirk. In *The Education of Exceptional Children,* Forty-ninth Yearbook, Part I. National Society for the Study of Education. Chicago: Univ. of Chicago Press, 1950.

GIFTED CHILDREN IN AN ENRICHED PROGRAM

by James M. Dunlap

UNIVERSITY CITY PUBLIC SCHOOLS

Most elementary-school children who test in ability in the top 4 or 5 percent of the general population, IQ 125 or higher, also achieve at least one or two years above their grade level. However, this is

[Reprinted from *Exceptional Children,* 21, January 1955, 135-137, with the permission of the Council for Exceptional Children and the author.]

not always true of the brightest of this gifted group. One fifth-grade boy, for example, having a Stanford-Binet IQ of 150, never rated better than average in achievement. When asked what trouble he was having with his school work, he replied, "None at all. If you are referring to my achievement test scores, I do poorly so my teacher won't expect too much of me. Then I can fool around and have fun." Teachers are often baffled and concerned by the mediocre achievement of supposedly capable students. "They do such poor work for me I can't believe they are gifted," said one teacher referring to two eleven-year-olds with Stanford-Binet IQs of 181 and 199; "They don't even write legibly."

Perhaps these instances are exceptional but, when a teacher has 30 or 40 pupils in her class, it is difficult in a crowded schedule to provide for the individual needs of children at the extremes. Because positive motivation can be overlooked so easily, gifted children often need a definite program which is enriched specifically to stimulate their interests and to challenge their dormant abilities.

University City, like many residential suburbs, has a high proportion of brilliant children. The program which has been developed there, however, is one which could be organized in any school district, large or small, even where only eight or ten gifted children have been located. Organized three years ago with 50 gifted pupils in six elementary schools, the program reached an enrollment of 197 the following year. In the first two years, a total of 239 different pupils participated in enrichment. At the present time, 275 children in eight elementary schools receive special instruction from two and one-half full-time teachers in 30 different groups.

WHO ARE THESE GIFTED CHILDREN?

Pupils are selected from grades two through six on the basis of a review of all previous school marks, standardized tests of ability and achievement, teachers' recommendations, a group screening test, and finally an individual intelligence test. This variety of methods must be used because all gifted children do not make good marks on standardized tests or in the classroom, and teachers, without special help, often fail to recognize many of their brightest pupils. Generally, a Stanford-Binet IQ of 140 at least is required, but this IQ is not always the minimum. Depending upon the number of qualified candidates found, this figure may be higher in some schools and also may vary from grade to grade within a school.

WHAT IS THE ENRICHMENT PROGRAM?

Pupils meet with their enrichment teacher in groups of eight to ten for periods of 40 or 50 minutes twice each week during regular school hours. For the most part, they explore topics not generally included in the prescribed curriculum or, if prescribed, not studied intensively. These topics emphasize language, social studies, and science. They are given such titles as The History of the Wheel, Children in Other Lands, Prehistoric Times, St. Louis Industry, Mythology, Great Inventions, and Sky Pictures. The children themselves, with the help of their teacher, usually choose their own topics.

In these study units, reading, discussions, and written and oral reports are supplemented by lectures given by outside authorities, by experiments, by trips to make first-hand observations, by construction of models or equipment, and by preparation of charts, graphs, maps, and pictorial representations which the children need to illustrate their projects. The original plan was to study two or three different units each year. The pupils, however, in every instance since the beginning of the program have insisted on continuing their initial topic. Such sustained interest not only indicates gifted children's ability to concentrate on a subject for a long time but also suggests their eager acceptance of the special opportunities offered by an enrichment program.

Sixth-grade enrichment pupils, in addition to their usual studies, plan and carry out projects for the week-long school camp program which all sixth graders attend each spring. Last year, one group constructed a weather station which was used by pupils of every school. Predictions compared favorably with the United States Weather Bureau forecasts. Other groups prepared aluminum signs identifying flora and fauna of the camp area and formulated provocative questions for campers on nature hikes.

These unit studies are not the only means of enrichment. Parts of some periods are devoted to discussions of current happenings using such references as newspapers and periodicals or the map, *World News of the Week.* At other times, a series of questions stimulates lively discussion. Provision is made for creative writing, for the study of good human relations, for the examination of current popular magazines, and for games, puzzles, and the like. Typing was introduced recently not as a skill but as new adventure and as an additional means of communication.

These activities in themselves are not of major importance. It is the attitudes, study habits, and ways of getting along with people that are the objectives of the enrichment studies. The variety of challenging activities that can be introduced in an enrichment program by an imaginative teacher is surprising, particularly in view of the limited amount of time devoted to the special program. The 40- or 50-minute periods twice a week are a total of only two or two and one half weeks out of the entire school year.

DO GIFTED CHILDREN BENEFIT FROM ENRICHMENT?

Gifted children evaluate their own programs. They *know* when school work is fun, when their teacher requires their best effort, and when their activities have real meaning for them. Recently, when all sixth-grade pupils were sent home while their classroom teachers had regular, scheduled conferences with parents, the entire enrichment group came back to school *in the middle of the afternoon*. They explained, "We have enrichment only twice a week and didn't want to miss half of it."

A principal who was showing his school to out-of-town educators finally conducted his guests to the enrichment room during the noon hour. There they found six children quietly at work when they could have been out playing. "Of course," the principal explained, "these children are perfectly capable of working without supervision." A classroom teacher reported to the enrichment teacher, "I want you to know how much you are doing for these children. John has gained so in self-confidence and Mary has just blossomed since being in enrichment." A parent explained, "My boy describes enrichment as 'the icing on the cake.'" A father acknowledged, "It keeps the old man on his toes too." A mother reported, "Enrichment isn't just for the children. It is an experience for the whole family and the whole family enjoys it."

However, these comments do not imply that all reactions are positive. In two and one half years, questions have arisen concerning 25 out of the 340 children who are or have been in enrichment. In 13 instances the program did not meet their needs. These children were not temperamentally suited to the extra work or the extra responsibility. Occasionally, a teacher complains that the wrong child is in the program. "Why," she asks, "is Dick in enrichment when he takes no interest in his class work while Jane is not in the program and she is my best student?" Seldom has a parent objected that enrichment is not beneficial to his child. Occasionally, a mother asks why her child is *not* in enrichment but not a single parent has further questioned the school's decision after an explanation has been made. Enrichment has always been an integral part of the whole school program just as are music, art, school patrol, remedial teaching, speech correction, and similar activities which take children from the classroom. Enrichment is just another way of meeting an individual need.

A follow-up study of the first 23 enrichment students to enter junior high school also gave an opportunity for evaluation. The pupils were matched for intelligence as measured by a group test (The Hermon Nelson Test of Mental Ability, grades 7-12), administered to all entering seventh-grade students, and also for sex in order to make up a control group. These groups were compared with the honor-roll pupils, with the entire seventh grade, and with each other. Although the number of cases is small, it represents all of the available enrichment students.*

The seventh-grade honor roll at the end of the first nine-weeks marking period was made up of 62 pupils out of a total of approximately 440. To this group, enrichment students contributed 14 as contrasted with only four from the control group. This is a ratio of three and one half to one. The medians of the enrichment and control groups, each 23 in number, were 10 IQ points higher than that of the honor roll as a whole. If the enrichment and control honor pupils were omitted from the entire honor roll, the median of the enrichment and control groups as a whole would be 13 and 18 IQ points higher respectively than that for the remaining honor-roll pupils. The median of the total honor-roll group itself exceeded that of the entire seventh grade by 11 IQ points.

* A tabular summary has been omitted.

Factors other than the enrichment experience which might have influenced the three and one half to one ratio were carefully considered. Age, previous school attended, section assigned in junior high school, and the number and kind of extracurricular activities chosen were substantially the same for both groups of children. They also were almost identical to comparable data for the honor-roll group. The findings remained the same throughout the school year.

That the honor pupils of the enrichment group were representative of the enrichment group as a whole is shown by the fact that the median and quartiles were identical or varied only one IQ point. For the control group, the honor pupils rated from two to five IQ points higher, and in view of the limited number of cases seem to be representative of the entire control group.

IMPLICATIONS

Evidence from spontaneous comments of children, principals, teachers, and parents indicates that the enrichment program fosters certain desirable outcomes for a large majority of gifted children. Statistical data, within the limits of this small study, point to the fact that the bright, but not the brightest, pupils are frequently the best students. However, more important is the evidence that the enrichment program helps to motivate a substantially greater number of the *most* able pupils to make more effective use of their abilities.

Whatever the provisions may be for gifted children, their effectiveness and success as adults in a democracy depends not only upon their general intelligence but also upon their motivation, drive, personal adjustment, and desire to serve their community and nation in ways for which they are best qualified. To help direct their adjustment and to stimulate their desire to put forth their best effort, appropriate provisions must be made for gifted individuals while they are still children. From the beginning, they must learn to *want* to direct their abilities toward solving the important problems of living together whether their interests be business, industry, education, science, religion, or human relations.

5

MORE SPECIAL PROGRAMS AND PROVISIONS

PROVISIONS FOR MENTALLY GIFTED CHILDREN

A HIGH SCHOOL FOR GIFTED STUDENTS

DEVELOPING A SCIENCE PROGRAM FOR RAPID LEARNERS

A SEMINAR FOR SUPERIOR STUDENTS

A STIMULATING SEMINAR FOR RURAL YOUTH

A MULTITUDE of unique provisions for gifted children exist in the United States. For the most part, private institutions are the only elementary schools purposefully to utilize variations of the Hunter program of complete segregation by ability. On the other hand the geographic setting of some public schools yields a population rather similar to the one at Hunter (average IQ in the top 10 percent; the Hunter average falls within the top 1 percent). Even in those schools, however, three, four, or five students in each room of 30 pupils are of only average intelligence. For these children some special de-enriching procedures are needed to insure their learning of the basic fundamentals.

Special classes, either for part or all of the day, are not the only answer to the problems presented by the gifted. In Quincy, Illinois, the schools enroll approximately 400 children in each grade and could easily have some ability-grouped classes. Instead, enrichment in the regular classes with an extensive use of community resources in curricular and cocurricular activities is favored by the professional staff. Some special educational opportunities are provided in both the school and community for the upper 1 or 2 percent of the pupils, however. The teachers in Quincy are significantly involved in the identification process, perhaps more so than in most communities. No effort is made to segregate the gifted for instructional purposes in Cedar Rapids, Iowa, either. The program is designed to enrich the experiences of the student through individual attention in the classroom. A detailed report containing information about interests, abilities, achievement, and social and emotional adjustment of each mentally advanced pupil is supplied to his teacher. On the basis of this report each teacher attempts to provide broader and more advanced experiences for the gifted students in mathematics, science, language arts, and social studies. One teacher works full time with the other teachers, helping them secure suitable books and other materials. A bulletin is also published, giving specific suggestions for activities and techniques for use with gifted pupils.

Portland, Oregon, has a program similar to those in Quincy and Cedar Rapids. A distinguishing feature of the Portland program, which has been quite instrumental in its success, is the practice of designating a teacher in each building to act as coordinator for the program. Each coordinator is partially released from teaching duties so that half of each day can be spent in scheduling consultants, programing and counseling students, ordering books and materials, and keeping records. The importance of a coordinator, assigned specific duties and allotted time to work, cannot be overestimated. Although it is not the policy to group gifted pupils separately in Portland, some small special-interest groups meet for short periods two to five times a week for special studies in such areas as mathematics, foreign language, science, creative writing, rhythms, music, creative drama, and social leadership.

In determining how much segregation of pupils is desirable an educator must consider all students. If pupils are to be divided into subgroups, whether within a classroom or among classrooms, such a division should be only on the basis of what is best for each child. If sectioning is on a basis other than chronological age, it should not only improve the learning for those selected for the new class but should improve, or at least not detract from, the education of the selected groups. It is unwise to allow the development of the idea that a new class is a special class. Rather, children should be selected for or segregated into the class in which they can achieve maximum growth. Then every student will be enrolled in a special class—the one that is best suited to his needs. Available evidence indicates that just as a teacher cannot provide optimum learning experiences for children with a wide range of chronological age neither can she effectively teach one age group when the IQs span more than 50 to 60 points. When a child's IQ differs more than 25 to 30 points from the class average, he can probably be more efficiently taught in another group, at least some of the time.

In the secondary school the situation is quite different. In many high schools students have been enrolled in a section of a class according to their ability for years. As schools have been able to provide an increasingly large number of elective subjects, the basic curriculum of the school has been modified to fit the varied talents and aptitudes of all students. Since students traditionally have different classmates and teachers as they move from class to class through the day, it has been relatively easy for a given student to be in an honor section of one class and an average section of another. Consequently, the violent arguments that flare up about the varying degrees of segregation in elementary-school circles are diminished almost to nonexistence in discussions of secondary-schools.

New York City has special high schools of science, mathematics, technical training, homemaking, music and art, and the performing arts. These schools exemplify the most extreme form of ability grouping and are feasible in only a few of the large cities. A more generally accepted approach to ability grouping than the special high school is a "multiple-track plan" within the comprehensive high school. A large high school may be divided into several little schools, or "tracks." This might take the form of an "honor" school for the intellectually gifted, a "general" school for those of average ability, a music and/or art school for youth with these special talents, a commercial school for specialization in that area, and a vocational school for students preparing for the trades. A student from any one school might find himself in several of the basic courses with students from other schools.

A modification of the multiple-track plan results in honor classes rather than an honor school. Under this plan a student with outstanding ability in a given area is put into a special honor class in that area but remains in regular classes for his other work. The fact that students develop in different areas at different rates makes this program easier to fit to individual needs and allows honor classes to proceed at a rapid rate. Talented students have an opportunity to associate and learn from other students in a variety of classes and at the same time receive the necessary stimulation to perform commensurate with their particular aptitudes. It would be possible for a given student of high ability to be in from one to five or six honor classes in a given semester. In any event, he still has an opportunity to meet with some regular classes and with all students in various cocurricular activities or the homeroom. This approach has been found to work well with both academic and nonacademic areas. The qualifications of the school staff, the funds available, and the aptitudes of the students combine to determine the number of honor classes to be provided in a given school system.

In some schools cocurricular activities provide the only ability grouping. In clubs or after-school classes, talented students have an opportunity to do things the regular program does not provide. Dramatics, speech, art, music, foreign-language, literary, science, mathematics, and civics clubs are sometimes created and are open only to those with some aptitude for these activities. In addition, school facilities such as art rooms, laboratories, libraries, shops, and gymnasiums may be open for the students in the evenings and during the weekend.

Of course, the cocurricular program does not need to be reserved for the schools. The children's librarian in Dallas, Texas, directs creative-writing groups of elementary- and secondary-school pupils. Classes meet separately to read and discuss poems, essays, and stories before trying their hand at composing. In other cities librarians provide considerable help to organized groups or individuals in the search for resource material or books for pleasure. Many short classes are offered to help the children learn efficient use of the library.

The Children's Summer Studio is an art studio for children from kindergarten through secondary school sponsored by the Recreation Council of Lawrence, Kansas. The workshops meet in a school building on a voluntary basis. Kindergarten and first-grade children form a class in which they are directed in a large number of activities. All other children choose the shop in which they work for the first half of the session and may change shops only at the half-way point. In Lincoln, Nebraska, special art courses for talented elementary-age youth are offered at the University of Nebraska on Saturday mornings throughout the school year. The youth are selected on the basis of promise shown by original paintings submitted to the faculty. The Worcester, Massachusetts, Art Museum offers professional instruction in art for children of ages 4 through 13. The purpose of the activity is to provide all interested young people with early practice in, understanding of, and enjoyment of art. The Rotary Club of Dayton, Ohio, sponsors a choir of about 90 boys from the ages of 9 to 18. And so the story goes. Some California towns develop talented tennis players while many other communities choose to encourage swimming or baseball. The environment for learning is a great determiner of the development of talent.

The readings in this section are concerned with some of the more formal programs in the schools and were selected to show how programs can come into being. The Malden, Massachusetts, school program is patterned after the major work classes. Superintendent of Schools Chester Holmes describes the development of the program and his plans for accelerating the students who stay in the program by giving them a year of work equivalent to the freshman year of college. The article by Francis E. Morhous and Elizabeth Sherley describes the "competent-child project" in Schenectady's Mont Pleasant high school. The project includes enrichment and acceleration in the departments of mathematics, science, English, foreign language, and citizenship education. Then, breaking away from the schoolwide program, I have selected an article by Dr. A. Harry Passow which provides the guidelines for developing programs in other areas. The last two articles suggest the use of a seminar for a large secondary-school English class and for a group of rural juniors and seniors. The seminar in sophomore English was first tried by Jackie Mallis in Tucson. She felt it to be so successful that she adapted it to a junior-level American literature class and now, in San Jose, California, she is using the plan exactly as it is described in her article. A seminar for rural youth, such as Glyn Morris describes, could be effectively used from the upper elementary years upward.

PROVISIONS FOR MENTALLY GIFTED CHILDREN

by Chester W. Holmes

MALDEN PUBLIC SCHOOLS

In this report I have attempted to outline the provisions which we have made to meet the needs of some of our gifted children. While most of the work in this field is being done on the junior high and senior high levels in other cities, we became convinced that the proper place to begin was on the elementary level and, as you will see, in the fourth grade.

In the fall of 1952 I suggested to those members of our staff, who had discussed with me from time to time the desirability of making more adequate provisions for mentally gifted pupils, that we study the problem intensively to see whether we could do something really constructive within the framework of our own school system. We arranged with the Harvard-Boston University Extension Service to offer a course here in Malden one afternoon a week for a semester, carrying two or three hours of graduate credit, and dealing directly with what was being done then to meet the educational needs of the bright pupils throughout the country. Thirty of our teachers, supervisors, principals, and nurses, including myself, enrolled in the course, which ran from October 1952 through January 1953.

At the close of the course I invited any members of the class who would seriously like to have a hand in the organizing of such a class on the fourth-grade level in the fall of 1953 to meet with me for two hours once every two weeks during the spring of 1953 and to study the possibilities. Fifteen agreed to do it; and we spent the time in setting up criteria for the selection of the members to compose the class.

In May 1953, when we had a report ready for our school committee's favorable action, we ran into some opposition; and the program was postponed for further consideration. During the

[Reprinted from *Provisions for Mentally Gifted Children*, Malden, Mass.: Office of the Superintendent, February 1957.]

school year 1953-1954 we reworked somewhat but came up again in May 1954 with substantially the same recommendations; this time we were successful and were authorized to open such a class with the reopening of schools in September 1954.

We chose the fourth grade as the one with which to begin our program because our study of current practices had indicated it was really the earliest grade at which a reasonable and wise selection of pupils for the experiment could be made. Therefore we proceeded to the selection as follows, selecting the pupils for the advanced *fourth* grade for 1954-1955 from those who were in the *third* grade in May 1954.

PUPIL SELECTION

First, we agreed that the selection should be made on a citywide basis and not confined to third graders within a particular school or local area. We further agreed that the class would be instituted in a new school which was to open in September 1954, even though this new school was not centrally located and was really a periphery school requiring either bus or private-car transportation for many of the class members.

Secondly, we agreed to limit the class membership to 20 as a minimum, 23 as optimum, and 25 as absolute maximum. Our problem was to select as wisely as we could, then, not more than 25 pupils from a citywide third-grade population of 650 pupils.

The head of our testing department prepared a questionnaire to be circulated among all third-grade teachers in April 1954 (anticipating by a full month the approval of the school committee!), calling for nominations of the most promising pupils.

Our testing department, after some eliminations of doubtful cases, came up with the names of 33 likely candidates and administered to each the Binet test. The results of the Binet tests were collated with all other available data about the candidates. We also used the Iowa Arithmetic and Reading Tests and the California Short Form intelligence test before giving the Binet test.

The difficulty then was to reduce the list from 33 to 25. We held a reception in our teachers' library for the parents of the 33 pupils on the list, and the parents were told of the purpose of the class and the proposed curriculum. The chairman of the school committee, the superintendent of schools, the principal of the school where the class was to be set up, and the teacher selected for the class were present to speak to the parents and answer their questions. The parents were plainly told that we had to cut the number of pupils from 33 to 25. Parents of two candidates said they would not press for the inclusion of their children; that left six to be dropped. Finally, the superintendent of schools, the head of the testing department, and the principal again reviewed *all* the qualifications of the 31 remaining candidates and removed the names of the six who seemed the least likely to succeed. This action, unfortunately, had to be somewhat arbitrary.

We selected our teacher for the class on a citywide basis and not because she happened to be a member of the faculty of the school which was being replaced by the new structure. She had been, during the previous two years, frequently mentioned by various members of our supervisory staff as doing unusually good fourth-grade work; as having initiative, imagination, inventive capacity; and as having developed her work on a unit basis to a high degree of success. She did a very acceptable job of organizing the class but had to leave us for maternity reasons at the Christmas holidays. We scanned our teacher abilities again for her successor and believe that the teacher who took over the class has done a splendid job in every way.

The work of all the advanced grades has been *basically* that of our regular grades throughout the city, but it has been both more *in*tensive and *ex*tensive. Much more has been done in the matter of class visits to points of interest—historical, industrial, and commerical. The members of the class have done a great deal of creative writing, both poetry and stories; they have written essays or reports on projects they have developed. They have completed a large globe of the world in papier-mâché, have molded jungle animals in clay, and have made soap carvings of animals. In short, their imaginations have been stimulated, and they have had at hand adequate resource materials to give substance to the products of their imagination.

TEST RESULTS

We tested the advanced fourth grade at the close of the year in June 1955. The class had IQs ranging from 122 to 158. Their grade placement was 4.9; the battery median on the Stanford Achievement test for the class was 6.6; and the median for paragraph meaning was 7.0; for word meaning, 7.4; for average reading, 7.3; for spelling, 6.2; for language, 9.2; for arithmetic reasoning, 6.2; for arithmetic computation, 5.2; average arithmetic, 5.8. It is clear that the greatest weakness of the class was in the field of arithmetic, and more attention is being devoted to the development of the basic skills in that field in both the present advanced fourth and in the advanced fifth grade whose medians have just been quoted.

In June 1956, we tested the second advanced fourth grade; its IQ range was from 126 to 153. The battery median on the Stanford Achievement Test for the class was 7.4. The median for paragraph meaning was 7.6; for word meaning, 8.0; and for average reading, 7.8; for spelling, 6.5; for language, 8.3; for arithmetic reasoning, 7.3; for arithmetic computation, 6.8; and for average arithmetic, 7.0.

Comparing the data in the foregoing paragraph with those in the paragraph preceding it, it will be noted that although the spread of IQs in the second group is slightly narrower, it was from a half grade to more than a full grade higher in achievement in some of the areas. Only in language (9.2 for the first group against 8.3 for the second) did the first group excel.

One thing is noticeable about both classes: they do their poorest quality of work in the area of arithmetic computation. Drill work is something of little interest to bright children; it is on the boring side! We feel, however, that there has to be a reasonable amount of drill work in arithmetic until the fundamentals are mastered, regardless of how boring it may be.

Comparatively little school-plant adjustment is ordinarily necessary. For such a class in our new building we used a regular classroom which had a sink with hot and cold water. Because we wished to keep the two classes together in the next school year and because the new building in which the first class was established became overcrowded, we were obliged, in September 1955, when schools reopened, to move the two classes for the mentally gifted into two rooms made available in our high school. This we did most reluctantly because we firmly believe that these children should be in a building with their peers and not in a high school. Thus, we had to compromise our theory and beliefs with expediency; we planned to move them back into an elementary school as soon as either of two buildings about to be constructed are completed. Again, in 1956 when the third advanced fourth grade was established, we had to put it also in the high school building. Yet at a recent meeting with the parents of the pupils in these three advanced grades, when we asked them whether they would like to have their children continue to be taught here in the high-school building, they voted overwhelmingly in favor of it for 1957-1958. They said their children loved attending the high school and that they were entirely satisfied with the existing situation. That has given us food for thought!

I must add here that there are a few advantages to these three classes being in the high school; they have the use of the gymnasium and of the library and have evoked the interest of the heads of departments of science and industrial arts who have allowed individual members to capitalize on their interest in those fields. The head of the modern language department teaches classes in French for twenty minutes three times weekly.

THE OUTLOOK

Of the original 25 pupils in the first class formed, only two left it during the year: one because of removal from the city and the other who showed such signs of social immaturity and lack of adaptability that we returned him to his regular fourth-grade class in April. In September, when this class became the advanced fifth grade, we filled these two vacancies by moving into it the two pupils who stood first and second on our "waiting list."

What is the outlook for these classes? In planning their future we have to count on the continued support of the school committee. As a new advanced fourth grade comes into being each year and the current classes move up, we shall have to take them on through the junior high school and senior high school.

We estimate that when they have finished their three years of junior high instruction, they will actually have completed the sophomore year of senior high work and be from about one quarter to one third through the work of the eleventh grade. They should be eligible for a senior high diploma upon completing their eleventh year of study, but we plan to hold them in the senior high school for their normal twelfth year, during which they will complete the equivalent of college freshman work.

Naturally the plans have to be tentative and will be subject to such changes as local conditions may impose from time to time; nothing in this type of work can be locked up as inviolate or inflexible; and we shall feel free to adapt both organization and methods of instruction in the years ahead according to the best thinking and experience we can find.

A HIGH-SCHOOL PROGRAM FOR GIFTED STUDENTS

by Francis E. Morhous

MONT PLEASANT HIGH SCHOOL

and Elizabeth Sherley

SCHENECTADY PUBLIC SCHOOLS

For the many material benefits enjoyed by this country's population of 160 million we are indebted to a few—those designers, creators, and leaders in every area from engineering to foreign problems. These few comprise the "gifted" segment of our population which is as valuable to this nation as any national resource.

Recognizing our obligation to contribute to this human resource pool, we at Mont Pleasant High School in Schenectady have launched what we call our competent-child project. Through this program we seek to identify the gifted youngster whose unusual abilities, eagerness to learn, initiative, and originality distinguish him as a future leader—be he a scientist, diplomat, businessman, or educator—and provide him with an enriched and accelerated curriculum that will develop his potential.

Mont Pleasant is a typical senior high school with 1300 stu-

[Reprinted from the *School Executive*, 75, July 1956, 39-44, with the permission of the *School Executive* and the authors.]

dents and a sound core of experienced and interested teachers, and it is bound by the usual limitations of budget and curriculum. It is located in an industrial city, the home of the General Electric Company.

The city has a progressive school administration which began four years ago, in the elementary division, the process of identifying the gifted child. It has several alert community groups that have studied the problems of initiating programs for gifted youngsters. Our competent-child project was worked out in conferences between school staff members and two of these local citizen groups.

Our approach to the project was tentative. Extensive research had disclosed accepted basic means of identification, the level at which identification should be made, and the characteristics of gifted children. But actual methods for application in an average high school were mainly plans. Fears of the possible ill effects of class segregation or acceleration were expressed and curriculum obstacles seemed insurmountable, but with the permission of the administration and the blessing of the community representatives, we decided to work with what we had, establishing all possible safeguards so that no child would suffer.

The satisfactory results obtained thus far in working within prescribed limitations have compensated for any doubts as to the validity of "doing" before all the paper procedures received the gold star of approval.

The project includes enrichment and acceleration in the departments of mathematics, science, English, languages, and citizenship education. This is how it works.

MATH ACCELERATION

The chairman of the mathematics department had become convinced that a special math class for the gifted students was needed. An earlier device had been tried by which the gifted members in a heterogeneous group were called upon to develop the more difficult problems for the entire class, but this had reacted to the disadvantage of the slower members. Why try for the solution, they reasoned, if someone else would develop it?

Through special math classes, the gifted child is stimulated by his peers and the average child feels less resentment and greater incentive to work out his own solutions. Selection of the special group is based on IQ tests, the achievement success in elementary algebra in junior high school, and the recommendations of the junior-high-school guidance counselors.

The math program utilizes segregation and acceleration. This group proceeds as rapidly as desirable from one level of accomplishment to the next and will complete the usual three years of mathematics in two years. In the third year of their high-school mathematics course they will take the equivalent of a freshman college math course so that they may enter college with advanced standing in this field.

As a safeguard for the pupil, a careful check of the individual's math progress is made. If a youngster is unable to keep up with the class, he is transferred to a regular class without loss of time on his part. This program is based on the Kenyon Plan with modifications necessitated by New York State syllabus requirements in mathematics.

Enrichment is looked upon more kindly than segregation; it arouses less public prejudice and causes fewer curriculum difficulties. The best type provides development of essential skills or understandings and opportunity to exercise initiative and originality. In a heterogeneous group, enrichment means infinite planning and a vast expenditure of the teacher's time as she tries to meet the needs of the gifted *and* the average child. Enrichment, properly used, is not simply assigning "more of the same."

The departments of English, languages, and citizenship education use mainly enrichment, although some segregation on the basis of achievement or interest has been included.

CREATIVE WRITERS

An elective course in creative writing is offered. It is segregated only in the sense that common interest has brought the group together. The intelligence quotient is not the deciding factor here, although individuals are chosen with the recommendation of their English teachers. Pupils participate in planning the types of writing they wish to study and practice—short stories, poetry, drama, essays, or radio and television scripts. Sources for ideas, plots, and models are explored and developed. Magazines and anthologies are examined. The students and teacher discuss problems in writing such as the wisdom of specializing in one type of writing, forms of manuscripts, plagiarism, and refinement of ideas. Private pupil conferences are held during and after class.

The writing-class members outline the plots of their short stories to the class for comments and criticism. Every member is heard and everyone listens. They polish their own ideas by reading to each other examples, say, of expressions describing sound, touch, and sight from outstanding published works. Plots from various sources—themes, newspaper stories, personalities, localities—are worked out. As proficiency develops, the youngsters submit their best work to magazines. Some work individually or in groups writing alma maters; some write for the school yearbook; others write essays for various local and national contests.

"ICI ON PARLE FRANÇAIS"

The language department carries on a valuable laboratory course for pupils of superior ability. Spoken French, designed as a supplementary course for the work covered in the French II and III classes, enables those students to hear and speak more French than is possible in the regular classes. A language laboratory in the rear of the classroom is equipped with tape recorders, eight pairs of earphones, individual booths for four students, and listening space for four more students, two on each side of the machines.

The basic text is *Spoken French,* with accompanying tapes in French. While half of the class is listening to tape recordings, the other half is practicing the sentences heard on the tape or engaging in informal conversation in French. Tape recordings of French conversation, made by two French exchange students, are used in the course. Playlets and skits in French are presented as experience increases fluency. Monthly social events at which only French is spoken are planned and enjoyed by this group.

A program for enrichment of the Latin II course makes use of acceleration. The syllabus requirements are met in the first semester, concluding with final testing. The second semester is designed to give the pupils a broader study of Latin literature and the contributions of Roman civilization. Excerpts from Cicero's orations and essays, Vergil's *Aeneid,* Ovid's *Metamorphoses,* and Marcus Aurelius's *Meditations* are read, some in the original Latin and some in translation. A tape recording is used of portions of Cicero's first oration against Cataline, with an introduction and conclusion in English. The stressing of Latin phrases used in English and both Greek and Latin roots or stems in English words creates a broadening in vocabulary usage and semantics. Since many pupils take only two years of Latin, this program considerably enriches the usual course in Latin II.

ENRICHMENT IN HISTORY

The curriculum in history provides the use of a three-year sequence—world history in the tenth year, American life and institutions in the eleventh year, and American problems in the twelfth year—which offers the best preparation for academic pupils with a special interest in history. In possibilities for the gifted child, the course offers almost unlimited opportunities for research, interpretation, development of fluency in both oral and written expression, and practice in integrating past world movements with current history.

In Social Studies 12, a simple program is used for a heterogeneous group with satisfactory results for the whole class, whether the individuals are gifted or average. The class selects a number of large units of work, such as, say, nationalism or colonialism, and the pupils choose for individual study those which interest them most keenly.

Each student subscribes to a basic magazine, chosen for its diversity of news and impartial reporting. Each pupil keeps his own file of current material relating to his chosen topic. If several pupils choose the same topic, each finds it necessary to search out material from other sources, since duplication of material is discouraged. One day each week panel discussions are held as the class explores the modern scene in as many areas as time permits. A summary of the discussion is written each time by a different member of the group so that each gains experience in reporting.

At the end of a ten-week period a comprehensive summary of background research on the chosen topic is written. Thus, current history is integrated with the past, individual initiative in research is pursued, group discussions become vitalized, and a continuing review proceeds. Practice in presenting ideas and organizing material is achieved by panel discussion and written summaries.

A science seminar whose membership is restricted to eleventh- and twelfth-year students who have shown high proficiency in science as determined by grades and interest in previous science courses is held after school. The purposes of this seminar are to offer pupils an opportunity to report on, demonstrate, and discuss topics of scientific interest and to acquaint members with opportunities offered in science as a career. Speakers from the student group, faculty members, and industrial leaders from the community present topics of immediate interest. This is followed by a discussion and question period. From this very competent and interested group some students have been encouraged and helped to do original experimentation worthy of entrance in science fairs and science talent-search contests.

A course in the appreciation of the visual arts—architecture, painting, sculpture, and the minor arts—is offered to twelfth-year college-preparatory students. An introduction to and an appreciation of art forms from earliest times to the present day, including a study of the modern movement and its various roots, is developed. General aesthetic values are stressed as well as the cultural significance.

And now, one may well ask, what has happened? We know that no child—gifted, average, or less capable—in our high-school population has been neglected. The faculty has been stimulated to take a new look at procedures and courses to see what changes would be beneficial to all students. Gifted students have expressed an interest in the continuation and enlargement of the programs already under way. Evaluation of several of the projects by the students themselves has shown the faculty that the program is challenging and stimulating but that some improvements are needed.

NOT AN "HONOR GROUP"

The teachers participating in the projects feel that to obtain the best results, homogeneous grouping is necessary. There is no wish to create an honor group which will be kept together in all subjects. A student may be "gifted" in music or art, but possess little interest and ability in history. Groups of pupils with like interests and abilities achieve more since they are competing within a group of their peers.

The average pupil in a heterogeneous group expresses resentment at the inescapable dominant influence of the "gifted"— inescapable, because the gifted child often possesses the ability to lead, initiate, and influence. Grouping by ability in a heterogeneous class is an artificial device which fools no member of the group. The limitations of time and the number of groups make it difficult, if not impossible, for the teacher to work with each group and develop the varied potentials of each member.

One of the most interesting responses to the program in mathematics came from a group of eleventh-year pupils. They proposed attendance at a summer-school session to study advanced algebra and solid geometry with the understanding that the chairman of the department would offer the course in calculus and analytical geometry a year ahead of the planned time for the pilot group, begun this year. This group reflects the eagerness to learn, so characteristic of gifted children. If we offer them a way, they will be quick to grasp its challenge.

"I HAVE LEARNED HOW . . ."

The creative-writing group made a number of thoughtful appraisals. This is what some of them wrote: "I have learned how to express my ideas in writing—also many writing hints such as simplicity." "Particularly important is the fact that the students are able to help plan the course." "I have begun to appreciate what I read." "The practice of dissecting each other's stories has helped me see some of my own particular errors in writing."

Spoken French appeals to pupils who have professional careers in view. One boy seeks to acquire fluency in French because he is interested in preparing for the diplomatic service. Another plans to be a geologist and believes his work will take him to various parts of the globe. One plans to be a teacher of French. Ambition to qualify as an interpreter in government service or in some commercial house leads another to plan for a college major in modern languages. All pupils feel that the fluency attained in spoken French will be helpful to them now in their regular French II or French III classes.

The administration has experienced profound satisfaction in actually working with the students in such a program, instead of delaying until a perfect plan is evolved. True, the "bugs" appeared; but the plans are not just on paper, not just theories. The results achieved, not as perfect as were envisioned, show what can be done by a typical school within the restricted limits of time, money, and curriculum to develop the potential of the gifted.

DEVELOPING A SCIENCE PROGRAM FOR RAPID LEARNERS *

by A. Harry Passow

COLUMBIA UNIVERSITY

The impact of science and technology on our life and culture in the twentieth century needs no elaboration to science teachers. Almost nothing has remained untouched by the discoveries, inventions, research and creativity which have marked the past fifty years. If the achievements of the period since 1941 foretell anything, it seems likely that the next few decades will bring science revolutions which are staggering.

There is no question that science will go on playing a significant role in our lives—even, perhaps, determining our existence. There can be no question that we will need many scientists, not

* Paper presented at the National Science Teachers Association meeting, March 15, 1956, Washington, D. C., published with permission of NSTA.

[Reprinted from *Science Education*, 41, March 1957, 104-112, with the permission of *Science Education* and the author.]

only to replenish the talent reservoir but to feed the ravenous manpower shortages which threaten us in the extended cold war. Our manpower needs intrude themselves daily and persistently. As specialization breeds more specialization, our requirements for trained scientific personnel increase geometrically. We stand now on the threshold of new discoveries; yet we may wonder soberly if creative, free scientists in sufficient numbers will be prepared to lead us knowingly into new eras.

It is a truism, of course, that the scientists of tomorrow are in our schools today. It is highly probable that these potential scientists are among our rapid learners—those students with high intelligence as measured by our standardized tests. Research by Brandwein, Haslett, Roe, and Wrenn points to high intelligence as one characteristic of the scientist. Wolfle's researches indicate that high intelligence marks individuals in the specialized talent areas. Intelligence alone, of course, does not make a scientist but we can be reasonably certain that as we develop science programs for rapid learners, we will be including most of our potential scientists.

What directions shall we take in developing science programs for rapid learners? In developing any program, one must heed several things: the characteristics of the learners, the nature of the discipline, the needs of society, and the function of the school. Saying this another way: we have to be clear on the students for whom the program is intended, the goals of a program, the possible content and methodology, the levels at which it should be developed, and its relation to the total school program.

It seems to me that if we are to develop adequate science programs for rapid learners, we must attack the problems from new vantage points. Our past techniques have illustrated the old saying, pouring new wine into old bottles. That is, we have picked up existing sequences, materials, and methods, and by modifying them, we have tried to increase or decrease the difficulty of a subject or the tempo of instruction. Certainly changes have been made and there has been some improvement, but the paucity of good scientists and the general lack of public understanding of science are, in part, an indictment of existing programs. I would like to raise some of the issues and problems involved in developing programs and suggest some possible new directions.

SCIENCE PROGRAMS—FOR WHOM?

The development of the sciences and their influence on our culture make an understanding of the nature of science and its meaning to society essential for all rapid learners. This should not delude us into seeing a future scientist in every rapid learner. Realistically, some will become scientists, technicians, science teachers, and engineers; others will not. However, all need science understandings and meanings which a program must provide.

As we look at those who will become scientists, we should remember how the nature of science itself has changed in the past few decades. Some of our previous large divisions have subdivided while at the same time several other areas of science have been synthesized. We have many different kinds of sciences and scientists. There will be youngsters who eventually will become research and theoretical scientists; others who will go into the applied sciences; and still others who will turn to science teaching. To what degree should the programs for these breeds of scientists be similar and at what points should they diverge?

Even the nonscientist who is to make a real contribution in his chosen area must, in a scientific world, absorb the meaning and the method of science. Problem solving is not confined to natural science pursuits alone; the method of science is equally applicable to other areas of learning. Terman's study of scientists and nonscientists found real differences in the interests, abilities, and social behavior of the two groups. Yet if we are to progress, the scientist and the nonscientist must understand each other and the world of science. Such understanding can come from adequate science programs which are appropriate for different kinds of rapid learners.

WHAT ARE SOME GOALS?

Adequate science programs will have varied purposes. For all rapid learners, whether potential producers or consumers of science, the program should result in basic understandings and meanings which constitute science in general education. The emphasis should be on ideas, concepts, and relationships, and not on information alone. The program should stimulate intellectual attainment and scholarship for all. It should develop inquiring minds, ignite curiosity and reward constant seeking of responses to the question "Why?" It should provide students with problem-solving experiences and an understanding of the processes involved. The program should stimulate a desire for learning, seeking, and studying. It should develop understandings of the relationship of science and the scientific method to other aspects of our culture. It should deepen students' understandings of the knowledge we have and the sources for extending that knowledge. These things the science program should do for all rapid learners.

In addition, the science program should provide the special skills, knowledge, and attitudes needed by those students who are potential scientists. It should develop interests and motivate rapid learners into seeking the means for developing their science potential. Specialization which differentiates the pure scientist from the applied scientist probably should not come until college. The basic program in secondary school should be essentially the same. For students who have the interest, critical judgment, creative ability, motivation and other characteristics which in combination with high intelligence make them potential scientists, the program should serve both to recruit and educate. For these rapid learners, the science program must serve both general and special education function.

Objectives like these—and many science teachers can develop better and more comprehensive lists—emphasize the unique characteristics of the rapid learner and the goals we should have for him. While these same goals are desirable for all children, they cannot be attained to the same extent by all. The rapid learner can think abstractly; he is curious, handles concepts and ideas easily, sees relationships, and has an extraordinary memory. Persistence, insight into complexities, ability to generalize, willingness to challenge, are characteristics ascribed to the rapid learner. Such traits point the way toward a program which places great emphasis on meanings, ideas, generalizations, concepts, and abstractions. The program should stress acquisition of facts and skills as these relate to meanings and relationships. All rapid learners need basic scientific information but beyond that they need an understanding and appreciation of problem solving processes which we sometimes call the scientific method. They need experiences which emphasize the universal applicability of the problem-solving process and research methodology to all areas of learning. One of the unique aspects of science teaching is the possibility of stressing the method of science so that it becomes part of personal behavior in various kinds of problem situations.

DEVELOPING THE SCIENCE PROGRAM EARLY

A science program for rapid learners must begin early, long before the secondary school. It may not be possible in the elementary schools to determine who will be the scientists and who the nonscientists. But the rapid learner is marked by intellectual precocity which could benefit from early discipline of work habits, attitudes, and study skills. We cannot and need not commit rapid learners to science careers during the elementary years, but we can provide them with the kinds of experiences which enhance interest and stimulate understanding of the meaning and importance of science. By science programs which are sterile, routine, and practically divorced from desirable objectives, we have frequently nipped interest in the bud and driven youngsters from pursuing science and mathematics careers. It seems reasonable to assume that science experiences which embody the excitement, challenge, and discovery of modern science could have a positive result with young boys and girls.

Science has filtered down into elementary-school programs but on a limited scale. At this level, science need not be confined to nature study or watered-down experiments. Young rapid learners are capable of projects and independent study. They can pursue in greater depth and breadth problems with which they are concerned if they are helped with additional resources. Usually rapid learners can read and comprehend materials far beyond grade level; they can work with a variety of resources.

Surrounded by television, motion pictures, toy laboratories, books of all kinds, and all types of do-it-yourself kits, the youngster of today is ready for real science experiences earlier than ever before. We can either encourage and foster this interest and channel it into constructive paths, or we can delay and discourage it and thus effectively kill interest and motivation.

The need for opportunities for individual searching leading

to reflection and discovery is important at early ages. In our culture students often fail to discover that it is possible to find things out for oneself. We need to create conditions at all levels which help youngsters learn that they can satisfy their curiosity by their own efforts. It is not the magnitude of the discovery but rather the fact of discovery by the youngster himself that is important. One way to teach problem solving is to let students engage in the problem-solving process—with problems real to them.

The elementary science program can be enriched in many ways—by differentiated assignments which encourage depth of activity, by group projects which deal with topics at an advanced level, by extended materials which are commensurate with the learner's abilities and desire to delve deeper, by opportunities to work independently with difficult materials. These few enrichment activities are only indicative of many ways of making it possible for rapid learners to have intensive experiences in science, to explore science interests, to experiment, to create, to discover for themselves. All rapid learners should have these kinds of opportunities and experiences at the elementary level. These are essential for their basic education and can serve to develop interests in further study.

Like all children, the rapid learner needs help in developing and focusing his special interests. Once these have been identified and welcomed, he is in a position to push ahead with his choices. The elementary-school program is typically one of developing basic skills, of general education, of exploration. There is a need for individual guidance and instruction which encourage the child with interest and some aptitude to develop his potential in science at this level just as readily as we encourage the young musician or Little Leaguer. The rapid learner who has already acquired an interest in chemistry need not have to wait until he reaches senior high school for worthwhile experiences.

We must recognize the real difference between encouraging and manipulating, between making experiences available and forcing youngsters. What is needed is to provide opportunities for real, challenging experiences as early as children are ready so that they can come to understand the meaning of science and acquire the attitudes, skills, and knowledge which will enable them to develop further in whatever areas are chosen when interests and aptitudes are matured.

A rich elementary science program will make experiences available for rapid learners which are not available for all. Programs which use the seminar approach at the intermediate level hold much promise. Individual projects which involve use of advanced materials and equipment under teacher guidance are fruitful. Whatever modifications make it possible for students to develop positive attitudes toward the sciences and to acquire desirable work skills and study habits should be explored—both within and outside of the regular classroom structure.

A good elementary-school science program makes possible sustained effort by individual and groups of students. Such programs enable youngsters to acquire the "feel" of science and the scientific method, to experience the thrill of discovery, to grapple with meaningful problems. How much differentiation is desirable in elementary programs still needs a great deal of study and exploration. But we can be sure that opportunities for individual creative thinking which may or may not be shared with other students in the class need to be developed to a much greater extent. We cannot predict accurately at the elementary level which students will be our future scientists, but we can be sure that the quality of the program at this level can do a great deal toward encouraging or discouraging their development.

The elementary-school teacher is primarily a generalist. He is required to provide experiences of many kinds and he is responsible for practically all of the student's program. He is seldom a science specialist and frequently lacks the equipment and facilities necessary for an adequate science program. He needs in-service help to extend his competencies in science. As he develops understandings of the ideas of science, he will know how to integrate these with other foundation areas. Some schools have provided these in-service experiences using specialists from nearby colleges or have brought in researchers and specialists from industry to enhance teacher competence.

Another promising procedure has been that of closer cooperation between the elementary and secondary schools in the use of staff, equipment, materials, and developed competency. Rapid learners in high school have been used with success as seminar leaders, demonstrators, laboratory assistants, and equipment handlers in the elementary school. Such experiences, coupled with teacher guidance and instruction for the advanced students, can be valuable for both groups of rapid learners, elementary and secondary. High-school science teachers have assembled kits and equipment for use by the elementary teacher, thus making additional facilities available. This cooperation also makes possible increased articulation between various levels. In many of our school systems, this acceptance of responsibility and leadership by the secondary-school science teachers has been invaluable in developing the total program.

CREATIVE APPROACHES NEEDED

Many of the same problems exist at the secondary level as at the elementary. We have tended too often to expose students to a routine acquisition of "basic facts" without meaning or method. Our so-called laboratory experiments have taken on some of the aspects of recipe filling with students knowing that if they manipulate data sufficiently, they will arrive at answers already determined. We have not set the conditions in our science courses which encourage the student to work through a problem as a scientist might work it through—learning how to phrase answerable questions, how to use past experiences in the solution of new problems, how to test possible solutions, how to acquire meanings from problem solving.

Science at the secondary-school level has a place in the general education of all rapid learners. How much differentiation should take place in the science programs of the potential scientists and nonscientists has not been determined. In most secondary schools, there has been no distinction made with the possible exception of numbers of courses and sequences taken by the students. Some schools have divided courses into "producer" and "consumer" sections but the latter have usually been watered-down versions of the former. Within the "producer" section no distinction has been made among rapid learners interested in science, others not especially interested, or still others who are disinterested. We have not viewed the advanced high-school sciences (biology, physics, and chemistry) as part of special education but as part of the basic general college-preparatory sequence for certain students. Differentiation in programs has come usually at the college level.

However, all rapid learners are not cut from the same pattern.

They differ in aptitudes, interests, motivation, and purposes. They have some common needs but they have individual, different needs as well. Science programs will have to be developed at the secondary level which meet both common and individual needs. These may take the form of separate courses and sequences or differentiated learning experiences within the same course.

We need to carefully re-examine present organization, materials, content, and methodology for the means they provide in attaining desired goals for different kinds of rapid learners. New approaches are needed in both classroom and individual instruction. Cohen and Watson in *General Education in Science*[1] describe our present situation as follows:

> Rather than presenting the exciting adventure that science should be, all too many of our secondary schools tend to teach the student how to solve a limited number of numerical problems, ask him to memorize formulas and definitions, and generally overload his mind with dogmatic assertions—while the great adventure of logical deduction, concept formation, and theory construction never enters the classroom. It is no wonder that so many of our students, their minds offended by rote learning, come to us with open hostility for, and even hatred of, science.

For all rapid learners opportunities for individual research, independent study, and project development should be provided. The nature of these activities may differ in terms of content or quality or depth. The nonscientist, for example, may deal with certain science topics in relationship to his special interests while the same topic is examined quite differently by the rapid learner interested in science. Students may tackle different kinds of problems and units. Independent activities should be coupled with seminar-type activities in which students can deal with ideas and meanings, with problems and their possible solutions. Basic courses in science need restudy in terms of their effectiveness in developing understandings and techniques.

We need new approaches in developing science programs for rapid learners—approaches which will provide the flexibility required for appropriate experiences. We can explore teaching methods which encourage concept formation, establish relationships, and produce meanings instead of rote memorization. The kinds

[1] Bernard Cohen and Fletcher G. Watson, *General Education in Science,* Cambridge, Mass.: Harvard Univ. Press, 1952.

of planning we do with students, the ways we provide for individuals and small groups, the resources we use, the evaluation procedures we employ, all effect the nature of learning which takes place.

Differentiated assignments and activities are possible and desirable at all levels. These are not necessarily used at all times but only when differences in ability and interest warrant their use. Differences may be in problems assigned, resources to be used, or methods of attacking the problem. When this kind of flexibility in needs is provided for, a variety of instructional materials is necessary and different kinds of classroom organization can be used when appropriate. Sometimes students will meet as a total class or in small groups or individually. Here secondary-school teachers can borrow some of the flexibility prevalent in the elementary grades.

Laboratory work is essential for developing science understandings. But meaningless manipulation of materials and equipment do not develop the skills, attitudes, or knowledge. Only as students face laboratory problems as challenging experiences can they acquire desired ends. Precision of measurement, effective technique, understanding of the processes, utilization of varied resources are the goals for rapid learners. Laboratory experiences which focus on problem solution rather than on material manipulation are needed.

Arguments of demonstration versus laboratory method still continue as if these were our only alternatives or mutually exclusive. Encouraging, indeed, is the use of the research seminar in the secondary school. Such seminars operate as a research team might function. Youngsters are encouraged to develop individual research projects in areas of personal concern, to desire and carry out experimentation, to report and discuss their research with their peers, and to critically examine the work of their peers. Such a seminar cuts across usual subject divisions; it builds on the foundations acquired in previous courses but puts a premium on problem solving. We need to experiment with seminar approaches as well as with modifications in more traditional classes (even those involving college-level material) to attain desired goals.

Our traditional science sequence of general science, biology, physics, and chemistry has recently undergone some modification. Advanced and special courses have been added; earth sciences, electronics, radio, physics, and similar courses have been provided, usually for rapid learners. Ford Foundation's Kenyon Plan has given importance to college-level courses in physics, biology, and chemistry.

However, our course sequence and content can stand further re-examination. As we study this structure, we may find out that some of our present courses should be abandoned and new courses developed dealing with natural and physical sciences. We may find that the content of our existing courses can be acquired by rapid learners in far less time than now spent, opening possibilities for individual experimentation, advanced studies, or seminars. We may find that we will need to establish multiple tracks within a class or among several classes. We may find that we need to integrate science with other disciplines—mathematics, humanities, or social studies. Or, we may find that modifications are required only in the methodology used or the materials and facilities required. But we can only determine which approaches are effective for developing science programs for rapid learners if we will bring to the problem open, experimental minds, and fresh perspectives. A joint effort by teams of high-school science teachers, college specialists, science educators, and representatives from industry may open new channels for designing fresh approaches.

Field experiences are very desirable for rapid learners—not as excursions but as means for extending the science classroom. Technical libraries, industrial laboratories, science museums, commercial processes, natural resources can all serve to enrich the learning of the rapid learner. We have heard a great deal recently about extending our science programs by drawing from the technological ranks of industry. A good research scientist may lack the qualities of a good teacher and be unwilling to acquire the essential teaching skills. However, the scientist can make a contribution for specific activities, working with an individual student or a class. In our haste to reject General Sarnoff's proposal,* we should not

---

* In February 1956 Brigadier General David Sarnoff, board chairman of Radio Corporation of America, proposed "the establishment of a 'National Educational Reserve' comprised of qualified teachers in mathematics, physics, chemistry, engineering, and related subjects, to be drawn from the technological ranks of industry." Each year, according to the plan, American corporations would release, at full pay, a number of men and women to teach in local schools. The plan was described as an interim solution (five years) to help with the training of scientists.—EDITOR'S NOTE.

dismiss those aspects of his suggestions which have real merit. Teachers can plan rather directly and specifically with the specialist for helping individuals or groups develop projects, for providing technical assistance, for making resources available, for leading lecture discussions, for judging projects. These are supplemental activities which require close teacher-specialist cooperation.

The adequate use of instructional materials needs a great deal of exploration and study. For example, the use of open- and closed-circuit television has been proposed. While industry is exploiting this new media, schools, because of numerous complications, are just slowly entering the field. Possibilities exist for rapid learners in television both as viewers and as producers. Just as television has brought great cultural resources into schools and homes, it can bring science opportunities into the classroom. The educational potentialities of television, films, radio, and even correspondence-school courses have not been adequately realized. We need to experiment with individual use of instructional materials. Just as we have begun to recognize that there are books and pamphlets which are appropriate for one or a few students, we are beginning to find that individualization applies equally well to the use of films, filmstrips, other instructional materials, and field trips. Not all students need to use the same materials or take the same trip.

Science programs can continue to be supplemented by extra-curricular activities. Science and mathematics clubs, science contests (i.e., the Science Talent Search, Bausch and Lomb Scholarship Contest). Science fairs can continue to play an important role in stimulating and motivating rapid learners. To these, some schools are adding technical work experience, participation in science-related community activities, apprenticeships, museum experiences. The extent to which these features of the extra-curricular programs can be incorporated into regular science instruction needs careful study.

SOME OTHER CONSIDERATIONS

We have not discussed some of the usual areas which are considered in planning programs for rapid learners—problems related to acceleration, grouping, or special provision within regular classes. These are primarily administrative means for facilitating enriched experiences. Research has indicated that each of these administrative plans can contribute to certain desired academic goals without necessarily creating personal or social problems. Decisions concerning administrative modifications effect the nature of the instructional program. These decisions, however, should be made in terms of the ends desired and the possibilities of the administrative modification helping in goal attainment. Whether we use one or a combination of these plans depends on what it is we are trying to accomplish, the size and location of the school, and the available resources, both human and material. In developing science programs for rapid learners we should examine each of these administrative arrangements for its possible effect on flexibility in time, instructional activities, materials, class structure, and learning opportunities. And, we ought to examine these with an open, scientific mind, avoiding the emotional heat which is sometimes generated by advocating any particular arrangement.

The balance between science and the remainder of the rapid learner's program needs careful analysis. If we increase the challenge and level of difficulty, if we encourage experimentation and guided study, if we extend the range of resources—how can we relate these to the load the student is carrying and the total demands we make on him? Guidance, integration, and articulation need consideration by the teaching and counseling staff. Differences in interests, motivation, and purposes of rapid learners will mean that their commitment to science and involvements in other phases of the school program will vary. In some schools there is a keen competition among departments, each grabbing as many rapid learners as possible and holding on to them for specially sponsored programs. While it is normal for a high-school student to begin to focus his efforts, he requires guidance in developing a balanced program in terms of his personal educational needs. Interdepartmental study of this problem is needed with all teachers concerned sitting down with school counselors to examine each individual case in order to come to agreement and learn to guide the student. The counselor frequently has a more balanced picture of the individual child than any single department. Through such guidance meetings decisions can be made with regard to courses and sequences for different kinds of rapid learners.

There is frequently a question on the effects college admissions officers and faculties have on such programs. If past experience is any guide and present trends continue, we can assume that colleges are interested in securing the best-prepared students they can get. There is reason to believe that colleges will accept, with little hesitancy, rapid learners who have had science preparation which has not followed the normal sequence.

SCIENCE TEACHERS AND THE SCIENCE PROGRAM

The bulk of research implies, when it does not flatly state, that the key to an effective program lies in the quality of the teacher. If the teacher is inspired and inspiring; if he understands the meanings of science and the relationship of science to the world in which we live; if he is flexible and makes possible the flexibility needed for adequate programing; if he encourages individual excellence and devotes the time and effort required to guide the student to locate necessary resources; if he is sympathetic to rapid learners and their particular needs; if he knows his science and his techniques; if he is willing to adapt his teaching methods to stimulate problem solving—then the teacher has the attitudes and competence which comprise "good quality."

Study after study points to the importance of the teacher as a motivating factor in creating a scientist or science teacher. He needs to find and encourage as many youngsters as possible to acquire scientific skills. He needs to provide experiences in the kind of atmosphere in which interests are developed and students are motivated to high achievement.

Yet the shortage of qualified science teachers increases even faster than the general scarcity. We need to get more young people into science education and we need to retain what good science teachers we have. What rewards and motivations can we provide? The Science Teaching Improvement Program and the National Science Foundation have explored higher salaries, better working conditions, special awards, scholarship aid, and consultants for teachers. New York City is exploring ways of increasing the salaries through "additional services." The crisis for good science teachers has rallied industries, professional educators, science associations, and colleges to cooperatively plan means for recruiting and holding good, trained, qualified personnel. It is to be hoped they are successful in their efforts for as Dr. Vannevar Bush pointed out in *Science: The Endless Frontier:*[2]

Improvement in the teaching of science is imperative; for students of latent scientific ability are particularly vulnerable to high school teaching which fails to awaken interest or to provide adequate instruction.

THE CHALLENGE IS GREAT

The times are such that the demands for scientists and mathematicians become increasingly insistent. We can make the error of indiscriminately recruiting or forcing or pirating students into science programs to meet manpower shortages. Recent magazine articles have described how the USSR has reorganized its entire school system so that it concentrates on training scientists, and then creating conditions which have made of such youth "an elite generation." We cannot follow this direction. However, we can begin to examine carefully the nature of our rapid learners and the nature of science, and build the kind of programs which will stimulate students to move into these areas in increasing numbers because there is a promise of excitement and personal fulfillment. Rapid learners like the challenge of problem solving; they like to handle ideas and see relationships.

The need is great and the challenges which face science teachers as they develop programs for rapid learners are many. Some of the problems could be solved by salary schedules which attract and keep competent teachers. But money alone would not be enough. I. I. Rabi, the Nobel-prize-winning physicist, pointed out in a speech reported in *The New York Times* recently that, despite their recognition that science is playing an increasingly important role in our national economy and security, Americans hold science and the scientist in lower esteem than ever. "What disturbs and frightens the scientist," he said, "is the increasing tendency to treat science and the scientist as a commodity with all the appropriate export and import regulations which relate to important strategic materials." Our science programs have the difficult job of encouraging and developing those rapid learners who, by potential ability, interests, and aptitude can become our future

[2] Vannevar Bush, *Science: The Endless Frontier,* Washington, D. C.: U. S. Government Printing Office, 1952, p. 21.

scientists and teachers. It must also help the nonscientist understand the meaning of science and the emotional commitment of the scientist. It must contribute to an understanding which will restore the prestige of the scientist and the science teacher to its rightful place.

Questions of sequence, administrative organization, scholarship aid, and others are all part of developing an adequate program. But an appropriate science program for rapid learners will emerge only as we understand our end purposes and use ingenuity and creativeness in building new programs. No single formula can be developed which can be followed by all schools and all science classes. The best place to begin is with a critical analysis of existing programs as a first step in creating new and different approaches.

In a struggle in which we are hopelessly outnumbered, our strength must come from free, creative, thinking individuals who understand the nature of science, its meaning in our society, its relationship to the future. We need to develop individuals with the moral and ethical values which are so essential to modern scientists. These are the kinds of persons our rapid learners can become if we are able to meet the challenge of developing adequate programs for them.

A SEMINAR FOR SUPERIOR STUDENTS

by Jackie Mallis

JAMES LICK HIGH SCHOOL, SAN JOSE, CALIF.

An ever-present challenge to the serious teacher is the superior student in any class. Teachers of required courses such as social studies and English, particularly on the high-school level, tend to have an especially difficult problem finding ways to keep these students profitably busy while devoting most of the class time to average and

[Reprinted from *The Clearing House*, 31, November 1956, 175-178, with the permission of *The Clearing House* and the author.]

below-average students who constitute the majority of rather large classes. Too often enrichment assignments for superior students result in mere busywork, which is not enriching at all but simply time consuming, and the pupils, recognizing such work for what it is, give it only perfunctory attention, actually gaining little from it except another grade of 1 or 2 to add to their already easily won string of 1's and 2's.

Faced with a number of such students in each of three classes, I realized I had to do something uniquely inspiring to stimulate them to maximum achievement. The answer was a seminar. Although designed for sophomores in an English class, it could be equally successful for freshmen, juniors, or seniors in English or social studies.

Deep thought preceded the actual planning and preparation of the seminar. Before I could settle to typewriter and ditto stencil, I had to answer several questions: What theme would offer the right scope for individual interest and promote the best growth? What materials were available? What procedure would guarantee the greatest measure of initiative and self-reliance? How could I encourage leadership qualities?

Since most of the work for the seminar would have to be done in the library without my direct supervision, I had to be certain the individuals chosen were as competent as their discussion and composition, their speed in doing assignments, and their eagerness to tackle homework for honor grades made them seem. I administered a diagnostic test of English fundamentals, then checked Iowa Reading Test scores, IQ (Otis) scores, and percentile ranks for those whose diagnostic scores suggested considerable ability. It was no surprise that these individuals had scored twelfth grade and above on the reading test in the spring of their ninth year and that they had IQs ranging from 112 to 135.

On the first Monday of the new six-week period, I sent my classes to the library but kept the seminar pupils in the classroom, telling them they had been chosen for an experiment. Since none could define "seminar," I explained the term, its usual reference to a college group, and my reasons for inviting them to share this experiment. "High mental ability" (instead of specific IQ ratings) was mentioned, and definite grade scores in reading were named (though not in personal terms). I distributed and discussed the dittoed assignment sheet included below. The very next day the seminar students signed out for the library and every day thereafter until the last week of the marking period when they had to be in class to present their final exam—No. 6 on the sheet—and to listen to the presentations of the others in the seminar.

SEMINAR THEME: *"Problems of Our Society"*

PURPOSES: To develop self-direction in investigating a problem; to learn to use a variety of sources in finding out about the problem; to learn to communicate effectively with others about the problem; to develop specialized skills and techniques in analyzing the problem: note taking, outlining, interviewing, reference and research ability; to learn to work independently and cooperatively and to assume responsibility for accomplishing the maximum results in each period.

PROBLEMS TO CONSIDER: Crime (juvenile delinquency), war (relations with other countries), Indians, prejudice, education, immigration, religious differences, threats to freedom, leadership (of a powerful nation), the handicapped, poverty, marriage and/or divorce—or another problem that affects large numbers of people.

MATERIALS TO USE (including those from our school library, the city library, and the university library): (1) encyclopedias, *The World Almanac,* other reference books, fiction and nonfiction books, short stories, poems, plays, magazine stories and articles (see *Readers' Guide to Periodical Literature*), newspaper articles; (2) radio or television programs or movies; (3) interviews with appropriate persons.

PROCEDURE: 1. Choose a problem and sign out for library. Skim an encyclopedia article on the subject to see major phases of problem. Then compile a working bibliography (author, title, call number, *or* magazine, date, page) of all available material suited to your interest in the problem. Submit to the teacher with your working bibliography a plan for six weeks' work set up so that a specific phase of the problem is indicated for each week.

2. When your plan sheet and bibliography have been approved, start reading and taking notes. At the end of each week (on Friday or the following Monday) submit a weekly job sheet like the sample below:

WEEKLY JOB SHEET
for

_____
(date)

This week I did the following:

Monday: Went to library to find short story, "Whose Children Are These?" by D. J. Petersham. Used *Readers' Guide* to locate magazine, then had library clerk get magazine for me. Read and took notes on story.

Tuesday: Outlined ideas for a story suggested by a sentence in story read Monday and wrote rough draft.

Wednesday: Revised my story.

Thursday: Started reading book, *Let's Mend Our Own Fences,* by Bishop Robert Kelley, pages 1-74.

Friday: Worked on water-color illustration for my story and prepared cover for it. Also read more of book started yesterday, about thirty-four pages.

Evaluation of week's work: My greatest gain this week, I think, was the contact with Bishop Kelley's book. I have never read such an inspiring and provocative book. For the first time I was led to think about the many children we cheat of their rights and opportunities by letting them become delinquents.

Homework: 2½ hours Friday evening finishing the story I wrote and reading another fifty pages in Bishop Kelley's book.

Vocabulary learned:

homogeneous—adj. (hōmō jē'nē ŭs)—of the same kind or nature. "A more or less *homogeneous* group of boys in each craft class." Kelley, p. 71.

penchant—n. (pĕn'chănt)—strong leaning or attraction. "She had a *penchant* for evil." Petersham, p. 64.

—————————————————————————————

(Signature)

3. Hand in each week *at least* one well-organized theme on your problem, choosing a different phase for each theme.

4. Hand in *as much creative work as you have time for:* an original play, a script of a story, an original short story, a series of appropriate poems, a collection of poems or other works related to the topic with critical or comparative comment, drawings related to the problem, charts, graphs, maps, cartoons, and so on.

5. Report to the group now and then (as the opportunity arises) on findings of special note or on difficulties encountered.

6. Prepare alone or with others working on the same or a similar problem a *program* that will use one entire class period. Suggested activities: panel, debate, recordings, movies, dramatic presentations, speeches, monologues.

7. Write a thoughtful *evaluation theme* of the seminar and of your part in it, noting any special gains in your general background, in your work habits and research skills, in doing new things, in important attitudes you have developed, in language fluency, and so on.

NOTE: For this work you will need an 8½ by 11 spiral notebook for all written assignments except job sheets, a pen, and an average grade of 2 to remain with the seminar.

CLASS PRESENTATIONS

Except for part of a period here and there (no more than four times altogether), I did not meet with them as a group, nor did I give more than occasional assistance to individual problems of locating references or developing theme material. Such help had to be squeezed into the class routine, but on the whole it seemed to be all that these superior students needed to keep them from bogging down.

The full-period presentations proved most interesting and instructive, not only to the classes but to the other members of each seminar. In one group four girls had chosen the same subject: juvenile delinquency. Since each had covered a different aspect, they decided to join forces in a panel. One girl studying problems of immigrants read a story to the class which seemed to her to typify the general theme of her research. A boy lectured to the class on the economics of war, using blackboard charts and graphs to illustrate his points. A boy and a girl who had pursued different lines of prejudice showed movies chosen after careful study of catalogues and previews at the University of Arizona Visual Aids Bureau. The movies were supplemented by introductory and concluding speeches. Two girls investigating the plight of the handicapped brought directors of local institutions for the handicapped to serve as experts in a question period.

Of all the presentations, the most impressive by far was a panel by community resource persons (including the mayor, a social-service worker, a parole officer, and a minister) on juvenile delinquency. The painstakingly detailed planning by the girl responsible for gathering these people together brought to light unsuspected talent for organization, and her chairmanship of the panel revealed a rare maturity of charm, wit, and diplomacy which ordinary classroom activities had failed to recognize.

Of the creative work submitted, a series of poems depicting the changes in religion from pagan worship to Christianity and the one-god religions of the East unearthed genuine creative writing talent.

EVALUATIONS

Typical comments in the final evaluation themes indicate to what extent the seminar had exceeded my hopes and aims:

For the first time in my life I learned to depend on myself to figure out how to go ahead; before, I kept plaguing the teacher for directions.

At first I thought, "So this is the punishment for being able to read well, having all this extra work to do," but I soon found myself being able to take part in discussions with my mother's university friends and actually being asked questions about the stuff I was reading on the Negro.

I used to be embarrassed to be what is called "a brain." No one seemed to appreciate my ready answers in class or my good grades. In fact, they resented them. So I learned to "get by" with the others. When the seminar began, I was thrilled and excited by the challenge, but suspicious and uncertain. Then I found I really had to work to satisfy the teacher's high standards. It was fun and I've discovered that there is a satisfaction in doing something well that outweighs ridicule. I'm proud now of my grades, for if I hadn't had the ability, I wouldn't have been asked to join the seminar.

The only failures in the group of twelve participating in the seminar were those with the highest IQs—128 and 135 respectively. This was the rather illuminating evaluation by one:

For nine years I have been getting 1's because I was a good little girl and smiled sweetly. It began in first grade and has happened all through parochial and public school. I always finished my work in the first ten or fifteen minutes of classtime and had the rest of the time to play. It got easier and easier to play first and then make up excuses if I neglected to do the assignment. Today my past caught up with me. For the first time in my life I have a 5 instead of a 1. My "little girl act" didn't work. It's a funny feeling to be flunked. I couldn't hand in my notebook because I went out with S— last night when I should have been writing themes to make up for the days I "happened" to be absent. I couldn't do the final because I realized I couldn't bluff my way through a 53-minute class period for which I had made little preparation.

Probably the most representative evaluation was that made by the writer of the poems on religion, who said, in a report for *Student Life*:

None of the students who took part in the seminars will ever forget them. It was perhaps the hardest thing they had ever attempted in all their ten previous years of schooling, but it was without a doubt most satisfying. . . .

In the six weeks the students felt they had made several important gains. Their knowledge of the world had broadened, not only as they pursued their own course of study but as they listened to the programs given by the others. Research materials and methods were no longer a mystery. Vocabularies had grown. Perhaps, most important, their ability to plan and execute a detailed study had been proved. They were no longer children awed by too big an assignment, but capable young people ready to tackle any subject, step by step, with a purpose, a plan, and a progressive procedure.

Considering all factors, I am convinced that the seminar approach to gifted students is the most feasible method of spurring such youngsters to developing their greatest potential on their own.

As for the attitude of those students not selected for the seminar, I found only overwhelming relief at not having "all that extra work" to do. Shy, inarticulate pupils relaxed once they were away from the critical scrutiny of their superiors, volunteered answers, asked questions when a point was not clear, and really settled down to learn. The smaller numbers in each class enabled me to concentrate on the specific bugaboos of each student, and group work produced more constructive results.

As a teacher, I learned new approaches to both the slow learners and the superior students that I have since adapted for other classes. As for the seminar plan, I am now developing a new one, America, a Land of Progress, for my American literature classes, and I am tremendously pleased with the eager interest and enthusiastic response of those who elected the seminar over two much easier plans under which the course is currently operating.

A STIMULATING SEMINAR FOR RURAL YOUTH

by Glyn Morris

LEWIS COUNTY BOARD OF EDUCATION

The task of meeting the special needs of talented pupils is challenging under any circumstances. This is particularly true in rural

[Reprinted from the *Journal of the National Association of Women Deans and Counselors*, 21, October 1957, 31-34, with the permission of the *Journal* and the author. Technical assistance for this seminar was provided by Dr. A. Harry Passow, director of the Talented Youth Project, Teachers College, Columbia University.]

areas. Here, in the small schools, there are relatively few pupils in the talented end of the spectrum of abilities, which makes grouping in an individual school for special purposes frequently impossible. Geography and climate likewise are obstacles in bringing gifted and talented pupils together in groups. They would have to consume so much time in travel in a county where some schools are as much as 41 miles apart and where snow falls early and abundantly, and stays on the ground a long time.

Despite these difficulties the district superintendent and principals of six schools in Lewis County, New York, have launched an experimental program for talented youth. Once each week, on alternate Tuesdays and Thursdays pupils from grades 11 and 12 are brought together in cars and station wagons for an afternoon of experience designed especially for them and called The Youth Seminar. Their official meeting place is in the homemaking room of the Lyons Falls School, but they use other resources in the village, particularly a large living room containing a good record player. The present faculty for this group consists of a homemaking teacher, a guidance counselor, and the county director of pupil personnel services, who serves as chairman of the group. Other teachers served in an advisory capacity. The choice of faculty members was primarily determined by two factors: availability of the teacher and his interest and ability to work in a flexible and evolving program.

The program was started in 1955. At the outset, the focus was not clear, although there was considerable initial emphasis on developing skills and knowledge useful in improving scholarship. However, as the program unfolded in the long and frequent planning sessions held by nine teachers, and subsequently got under way, the limitations as well as new possibilities became clearer. For instance, it was evident that the seminar must be conducted without laboratory or other expensive and specialized equipment. Teachers also agreed that the most desirable and needed kind of program was not "more of the same" school experiences the pupils had been having, but opportunities to integrate knowledge, clarify, and deepen concepts and develop appreciation. These aims would be best attained by giving pupils the opportunity to ask questions and to follow through on answering them without concern for grade or credit.

During the past year all experiences of the seminar were related to the topic Communication, a theme selected by the faculty because it seemed both urgently needed and inclusive. At the end of the year, when the pupils evaluated their experiences, several stated that at first they "couldn't see how we could spend a year on that!" "I thought of telephone wires," one said. And another stated, "I never thought communication was important." But they did spend the year on this topic, and discovered to their amazement that there was much more to learn.

They began with a general question: "Can more effective communication improve living, and how?" After spending several afternoons in asking questions about the meaning of communication and indicating the implications of these questions, the group visited the small church next to the school. This was the first visit to this church by many of the pupils. While the students were there the symbols and ritual of the church were explained; then communication was discussed in relation to these. This proved to be a strategic experience! Questions of all kinds were asked: "What makes people respond to art?" "Why are beliefs right for some but not important for others?" "How does God communicate with man?" "How is knowledge obtained?" "What is the difference between esthetic appreciation and knowledge?" "How are values established?"

Eventually these questions and many others were arranged on a large chart to show their relationships and implications. The faculty in this case thought it desirable to emphasize the relatedness of the several ways by which the study of communication aspects of life may be approached, as well as to chart progress as the group moved along.

The seminar had a peripatetic character. There were trips to other churches, the art museum, and the courts. All went to see the film *Friendly Persuasion,* and later discussed this story of a Quaker family torn by conflicting values. The concept of "relativity" of values became alive for them. Whenever possible, all viewed selected dramas and programs of the better type on television, and listened to selected radio programs. For some, music of the opera took on meaning for the first time. Several stated that this was their first experience of listening to serious music "all the way through." They read poetry aloud and listened to records of poetry expertly read, the aim being appreciation rather than analysis. At one point each pupil read *Patterns of Culture* by

Ruth Benedict. A number of films on culture, religion, and communication skills were viewed. For the first time for some, Emerson's essays were read and discussed both as to content and form. One boy had what was for him the unique experience of rereading an essay, and summarizing another for the school paper. They were introduced to semantics through Hayakawa's *Language in Action;* some thought that this was one of the most outstanding experiences of the seminar. They compared and noted the different ways the same news was presented in a number of newspapers of the same date, and especially noted the ways in which editors and feature writers made words work for them. Each pupil was provided with a paperback dictionary which he carried with him. The faculty used new words frequently in their conversation and encouraged the pupils's interest in and use of new words; soon looking up the meaning of words began to have an element of discovery for them. As a result of considerable emphasis on the role of perception in communication, pupils seemed to grow in understanding the validity of points of view, especially in their consideration of world religions. Several boys did independent reading in philosophy, and one girl "discovered" Walt Whitman.

At the close of each afternoon session the faculty summarized the proceedings on a tape recorder, and asked two students selected at random to make any comments they wished. These summaries are replete with enthusiastic comments as well as frank appraisals. The following comments are typical: "This is entirely different from anything we have had in our school." "We had the opportunity to think aloud and develop our thoughts orally without fear of criticism." "We went into things deeper." "It made me think more deeply on subjects I didn't think were important." "In regular classes the answer is right or wrong—but in seminar you examine what everyone says." "Now I look up more facts." They appreciated the opportunity and stimulation of meeting with pupils of their own caliber from other schools. One boy summed up the experience when he said, "Why can't this kind of thing be done for all pupils?"

After two years of this experience, several points seem clear:

1. The teachers found the experience personally worthwhile. Throughout the seminar they remained enthusiastic. They began with interest in something not clearly defined, and developed convictions about the value of this kind of program for all concerned.

As evidence of their conviction of its value, they met voluntarily twenty-three times in the last year after school, several times at night, to plan and evaluate the program. As they followed through on the questions raised by the pupils they found themselves involved in a rich educational experience, ranging from long discussions on complex topics to reading books out of sheer curiosity. One teacher remarked, "I've learned more during the last two years than during any other similar period." They did not experience undue discomfort when it was necessary to respond to spontaneous and unplanned parts of the program. They were not embarrassed when they had to say, "I don't know. We'll have to look it up."

2. It became clear that talented rural high-school youth have serious questions to ask but have not had adequate opportunity to ask or answer these. For example, after the first year, the faculty learned that discussion on such topics as What Is the Good? and What Is Evil? were highly appreciated by the pupils. They also felt the need of more opportunity to discuss human relations and problems of family life.

3. Experiences somewhat similar to the seminar could be carried out in small schools. The group might include mature pupils above the ninth grade. A plan is being developed in Lewis County for preparing at least one teacher in each school in this "free-wheeling" approach.

The seminar is another example of the desire of pupil and teacher to grow. It shows that, when the circumstances permit, they have within them resources for growth, and discover that learning is a joyous, creative quest.

6

ACCELERATION

❧❦❧

AFTER PONDERING the advantages enjoyed by the 29 percent of his subjects who were accelerated (see p. 48), Terman was disturbed by the thought that "the schools are more opposed to acceleration now than they were thirty years ago. . . . The lockstep seems to have become more and more the fashion, notwithstanding the fact that practically everyone who has investigated the subject is against it." The proponents of limited acceleration for certain individuals feel that advancement should not be based on sheer time spent on a subject, but on the level of competence attained. When competence is achieved, the student will become bored and frustrated unless he is challenged by more advanced and interesting material. Some students will be able to finish the necessary training or instruction in shorter than average periods and that by making their way through the instructional program at their natural rate, they will be able to become productive for both themselves and society, and more rapidly. Even though Terman, Pressey, Worcester, and groups such as the Educational Policies Commission have spoken realistically of the values and advantages of acceleration, many other groups have opposed it.

The arguments of those opposed to acceleration center around the feelings that (1) it is very important to keep the child with those of his size and social and emotional level, (2) no one is accelerated to the same extent in all areas, and (3) the child will skip some vital material because of large classes and rigid courses of study. These educators point to a few accelerated students who are maladjusted, without realizing that they may have been as maladjusted or even more poorly adjusted had they not been accelerated. These educators may fail to recognize the many who have been quite successfully accelerated because their adjustment has been no different from, or better than, the average.

A child should not be accelerated if he moves into a group that is superior to him in physical, social, and/or emotional maturity. The intellectually mature tend to be mature in other respects, and so the gifted are often moving into a group which is more similar to them in physical, social, and emotional development as well as intellectual development. For acceleration to be effective, an assessment of developmental status requires time and technical

278

skill. Capable people interested in human development need to evaluate each child considered for an accelerated program to make certain that the child does not skip any vital material and that he is accelerated only in areas in which he will profit academically and personally. Teachers, counselors, and school psychologists can determine which individuals can be advantageously accelerated. An IQ alone is not an adequate predictor, but the information in a comprehensive case study should be of great assistance in determining the advisability of accelerating individual pupils. IQ is quite important, however, because acceleration has been inappropriately used with high achieving individuals of only high average intelligence. When these people who were achieving to the limit of their ability were requested to achieve at even higher levels, they were unable to do so. Their reactions to this unreasonable request have been varied but generally undesirable.

Perhaps some of the emotionalism found in the arguments of those opposed to acceleration hinges on the words "grade skipping." Grade skipping is more synonymous with double promotion than with acceleration. When one is promoted from the third grade to the fifth grade without attending the fourth grade, the child has been accelerated by one of the many, but probably by the worst, method—grade skipping. Because grade skipping involves disjunctions in school programs and social contacts, most people try to avoid such skipping. Rapid progress is a more desirable term to many because in such a plan the disjunctions are avoided. Acceleration through rapid progress is easiest to accomplish in primary pools, selected classes, ungraded units or combined classes, and one-room schools, but with good teachers acceleration or rapid progress can be effectively accomplished in the regular classroom without any omissions. Rapid progress allows a person to move forward at approximately his own pace, being neither hurried nor held back, yet covering all of the desirable material. It seems as though normal or natural progress might be a better term to describe academic progress.

Much success has been found in early-entrance provisions all along the educational ladder from kindergarten through advanced professional work. Programs for early entrance to kindergarten on the basis of intellectual ability have been used successfully in Massachusetts, Pennsylvania, and Nebraska for many years, and many communities have found ways of moving selected students into the junior or senior high schools in advance of their chronological age group. From the beginning of World War II colleges and universities have increasingly allowed various forms of early entrance. (In Section 10 the Ford Foundation report evaluates 12 major college experiments in admitting high-ability students prior to high-school graduation.) It is possible for upperclassmen to enroll in beginning graduate courses before completing the bachelor's degree. The work will not be counted towards both degrees in most schools, but it can count towards either degree in many schools.

Another frequently used plan which minimizes the disjunction with the age group is found in advanced-placement programs. In these plans students take work (one or more courses) either in their institution or in the next higher school, often in addition to their regular load, that will allow them to receive credit when they officially enter the next higher institution. Advanced standing in a school can also be earned by satisfactorily passing a proficiency examination. Such examinations in colleges have most frequently been given in English, foreign languages, math, and science but in recent years capable students have been bypassing more and more introductory courses. When advanced placement is attained, some schools add a more difficult course to the requirements in that area, while other schools force the student to take any course in another area to broaden his experiences; still others leave the choice up to the student. Even for those who achieve advanced placement, very few colleges shorten the semester-hour requirements for a degree, so that acceleration in this sense is seen as learning at a more advanced level rather than leaving the school at an earlier date. The student can often prepare himself for entry into graduate work with advanced standing. In addition, acceleration is also accomplished by giving students heavier loads through additional classes, or correspondence courses, private lessons, and clubs.

The following readings by authors who have completed intensive investigation of acceleration indicate that acceleration should enjoy more favorable consideration than it has had in recent years. The introductory article by Sidney Pressey lays the groundwork for the more specific studies that follow. The next articles are grouped along the age scale. The first is by Dr. D. A. Worcester, a Visiting Lecturer at the University of Wisconsin and Emeritus Professor at the University of Nebraska. Dr. Worcester is known to many as the father of special education in the Midwest and as a diplomat of clinical psychology. His interests in mental tests, learning, and gifted children led to the formation of a statewide program of entrance to kindergarten on the basis of ability. His article reports the research dealing with early entrance to kindergarten. In the third article Dr. Joseph Justman, assistant director of the New York City Bureau of Research, discusses acceleration in the junior high school. The views of both the proponents and opponents of acceleration are presented and the research in the area is reviewed. (Reference 4 at the end of this article will be helpful in understanding the personal and social adjustment of accelerated and nonaccelerated junior-high pupils.) An evaluation of the "Academic Achievement of Intellectually Gifted Accelerates and Nonaccelerates in Junior High School" in New York City is reported by Dr. Justman in Section 10 (pp. 480-489).

Articles dealing with two of the many programs for the accumulation of college credit by passing proficiency examinations and the teaching of college-level courses in high school follow. Dr. W. Leslie Barnette, Jr., a director of the University of Buffalo's Vocational Counseling Center since 1950, is the author of the article pertaining to the proficiency examination program at that college. Dr. Morris Meister was principal of the Bronx High School of Science when he wrote "Cooperation of Secondary Schools and Colleges in Acceleration of Gifted Students." Dr. Meister is now president of the newly formed Bronx Community Junior College.

In the final article Dan C. Shannon presents a summary of the available research on acceleration. He concludes that published research indicates that acceleration of gifted children, when properly used, is helpful to many and does not handicap gifted individuals personally, socially, or academically.

ACCELERATION: BASIC PRINCIPLES
AND RECENT RESEARCH

by Sidney L. Pressey

OHIO STATE UNIVERSITY

Sometimes a topic becomes so involved with situations emotionally charged that dispassionate consideration of it seems almost impossible. Occasionally an unfortunate label leads thinking astray. Educational acceleration is a subject which has suffered greatly from these handicaps—and more. It was closely associated with the war and two clumsy expedients then: college entrance without completion of secondary school, which aroused bitter antagonism in public school people; and lengthened college year, which burdened and antagonized college faculties. "Acceleration" implies hurry, probably superficiality. And every experienced educator has known bright youngsters double-promoted into an older group who there felt miserably out of place—perhaps he has been such a case.

In contrast, this paper will beg your open-minded consideration of the possibility that for abler students to progress through school at faster-than-average pace is normal *for them,* not hurrying; that there are ways of facilitating their progress which help rather than hinder good social adjustment; and that such steps can lessen the load and facilitate the work of our overcrowded schools. An additional gain should be very timely. Russian universities and technical schools appear now to be graduating about three times as many engineers and twice as many scientists a year as American institutions.[1] Multiple evidence indicates that facilitating the progress of able students leads more of them to complete collegiate and professional training; also probably the occasional notable

---

[1] H. A. Meyerhoff, "United States Shortage: Scientists," *U. S. News and World Report,* January 15, 1954, 46-49.

[From an address delivered at the 1954 Invitational Conference on Testing Problems sponsored annually by the Education Testing Service, Princeton, New Jersey, with the permission of the ETS and the author.]

genius (the Edisons or Einsteins) will thus be more likely to reach full fruition.

TWO MAJOR NEGLECTED FACTS OF HUMAN DEVELOPMENT

Of basic importance are two conclusions from recent developmental studies regarding the gifted—in childhood and youth, *and* in adult career. First, gifted children tend to develop more rapidly than the average youngster, not only intellectually and educationally but also physically and in personality. The bright six-year-old is likely to be advanced not only in intelligence, but also in reading and physique and social assurance, more like a second- than a first-grade child. The bright sixteen-year-old is probably not only in ability and in general knowledge up with the general run of eighteen-year-old high-school seniors or even nineteen-year-old college freshmen; he probably reached puberty earlier than average and is in physique, interests, and social adjustment more mature than the average for his age. To have him in the eleventh or twelfth rather than the tenth grade, or to start the bright six-year-old in the second grade, is not to hurry him but rather to have him progress according to his real growth rate. Terman remarks that, "The exceptionally bright student who is kept with his age group finds little to challenge his intelligence and too often develops habits of laziness that later wreck his college career. I could give you some choice examples of this in my gifted group." [2] There is also evidence that holding a bright youngster back with his age group is less favorable to good social adjustment than carefully advancing him into a group more like him in ability and maturity of personality.

A second major question of educational policy regarding the able student is usually not faced squarely: if he is to be most productive in career and most adequate as a citizen, at about what age should he be through with full-time school and really begin his adult life? Vital statistics show the late teens and early twenties to be the healthiest years; physical tests and athletic rec-

[2] L. M. Terman, "The Discovery and Encouragement of Exceptional Talent," *American Psychologist,* 9, 1954, 221-230; also *The Gifted Child Grows Up,* Stanford: Stanford Univ. Press, 1947.

ords show them to be physically the most vigorous. And Lehman's very extensive findings regarding ages of most brilliant scientific discoveries, most important inventions, best writing, most remarkable paintings, all indicate that the most outstanding creative work is done early in the adult years—often in the twenties, sometimes even in the teens.[3] The total of such evidence is impressive. Nevertheless, American educational programs for our most able young people are being more and more lengthened; they must have not only college but also graduate or professional training, perhaps an "intern" experience—possibly even some postdoctoral work. Before the Second World War, the median age of receiving the Ph.D. degree in this country was 30; now, it tends to be a little later. By the age of 25, Edison and Einstein were doing important creative work. If they were of that age in this country now, they would instead probably be worrying about their language requirements!

The argument thus is that *able students should progress more rapidly than the lockstep rate through school and college because they develop more rapidly than the average young person, and should get into their productive careers earlier than occurs with the lockstep.* But what about possible social maladjustment, gaps in training, or damage to health?

MEANS OF "ACCELERATION"

By a historical perversity, the worst means for rapid progress—grade-skipping in school and the lengthened school year in college—have been so much more used than better methods that, to many people, these worst ways are synonymous with "acceleration." The boy who is skipped from fourth grade to sixth (obviously a half-grade skip is less risky) may suffer at least briefly from ignorance of some arithmetic process taken up in the fifth grade. If he is a conspicuous only one thus to be advanced into a close-knit little sixth-grade social unit, he may initially meet hostility—and parents may talk. But even this clumsy method, grade-skipping, need not cause much trouble. Bright children are usually ahead of their age in their reading and other subjects; a little help from a teacher or

[3] H. C. Lehman, *Age and Achievement,* Princeton, N. J.: Princeton Univ. Press, 1953.

parent usually takes care of any omissions. If grade-skipping of bright pupils is made fairly common and if (as is common nowadays) changes in the membership of a grade group are frequent for other reasons, social difficulties are usually minimal. Trouble is likely only if the "accelerated" child is not really of superior ability but is pushed ahead because of parental pressure, or schoolwork neurotically superior in compensation for a social maladjustment already existing. Grade-skipping is the easiest method of advancing a pupil, especially in a small school; and if "skippers" are selected carefully on the basis of adequate measurement (and a little help is given in adjusting for the skipped work and to the new group), outcomes are usually good—as will be seen shortly.

However, there need be no skipping over possible needed school content, or moving an occasional child into a strange room. Children may be admitted to the first grade (or transferred from kindergarten) on the basis of mental age and reading readiness rather than chronological age; and some half-dozen investigations have all shown bright five-year-olds, so admitted, thereafter excellent in schoolwork and in relations with other children. Or bright six-year-olds with some initial skill in reading may be started in the second grade. Or, a "primary pool" may throw together all children usually in the first three grades, and move each on into the fourth grade when he is ready. Large junior high schools may have rapid-progress sections, made up of bright youngsters with excellent school records to date and good social adjustment, which do the usual three years' work in two. Several careful investigations have shown these rapid-progress pupils doing as well in senior high school, academically *and* in relations with other students, as pupils of the same general ability and total record at the beginning of junior high but who spent the usual three years there. Similar rapid-progress sections (three years in two) in senior high have shown similar success in college.

A few college students may be really fatigued by a lengthened school year, though a total of six weeks or more of vacation usually still remains; both fatigue and protest seem greater in the faculty. A few students who need the earnings or the experience of summer employment may miss these benefits. But the questionableness of a double assumption in the method must be stressed: that bright students can learn only in college courses, and that they must spend as much time in these courses as average students. A substantial number of studies have shown that students who obtained credit for a course by passing a comprehensive examination in it instead of going to class (preparation having been obtained from superior or extra work in secondary school, from independent study, travel, or otherwise) do excellently in later courses in that subject and also in total college record. Streamlined sections of college courses, with methods adapted to the superior student and with reduced hours in class to facilitate acceleration, have been reported as successful; so have been honors programs, combining or replacing several courses, and guided independent study. *In short, the progress of superior youngsters may be facilitated in a variety of ways; most of them are better than grade-skipping or lengthened school year.* It need hardly be mentioned that wise use of each requires initial testing to assure superiority, and continuing measurement thereafter to guide progress and determine outcome.

Whatever the methods for rapid progress, modification should be attempted of the present powerful social pressures for the lockstep. Thus, from the day of entrance, the college is designated a member of the class which is to graduate *four* years later; the entrant in 1954 is a member of the class of 1958 (English universities are wiser; there, an entrant in 1954 is a member of the class of 1954). Each of the four years is given a distinctive name and status; special opportunities (as for presidencies of student organizations) are open only to students in their fourth year. A student who finishes college in three years soon becomes a social anomaly who belongs nowhere. Instead the feeling should be fostered of belonging to the school not the class, associations and friendships should be freely formed within the total student body without class distinction. And status should be determined by academic progress and other accomplishments, not time served. That would be the democratic way; and it would benefit not only the gifted but also those who for some reason take longer than the usual time to finish an academic program.

OUTCOMES OF "ACCELERATION"—AND THE COLD WAR

As already indicated in passing, the evidence is that most able students do not suffer from acceleration. But much evidence goes further. *They actually seem to gain!* When Terman compared those in his gifted group who graduated from high school young (under 15½) with those graduating near the usual age (over 16½) he found that 16 percent more of the younger group graduated from college, and 19 percent more took one or more years of graduate work. The young group married over a year younger and had fewer divorces. Twice as many of the younger group were highly successful vocationally. Results to date of the Fund for the Advancement of Education and of the Ohio State University investigations are similar; these last studies show both those entering young and those taking a four year program in three years doing better in college, *and* having more successful careers after, than matched cases of the same ability but entering at the usual time or taking the usual four years for a degree.[4] And in most of the investigations to date the accelerates were not carefully selected as capable of rapid progress, or given guidance in acceleration: also, they moved forward mostly by these least satisfactory methods—grade-skipping or lengthened school year. There is every reason to suppose that better selection, guidance, and methods would bring yet better outcomes. For instance, 25 percent more of a group of bright freshmen selected as capable of acceleration and given guidance in so doing, finally obtained a degree than a controlled group not accelerating. A more effective education in *less* time—how can this be explained? Presumably because more rapid progress is normal for the gifted, and the beginning of adult career (and marriage and responsible citizenship) without long delays is biologically sound. There are of course certain obvious advantages; saved time and funds leave more of both for advanced training. There are also motivational gains of possible pervasive importance. It is in the American tradition, and stimulating to the bright and ambitious youngster, that there be opportunity to get ahead. The lockstep negates all that. You may have heard the jibe that a certain state penitentiary had a major advantage over the neighboring university: you could get out of the pen sooner if you did well. *Wise means for "acceleration" are legitimate opportunities for the able to forge ahead, which encourage a general climate of enterprise and lively effort.*

[4] The Fund for the Advancement of Education, *Bridging the Gap between School and College*, 1953; S. L. Pressey, *Educational Acceleration: Appraisals and Basic Problems.* Columbus: Ohio State Univ., 1949.

IN RÉSUMÉ AND FINAL APPLICATION

Numerous studies of human development thus show that able youngsters should progress in school faster than the lockstep rate of a grade a year, not only because they develop faster but to prevent long, drawn-out education from delaying productive careers. Wise methods of acceleration expedite progress without hampering social adjustment. With acceleration, more able students complete advanced training; they get into productive careers earlier. And these careers tend to be more fruitful. In addition, congested schools are relieved to some degree. It seems a not unreasonable estimate that each year there remain in the secondary schools perhaps 300,000 bright youngsters who ought well have been graduated. *More trained men, sooner, at less cost,* to counter the Russian technological threat! Clearly such a program calls for frequent appraisals from the primary years to graduate school, continuing guidance, and informed educational statesmanship. Surely, then, the topic is most appropriate to this conference.

ADMISSION TO KINDERGARTEN ON THE BASIS
OF MENTAL AGE

by D. A. Worcester

UNIVERSITY OF WISCONSIN

PUBLISHED STUDIES

Hobson (2) reported a few years ago a long-time accounting of children in the Brookline, Massachusetts, schools. In general children were admitted to kindergarten if they were 4-9 (four years, nine months) of age by October 1. Beginning in 1932, younger

[Reprinted from *The Education of Children of Above Average Mentality*, Lincoln: University of Nebraska Press, 1956, pp. 13-29, with the permission of the University of Nebraska Press and the author.]

children were admitted on the basis of mental age. At first, only those who were 4-6, chronologically, by October 1 were tested, but later the age was left to the discretion of the superintendent of schools, and some children as much as nine months below the regularly adopted age were accepted.

Originally, the MA (mental age) requirement was 4-10. This was raised to 5-0 in 1936. (It is seen that in terms of IQs, these early entrants would vary from a minimum of 107 for those nearly at the "standard age" to 125 for the youngest in the group.)

Results of this plan were reported by Hobson in 1948.

1. The teachers' marks and the children's readiness as indicated by achievement tests for the kindergarten and first grade over a ten-year period showed that: (a) In kindergarten, the older children made more A's, while the younger (admitted by test) made more B's and fewer C's. On achievement tests, the difference was very slight, but what difference there was, was in favor of the younger ones. (b) In the first grade, in each of the ten years, the younger children made more A's, more B's, had fewer failures and trial promotions, and were higher on test scores.

2. The grades and test scores for two classes were followed through the eight grades, and were higher in *every* grade for the younger children. In several instances, the younger ones had twice as many A's as the older. Those admitted by test in 1933 had no trial promotions after the first grade and no failures after the fifth. Of the 1934 younger ones, there were no trial promotions after the third grade and no failures after the second. It is clear that, for eight grades, those admitted by mental age made the best records. There was no lessening in the quality of achievement as they became older.

3. All children in the elementary grades were studied in 1942-1943. In every grade, the children who entered by test were doing better than the older ones in terms of both teachers's marks and achievement test scores. On achievement tests, the younger ones excelled by two to seven months. Those who entered by test were uniformly getting higher scores than those of underage who had transferred from other schools.

Hobson states that, after the kindergarten age, the two groups cannot be distinguished physically and that the younger are less often than the older referred for emotional, social, or personality problems. At the time of his report, the plan had been in operation for fifteen years and was receiving general support from administrators, teachers, and patrons.*

Another study, by Birch (1), reports on children admitted to first grade in Pittsburgh schools. In Pennsylvania, the minimum age for entrance to first grade is five years, seven months, as of September 1. Children over five years, but younger than the above minimum, may enter on recommendation of a public-school psychologist. Children were evaluated by interview for social, emotional, and physical maturity, and by test for reading readiness and superior mental capacity. Usually, though not always, an IQ of 130 was advised. A follow-up after one to three years "indicated that an overwhelming majority of the children admitted early to first grade were making satisfactory school adjustments in all areas—academic, social, emotional and physical."

Still another study, this time of rural children in Berks County, Pennsylvania, showed very similar results. Of 21 children, 16 were in the best reading group and 4 were in the middle group; 16 were in the highest group in number work; 20 "got along well with other children."

NEBRASKA STUDIES OF EARLY ENTRANCE

In 1939, the legislature of the State of Nebraska, at the request of the State Department of Public Instruction, passed a law to the effect that no child may enter kindergarten unless he is five years of age on or before October 15 of the current year and that no child

---

* In his presidential address to the American Psychological Association's Division of School Psychologists in 1956, Hobson described a follow-up study of Brookline's 550 underage children graduating from high school between 1946 and 1955. In high school the underage children increased their margin of academic superiority over the 3891 students admitted to the school through normal channels as measured by grade-point average, average rank in class and sex group, and in percentage graduating with honors. The underage students engaged in a significantly larger number of high-school extracurricular activities and were no different from their classmates in athletic and social honors and elective positions. The underage boys and girls exceeded their fellows by a ratio of two to one in honors, awards, and distinctions at graduation. When compared with classmates of the same sex, a significantly larger percentage of underage graduates sought and gained admission to accredited four-year colleges. —EDITOR'S NOTE.

may enter first grade unless he is six years of age by October 15 or has completed kindergarten, provided that a school may admit to kindergarten a child who is younger than the stipulated age if he shows readiness as determined by criteria set up by the State Department.

For the past few years, the State Department of Education has set a mental age of five years and three months as of September 1,* on the basis of an individual mental test, plus the examiner's judgment of social and physical readiness, as the criteria for early entrance. It should be pointed out that a school district may refuse to admit anyone on the basis of the test, may demand a standard higher than that set by the State Department, and may determine the date after which it will no longer accept children on the basis of examination. The date, December 31, is the one most often used as the deadline, regardless of the giftedness of the child.

A few schools in the state had a program similar to the present one before the new law was enacted. In the last three or four years, we have been accumulating evidence concerning the progress of children who have entered under the plan based on mental tests. It is hoped that we may continue these studies so that we can know what happens to these individuals as they progress through their school life.

We should like to call special attention to two considerations in connection with these studies:

1. The amount of acceleration achieved in this program is small. If new classes were started at midyear, all of these children would be regularly admitted the second semester; so, in effect, they are only one semester accelerated from their fellows. However, as few schools have midyear promotions, to be admitted at this earlier date will save a full year of the child's life.

2. The children in this group are not classified as gifted children. The minimum IQ which will qualify for early entrance is 109. Actually, the average IQ of those in the studies which we have is about 116. Hobson's study is the only other one of which we know on the effects of one-year acceleration on children of this mental level.

* In 1955, the mental-age requirement was to be raised to 5-6. This change is not on the basis of evidence but on the "feeling" of some that success of children so admitted will be even more assured.

LINCOLN AND LANCASTER COUNTY SCHOOLS

Prior to the present state program, the Lincoln, Nebraska, public schools admitted to kindergarten children who became five years of age before February 1. A study was made by Smith (7) of a group of these children. It should be remembered that there was no mental-age limitation in this instance.

The cases of 175 early-entrance children in grades one to five were compared with an equal number of children in the same grades whose birthdays came before October 15. Comparisons were made in relation to school marks, standardized test results, a sociometric rating, and a rating by teachers as to social and emotional adjustment.

After having entered kindergarten, the children were given the Pintner-Cunningham test and 27 of those who were underage were matched with 27 chosen at random from the same grade and of the same sex. None of the younger ones who rated strong-average or above-average in mental ability were found at the beginning of the first grade to be less ready for reading than those in the control group. In the *third* grade, the children in Lincoln were given the Otis Quick-scoring Test. Twenty pairs were made on the basis of Otis IQs. The early entrants were shown to be reading, as measured by the Progressive Reading Test, as well as or slightly better than those in the control group. If we can assume constancy of the IQ and judge on the basis of the Otis test whether or not a child would have made a score sufficiently high to allow early entrance to kindergarten, then *no child* of the younger group who would have been admitted by test was below average achievement in the third grade.

A group of 17 early entrants were matched for Otis IQ scores at the third grade and were followed through the sixth. The younger ones received higher marks in the kindergarten through the fourth grade with no differences in the fifth and sixth grades.

Each of the children was asked to write the names of three children in his room whom he considered to be his best friends. The younger ones on this rating equaled or slightly surpassed the control, but no statistical differences in numbers liked were found. Teachers were asked to rate children as to social and emotional adjustment. Again, there were no statistical differences. In the fourth grade, the control group was slightly higher; in the fifth, the experimental group. It should be noticed that almost always, though not universally, those who rated high on mental ability were rated high by the teachers on social and emotional adjustment.

There were no differences at the fifth-grade level in the numbers wearing glasses.

In Lincoln, other studies are in progress. In 1950, on the basis of testing, 74 children were admitted to kindergarten. The mean IQ of these children was 117.4. In 1953 of these 50 were still in school. Their mean Otis IQ was 120, and at the beginning of the third grade their mean grade placement on the California Reading Test was fourth grade. That is, they were one grade ahead of standard norms, which in this instance was almost exactly the average for their class. Similarly, in 1951, some 132 children were admitted, again, the mean IQ of Stanford-Binet was 117.4, and in 1954, the 103 who were still in school at the beginning of third grade had a mean Otis test IQ of 120 and a mean grade placement on the California Reading Test of 3.8, or .8 ahead of standard norms and the same as the average for their class.

Kazienko (3) studied pupils of rural schools in Lancaster County, Nebraska, whose initial school experiences were in a beginner grade, or in a first grade without the benefit of a beginner grade. All of the children started school at five years of age or younger. Those who started in the beginner grade were further divided into those whose teachers had emphasized reading readiness and those whose teachers had given little attention to readiness. Each child was given a mental-ability test and an achievement test during the seventh month of the fourth grade. Through analysis of multiple regression, Kazienko found that the factor of mental age is very significantly more influential in determining fourth-grade achievement than chronological age, intelligence quotient, or the combination of those two. This is a tremendously important finding, one which in itself *should* be enough to do away with rigid chronological age requirements for school entrance.

ALLIANCE STUDY

In Alliance, Nebraska, a program for admitting by test had been set up before the present law became effective. Here, children were admitted on the basis of a mental age of five as of September 1. None of the 13 children in the seventh grade in 1955 had average marks below C and 10 of the 13 had average marks of A or B. Of these children 11 were in the sixth grade. One of these had been retained in the second grade. All of the others averaged A or B.

Six of the 20 children who were admitted by test and who were in the fifth grade in 1953-1954 had made unsatisfactory progress at one time or another. Five of these were in a group tested at one time. It is suspected that since this group differs so much from others, some accidental factor was involved. Even then, 14 of 20 did make good progress.

MONDERER'S STUDIES

In Fairbury, Nebraska, Monderer (4) was able to follow through five grades children who had been admitted by test. Grade by grade, he compared the early entrants with the other children in the same grades but who had been admitted regularly. In every grade the early entrants surpassed the control groups in academic subjects and in the teachers' ratings of social adjustment.

The differences were significant beyond the one-degree level of confidence, and the differences were greater in the fourth and fifth grades than in the first three. Similar superiority was shown on scores on the Stanford Achievement Test.

Monderer also studied two other groups formed after the law limiting entrance—one group of city children and another of rural children. In neither of these groups were there significant differences between the early entrants and their controls in achievement, social acceptance by peers, or ratings by teachers. In terms of physical development, there were no statistical differences shown in the first three grades (which is as far as he carried his study here) on development as measured by the Wetzel grid. The median heights of the two groups were the same. In other words, those admitted by test were as far advanced mentally, socially and physically as the others in their classes.

MUELLER'S STUDY

One argument *against* taking younger pupils is that they will do much better if they enter school when they are older. It is most difficult to get real evidence upon this point. When children pass tests, they are usually enrolled in school; so it is hard to know what would have happened if something else had been done. Oak-Bruce (6) points out that readiness is not necessarily increased by staying home for a year. And if a child is ready to go now, to stay out of school may result in maladjustment.

Evidence leading toward this question lies in a study by Mueller (5) in which comparison has been made between those persons who took the early-entrance examination and passed it; those who took it, failed, and therefore entered school a year later; those who entered regularly, being of such age as not to require an examination, and those who, though eligible to take the test, did not, and entered school a year later. It is obvious that those who entered by test were around eight months younger than their regular classmates and a year younger than those who took the test and failed it. Those who took the test and failed it, for the most part, were average or above average in mental ability, but not quite high enough to make the critical test score.

There was also a very small group who took the test and passed it, but who for some reason did not enter school until a year later. There are not enough of these children to justify conclusions, but no trend seems to be appearing to show that waiting benefited them.

Mueller studied the results obtained from 4275 pupils from the cities of Grand Island and Hastings and from many small towns and rural districts of Nebraska. Teachers were asked to rate all members of their class as to (1) achievement, (2) health, (3) coordination, (4) acceptance by other children, (5) leadership, (6) attitude toward school, and (7) emotional adjustment.*

The results of this study are unequivocal. If a child is ready mentally, it is clearly to his advantage to enter school even though he be slightly younger, chronologically, than the average.

Remember, these ratings were by teachers. In every quality, those entering by test stand better, whether in terms of the number of those receiving high ratings or of the few receiving low ratings. The younger, but brighter, group not only were significantly higher than those of the regular class in achievement, but also in health, coordination, acceptance by others, leadership, atti-

* The results, summarized in seven tables, have been omitted.—EDITOR'S NOTE.

tude toward school, and emotional adjustment. Their advantage also obtained over those who took the test and failed.

The differences between those who took the prekindergarten test and received a satisfactory score to enter school that year and those who would have been eligible to take the test but who did not and entered school the following year were slight, and probably not significant in leadership and coordination. What difference there was was in favor of those who took the test and entered school. These two groups were, of course, of the same chronological age.

While those who entered school without testing were slightly taller and heavier than those who entered by test in the kindergarten year, this difference had disappeared by the fourth and fifth grades.

It must be noted that the early entrants were a little higher on intelligence tests; so the two groups were not completely comparable. But those who were delayed had as high MAs when they entered kindergarten as did the early entrants at the time they were admitted. There is no evidence that a child four years and nine months old with an MA of six years now will be any better adjusted to a kindergarten group if he is required to wait a year and join such a group when his MA then will be more than seven years.

To summarize some of these findings, children in these Nebraska studies who were admitted to kindergarten on the basis of individual mental tests were, on the average, approximately eight months younger than those admitted regularly. There were no statistical differences in physical development. In academic work, the younger did as well as or better than their older classmates. Judged by their peers or by teacher's ratings, they are socially and emotionally as well or better adjusted. They have as good or better coordination. They are accepted by their peers. They like school. They do as well as or better than those of the same age who were a year later in getting started in school. Indeed, no negative effects have been discerned. As compared with those who took the test but did not pass it, the younger ones had gained a year of school life without loss in social adjustment.

In the light of these findings, and in agreement with similar studies, it would seem that to admit to kindergarten children who will become five years of age before the first of January following their admission and who show readiness on the basis of mental ability equivalent to an IQ of 110 or more, is a justifiable educational policy. It would not seem justifiable to refuse to do so.

VALUES OF ACCELERATION BY EARLY ENTRANCE

1. Early entrance has the advantage of any form of acceleration in that it saves a year of the pupil's life. If there be no further acceleration, the child has the regular number of years of education with all the possibilities of enrichment and still can enter college and, after that, post-college training at an earlier age. For very many of these bright children, the extra year will be spent in advanced education in order to prepare for the exceedingly complex tasks of the professions, technology, business, and government.

2. The child will be placed from the beginning with those more nearly his mental and social equal and will, therefore, be less likely to develop habits of dawdling and laziness.

3. His education will be directed. In some homes, to be sure, the mentally ready child who has to "sit and wait" will have the advantage of enlightened home training. For many, it will be haphazard.

4. The problem of skipping material in the curriculum is obviated.

5. Teachers are made more aware of the particular needs of bright children by recognizing them at the beginning of their school careers.

6. The school system as a whole becomes sensitive to the problem of the gifted.

REFERENCES

1. Birch, Jack W. Early School Admission for Mentally Advanced Children. *Exceptional Children,* 21, December 1954, 84-87.
2. Hobson, James R. Mental Age as a Workable Criterion for School Admission. *Elem. School J.,* 48, February 1948, 312-321.
3. Kazienko, Louis W. Beginner Grade Influence on School Progress. *Educational Administration and Supervision,* 40, 1954.
4. Monderer, J. H. *An Evaluation of the Nebraska Program of Early En-*

trance to Elementary School. Unpublished Ph.D. dissertation, Univ. Nebraska, July 1953.

5. Mueller, Karl. *Success of Elementary Students Admitted to Public Schools under the Requirements of the Nebraska Program of Early Entrance.* Unpublished Ph.D. dissertation, Univ. Nebraska, 1955.

6. Oak-Bruce, Laura. "What Do We Know—For Sure? *Childhood Educ.,* March, 1948.

7. Smith, Janet. *The Success of Some Young Children in the Lincoln, Nebraska, Public Schools.* Unpublished master's thesis, Univ. Nebraska, 1951.

ACCELERATION IN THE JUNIOR HIGH SCHOOL

by Joseph Justman

NEW YORK CITY BOARD OF EDUCATION

The development of an appropriate educational program for the pupil of superior ability has been the concern of American educators since shortly after the Civil War. In general, early approaches to the problem utilized some technique of acceleration through the grades as a means of meeting the challenge presented by the superior pupil. Shortly after the turn of the century, however, educational authorities began to use a variety of multiple-track plans as a means of providing for such pupils, and virtually eliminated acceleration as an administrative measure. This emphasis upon enrichment lasted until the manpower needs of World War II led to an increasing demand for acceleration in educational programs, particularly at the higher school levels. In spite of this development, a survey conducted shortly after the war reported only limited use of acceleration as an administrative device (6). Within the past few years, however, a large number of communities have reported the adoption of experimental programs, embodying some degree of acceleration, for their able pupils. The indications are that a new trend in administrative practice is well under way.

[Reprinted from the *High School Journal,* 40, December 1956, 121-126, with the permission of the *Journal* and the author.]

Historically, acceleration of the pupil of superior ability has taken two forms: (1) double promotion, where the pupil "skips" a grade or (2) completion of the normal work of two or more grades in less-than-normal time. The feeling that the child who omits a grade misses contact with important units of instruction has led to a considerable drop in double promotions, particularly since the transition from semiannual to annual promotion in many communities. On the junior-high-school level, where the pupil is introduced to so many new concepts in so short a time, this feeling has acted as a deterrent to even the limited adoption of "skipping" as an administrative device.

Rather, the second approach is much more frequently observed, particularly in large communities. Where the population on the junior-high-school level is large enough, it is possible to organize special classes composed wholly of able pupils who can complete the three-year junior high school in two years. This pattern of acceleration is apparently becoming more common throughout the country.

Criteria for the selection of pupils for such special classes differ from community to community. All of them, of course, require that the pupils have shown high academic achievement; others set minimum age and minimum IQ requirements. The minimum IQ that is demanded varies. New York City, for example, calls for an IQ of at least 130; in other communities, an IQ of 120, or even of 110, may be set as a standard for admission to a special class. A good attendance record and freedom from social or emotional maladjustment are common criteria for placement in the special group.

School administrators are by no means unanimous in their opinions concerning the adequacy of the special class in meeting the needs of superior pupils. In a study (5) conducted in New York City, for example, 79 junior-high-school principals were asked, via an anonymous questionnaire, whether they felt that such "special-progress" classes, as they are called in that community, should be retained or abolished. Of the 74 principals who responded to the question, 46 voted for retention of the special-progress class, 28 for abolition.

Proponents of a program of acceleration within the framework of a special class generally cite the following outcomes in support of their point of view:

1. By providing for cooperation and competition with a peer group, the superior pupil is stimulated to work to capacity. The more able pupil is not held back by the slower progress of others and, because he must exert himself, does not develop habits of carelessness and indolence.
2. Curricular enrichment is actually facilitated, even though the pupils' total time in school is curtailed. The superior ability of the group makes it possible to complete the normal course of study at a very rapid pace, and leaves room for the inclusion of many activities of educational value.
3. The class serves to bring to the fore such leadership qualities as the pupil may possess. By stimulating the development of leaders, it becomes a reservoir of key pupils when school-wide activities and school-community projects are undertaken.
4. A class composed wholly of superior pupils constitutes a challenge and a stimulus to the teacher. Assignment to such a group is reflected in greater teacher satisfaction.
5. The saving of time is another important factor to consider. The superior junior-high-school pupil is the future college student. Acceleration means earlier entrance into higher schools and, ultimately, into professional life.

Opponents of acceleration via a special class also have recourse to a number of typical arguments:

1. The special class is conducive to snobbery and self-conceit. The pupils tend to look upon themselves as out of the ordinary, considerably better than the common herd.
2. The class tends to overemphasize academic achievement, at the expense of other outcomes equally important. This apparently stems from the weight given academic achievement as a factor in the selection of pupils for the class.
3. Organization of a special class makes for disharmony within the school and the community. Not only is there a tendency for the other pupils in the school to reject pupils enrolled in the special class, but teachers must cope with the difficult problem presented by the disappointed child who is not admitted. Moreover, snobbery develops among the parents of children who are selected for the special class. The resulting hostility of parents of children who are not admitted becomes another source of difficulty.

4. Obtaining suitable teachers is also a difficult problem. Any special class calls for a teacher who has special skills. Few teachers are now equipped to meet the needs of a high-ability, accelerated group. To prepare such teachers would entail the organization of a comprehensive program of teacher training, including in-service courses, workshops, demonstrations, and conferences.

5. Withdrawing high-ability children from other classes on the grade to form a special class is unfair to the other children on the grade and to their teachers. The superior pupil serves as a valuable stimulus to other children in his class. They learn from his contributions to class discussion and profit from his suggestions in committee work and other group activities. To the teacher, too, her occasional pupil who stands out makes her often cheerless task not only palatable, but sometimes a veritable joy.

The pros and cons summarized above represent the personal reactions of school people with many years of experience who have observed accelerated groups in action. Of course, personal experience should not be dismissed perfunctorily as of little value in appraising the advantages and limitations of acceleration. Yet, too often, even experienced observers see only those outcomes that support their previously established conclusions. A truly objective appraisal of the gains and losses associated with enrollment in an accelerated group must rest upon carefully controlled research studies.

What, then, does research show? Unfortunately, there have been few *carefully controlled* research studies contrasting accelerated and normal progress pupils of equal ability, particularly on the junior-high-school level. Moreover, such research as has been conducted has not been directed to the specific allegations advanced by proponents or opponents of acceleration.

Although the research in the field has been relatively scanty, the following generalizations appear to have been established on a fairly firm basis:

1. Able pupils can complete the academic work of the junior high school in two, rather than three, years without loss (2).
2. Junior-high-school accelerants suffer no ill effects in academic areas in their subsequent high-school careers (1, 3).
3. The personal and social adjustment of the accelerated pupil

is generally equivalent to that of his normal progress peer during the junior-high-school period (4).

4. The social adjustment of junior-high-school accelerants proves to be similar to that of nonaccelerants when the two groups are followed into the high school (1).

In general, research in the field has been restricted to a consideration of the relative academic achievement and social adjustment of accelerated and nonaccelerated groups. Certainly, research has not yet succeeded in presenting a complete answer to the question, "Can able pupils be accelerated without loss?" Bearing in mind the narrow range of problems that have been considered, the weight of the evidence points to the conclusion that differences between accelerated and nonaccelerated pupils of equal ability are generally small, and that moderate acceleration is not accompanied by a decrease in academic attainment or social adjustment.

It is true that many other aspects of the problem still remain to be studied. Even on the basis of the limited evidence now available, however, a strong case can be made for the inclusion of special classes following an accelerated program within the framework of the junior high school.

REFERENCES

1. Herr, William A. Junior High School accelerants and Their Peers in High School. *School Rev.*, 45, March-April 1937, 186-195, 289-299.
2. Justman, Joseph. Academic Achievement of Intellectually Gifted Accelerants and Non-accelerants in Senior High School. *School Rev.*, 62, March 1954, 142-150.
3. ——— Academic Achievement of Intellectually Gifted Accelerants and Non-accelerants in Senior High School. *School Rev.*, 62, November 1954, 469-473.
4. ——— Personal and Social Adjustment of Intellectually Gifted Accelerants and Non-accelerants in Junior High School. *School Rev.*, 61, November 1953, 468-478.
5. ——— and J. Wayne Wrightstone. The Opinions of Junior High School Principals concerning the Organization of Special Progress Classes for Gifted Children. *Educational Administration and Supervision,* 37, November 1951, 396-404.
6. Wilson, Frank T. A Survey of Education Provisions for Young Gifted Children in the United States, and of Studies and Problems Related Thereto. *J. Genet. Psychol.,* 75, 1949, 3-19.

ADVANCED CREDIT FOR THE SUPERIOR
HIGH-SCHOOL STUDENT

by W. Leslie Barnette

UNIVERSITY OF BUFFALO

The College Entrance Examination Board recently announced a plan of advanced placement which it offers "in the interest of able students, secondary schools which enable these students to undertake work commensurate with their abilities, and colleges which welcome freshmen who are ready for advanced courses."[1] A program devised to aid superior high-school students to use their ability toward acceleration and enrichment of their college programs, long used by the University of Buffalo, is evaluated here.

The program of college-credit examinations at Buffalo, in operation for over twenty years, was designed to serve two main functions: to achieve better articulation between high school and college, and to provide special attention for the superior student and to encourage independent study on his part. Studies of the effects of the program have been reported by Edward S. Jones, Gloria K. Ortner, and M. E. Wagner. These previous surveys have shown that other schools have used the examination principle in similar ways; several of them made a start in this direction when extending advance credit to veterans after the Second World War; many schools also use "placement" examinations to section classes. Little attention, in general, has been paid to the superior student who has excess high-school credits which might duplicate certain college courses.

While the program of college-credit examinations at Buffalo has other functions, the main intent is to aid and attract the superior high-school student and to provide him with an advanced start on

---

[1] Commission on Advanced Placement, *Advanced Placement Program,* New York: College Entrance Examination Board, 1956, p. 7.

[Reprinted from the *Journal of Higher Education,* 28, January 1957, 15-20, with the permission of the *Journal* and the author.]

his college work.[2] To be eligible for such examinations, the student is required to have a minimum New York State Regents average of 82, with 87 in the subject of the examination. In addition, he must furnish a letter of recommendation from the high-school principal or a teacher and present more than the required 16 high-school units for admission. Students already in college may also take advantage of the program; to do so they must present a quality-point average of 1.7—that is, be approximately within the top third of the college group.

A counselor is always available to talk with these students and, on occasion, the counselor may visit the high schools on invitation in order to explain the program. College syllabuses and sample examinations are made available to all interested students; a high-school teacher may even help the student to prepare for such examinations. In the majority of cases, since the areas of mathematics and modern foreign languages are most frequently chosen, the student may report for the examination with little or no extra preparation. In other areas, however, considerable independent study may be involved—something which the college faculty definitely wants to encourage. All examinations are graded by faculty members; they are paid for this work.

Edward S. Jones and Gloria K. Ortner recently completed an evaluation study of the entire Buffalo program using matched groups: the records of students who took nine or more hours of college credit examinations were compared with those of students who took at most three hours. Their study showed that the college performance of the two groups presented a strong argument for the program. The nine-plus group surpassed the control group significantly in the frequency with which these students completed their work for the degree. Since these students spent the equivalent of one semester plus one summer shorter time in college and were, on the average, one year younger, it is significant that their performance throughout their college years was comparable to that of students who spent the full four years in attendance. The faculty rated this nine-plus group higher in pleasantness and initiative; later follow-up showed no lack of community leadership and participa-

[2] The program also acts as a kind of scholarship aid since student fees paid for such examinations may be deducted from tuition. The Buffalo experience, which involves small financial layout, may stimulate other colleges to adopt similar programs.

tion on the part of this group. More of this nine-plus group went on to graduate school.[3]

I recently completed a summary report of the entire program by taking a sample (all sudents participating in the program with surnames beginning with A or B) and using this as a basis for an overview of the entire twenty years of experience. The records produced a total of 205 individual students who had taken 484 examinations. The earliest date of such examinations was June 1932, practically at the formal beginning of the Buffalo program; the most recent was July 1955. The largest number of such examinations (55 percent) were taken by students before they enrolled as full-time students at the university; mathematics and modern foreign languages were the two most frequently chosen areas. Examinations in freshman English were the next most popular (13 percent). While, in theory, any and every university subject area is open for examination, few social-science areas are selected for examination purposes—not surprising in view of the lack of opportunity in high-school courses to make any beginning in the area. On the other hand, few students now elect to take examinations in the natural-science area. This may be due in part to the actual discouragement by college counselors unless the student is especially able; faculty members also believe that the laboratory aspects of these college courses cannot be adequately mastered by unsupervised study. Regardless, students do show wide variation in choices, and examinations are administered in accountancy, economics, geography, statistics, Latin, music history and theory, and engineering drawing.

The modal student takes only one college-credit examination, either before or after enrollment here. Such a statement, however, greatly obscures the facts. Many students take two or more such examinations. It is by no means uncommon for a student to take two, three, or four examinations; one ambitious candidate took 14 different examinations, all of them before full-time registration at the university. The average per-student number of before-enrollment examinations was 2.45 and the average per-student number of after-enrollment examinations was 1.87.* Jones and Ortner report an average of 1.8 examinations per student—covering the entire

---

[3] *College Credit by Examination: An Evaluation of the University of Buffalo Program,* University of Buffalo Studies, Vol. XXI, No. 3, Buffalo, N. Y.: Univ. Buffalo, 1954, pp. 166-168, 172-174.

* Table 1 and an expansion of this data have been omitted.—Editor's NOTE.

program to the summer of 1953, and involving a total of 2949 examinations administered to 1618 students.[4] A student may take these examinations both before and after enrollment; there were only 10 such cases in the A-B sampling, however.

Discussion about the "modal" and "average" student who participates in this examination program completely obscures the unusual and remarkable students. In connection with the comment concerning the large numbers of college-credit examinations that a few students take, the following case is presented as an illustration:

A premedical student took a total of 10 college-credit examinations (seven before enrollment at the University of Buffalo; three after). His father, with only a grammar-school education, was in the produce business; his mother was a high-school graduate. He had been the high-school valedictorian; he came to the university with a New York State scholarship as well as two University of Buffalo scholarships. At entrance to the University of Buffalo he reported an extensive extracurricular activity in music (organ; high-school glee club, band, and orchestra); he was also the pianist for his church group for a period of ten years. Furthermore, as evidence of other interests, he reported enjoyment and participation in public speaking and horseback riding.

Before enrollment at the university he took seven college-credit examinations with the following marks: elementary French, B, B; intermediate French, B, C; freshman English, C, D; and European History, first half, C. One year after enrolling he took three additional examinations; history of music, B, F, and European history, second half, B. The total semester-hours of credit earned by these college credit examinations was 26 hours.

He attended the University of Buffalo for about two years. He was a biology major (all tutorial work was graded A) and accumulated a total of 95 semester-hours of credit with 202 quality points or a 2.12 grade-point average. He received his B.A. degree (*cum laude*) in two years.

The records further show he was granted his M.D. degree from the Medical School three years later.

Inspection of Table 2, wherein are recorded the marks earned in such examinations before and after enrollment at the university, will show that the college-credit examination program is no "easy way" in which to achieve high marks. Approximately 20 percent of

[4] *Ibid.*, p. 143.

these examinations are graded D and F in the case of students attempting them prior to enrollment; the figure increases to 25 percent after enrollment; C is, by all counts, the most frequent awarded mark.

Superior quality is evident in the performance of these students in examinations taken before enrollment. Such students are probably very well motivated and well prepared. Students who attempt these examinations at a later date probably are more "relaxed"; many of them would have had satisfactory experiences with these examinations earlier and so may think the examinations are easier than they really are. In actuality, however, the performance for the "before" and "after" group is not very different.

TABLE 2

Marks Earned with College-credit Examinations
Before and After Enrollment

Mark earned	Before enrollment	After enrollment
A	54	37
B	73	36
C	73	49
D	36	19
F	21	21
Totals	277	162
Median Mark	C−	C+
Percentage of D's and F's	21	25

A measure of the "staying power" of these students as well as an index of the seriousness of their college plans is shown by the percentage that received degrees. Fifteen of the 205 students we are considering entered the university too recently to have had time to complete the work. Out of the remaining 190 students who could be checked to ascertain degree status, the records show that 84 percent obtained degrees.

The significance of this figure may be seen when it is compared with the results of a follow-up study of the records of the 1949-1950 freshmen in the College of Arts and Sciences made by the Registrar's Office at Buffalo. A total of 507 freshmen were involved; 194 of these, or approximately 40 percent, were found to have obtained the B.A. degree or were in attendance in some professional school. This finding agrees with national figures for privately supported universities and colleges. The ratio of the percentages 84 to 40 points to the superior quality of the group as well as to their superior motivation.

Not to be disregarded, of course, is the problem of values— "enrichment" versus "acceleration." This is a difficult item to disentangle and the terms are unfortunate. The present writer prefers to think of this classification in terms of two groups of students: one that used the college-credit examination courses as background for further work in an area, and the other as students who terminated their work in a particular area. This is not to deny benefits accruing to this latter group; for example, these would have gained (as indeed they say themselves) values from independent study that was involved. Actually both aspects might be claimed for the same student: the student who benefits from the independent study, even if he does not continue further in the area, has been "enriched" and has obtained values that might well spread into other areas.

Acceleration, of itself, however, has generated a good deal of controversy. Opinions, especially those against the idea of holding all college students to the same pace are reviewed by M. E. Wagner.[5] Jones and Ortner summarize the pertinent arguments against acceleration and conclude that we should encourage able students to "break out of the academic lockstep in both school and college." These same authors report that approximately 80 percent of 40 high-school teachers interviewed were in favor of the program of college-credit examinations as a technique for acceleration. They also point out that "enrichment is a natural corollary of acceleration, if a college encourages it," but that the teacher needs time and the disposition to work individually with superior students.[6]

Both these studies report student attitudes concerning this issue. Questionnaire returns were analyzed for students who obtained nine or more hours by college-credit examinations. The most frequent advantage mentioned was the time and money saved so that more advanced courses could be taken relatively early.[7] Other advantages indicated by Wagner involved such psychological factors as security, confidence, and feelings of accomplishment

[5] *Anticipatory Examinations for College Credit: Twenty Years of Experience at the University of Buffalo,* University of Buffalo Studies, Vol. XX, No. 3, Buffalo, N. Y.: Univ. Buffalo, 1952.
[6] Jones and Ortner, *op. cit.,* pp. 129-132, 142.
[7] Wagner, *op. cit.,* p. 126; Jones and Ortner, *op. cit.,* p. 147.

which such advance college credit brought. Other students mentioned that the program provided an incentive to go to college and taught them something about the values of independent study. Seventeen students (8 percent of Wagner's sample) specifically mentioned enrichment; they said they were thereby enabled to take certain courses "for fun" which were outside departmental requirements.[8] It would then seem that acceleration has greater appeal for students; they are not, however, unaware of the enrichment aspect.

To examine this problem further, a study was made of students in the A-B sampling who took a minimum of six hours of college-credit examinations. We then checked to see if these students later registered for further work in the area: 86 students were involved. Of these 40 took no additional work in the area of their college-credit examination; 27 took some additional work; 19 registered for more than six additional hours in the same area. Most of the students who took further work in mathematics did so mainly to fulfill departmental requirements and no more; there were three students, however, who went on for extensive work in mathematics (29, 31, and 32 additional credit hours in mathematics). In the area of modern foreign language, the report is rather different; six students continued with modern foreign languages and accumulated a considerable number of credit hours:

Credit hours	Areas
12 (additional)	German literature and history
12 (additional)	German and French
15	French
25	French, Italian, Spanish, German
36	French, Latin, German, Greek
62	German, French, Spanish, Greek

An over-all estimate would suggest that approximately 12 percent of this student group made real use of the college-credit examinations in the sense of enrichment. But, of course, they were also accelerating.[9]

The extent of the college-credit examination program is considerable. Wagner, reporting on the program almost since its inception in 1932 through 1949, indicated a total of 2730 examinations administered to 1496 students; Jones and Ortner, bringing the totals

[8] Wagner, op. cit., p. 131.
[9] Thanks are due to Dorothy Adema of the Office of the Dean of Students for these results.

up to the summer of 1953, reported 2949 examinations with 1618 students. Estimates were made by the present writer, based on the A-B sampling by extrapolating these data to arrive at the totals for the entire file in the Registrar's Office. The grand total thus becomes 4010 examinations taken by 1700 students.

Costs to the students participating in this program would amount, at the standard rate of $5 for each semester examination, to $20,050—a sum which may well be thought of as scholarships since students, when they enroll at the university, may have such fees deducted from their tuition charges. At the present tuition rate of $19.25 per semester-hour of credit (not, however, the tuition rate for most of the period involved), this represents a possible tuition "loss" of $231,477.50, a sum which may be thought of as an investment by the university in the superior student. This figure is predicated on the assumption, generally true, that all of these 4010 examinations were for three semester-hours of credit. These figures show that the program acts as a scholarship award to the student since fees for such examinations paid by him are deductible from his tuition. Over the years this practice amounts to a sizable investment by the University of Buffalo in the encouragement of such superior students.

COOPERATION OF SECONDARY SCHOOLS AND COLLEGES IN ACCELERATION OF GIFTED STUDENTS

by Morris Meister

BRONX COMMUNITY JUNIOR COLLEGE

A dictionary definition of the term *articulation* is "an act of joining; a junction point." Applied narrowly to the theme of our con-

[Reprinted from the *Journal of Educational Sociology*, 29, January 1956, 220-227, with the permission of the *Journal* and the author. At the time the article was written, Mr. Meister was principal of the Bronx High School of Science.]

ference, this definition calls attention to the point where high school stops for most students and college begins for about 20 percent of them. Since only one in five can or wants to make the connection all we need is a good sieve, that is, an effective college-admission procedure.

Until recently, this has been the somewhat oversimplified view of the problem of high-school-college articulation. The point of view has worked fairly well so long as high-school population was decreasing and college population remained fairly stable. High schools have been so busy devising ways of caring for the needs of the large numbers who will never go to college that they have not worried much about the different kinds of barriers erected by colleges, in the exercise of their sovereign right to control admissions. At the same time, the colleges have been complaining, in a mounting chorus, about the quality of preparation for college work among those they do accept for admission. Some of the complaint is justified.

But the population picture is changing rapidly. The children are now born, and in the lower schools who, in a few years, will be crowding the high schools to the point of explosion. Increasing popularity of the college degree in American culture is already affecting college enrollments, and on top of this the colleges must get ready to receive the explosive pressure of high-school graduates in the near future.

Most important, the critical shortage of trained manpower in all fields and especially in secondary and college teaching threatens to erode still further the quality of learning at both levels of our educational system. Thus, the problem of articulation becomes serious in a new dimension. What we seek is a good junction point in a *living* organism. We know that a living joint functions properly not when mere friction is eliminated, but when muscle tone, blood supply, and healthy nerve action are also present.

REAPPRAISAL DEMANDED

This view of articulation demands a reappraisal, for which the writer offers a number of suggestions and considerations, as follows: First, *we must conceive of cooperation between school and college as a two-way process.* There must be some "give" on both sides.

About four years ago, when the Fund for the Advancement of Education announced what is now referred to as the Early Admission to College program, the National Association of Secondary School Principals reacted rather sharply. In a statement addressed to its 12,000 members, dated May 4, 1951, these were the recommendations:

1. That we oppose the acceptance of any plan which will result in the curtailment of secondary education for youth even though it may be on a limited scale. That we advise with students, teachers, counselors, and parents of our schools and school communities accordingly.

2. That we recommend for college only youth who have completed the requirements for graduation in keeping with the policies of our regional accrediting agencies. On the basis of this policy that we recommend for college only youth who have completed the twelfth grade.

3. That we award secondary-school diplomas or equivalency certificates only to students who meet the required and established standards for graduation from the secondary schools.

4. That we use every means at our command to present to all the educational, community, and other meetings the implications of the unsound practice of curtailing secondary education and the subsequent admission of students to college before graduation. That we point out as effectively and as forcibly as possible these dangers, even with the alluring inducement of funds provided by the Ford Foundation. We must make citizens generally aware of the sinister implications of such a program especially if a scholarship award is offered to their sons.

5. That you as a principal or superintendent write now to the Director of Admissions of one or more of the four universities, stating your position on general policy of curtailment of secondary education. Address the institutions in this "experiment" with which you have closest relations.

Nevertheless, thousands of students accepted these scholarships. Judging by their experiences in twelve different colleges no serious educational tragedies have resulted. On the contrary, these early admitted students have fared better than expected, in every way. In our own school we have been following the experiences of about 50 or 60 of them who were yanked out before receiving a diploma. More than half of them have answered questionnaires to which they were not required to sign their names. All who answered said they feel their decision to accept the scholarship was a wise one, that they were doing well scholastically, that they have adjusted well socially and that they have encountered no unusual difficulties. Two negative replies are interesting. One said, "Yes, it is possible my social adjustment would have been better had I waited another year or two." Another said, "There is some social stigma to being a Ford student, but discretion will subdue it and prevarication remove it."

OPPOSITION TO EARLY COLLEGE ADMISSION

Of course, opposition to early college admission came just as sharply from the colleges. Despite the good results referred to above, most colleges remain unreconciled to the idea, as are indeed most of the high schools. What is a bit unexplainable is the fact that several colleges, while steadfastly refusing to admit any freshman younger than seventeen, will accept Ford scholarship money for a substantial number of sixteen-year-olds each year on the early admission plan. True cooperation, then, between schools and colleges will require less absolutism, more willingness to abandon sovereign rights, and greater attention to the facts of life in schools and in colleges.

Secondly, *we must sharpen our understanding of the term, acceleration, especially in its relationship to enrichment.* There is such a thing as *raw acceleration.* For example, skipping a grade in the lower school or ejecting a tenth or eleventh grader from high school into college, might be considered raw acceleration. This, however, is not the same as what is sometimes called *enriched acceleration.*

Traditionally, "acceleration" describes a school procedure which permits students to obtain a given amount of education in less than the normal amount of time. "Enrichment" refers to a procedure which gives students more education in the same time. In practice, however, these definitions are not as simple as the statements indicate. When dealing with real children, in actual classrooms of specific schools, manned and administered by available teachers and principals, the concepts of acceleration and enrichment become complicated and intertwined. The child who can accelerate gets many enrichments in the process. Also, he may or may not be losing in some other ways, not readily measurable. Even assuming that there *are* some losses, the latter are usually determined by whether he deviates markedly from the norm of his group. In a large company of accelerants, he may not be subject to social or emotional imbalance. Should enrichments rather than acceleration be provided for him, his individualized demands quickly outstrip the possibilities of the teacher's available time, energy, facilities, resources, and training. As a result, only a modicum of enrichment can ever be offered and the needs in some areas for *all* individuals are often neglected.

Acceleration and enrichment cannot be treated as a dichotomy. It is not a question of either or; but of how much of each. Each has its values and each its evils. There is as much danger of social and emotional imbalance from retardation as from acceleration. The question, as Terman puts it, is "How much risk of maladjustment can one afford to take in order to keep the gifted child at school tasks difficult enough to command his attention and respect? . . . No universal rule can be laid down governing the amount of acceleration that is desirable."

The fact is that enriched acceleration does take place. Every teacher of an honors class will testify to that and support his conviction with data derived from many kinds of educational yardsticks. A class of high-ability youth learns faster and more deeply; they grasp concepts more quickly and retain them longer; they apply knowledge more readily and think more creatively. The duration of time of schooling is hardly as important as the quality of the learning and the degree to which all individuals approach their capacity potential.

Thirdly, *we need more facts and more studies in the area of both raw and enriched acceleration.* We will know when to take calculated risks in the education of children when we know more about the nature of intellectual and social growth in individuals of different ability levels. Can we identify at the eighth-grade level the kind of child who can do the four-year high-school course in three years or two? And what, if anything, does he lose in the process? By what techniques may this loss be minimized? What kind of individual can be safely accelerated and/or enriched, to what extent, and how?

The evidence on accelerated students assembled by Dr. Sidney L. Pressey of Ohio State University and by Dr. D. A. Worcester of the University of Nebraska are most impressive, in this connection. While not a complete endorsement of raw acceleration, this evidence points decidedly to numerous advantages for enriched acceleration.

Fourthly, *enriched acceleration is an essential need for high-ability youth.* Difference in ability among students must be accepted as a fact of life. Schools must become more aware of these differences and exert more effort to identify them. The great American ideal of education for *all* the children must be reappraised in terms of equality of educational opportunity with identity of educational exposure. It is the essence of democracy to give each individual the opportunity to develop his capacities to their maximum potential.

Whenever these basic premises are posited, a welter of discussion follows. What do we mean by "high ability"? High ability of what kind? Giftedness of what sort? What kind of talent and what do we mean by talent? Is high intellectual ability the only kind the world wants and seeks? Is success in school synonymous with success in society? What about social leadership? What about talent in art or music, and mechanical ability? What about emotional stability and creativeness? There are no ready answers to these questions because the facts are few or nonexistent. In the meantime, schools and colleges must carry on with what they have; they must do the best they can. A major fraction of the time that faculties and students devote to school pursuits is devoted to learnings and the attitudes and character traits called for by these learnings. What we encounter most of all in these activities are individuals who learn more or less rapidly.

Until we know more about gifts and talents, let us do what we can for our *rapid learners.* We can not do less and we can do far worse. There is some evidence, too, that a substantially high, though not a perfect correlation, exists between rapid learning and many of the other talents that society values. The probabilities are high that most of our leaders will come from the rapid learners. We will, in this process, find, stimulate, and develop more leaders of all kinds than we will lose. If the rare genius "will out" anyway, then why be concerned? An educational program geared to the near-genius will certainly contribute to the conservation of human talent and reduce its waste.

It is from considerations of this kind that our school [the Bronx

High School of Science] and several others gladly entered the demonstration sponsored by the Fund for the Advancement of Education known as the School and College Study of Admission with Advanced Standing. We introduced six of the eleven courses: English literature and composition, biology, chemistry, physics, and mathematics. There are about twenty to twenty-five students in each class. Some students are taking four of the courses; some are taking three; most are taking two of the courses; a few are taking only one course.

THE BRONX PLAN

When we announced the plan two years ago, 250 students and their parents came to an evening conference to find out about it. At that time there was no assurance that any of the colleges would grant the credit. We told the students and parents how uncertain we were about our ability to teach college-type courses and that lots of hard work was in store for every student who registered. Nevertheless, more than one hundred students volunteered. Their overall records and their past performance in the courses they wished to pursue were carefully scrutinized. Not all were accepted. The final, screened group of about sixty were among the best, but not *the* best, in the school. Their ability-level would place them in the top 2 percent of the general high-school population.

There were, of course, many administrative and programing problems. Among these, three are worthy of mention.

1. *Selecting the Teacher.* The teachers did not rush to volunteer. A Ph.D. in chemistry on our staff steered clear of the job. Fortunately, at least one courageous teacher came forward in each of the six fields. While each of them is a well-qualified, well-trained, experienced person, they are, nevertheless, typical of high-school teachers in New York City.

2. *Teaching Load.* It was felt these teachers should not be required to carry the full high-school teacher's program of five classes each day. Instead, we assigned to each of them three high-school classes and one college-type class. This made necessary an additional teaching position which costs New York City an extra $7000 a year. As one can imagine, this was not a simple thing to accomplish; but our Board of Education is interested in high-ability youth. After two years of operation, we are convinced that

one class fewer per day is really not adequate. Should future educational budgets remove from our staff the extra teaching position we now enjoy, we would certainly drop the college-type courses.

3. *Teaching Equipment.* The problem in the sciences is especially acute and could not have been solved had it not been for a Ford grant of $4000 for the purchase of laboratory apparatus and materials we did not possess. It was not possible to use the funds normally allotted to the school for equipment, since that would have been too great a drain on the high-school courses. The textbooks and a few other instructional materials required in the college-type courses were purchased by the students.

In May 1954 the same tests in eleven subjects were administered to thousands of high-school seniors and college freshmen. The achievements of the high-school-taught seniors compared most favorably with college-taught freshmen.

In May 1955 the College Entrance Examination Board administered advanced placement tests to several hundred high-school seniors in twelve subject areas; 1240 were written in the six subjects in which our school was interested. The results indicate, in general, that the high-school students achieved in superior fashion in all of the areas.

PARTIAL EVALUATION

How has the work been going? To begin with, our school has never encountered such enthusiasm on the part of teachers, students, and parents. We are a bit worried about this. We are trying to curb the overzealous. We are insisting on a reasonable program of extra-curricular activities for all. In a few cases we have had to call in every guidance influence in order to insure a well-balanced program of daily activity. We try never to forget that these boys and girls are young adolescents. In the main, the response has been satisfactory.

Now that the Ford Foundation has removed its financial support, we are charging each student an instructional materials fee of ten dollars. Finally, *all high schools can not and all colleges will not cooperate in accelerating the rapid learner.*

Before a high school can consider a special program for the rapid learners, it must have identified and segregated enough of them for administrative purposes. Not only is this not done generally, but it is often avoided as an undesirable practice. In the sparsely populated areas of the country, the high-school population rarely exceeds 150. It is futile to talk of high-school college cooperation on behalf of high-ability students in a school which presents every teacher with the entire spectrum of abilities in every class. In such situations, I can see but a few ways out:

1. Raw acceleration.
2. Correspondence courses.
3. Districtwide consultants and special services.
4. Individualized instruction on the part of a master teacher (the kind a small school can rarely afford).

Cooperation of high school and college on behalf of rapid learners is highly feasible when sufficient numbers of them are identified and grouped. Here, three school devices have been used with good effect:

1. Honors groups, such as are found in the schools of New York City, the major-work groups in Cleveland, and the seminar classes in Portland, Oregon, and elsewhere.

2. The school within a school. "This concept posits a group of rapid learners of superior general ability as distinguished from those who may excel in a particular subject area. It assumes that a pupil of high intelligence may be expected to do well in many areas. It functions on the principle that the honor school with its separate organization, adviser, and special guidance services can do a better job in providing a full and rich program for the bright youngster. Also it can direct its attention more effectively toward the pupil who is not working up to his capacity. All this can be done without depriving young people of the opportunity to work and play with children of their own age of lesser ability." [1]

3. The specialized schools. There are four specialized high schools for the gifted in New York City. They are Brooklyn Technical High School, the High School of Music and Art, the Bronx High School of Science, and Stuyvesant High School. Each of these schools has a philosophy, an organization, a curriculum and equipment centering around a specific purpose, and each is designed to meet special needs, interests, abilities, and aims. Hunter High School does not have a special "purpose" in this sense, but, in common with the others, it admits students as a result of a highly com-

[1] Leo Weitz et al., The Rapid Learner in Our High Schools, New York: High School Principal Association, 1956.

petitive examination, so that its student body is composed of moderately and exceptionally gifted children.

As for the colleges, there are many who frown upon any kind of acceleration. We still hear remarks from certain college professors that they would rather that high schools taught no physics or chemistry at all; so that they would not need to undo the poor teaching in high schools. There are also some colleges whose curriculum organization, especially in the freshman year, makes impossible any consideration of advanced placement.

While the number of high schools and colleges where genuine cooperation in the best interests of the rapid learner is very large, the number of institutions where cooperation is feasible is larger. This is the great hope for those of us who are concerned with bridging the gap between high school and college. Unless the gap is bridged, our nation will continue to suffer from deterioration in the quality of education and from the waste of potential leaders.

WHAT RESEARCH SAYS ABOUT ACCELERATION

by Dan C. Shannon

SAN DIEGO UNIFIED SCHOOL DISTRICT

Educators are increasingly concerned about the education of gifted children. Some have attempted to enrich regular classwork. Others have accelerated the children. Many have talked about the problem of the gifted but have done nothing about it. Still others write negative articles using very fluent language. But what are the facts?

There has been a considerable volume of research done in the field of acceleration. While many educators dislike reading articles reporting research, they cannot escape the compulsion of the facts with which they deal. Just what does research say about acceleration? Let's take a good look.

A study was made by Keys and Wester among youths graduat-

[Reprinted from *Phi Delta Kappan*, 39, November 1957, 70-73, with the permission of Phi Delta Kappa and the author.]

ing from Oakland, California, high schools in the years 1934 and 1935. The group being studied was from one to three years younger than the control group, which was the normal age of high-school graduation. These two groups were matched by IQ, sex, father's occupation, and school class. Age was the only known variable. The findings were that the younger students took more scholarship honors, took part in more activities (even football), and were elected to more class offices. Shyness and timidity, which are terms often applied to gifted children who have been accelerated, were more common in the control group. "The few cases of serious problem behavior proved to be either bright but nonaccelerated controls, or accelerated pupils of only average intelligence." [1]

This isolated research might indicate that nothing is wrong with acceleration if used correctly, and it might indicate that acceleration used incorrectly can be harmful. Since the findings from one study cannot be considered conclusive, let us look at some more.

Margaret Alltucker gathered data from Berkeley High School in Berkeley, California. She states in her conclusions "that the pedagogically accelerated student is not as great a misfit in high school as he is commonly supposed to be." [2] She warns, however, that in cases where scholastic ability and physical development are not the same, careful counseling should be given. This is one accepted feature of any sane program using acceleration. Miss Alltucker's study was reported in 1924, and there are people who will say that children and schools thirty years ago were different. So let us look at a research project reported in 1953.

An experiment was conducted at the junior-high-school level. The experimental group completed a three-year junior high school in two years, while the control group completed it in the conventional length of time. It was found that the accelerated group measured slightly better in personal and social adjustment than the control group.[3]

These three research studies do not stand alone in their defense of acceleration as one practice to meet the needs of gifted children in school. Wilkins reported a study in which students were chosen

[1] N. Keys, "Adjustments of Under-age Students in High School," Psychol. Bull., 32, October 1935, 539.
[2] Margaret M. Alltucker, "Is the Pedagogically Accelerated Student a Misfit in the Senior High School?", School Rev., 32, March 1924, 193-202.
[3] J. Justman, "Personal and Social Adjustment of Intellectually Gifted Accelerants and Non-Accelerants in Junior High School," School Rev., 61, May 1953, 468-478.

by only one criterion, that they were at least one month younger than 17 years old at the time of high-school graduation. He has drawn the conclusion that "the activities of accelerated pupils in high school . . . are beneficial and healthful." [4]

At least one doctoral dissertation has been completed on the topic of acceleration. T. L. Engle did his work at the University of Indiana and studied children in some of the larger Indiana high schools. He reports that personal adjustment is not appreciably affected by acceleration.[5]

These studies have stressed the social and personal adjustment of the gifted children who were accelerated. What effect does acceleration have upon the academic success of the child? Since we can fairly conclude that acceleration, correctly administered, does not injure the child's personality, does it do him any good? What does research have to say to this question? Again, let us turn to the files.

As is the case of many thorough research studies, several phases of a problem were probed at one time in the project carried out by Keys and Wester in the Oakland Public high schools. For our purposes, however, the important finding was that the younger students did better scholastically than the older, matched groups. Remember that the two groups were matched for IQ, sex, father's occupation, and school class.[6]

One might feel by now that the author has "lifted" researches that support acceleration and left in the files those that do not support it. That is not the case. It is possible, of course, that researchers showing that acceleration is not useful and profitable have not been published.

It is true that not all researches have shown that the younger, accelerated group has done better in school than the control group of normal age youngsters. Unzicker,[7] Wilkins,[8] and Justman[9] all

---

[4] W. L. Wilkins, "The Social Adjustment of Accelerated Pupils," *School Rev.,* 44, June 1936, 445-455.
[5] T. L. Engle, "A Study of the Effects of School Acceleration upon the Personality and School Adjustment of High-school and University Students," *J. Educ. Psychol.,* 29, October 1938, 523-539.
[6] Keys, *op. cit.*
[7] S. P. Unzicker, "A Study of Acceleration in the Junior High School," *School Rev.,* 40, May 1932, 346-356.
[8] W. L. Wilkins, "High-school Achievement of Accelerated Pupils," *School Rev.,* 44, April 1936, 268-273.
[9] J. Justman, "Academic Achievement of Intellectually Gifted Accelerants and Non-Accelerants in Junior High School," *School Rev.,* 62, March 1954, 142-150.

conclude that there is little difference between the two groups in their achievement in high school or junior high. This is in itself significant, for if younger gifted children can maintain as good work as their older classmates, the fact strongly favors acceleration.

At this point we have seen that research has upheld acceleration on at least two points: (1) If properly used, acceleration of gifted children does not handicap them personally or socially. (2) Children who have been accelerated can maintain the quality of work done by their older classmates or even do better scholastic work at the high-school and junior-high level.

WHAT HAPPENS WHEN THEY ENTER COLLEGE

What happens, though, when these gifted, accelerated children leave high school and enter college? They were guided through the public schools without mishap and they did good classwork, even though they were younger than average. But when they reach college, will they be able to maintain this level of accomplishment? Again, research has the answer.

Two studies were conducted at the University of Buffalo. One, by Mary Sarabaugh, reports that younger students were compared with equally bright older ones. She found that the younger student keeps abreast scholastically, participates in extracurricular activities, continues his education as well as older matched pairs, likes his experience in acceleration, and would repeat it if he had the chance to do it again.[10] This is a pretty testimonial for acceleration!

THEY FOOLED THE PROFESSORS

A unique study was also conducted at the University of Buffalo by Ruth Eckert. This study came about because of a complaint of professors about the mature but bright versus the immature but bright students. The study consisted of a questionnaire asking professors to identify traits of maturity and to select, first, a bright and mature student, and, second, a bright but immature one. Cross checks were made of the completed questionnaires. In twenty-one

[10] Mary E. Sarabaugh, "The Younger College Student," *School and Society*, 40, December 15, 1934, 823-824.

cases, the same student was chosen both as mature and as immature. So it was shown that the professors could not agree on what constitutes maturity. Out of 135 mature choices, 44 individuals were chosen two times or more, but of the 123 immature choices only 18 were chosen two times or more. This shows that the professors could decide who were the mature students with more accord than who were the immature students. A comparison was made between the two groups of students and it was found that the mature group was *younger* at college entrance than the immature group. The mean age was 17.3 for the mature group and 17.4 for the immature group. This difference is not statistically significant, so it was concluded that chronological age is *not* the factor determining intellectual maturity.[11]

Perhaps the foremost authority of our time on problems of gifted children was Professor Terman of Stanford University. It was his opinion that acceleration should be encouraged. He arrived at this conclusion after performing a vast amount of research. He states that "children of 135 IQ or higher should be promoted sufficiently to permit college entrance by the age of 17 at latest . . . a majority in this group would be better off to enter at 16." [12]

As everyone knows, John Dewey stated that education is life. Many school people do not feel this way, though, and often claim that what might be all right for school is not good for life outside of school. The issue of acceleration is one that gets confused in this respect. Some educators claim that acceleration puts people through their schooling too quickly. Some speak of the oak tree that grows to full maturity in twenty to thirty years and of the squash plant that ripens in one season. To rush through school would make us like the squash. Such reasoning by analogy is absurd, of course. Why should anyone want to be like an acorn? Research, again, has an answer to the question about acceleration putting students through school too quickly.

S. L. Pressey has done a tremendous amount to research at Ohio State University on the topic of acceleration and its effect on adult life. Only two of his studies will be mentioned here. Pressey made a check of the graduates of Amherst College in relation to adult suc-

[11] Ruth E. Eckert, "Intellectual Maturity," *J. Higher Educ.*, 5, December 1934, 478-484.
[12] Lewis M. Terman and Metlita H. Oden, *The Gifted Child Grows Up*, Stanford, Calif.: Stanford Univ. Press, 1947, p. 281.

cess. Amherst College was selected because of its good alumni records. A rating scale, ranging from 7 to 0, was made that grouped successful persons as "internationally known," "nationally known," "locally known," "average success," "mediocre career," "unskilled worker," "failure (not self-supporting)," and "criminal or shady record." The alumni records of graduates were studied by two people who were not connected with the research study and were ranked according to the scale. If the two people made the same rating, it was accepted; if they disagreed by only one point on the scale, the lower figure was used. If there was more than one point in disagreement, a person working on the research study arbitrated the score. The following table gives a picture of the results of this research.[13]

Age of graduation		19	20	21	22	23	24	25	26	over 26
No. of graduates		24	114	216	235	132	59	47	37	60
After-college success	Nationally known (percent)	29	22	15	12	10	3	2	3	—
	Failures (percent)	4	6	6	5	2	3	6	11	15

Note how the percent of nationally known increases as the age at graduation decreases. This suggests that acceleration in school would not be harmful in adult life. Pressey states in his report that perhaps one reason the percent of nationally known graduates drops as the graduating age increases is that higher graduating age shortens the productive career. This line of thought was examined more thoroughly in another research by Pressey. In this study, two volumes of the *Dictionary of American Biography* and the 1942 volume of *Current Biography* were checked. It was found that the twenties are a very productive period in a person's life. This study indicates that early age in entering professional life is an argument in favor of acceleration of the gifted in school.[14]

Marie Flesher did a follow-up study of graduates from the College of Education at the University of Ohio. She paired 19- and 20-

[13] S. L. Pressey, "Age of College Graduation and Success in Adult Life," *J. App. Psychol.*, 30, June 1946, 226-233.
[14] Pressey and Arthur Combs, "Acceleration and Age of Productivity," *Educ. Res. Bull.*, 22, October 13, 1943, 191-196.

year-old graduates with older graduates of the same sex, general ability, and grade average. She thus avoided any argument that the accelerated students would have better success because they had been better students.

YOUNGER GRADUATES MORE SUCCESSFUL

Did they graduate too young? Were they immature? She concludes,

. . . the answer is an emphatic negative. These younger graduates outdid their elders in securing advanced degrees. A greater number of them secured teaching positions immediately after graduation. The younger women demonstrated success equal to that of their olders sisters in securing mates. More of them were able to secure top salaries in the teaching professions. They impressed their school administrators more favorably as teachers. Throughout, the record of the younger graduates is as good, or better than, that of the olders.[15]

Research, cold research, is the reporting of fact as discovered by scientific probing. Many educators prefer not to listen to research. It may say things that they are not willing to listen to. This seems to be true in the area under discussion.

ACCELERATION STILL UNDER SUSPICION

Frank Wilson[16] discovered that fewer than half of the respondents to a questionnaire he devised favored acceleration to the extent that Professor Terman does. Wilson asked in his questionnaire if the respondents agreed with the opinion of Professor Terman as quoted earlier in this article. Wilson found that people connected with colleges and universities agreed with the Terman statement more commonly than public-school people. Could this indicate that those connected with colleges and universities tend to form their opinions from research findings more readily than those connected with public schools? Hardly.

[15] Marie A. Flesher, "Did They Graduate Too Young?", *Educ. Res. Bull.*, 24, November 14, 1945, 218-221.
[16] F. T. Wilson, "Educators' Opinions about Acceleration of Gifted Students," *School and Society*, 80, October 16, 1954, 120-122.

The real significance of Wilson's research is that nearly 50 percent of all the respondents favored some acceleration. With this fact in mind when he reads articles that debunk acceleration as a means of adjusting the school's program for the gifted, one can retain his sense of balance. There are many believers in the value of acceleration, even though they may not be heard from often.

7

ADJUSTMENT

THE ADJUSTMENT of gifted individuals has been of considerable concern to parents and teachers recently. Fortunately, we are outgrowing the idea that the bright and gifted are eccentric and destined to lead poorly adjusted lives. But as we outgrow some of the misconceptions which have hindered public acceptance of giftedness, we are learning more of the complexities involved in the personalities of the gifted. The very characteristics of giftedness cause some adjustment problems.

Early development, wide interests, and ease of understanding help gifted children to solve their problems more quickly, but also create many problems. In the studies that have been reported so far it has been found that gifted children are on the whole superior to the average in personal adjustment. Terman and Oden found their large sample to be well adjusted socially both in childhood and adulthood. Moreover, in comparing the people in their study who possessed the highest IQs (1 out of 1000) with those of relatively lower IQs (1 out of 100), they did not find more maladjustment among those with the highest IQs. Leta S. Hollingworth, however, found that children with the highest IQ (1 in 1000) are likely to have special adjustment problems. Most studies have indicated that the truly gifted person is usually endowed with a superior physique and mind. His physical vitality and his mental ability enable him to deal with stresses and to correct undesirable emotional conditions or personality trends. Another characteristic of the gifted is a superior capacity for self diagnosis. Whether insight is evidence of adjustment or a step toward adjustment, it probably requires a fairly high degree of intelligence. Despite their superior insight and adaptability, some gifted individuals are so emotionally disturbed that they fail to make a satisfying social or personal adjustment. Almost all of the problems of the gifted result from the blocking or denial of normal satisfactions.

Like other children, the gifted must be considered and treated as individuals. There are two reasons why investigations do not always reveal the role of intelligence in personal adjustment: (1) The sampling may not have included emotionally unstable bright children, who would have been unable to show their true capacity on

328

the tests, and (2) the major measures of personality that have been used may also be, to some extent, measures of intelligence.

Gifted children sometimes experience feelings of inferiority even though they are superior in so many ways. A gifted child is especially likely to feel inferior in developing physical skills or in other activities where it takes him longer to become proficient than in mental activities. When the gifted child loses interest in thinking, playing, and working at the relatively immature level of his chronological peers, he sometimes withdraws from social contacts and engages in solitary pursuits. The ability to deal with problems by reasoning is so highly valued that it is sometimes used to excess. Such is the case when the gifted child uses his intelligence to gain the approval of parents and teachers, but in so doing he over-emphasizes the intellect and fails to receive the greater gratifications based on emotional acceptance and belonging. Other causes of poor adjustment are parental or teacher pressure and exploitation, and the opposite reaction by adults—indifference and neglect. Poor school achievement is also associated with adjustment problems, but that aspect of the problem is considered in Section 8. Each case has its own peculiar combination of factors which are likely to be complexly interrelated.

The material in this section pertains to students enrolled in traditional classes. Some additional information about the personal and social adjustment of pupils in special classes is found in Section 10. The articles by Barbe, Mann, Smith, and the Ford Foundation are particularly appropriate. Other related data by Terman, Lewis, Laycock, and Doll is found in Section 2.

The first article in this section is a summary by Douglas A. Thom and Nancy L. Newell of a follow-up study of 43 children with 1916 Binet IQs of 130 or above who had been referred to the Massachusetts Division of Mental Hygiene approximately 11 years prior to the study. Upon retesting, their IQs were uniformly high and most of the disciplinary problems, for which they had been referred, had disappeared under the guidance of the clinic. A description of the family and subject backgrounds is provided.

In the second article James J. Gallagher and Thora G. Crowder processed 35 gifted children attending grades two to five by the case-study method. These subjects possessed a Stanford-Binet IQ of 150 or above, and were drawn from the schools of the community. The purpose of the study was to discover the extent to which highly intelligent children have difficulty adjusting to a regular classroom situation academically, intellectually, socially, and emotionally. Gallagher and Crowder were both affiliated with the University of Illinois Institute for Research with Exceptional Children when the project was underway.

In the following study Robert V. Miller analyzes the differences between mentally superior, mentally typical, and mentally retarded children in upper elementary classrooms with regard to sociometrically ascertained social status and socioempathic abilities.

"The Temperament of Gifted Children" by Marcella Ryser Bonsall and Buford Stefflre is an analysis of the scores of over 1300 white secondary-school senior boys who took both the SRA Primary Mental Abilities test and the Guilford-Zimmerman Temperament Survey. Bonsall and Stefflre concluded that the superior temperament of the gifted stems much more from the socioeconomic level at which most gifted children are found than from any other difference in gifted children as such.

The final article is an analysis of compositions on the subject "How It Feels to Be Growing Up" written by 1124 pupils in grades seven through twelve. The analysis by Ruth Strang contributes to our understanding about the way in which gifted adolescents perceive the growing-up process and the ways in which they are alike and different from their age mates of lower intelligence. Dr. Strang, a professor at Columbia University since 1940, has long been regarded as an authority on child and adolescent psychology.

HAZARDS OF THE HIGH IQ

by Douglas A. Thom
and Nancy L. Newell

Very little recognition has been given to the fact that extremely high intelligence is as far from normal as is mental deficiency and that it creates problems of its own that may be acute, though not as depressing, as the problems of inferior intelligence. In psychological theory, the range of normal intelligence runs from the dull, borderline mentality, at 70 IQ, to the very superior level of 130 IQ, or thirty points of divergence from 100 IQ, which represents the average performance of children at given age levels.

An eight-year-old child with an IQ of 70 may be normal in size and appearance, and mannerly if he has been well trained. He has, however, the mentality of five and one half years and is hardly ready to learn to read. If he is placed in first grade, he may be embarrassed by his size and be subjected to teasing and to the humiliation of failure. He cannot hold his own with children of his own age and may become quarrelsome, or take refuge with adults who give him special consideration.

On the other hand, the eight-year-old child with an IQ of 130 may also be normal in size and appearance, but he has the mentality of ten and one half years, which throws his adjustment to his group also out of balance. He learns his lessons quickly, is bored with the activities of third grade, and may work off his excess energy in unprofitable mischief. He attracts attention by his clever remarks and develops a desire for the center of the stage. He bosses children of his own age, but is rejected by older and larger children whose interests fascinate him and challenge his ability to compete with them. He is still only eight years old in physical skills, in dependence upon parents, in emotional experience, and in a certain naïveté, which is charming, but which may be a dangerous pitfall if he tries to capitalize it.

[Reprinted from *Mental Hygiene*, 29, January 1945, 61-77, with the permission of *Mental Hygiene*.]

Children of high intelligence who develop personality problems are reported to be less likely to retain their problems than children of lower intelligence.[1] In the course of time, their intelligence enables them to recognize the advantages of conformity to established custom, and they discard undesirable forms of behavior which they see are going to be unprofitable to them. Nevertheless, disturbances of personality are deep-rooted; early environmental experiences leave their mark in conditioned reactions which, by repetition, become permanent traits.

In an effort to examine the interplay of high intelligence with personality factors, the authors, through the Massachusetts Division of Mental Hygiene, made a follow-up study of 43 children of IQs above 130 who had been seen in the child-guidance clinics between 1927 and 1934. The interval of time between the first contact and the follow-up averaged eleven years. The children came to the clinics because of some problem of management or educational placement sufficiently troublesome for the parents to seek advice.

The objects of the study were to check the correctness of the original diagnosis and treatment; to learn what methods of training the parents had used; to find out how the children had reacted to the problem of their own superiority; to discover what factors had contributed to success or failure in their adjustment.

THE HIGH IQ PERSISTS

Of the 43 children 38 were available for re-examination, and tests were selected which corresponded as closely as possible to the original Stanford-Binet (1916 revision) which had been given when the children's ages ranged from two to ten years. Their IQs on this test had ranged from 130 to 166, with the mean or average for the group at IQ 139. The results of the re-examination were unexpectedly consistent. The children at this time were from ten to twenty years of age, their IQs ranged from 106 to 161, but only one, a boy who had been twenty-three months of age at the time of the first test, fell below 120. The average for the group was 135 IQ on the Stanford-Binet (1937 revision) and 125 IQ on the Wechsler-

[1] See Leta Hollingworth, "The Child of Very Superior Intelligence as a Special Problem in Social Development," *Mental Hygiene,* 15, January 1931, 3-16, and D. A. Thom and F. S. Johnston, "Time as a Factor in the Solution of Delinquency," *Mental Hygiene,* 25, April 1941, 269-287.

Bellevue test. This decrease in average IQ was not significant in view of the advanced ages of the children and the well-known inadequacies of tests to measure the abilities of older adolescents.

Particularly interesting was the discovery that the IQs of 24 children who had been under school age at the time of the first examination fulfilled the predictions of superiority as satisfactorily as the IQs of children of school age, for whom intelligence tests are considered to be best adapted. Although intelligence tests may be unreliable in discriminating within the middle range of very young children, nevertheless, a child who shows exceptional ability in these early years may be expected to maintain superiority as he grows older.

STATISTICAL COMPARISON OF THE GROUP

For the entire group of 38 children, the problem of making a statistical comparison of the results of the first and second examinations presented difficulties because of the diversity of ages of the children and the variety of tests necessarily used in the second examination. A presentation of individual IQs would have been meaningless without prolonged interpretation. It seemed more reasonable, therefore, to present the results graphically in terms of deviations from the means or averages of the group in both tests.

In the diagram on page 334 the mean of the group in the first test is represented by the horizontal axis. Deviations from the mean in points of IQ are indicated above and below this axis. The mean of the retest is represented by the vertical axis, with deviations of IQ that are above the mean extending to the left, and deviations below the mean extending to the right.

It will readily be seen that the cases that lie in Section A were above the mean in both the first and second tests, as they are above the horizontal axis and to the right of the vertical axis. The cases that lie in Section B had fallen from above the mean in the first test to a position below the mean in the second test; whereas the cases in Section C had risen from below the mean in the first test to a position above the mean in the second test.

The cases that lie within the square are within the mean deviation on both tests, and represent children whose relative positions in the two tests were fairly consistent. The cases outside this square need explanation. In Section A, cases 1 and 2 are now college students, both of whom lost thirteen points in deviation on the second test. We may assume that their abilities are better represented by the tests given at the age of eight than at ages seventeen and nineteen, as both have made outstanding achievements. Case 3 shows perfect consistency of IQ at a high level. It is interesting that this boy has had a disturbed home life and has done indifferent work in school, but has always rated high in tests. Cases 4 and 5 were three years and seven months of age and four years and three

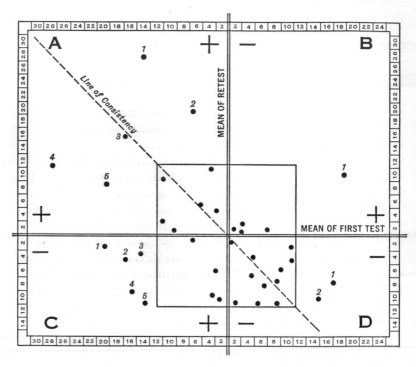

months of age respectively when first tested. Their gains in the retest, at ages eleven and thirteen years, probably represent the greater adequacy of tests at this age level and also favorable environmental factors.

In Section B, case 1 is the precocious infant whose IQ dropped from 148 to 106. He is doing good work in high school.

In Section D, cases 1 and 2 are those of girls whose environmental influences during the interval have been adverse.

In Section C, where significant gains have been made on the

second test, cases 2 and 4 were two years and four months of age and three years and eight months of age respectively at the time of the first test, and their abilities are probably better represented by the later test. Case 4 had special opportunities in a semiprivate academy, where she won a four-year scholarship, showed marked qualities of leadership, and graduated with the highest honors and a scholarship for college.

Cases 1 and 3 were seven years old and six years old respectively when first tested. Case 1 set his heart on a military career and deliberately failed in Latin School when the war broke out, in an attempt to force his parents to consent to his enlistment, but he gave his best effort to the psychological test. Case 3 was a "quiz kid" on a local program for more than a year. His school record was unsatisfactory as he had poor habits of work and neglected his lessons to concentrate upon his special interests, which were informational and literary.

Case 5 was at the time of the first test ten years old and was involved in the marital difficulties of his parents. The parental situation is now greatly improved. The boy is in college, and is mature and self-reliant. He shows a gain of IQ instead of the usual loss at this age and has gained significantly in respect to his position in the group (from 9 below the mean in the first test to 11 above the mean in the second).

In conclusion, difference of level between the first and second tests may be attributed to the varying efficiency of tests at different age levels and to favorable or adverse factors in the environment. It is with the appraisal of these factors that the latter part of this study is primarily concerned.

THE HOMES OF THE CHILDREN

The parents of these children were, in most cases, interested and willing to discuss problems of family life and to give information that would show what sort of homes produced these superior children. Were they prosperous homes, with advantages of leisure and luxury? Were they happy homes? Were the prosperous families happier than those with precarious incomes?

In 24 homes, there had been security and comfort, with varying degrees of luxury and expensive advantages for the children. In 19 homes, the incomes had been irregular or marginal, requiring careful economy; while in five homes there had been periods of actual dependency during the depression.

In 27 homes there had been a harmonious family life, with unity of aims and sharing of interests and privileges. In 16 homes, there had been indifference, selfishness, or conflict, which in five cases had resulted in divorce.

The question naturally suggested itself as to whether there was any correlation between the 24 families with comfortable incomes and the 27 homes in which there was solidarity or harmony, and whether there was any relationship between parental conflict and economic stress. Interestingly, there appeared to be no correlation between economic level and family solidarity, as harmony was found in 15 of the 24 prosperous homes and in 12 of the 19 precarious homes. In the latter group, the parents had compensated for financial restrictions by intelligent planning of family activities through the use of facilities that did not involve much expense. The planning of projects and the sharing of privation had contributed to the unity and happiness of the families. In those homes of the precarious group in which the parents were not harmonious, however, the conflict had been aggravated by financial stress.

In conclusion, it appears that the children of the study came chiefly from families of moderate degrees of both economic security and economic stress, and that financial status bears little relationship to the ability of parents to provide happy homes and to make satisfactory family adjustments.

THE PARENTS

One is inclined to expect high intelligence and advanced education in the parents of very brilliant children, so it was surprising to find an educational level that was moderately, but not exceptionally, high. Approximately one half of both fathers and mothers were graduates of high schools; eight fathers and nine mothers were graduates of colleges; four fathers and six mothers had not progressed beyond the elementary grades; and the remainder of the parents had had a smattering of high-school education.

Six fathers were practicing in professions; 14 others held positions of responsibilities; the remaining fathers who were living held various minor positions. Of the mothers, 22 had been engaged in business, 13 had practiced minor professions, two had been factory workers, and six had never been employed.

It was interesting that 41 mothers professed definite religious affiliations. In only three cases was there conflict in religious matters. More than half of the children were actively interested in church affairs and several were seriously concerned. The weight and quality of religious background was definitely high.

Nine fathers and 10 mothers were from foreign-speaking nations; 17 fathers and 20 mothers had foreign-born parents, many of whom had emigrated to escape poverty or persecution. Among the families of foreign extraction, there had been great effort to improve the status of the family, to take advantage of educational opportunities, and to prepare for vocational success. This was most marked among the seven Jewish families, some whose forebears were uneducated according to American standards, but had had a thorough training in Hebrew culture and were religious leaders.

There were four families with Indian blood, and the precocious infant had a mixture of French, German, Negro, and Indian ancestry.

Individual ancestors provided some interesting material, which can be reported only briefly. Three families were descendants of prosperous Tories who fled to Canada during the American Revolution. All three families had brilliant and talented members. One boy was fathered by a descendant of a famous inventor whose genius revolutionized the textile industry in England; collateral relatives had been active in colonial affairs, and there have been professional men in the family through four generations. The mother of this boy was descended from a Dutch pioneer who founded a religious settlement in America and traveled through the colonies teaching the art of grafting trees. This family includes a prominent politician and a nationally known philanthropist.

Other interesting forebears were the president of a college, the president of a large bank, a mathematical genius, several noted artists and musicians, two state governors, a celebrated actress, and several famous novelists.

Unfavorable tendencies occurred in 17 families. There were seven neurotic and four unstable mothers, two neurotic fathers, and two alcoholic and delinquent fathers, one of whom was "the black sheep" of a good family. Among grandparents, there were two cases of alcoholism and three cases of mental disease.

PARENTAL PERPLEXITIES

There was a good deal of bewilderment among the comfortably intelligent parents who had unexpectedly produced exceptional offspring. Their attitudes varied between the extreme conceit of the couple who were convinced of the genius of their child from the moment of birth, to the skepticism of the mother who would not admit any superiority in her daughter.

Seven parents had gratified their own vanity by boasting about their children and exploiting their cleverness at every opportunity. Eleven had pushed and overstimulated their children beyond their capacity to maintain a balanced adjustment. Fifteen had been possessive and overprotective to such a degree that the children had become seclusive, bookish, or abnormally shy. Seven parents were deferential to, or actually afraid of, the ability of their offspring to outwit or circumvent them. Seven parents, who had attempted forcibly to repress the effervescent precocity of their children, had become involved in an undeclared war in which mutiny, conflict, and antagonism were the order of the day.

Problems of discipline were much more in evidence at the time of the first contact when the children were younger. Twenty-two children were being handled with inconsistent methods because the parents or other relatives were operating on differing theories of management, or because the mother was at times overlenient and at other times oversevere. Seventeen children were being subjected to corporal punishment, and ten were contemptuous of authority. Most of these early disciplinary problems were resolved under the guidance of the clinic, and the cases were closed as improved or recovered.

During the years intervening between the first and the second contacts, problems of behavior had practically disappeared, but, in some cases, had been replaced by problems of personality and undesirable attitudes. Twenty-eight children were being managed easily by reasoning, while twelve remained difficult or defiant, and three had continued to rule tyrannically in the home. In general, the early misbehavior may be attributed to the aggressiveness and the self-assertion of the brilliant child who is testing his wit and will against the forces of his environment. With increasing maturity and understanding, he recognizes the value of social adaptation and turns his aggressiveness into acceptable channels, which lead to satisfying achievements and worthwhile pleasures.

No child in the group was without love from one parent or the other. Only 15 of the 43 children had received wise management, which had given freedom of activity within suitable limits so that they were able gradually to assume responsibility for their personal affairs.

HEALTH OF THE CHILDREN

At the time of the follow-up study, all of the 43 children were in good health. All but one had been full-term pregnancies; 36 were first-born and, although 22 had had instrumental deliveries, only four had been injured. Only 11 were "only children" and families were small, averaging 2.3 children per family. There were 14 children who had had serious diseases and 12 who had suffered from various chronic complaints previous to adolescence. There were 12 cases of poor vision requiring lenses.

Of this group, 15 children were left-handed or ambidextrous; six of them had been trained to use the right hand, four had speech difficulties, and six were extremely poor writers.

SCHOOL HISTORIES

The educational history of the group was relatively disappointing. Of the 43 children 24 had attended kindergarten and 15 had learned to read before entering first grade. At the time of the first contact, 12 had skipped a grade or had entered school a year early. At the time of the second contact, 34 had received high marks, 19 had been honor students, and nine had won awards, varying from prizes to college scholarships. At that time 16 had graduated from high school, three from vocational schools, and four from colleges.

Of 20 pupils remaining in school, 14 were a year or more advanced in grade placement. Nine children had disliked school, and five had done poor work.

Although these attainments appear to be gratifying, they seem to have been achieved principally through the energy and initiative of the children themselves. The schools had little to offer them in the way of special opportunities. In many instances, superior ability had not been recognized, particularly in pupils who were competing in an older group. In only five cases had any enrichment of program been provided.

One boy had been penalized by poor marks for lack of effort. He tossed off his lessons without effort and then relieved his boredom by attempting to run the class, which annoyed the teacher and provided him with some interesting diversion. Several boys were so antagonistic that they refused to do well lest they outshine their classmates. The boy of remarkable ancestry, whose psychological rating was close to genius, was submerged in a large high school. He was doing well in a college preparatory class, but, because of his retiring disposition, he was completely overlooked as an intellectual rarity. Three other children, who had made poor records in public school, blossomed into high accomplishment when transferred to private schools, where their potentialities and emotional adjustment were given individual attention. A bright girl from an impoverished home had been placed in a domestic-science course, which fitted her neither for further education nor for earning a living commensurate with her ability.

On the other hand, two children, whose parents had tried to impose scholastic advantages beyond their social and emotional maturity, had become so maladjusted that their education was a complete failure and they were unfitted to go on with the higher education which had been planned for them.

The boy who obtained the highest psychological rating was normally placed in school for his age in fifth grade. The clinic recommended that he remain there for the present because he was very small for his age and the school had nothing to offer other than double promotion. He was supplying his own enrichment by reading formidable literature which he preferred to playing childish games. In school he monopolized prizes and honors without effort, and he lacked the stabilizing influence of wholesome competition.

The children whose abilities had been recognized at school

were those who had been aggressive and socially well adjusted, and who had striven for honors and awards. The more retiring students had often been overlooked and, from the clinical point of view, had lacked guidance in utilizing their abilities and in making personal adjustments.

PERSONALITY PROBLEMS

The problems for which these children originally attended the clinic were chiefly the normal problems of childhood in connection with eating, sleeping, elimination, and discipline. The clinic looks upon such manifestations as symptoms indicative of emotional maladjustment and tries to correct or to modify the conditions that produced the symptoms instead of treating the symptoms themselves. As previously suggested, most of the immediate difficulties were eliminated under clinic therapy.

The personalities of the children were discussed with the parents on the basis of 36 character traits. The traits that appeared most frequently were happiness, energy, generosity, independence, and persistence. The traits that appeared least frequently were selfishness, dependence, and jealousy.

During the interval between the first and second contacts, there was an increase of confidence, conscientiousness, cooperation, and ambition, while a marked decrease appeared in the undesirable traits of stubbornness, defiance, negativism, and a tendency to "show off." The group as a whole gave a delightful impression of vitality, exuberant spirits, and worthwhile interests.

The social adjustment of these precocious children was difficult. The very young children, at the time of the first contact, were amusing themselves with imaginative play and with comradeship or conflict with their mothers. As they grew older, there was a tendency to prefer older playmates and to seek the companionship of adults. The discrepancy between intellectual and social development led to preoccupation with lonely pursuits, so that in some cases the parents were obliged to force the children to join groups at play. Some of the children who were leaders in school had few companions outside of school hours. Fifteen children, however, had developed qualities of leadership and were making an excellent adjustment in all sorts of activities.

In an attempt to analyze the factors that had contributed to the excellent development of some of the superior children, and to the less satisfactory developments of others, a division of the children was made into two groups on criteria not only of scholastic achievement, but also of personality factors and present adjustment to life situations. Half of the children (21 cases) had attained a high level of development and had fulfilled the potentialities that were found in the early contacts. The other half (22 cases) had achieved only mediocre success or were definitely maladjusted or unhappy.

TWENTY-ONE SUCCESSFUL CASES

In the group of successful cases, home conditions were predominantly good or had improved during the interval between first and second contacts; 15 children had had economic security, and 16 had had harmonious homes.

Of the 21 successful cases, 14 children had received wise and beneficial guidance. Training had been consistent in early childhood, and punishment had taken the form of penalties rather than of chastisement. Several mothers had profited by the advice of the clinic in avoiding the interference of relatives and in adopting less emotional attitudes toward childish self-assertion. These 14 children were so active and happy, and their lives so filled with engrossing interests, that they were refreshingly unconcerned with their superiority. The parents had made a special effort to preserve normality and to uphold good standards of conduct.

One outstanding girl, an only child, had been taught by her invalid mother to make decisions for herself, to use her gifts for the benefit of others, and to accept humbly the honors and admiration that were heaped upon her. Graduating from college at twenty, she was popular and gay, thoughtful of her parents, but not restricted even by the invalidism of her mother and eager to specialize in a profession in which she could render her best service.

Another girl, who also was graduating from college at twenty, had been guided and encouraged by a stepmother who had assumed the care of four small neglected children after the death of an intellectual, but highly impractical, mother. As the home was in a poor neighborhood, the girl had no suitable friends until she went to college. With her stepmother's help, however, she made a good adjustment, was prominent in college activities, and served as an assistant instructor. Her three brothers also made enviable records.

An interesting adopted girl, now in high school, has been so much more agile mentally than her adoptive parents that they have had their bewildering moments, but with patience and love they have guided her through some trying episodes and have been rewarded by her increasing stability and good achievement.

In the other seven successful cases, early training had been lax and inconsistent, or there had been antagonism and friction in the home, but these children eventually rose above these handicaps and, with increasing independence of family influences, were able to make satisfactory adaptation. In this group was the boy who deliberately flunked Latin School, but he was more effective than his parents in controlling his unruly younger brothers, and was a respected leader among his friends. Here also was the arrogant boy whose lack of effort had been penalized by his teacher. He was later entered in one of the larger private preparatory schools, where his desire for prestige may be both satisfied and curtailed.

A girl, now eleven years old, had been monopolized by her mother to compensate for the indifference of the husband, but in spite of overpossessive and indulgent training, she showed promise of well-balanced adjustment.

Another girl, who had been set on a pedestal as her father's favorite, was so upset by loss of prestige to her equally bright sisters that she failed miserably in a large high school, thereby further alienating her father. When she was transferred to a private school, she regained her confidence, took her college examinations against the advice of the school, and passed them "with flying colors." She felt herself restored to favor and gained self-reliance from the experience.

A boy, who had been taken by an elderly grandmother because his home had been broken by divorce, and who had languished in effeminacy and loneliness in a city school, blossomed into honors and leadership in a suburban town under the care of an intelligent young stepmother.

A twenty-year-old boy of exceptional ancestry had been bandied about among relatives as a result of the unfortunate marriage of his spoiled and willful mother, who had treated him with alternate overindulgence and cruelty. Escaping from his predicament at last by enlistment in the army, he earned rapid advancement in the artillery by his mathematical ability. His patience and generosity to his mother indicated a high quality of character.

In this group of 21 successful children, wise guidance and favorable circumstances contributed to the development of 14 of the cases, whereas the remaining seven overcame various handicaps by means of their own initiative and personal qualities.

TWENTY-TWO LESS SUCCESSFUL CASES

In the group of cases that showed only moderate success or actual failure, home conditions had been less favorable. Only nine families had had economic security, and 13 had suffered financial distress. In 12 homes there had been the scene of domestic conflict, and only one child had had security, harmony, and good training. This boy had been adopted to fill a woman's emotional need, had received devoted care, and had never been told of his adoption. His personality was charming, but his school work was only fair and he displayed no unusual ability.

In the 21 remaining cases of the less successful group, there was a greater degree of nervous instability among the parents or grandparents which may have affected the children either by inheritance or by association. Of the 17 families in which unfavorable familial tendencies had occurred, 13 were included in this group, whereas among the successful children only four instances of unfavorable family relationships were found.

The parents of the less successful children reflected a greater degree of vanity and more dissatisfaction when their children did not make a spectacular showing. Seven children had been overstimulated, and had reacted with a good deal of antagonism or fear of failure. Nine mothers had used corporal punishment, and three were still whipping boys who were from ten to fourteen years of age. Seven children had been overprotected, and in 16 cases marked favoritism had been shown for the child by one parent or the other. On the other hand, six mothers had rejected our clients in favor of a brother or sister. One such girl had transferred her affection to a brilliant and capable aunt, with unpleasant consequences in the household. She defied parental restraint, escaped to the aunt, and filled her time with expensive and erratic pursuits.

The child whose parents expected her to be a genius lived in a haphazard household where every one was allowed full liberty of self-development. At the age of eight, she had been removed from school after a quarrel about her placement, and had been irregularly instructed by tutors. At the age of sixteen, she had not completed the requirements of the eighth grade, but talked fluently and superficially on philosophy, psychology, and the arts. She was desperately trying to find a short cut to a profession that she considered worthy of her genius, and was becoming pathetically aware of her plight as she began to see the inadequacy of her preparation.

Two boys had been idolized and exploited by overdevoted mothers. One was submissive, seclusive, and unhappy. The other, the former "quiz kid," was so maladjusted scholastically that he was sent to a private school to be brought up to standards in subjects that he disliked and had neglected.

Another disturbed boy had been in bitter conflict with a stepmother who had taken him from a doting grandmother in order to give him the discipline she thought he needed. With her he adopted the attitude of a "whipped dog," but he retaliated by committing all sorts of petty misdemeanors in the community and by doing little else at school than reading and rating high in psychological tests. He flunked college after winning a scholarship. Finally he enlisted in the army and made a fine record in the air force. He adjusted well to the impersonal type of discipline, but was homesick. From the distance that lends enchantment, he expressed appreciation of his stepmother's efforts to bring him up properly.

Another boy, the only son in an ambitious family, had been forced ahead in various private schools at an early age. He had managed to evade fundamental courses and was not equipped for college, but he had developed dramatic and artistic talent and wanted to become an actor. No doubt the stage seemed to offer him publicly the recognition he had failed to obtain from his family. He finally specialized in accounting, to please his father, and astonished every one by an excellent record. He hoped, in spite of poor vision, to be accepted for war service, where he could use his mathematical ability.

A girl, who originally came to the clinic because of nightmares about fire, had been overexcited by a neurotic and timid mother, and favored by a clever and charming father. When he remarried after the mother's death, the daughter and stepmother engaged in a relentless duel which kept the home and the younger children in an uproar until the girl finally graduated from high school—where she had been a model of deportment—and became self-supporting. She was successful in her job, but was lonely and resentful, and continued to harass her family at long range.

A Jewish girl, who had been overawed by a tyrannical older brother, gained self-confidence away from home at a junior college. She was determined to defend herself, and the conflict resulted in a nervous breakdown in the mother.

Another girl, who had been suppressed by a dominating mother, found release for her abilities and expansion of her personality in the profession of nursing.

Three girls in this less successful group had been left fatherless by death or desertion, and had been casually supervised while their mothers took up the economic struggle. Two of them became headstrong and willful, refusing to be advised or restrained. They preferred to learn the lessons of life the hard way and were employed at very ordinary jobs. The third girl, who had been overprotected and indulged during her father's life, found uncongenial work in a factory. She insisted that because she was Jewish she was handicapped by racial discrimination, and used this as an excuse for her failure to make an effort to improve her position.

In this group of cases, emotional instability, false standards of the parents, and poor methods of training, as well as individual misfortunes and adverse circumstances, prevented the best development of the children, although psychological tests showed a persistence of their superior ability.

CONCLUSIONS

Although the number of children included in this study was small and an evaluation of the interplay of intangible factors was baffling in prospect, nevertheless, in the actual process of study, certain elements that had contributed to success or failure projected themselves in sharp relief.

The consistency of the later examinations indicated that the early psychological tests were reliable and predictive of continuing ability. The success or failure of the individual child, however, depended upon factors other than his numerical intelligence quotient.

Economic advantages above the low level of distress had little effect upon success or failure, but a happy and harmonious home life was definitely favorable to good development. Some children, however, were able to overcome adverse factors of home life as they approached maturity and were able to use their intelligence in the solution of their own problems.

Probably the most definite contribution to success was consistent and reasonable training in the very early years, because it accustomed the children to orderly and useful habits and attitudes. The acceptance of regulations that are for the good of all precluded the unfortunate philosophy so frequently observed among children that one must be naughty to have fun and that an audience must be secured at any price.

The children who had been kept in normal relationship in family and social life made the best adjustments as they matured; those who failed in fulfillment had been hampered by family instability or unfortunate environmental conditions.

From a clinical point of view, a need was revealed for a closer relationship of schools with social and clinical services in order to relieve emotional pressures and to help individual children to overcome their difficulties. Otherwise, they cannot utilize their abilities to the best advantage.

Public schools have, on the whole, offered little in the way of specialized opportunities for superior children because this group gets along creditably in the program geared to the average child. Handicapped and retarded pupils, who are unable to adjust to regular classes, have been provided with various types of special classes. For the superior group, there is no emotional appeal to pity or protection such as has been used to obtain appropriations for the education of the handicapped and retarded group.

It is time for the public to awaken to a realization of the neglect of a national asset that can be of inestimable value in the solution of the difficult civic problems that loom ahead. In a democracy, where many intelligent leaders are urgently needed, unusual abilities should not be allowed to go to waste, but should be developed for clear thinking and sound judgment, and should be directed toward goals of human service rather than those of self-aggrandizement.

~~~~~~

ADJUSTMENT OF GIFTED CHILDREN IN THE REGULAR CLASSROOM

by James J. Gallagher

UNIVERSITY OF ILLINOIS

and Thora H. Crowder

UNIVERSITY OF MISSISSIPPI

The increasing demand for persons with high intelligence to fill top-level technical and planning positions, both for national security and the advancement of our high-level technology, has focused attention on our educational programs for intellectually superior children. Summaries of previous work and present practices* have suggested that these highly intelligent children, as a group, achieve very well academically under a variety of special conditions and curriculum modifications. The effect of special services and provisions upon social adjustment and personality development of these children is not as thoroughly established.

Havighurst, Stivers, and DeHaan[1] have suggested that the success of various types of special provisions for gifted children depends upon size and socioeconomic level of the community. There also appeared to be a significant minority of these children, as reported in the above-noted summaries of research, who did not respond to educational adjustments and provisions and whose potential was lost to adult society.

To plan effectively for these intellectually superior children it is first necessary to know in what way the present educational system falls short of stimulating the ideal development of each child. If consistent patterns of poor adjustment are revealed in certain areas

* References deleted in reprinting.—EDITOR'S NOTE.
[1] Havighurst, R. J., E. Stivers, and R. F. DeHaan, "A Survey of the Education of Gifted Children," *Suppl. Educ. Monogr.*, 83, 1955.

[Reprinted from *Exceptional Children*, 23, April 1957, 306-312, 317-319, with the permission of the Council for Exceptional Children and the authors.]

of development, then special programs can be instituted to deal with these areas of difficulty.

The purpose of the present study was to discover to what extent highly intelligent children are having difficulty in adjusting to a regular classroom situation academically, intellectually, socially, and emotionally.

METHOD

SUBJECTS

The subjects in the present study were 20 boys and 15 girls attending grades two to five in a midwestern city of less than 100,000 population. All of these children had obtained a Stanford-Binet IQ of 150 or above as a prerequisite to membership in this group. Since this community had a highly favorable social, economic, and educational level (the major industry of the community was a university), the criterion of Binet IQ was set unusually high in an attempt to obtain the entire available sample of children at this ability level.

Table 1 indicates the sex and IQ distribution in the present sample. Almost one half of the present sample obtained Binet IQs of 160 or above and, although there were slightly more boys than girls, this difference was statistically insignificant. Since a Stanford-Binet IQ of 150 and above presumably occurs in approximately one out of every 1000 children, this community would have been expected to produce only three or four of these highly intelligent children at this particular age and grade level. While 35 children were processed by the case study method over a two-year period, there was still information available to the authors to suggest that the present sample by no means exhausted the supply of highly intelligent children in this community. It cannot be said, therefore, that

TABLE 1

Sex and IQ Distribution in Sample

Binet IQ range	Boys	Girls	Total	Percent sample in range
180-189	0	1	1	3
170-179	2	0	2	6
160-169	8	5	13	37
150-159	10	9	19	54
Total	20	15	35	100

TABLE 2

Family Background of Gifted Children

Father's occupation	N	Percent of total group	Educational level reached by mother	N	Percent of total group
College professor	17	49	Graduate work	4	11
Professional	5	14	College degree	14	40
Business	7	20	Some college	9	26
Skilled workers	4	11	H. S. diploma	5	14
Farm manager	1	3	Some high school	1	3
Military	1	3	Unknown	2	6
Total	35	100	Total	35	100

the present group represented a random selection of highly gifted children or the total available group that was originally sought.

Table 2 indicates the family background of the children in the present group. Approximately one half of the children came from homes in which the father was a college professor or connected in some academic capacity with the university. This was not too surprising a finding in view of the composition of the community studied. It is interesting, however, that 11 percent of the total group came from homes in which the father was a skilled or semiskilled worker and in which neither parent had obtained college training. Another 34 percent of the children were from homes in which the father was of professional background or a business man. These figures seem to correspond rather generally with the findings of other studies such as Terman's (5) concerning the employment level of the fathers of gifted children.

The level of education of the mother is suggestive also of a highly favored educational home background for these children. Over half of the mothers finished college and over three fourths of them had attended college at one time or another. Of the present group, however, 17 percent did not receive any education beyond high school. Since there are many factors which prevent women from obtaining as high a level of education as men, the level of education of the mothers of the present group is quite impressive.

One interesting note was that there was no history of divorce in the families of these 35 children.

PROCEDURE

These children were selected through two main sources, teacher referrals and group test results. The teachers were urged to look for other characteristics besides academic superiority, including the ability to see unique relationships, fluency of ideas, ability to think deeply, and so forth. Children who received a group test IQ result of 130 or above on the California Mental Maturity Scale were given individual Stanford-Binet tests to establish whether they qualified for admittance to the project. In addition, any other children who revealed unique or unusual talent to the school administrative staff were also given an individual screening examination.

If a child qualified with a Binet IQ of 150 or over, parents of the child were interviewed by the school personnel and asked if they would allow their children to participate in the program. All parents contacted agreed to allow their children to participate. Information gained through the study of each child was used to plan a series of curriculum adjustments within the framework of the regular classroom which, it was hoped, could aid the development of that child. An evaluation of the effect of the adjustment procedures on a long-term basis are now underway.

Each child who qualified for the study was given an extensive battery of test measuring intelligence, achievement, and personality development. A measure of social acceptance was obtained by administering a sociometric technique to each class that included a gifted child. In addition, the parents and teacher of each child were interviewed. The following measurements were administered to each child in the study:

A. Intellectual ability
   1. Stanford-Binet Form L
   2. Wechsler Intelligence Scale for Children
B. Achievement tests
   1. Stanford Achievement Test
   2. Special Diagnostic Tests when indicated
C. Social adjustment
   1. Teacher ratings
   2. Sociometric
   3. Parent and child interviews
D. Personality
   1. Rorschach test
   2. Teacher ratings

After the tests and interview material were collected on each child, this material was presented in a staff meeting attended by those members of the school district most directly concerned with the educational program of that child. An attempt was made to evaluate the total picture of the child and identify what areas, if any, the child was not developing to the limit of his or her potential. The curriculum adjustments were then planned in cooperation with the classroom teacher based on this evaluation.

RESULTS

INTELLIGENCE

The Wechsler Intelligence Scale for Children was administered to all of the subjects in order to obtain a comparison between the

TABLE 3

WISC Performance of Gifted Group

IQ levels	Verbal IQ	Performance IQ	Full-scale IQ
150-	5	2	6
140-149	17	10	17
130-139	6	14	7
120-129	6	8	3
110-119	1	0	2
100-109	0	1	0
Median IQ	143	138	144

verbal and performance ability of these children and to later compare these results against the success of the curriculum adjustment programs.

The numerical IQ results on the WISC were considerably lower than the Binet performances and are a reflection of the way in which the two measuring instruments were constructed. It is not possible to obtain an IQ of higher than 155 on the WISC whereas a child may obtain an IQ of over 200 on the Binet. It is clear that many of the children were performing at the very top of the WISC scale and their total capacities were not being measured by this test.

Although there was a tendency for the children to score higher on the verbal subtests (24 out of 35 had a verbal IQ greater than performance IQ) the median performance IQ of 138 should be proof that their superior intellectual talents range beyond mere verbal competence. The relatively superior results on the verbal subtests also must be evaluated in terms of the difficulty of obtaining a high performance IQ unless the testee performs the tasks with much speed as well as accuracy.

The academic achievement of the group is indicated by Table 4. The children in second and early third grade were administered the elementary form of the Stanford Achievement Test while the older children were given the intermediate and advanced batteries. The pattern of high achievement was the same with the younger and older groups but the older group showed a much more accelerated achievement in reading and allied subjects.

The median reading scores for the older group were more than four grades above their present placement and only one or two cases scored as low as their grade level. Other subjects which depended upon reading skills such as social studies and science, yielded similar superior performance. Thus the fourth- and fifth-grade teachers were faced with the problem of providing stimulation for these students who were competent to do high-school-level work.

Only when arithmetic performance was considered did the groups performance approach their grade placement. The median arithmetic computation score was only $+0.7$ grade units above grade placement. This result underscored the impression that the mastery of certain specific skills such as algebra and fractions was necessary for superior performance on standard achievement tests. No matter how intelligent the child, he or she was not able to advance much beyond his knowledge of specific arithmetic skills. This group revealed the ability to understand and deal with arithmetic reasoning problems effectively when reading and reasoning skills were more important than computational skills; 33 of 34 children obtained a higher arithmetic reasoning than arithmetic computational score.

The performance of the 12 children to whom the elementary battery was administered showed a less remarkable deviation between achievement and grade placement, perhaps indicating that educational planning for these younger children in the regular classroom might not be as serious a problem as that presented above by the nine- and ten-year olds. It is possible that this difference between younger and older children was due to differences in the maximum-obtained scores on the two test batteries. The median gain over grade level was between one and two grade units for each subtest as shown in Table 4.

SOCIAL ADJUSTMENT

A sociometric measure was given in each class where one or more of the children in the present study had been identified. Each child was asked to list the five people in the class who are his or her best friends. Care was taken that the choice be made on a friendship basis rather than a working-companion basis so that the popu-

TABLE 4

Stanford Achievement Scores Related to Grade Level

Advance and Intermediate Battery ($N = 23$)

Achievement score over grade level (by grade units)	* Parag. mean.	* Word mean.	* Arith. reas.	* Arith. comp.	* Spell- ing	Social studies	Sci- ence	* Lang. usage
+ 5.1 and over	5	9	1	0	3	3	4	6
+ 3.1 to + 5.0	10	5	8	1	7	11	12	10
+ 1.1 to + 3.0	6	6	11	10	9	5	5	5
+ 1.0 to − 1.0	1	2	2	11	3	4	2	1
Median gain	+ 4.2	+ 4.5	+ 2.4	+ .7	+ 2.9	+ 3.6	+ 4.2	+ 3.5

* Scores on one case were unavailable for plus comparison.

Elementary Battery ($N = 12$)

Achievement score over graded level (by grade units)	Parag. mean.	Word mean.	Arith. reas.	Arith. comp.	Spelling	Lang. usage
+ 4.0 and up	3	1	0	0	0	2
+ 3.0 to + 3.9	1	1	0	0	1	1
+ 2.0 to + 2.9	2	4	2	0	2	1
+ 1.0 to + 1.9	3	2	7	7	4	4
+ 1.0 to − 1.0	3	4	3	5	4	3
Median gain*	+ 1.9	+ 1.8	+ 1.4	+ 1.0	+ 1.4	+ 1.6

* Medians were calculated from ungrouped data.

larity could be evaluated apart from the advantage of being potential academic helpers.

The children in each class were then ranked according to the number of choices received and the class was divided on this basis into fourths or quartiles. Table 5* indicates the distribution of ranks achieved by the gifted subjects. There was strong indication that the gifted group of children were quite socially popular. Over half of

* Deleted in reprinting.—EDITOR'S NOTE.

the children in the group ranked in the top fourth of their class in social popularity. Over 80 percent of the group was above the median of their class in the number of choices received and only two cases fell at the bottom 25 percent of their class on this characteristic.

Although these results obviously were more favorable than chance, it seemed desirable to compare the gifted group against a random sample of their classmates. This random sample group obtained the level of social popularity that would be expected by chance. That is, 24 percent of them fell in the upper fourth of their class, 54 percent fell in the upper half, and so forth. A *chi square* test indicated a difference from chance at the one percent level of significance for the gifted group and supported the finding of superior social popularity of our group.

PERSONALITY

The Rorschach Ink Blot Test was administered individually in an effort to determine the status of emotional health of each child. Since it is the total picture that is presented on this test rather than individual scores that is important, evaluation of the results were made on the basis of over-all ratings of experienced judges. Two judges who had experience administering and interpreting Rorschach tests of children were given the protocols and asked to make judgments as to the emotional health of the subjects. One judge had previous knowledge of some of the cases while the other knew no more than the age and intellectual status of the child.

The correlations between judges were quite high for the characteristics of maladjustment, anxiety, and hostility. Although less high for ego control and creativity, the judges agreed sufficiently well to justify combining their ratings.*

Few of the cases revealed serious negative components in their personality. Only five cases were ranked as having marked disturbance, while 30 of the cases were rated as producing a predominantly healthy record. The same general results held for the characteristics of anxiety and hostility. In fact, there were practically no evidences of any hostility in 22 of the records. These favorable results were supported by ratings of teachers and over-all committee ratings of types of problems presented by these children. As always, there were notable exceptions to this favorable picture, and it would be unfair to brush aside as unimportant the five or six children who did show

* Tabular data has been deleted in reprinting.—EDITOR'S NOTE.

sizable problems in the emotional area. With one exception, these emotional problems did not seem related to the characteristic of high intelligence but were due rather to interrelationships within the family unit.

The judges were also asked to rate each child on the positive characteristics of ego control and creativity. On ego control the group again showed relatively good reality orientation, only one child revealing very poor reality contact.

In contrast to the other findings the judges were not positively impressed with the creative aspects of the records. They rated only seven cases as showing good creativity while 11 cases yielded some creative responses within the framework of a routine, uninspired protocol. Most unusual was the composite judgment that 17 of the cases revealed no originality or creativity in their records. Summing up these Rorschach results we can say that the group shows little emotional disturbance, good ego control, and unexpectedly poor creativity.

TEACHER RATINGS

Each child was rated by his or her classroom teacher as part of the original diagnosis of a case preliminary to the planning conferences. These ratings were made on nine aspects of behavior and personality that the writers assumed were observable within the classroom situation. The ratings were made on a four-point scale and the general findings are reported in Table 7. The teachers generally rated the children quite favorably on practically all aspects of behavior except creativity and leadership. On those characteristics related to classroom performance only two cases were judged as doing poor work academically, only four made infrequent contributions to the class, only two became discouraged and disinterested, and only four showed little enthusiasm for the school program. Since poor ratings might conceivably reflect on the teacher, there may have been a certain amount of unavoidable vested interest influencing these high ratings.

The ratings on creativity and leadership were less enthusiastic with only nine cases rated as spontaneously developing new ideas and 11 rated as not having creative work as a strong point. This finding corroborated the results obtained on the Rorschach test and raised the question of whether the schools could profitably spend more time on developing this characteristic.

TABLE 7

Teacher Ratings on Behavior and Personality Characteristics

Characteristic	Ratings			
Academic ability	Performs as well as ability allows	Does well but below capacity	Performance well below capacity	In trouble academically
N	21	12	2	0
Contribution to class	Makes contribution on practically all subjects	Frequently makes contribution	Sometimes makes contributions	Practically never makes contributions
N	20	11	4	0
Creativity	Spontaneously develops new ideas, new applications	Creative on occasion or in certain areas only	Creativity not a strong point	Regarded as an unoriginal person
N	9	15	11	0
Leadership	Generally accepted as leader of group activity	Can be leader; does not seek to lead group	Seldom reveals ability to direct others	Rarely attempts role of leader
N	10	18	5	2
Persistence	Works at task until finished, no matter the difficulty	Usually persistent; sometimes needs encouragement	Often becomes discouraged and disinterested	Noted for not finishing work
N	21	12	2	0
Enjoyment	Has great enthusiasm for school	Generally enjoys school	Shows little enthusiasm	Apathetic to school
N	19	12	4	0
Social ability	In social center of group	Well accepted by group, not most popular	Responds socially on occasion	Not a social participant
N	8	19	7	1
Behavior disorders	Rarely requires reprimand	Sometimes acts up; not a problem	Often disturbs class with antics	Constant discipline problem
N	23	9	1	1
Fears	Rarely shows fearful attitude	Some fears; emotionally stable	Often timid or fearful	Withdrawn, fearful child
N	25	9	1	0

On the characteristic of leadership, 10 of the children were rated as being the leader of their group and another 18 placed as a potential leader, although they might have been personally disinclined to leadership. Seven, or 20 percent, of the group seldom or rarely attempted leadership roles.

The ratings on social ability were in rather close agreement with the sociogram depicting the group as generally quite socially adaptable, although there was a sizable minority who were not doing too well socially. In the area of active behavior difficulties and emotional problems, the teachers saw few, if any, difficulties. Although this picture was in general agreement with other findings, it seemed clear that teachers were overlooking certain children who did have definite problems in this area. Both the Rorschach results and the total findings of the case studies identified from six to eight children in enough emotional difficulties to have been recognized by the teacher if she had known what to look for. Another discrepancy in the total results was the teacher ratings of high motivation and enthusiasm on the part of these children. The case-study findings revealed considerable lack of motivation and enthusiasm in a large number of the group.

IDENTIFICATION OF PROBLEMS

After all information had been collected on each child, a case conference was held which attempted to chart out the particular problems or difficulties revealed and to plan a program to deal with these problems. Agreement as to what type of problems were present in each case was made at the general planning meeting. Undoubtedly, this composite judgment was influenced by the selectivity of the psychologist's report.

Five cases were randomly selected and rated independently by the psychologist assigned to the project and the senior author of this paper, in order to establish the extent of agreement on the class frictions of problem areas. Here, 90-percent agreement was obtained on the types of problems present in these cases.

Table 8 shows the classification and frequency of problems in this group. Some of the categories listed in Table 8 need further explanation. Minor adjustment problem refers to the kind of incidental difficulties experienced by children which seemed to sap some of their potential without being serious or chronic enough to justify being placed in one of the other categories. Examples of these problems would be minor sibling rivalries, antagonistic relationships with another child in school, persistent minor altercations with one of the parents, and so forth.

Educational disability refers to particular problems in reading, spelling, arithmetic, and so on, when academic performance was compared to potential ability. Lack of academic motivation means

TABLE 8

Incidence of Problems Related to Grade Level

Problem type	Primary grades N = 16 (2, 3)		Elementary grades N = 19 (4.5)		Total * N = 35	
	N	%	N	%	N	%
No outstanding problem	7	43	3	16	10	29
Minor adjustment problem	9	56	8	42	17	49
Educational inefficiency	12	12	3	16	5	14
Motivation	7	43	7	37	14	40
Intellectual inflexibility	1	6	9	47	10	29
Social	2	12	5	26	7	20
Emotional: pervasive	0	0	1	5	1	3
Emotional: restricted	3	19	4	21	7	20

* The total number of problems may exceed the number of cases since several cases were listed as having more than one problem.

that the child indicated no interest in doing more or different work outside the normal curriculum and did not seem to be inner driven. Intellectual inflexibility refers to strict adherence to collection of facts without seeing new avenues of attack on problems or without presenting ideas different or more original than those voiced by their classmates.

The category, "Emotional problems in restricted areas," refers to the situation in which the child apparently was having difficulty in his adjustment in one of the three major areas of child experience —family, school, or peer relations—but was able successfully to keep it from spilling over into the others. Several of the children seemed to have sizable problems at home but not at school, and vice versa. These are to be contrasted with "Pervasive emotional problems," in which instances the disturbance is evident in all areas of adjustment.

In Table 8 the amount and type of problems present were divided according to primary and elementary grades. Two differences are worthy of notice in this comparison of younger and older gifted children. There were a larger number of cases in the primary grades that showed no outstanding problem and there was a marked increase in problems of intellectual inflexibility in the children of the elementary grades. While caution is necessary with such small samples and unknown selective factors operating, a hypothesis extending from this data could be that highly intelligent children have more problems adjusting in later grades and that these problems relate to a tendency to become less creative and more intellectually rigid and unimaginative.

It is significant that in the total group 29 percent of the cases revealed no outstanding problem. This would indicate that roughly one out of three of the cases observed had about as good an adjustment in the four areas of development—intellectual, academic, social, and emotional—as could be expected for a child of that age. This can be considered something of an achievement for these children considering the extent of the investigations made with the specific purpose of identifying problem areas.

Approximately one half of the group, or 49 percent, received a rating of minor adjustment problem. Actually, practicing school psychologists and social workers would be inclined to shrug their shoulders at most of these difficulties as being unimportant. Nevertheless, this rating did represent various conditions that might be improved.

Only 9 percent of the group revealed specific disabilities in educational work. Despite other difficulties, this group was able to work quite satisfactorily on academic subjects. Indeed the three cases that were rated as problems in the basic skills of reading or arithmetic were not seriously enough in trouble to be considered remedial cases in the ordinary sense of the word. It appeared that whatever difficulties this group may have had, they were still able to do enough in the academic areas to be comfortably abreast or ahead of their classmates.

Two areas that present the most real difficulties were those of motivational problems (40 percent) and intellectual flexibility (26 percent). The high percentage of occurrence of these problems indicates that there was a sizable minority of the present group who were unable to use freely their intellectual gifts and an even larger minority who did not seem to be inner driven to explore new things, create verbally or artistically, or do much of anything beyond what they are already accomplishing. The present group has been less than impressive in their spontaneous and creative work.

Social adjustment turned out to be less of a problem than other areas of adjustment. Only 20 percent of the cases could be classified as having some difficulty and these problems did not seem to relate to their intellectual status. However, subjective impressions led us to believe that some children were deliberately restricting their intellectual activity in order to insure their social status.

Only one case had an emotional problem which seemed to affect negatively all areas of development, but 20 percent of cases had enough of an emotional problem to cause personal difficulties which the child was able to keep isolated. For example, the child may have had distinct family adjustment problems which caused considerable personal tension but did not materially affect his school adjustment and vice versa. The total effect of these problems was hard to evaluate except to note that it did not seriously affect, in most instances, social and academic adjustment seriously enough so that attention was called to it.

Table 9 reveals a further breakdown of problem types in relation to school environment. The schools were divided into high-referral schools, or those which have contributed three or more children, and low-referral schools, or those which have contributed only one or two children to the project.

It is quite interesting to note the relatively high agreement in the proportion of problems from one type of school setting to another, with one outstanding difference—75 percent of the cases from the low-referral schools were classified as having motivational difficulties while only 26 percent of cases from the high-referral schools indicated this problem. It would probably be incorrect to jump to the conclusion that the poor motivation in the cases from low-referral schools were due solely to lack of stimulation and challenge from classmates. Many other possible variables such as family background, socioeconomic status, and so forth, were imponderables in the present comparison.

TABLE 9

Problem Type in Relation to School Environment *

Problem type	High-referral schools (N = 23, 74%)		Low-referral schools (N = 8, 26%)	
	Total † problems	% of cases	Total † problems	% of cases
No outstanding problem	7	30	2	25
Minor adjustment problem	12	52	3	37
Educational inefficiency: specific disability	3	13	1	12
Lack of academic motivation	6	26	6	75
Intellectual inflexibility	7	30	1	12
Social adjustment	5	22	1	12
Emotional problems: pervasive	1	4	0	0
Emotional problems: in restricted area	4	17	2	25

* Two schools were omitted from this data because they did not properly fit the criterion for either a high-referral or low-referral school.

† The total number of problems may exceed the number of cases since several cases were listed as having more than one problem.

SUMMARY OF RESULTS

1. Approximately ten times as many highly intelligent children were found in the local school systems at the grade levels two through five than could be expected by chance.

2. Extreme individual differences made it difficult to generalize

about the group without ignoring a significant minority of cases operating in opposition to the generalization.

3. A sizable minority of the present sample (29 percent) seemed to be adjusting as well as could be expected intellectually, socially, academically, and emotionally.

4. Relatively few members of the present group could be considered in serious academic, social, or emotional difficulties.

5. The major difficulties of the total group seemed to be lack of motivation, lack of creativity or originality, and minor personal-adjustment problems which tended to sap their total adjustment potential.

6. Teachers rated these children very favorably on practically all variables except creativity and leadership.

7. The older children in this sample had more problems of intellectual rigidity than the younger children. Proportion of other types of problems remained about the same.

8. Children in the present group coming from schools where there were few bright children showed more motivational problems than the children coming from schools where there were many other bright children.

DISCUSSION

One of the most significant comments the writers feel could be made in summary is that no general statement can be given concerning the present group without there being a great many exceptions to that statement. The variety of individual differences was constantly being impressed on the committee, particularly in the case-study conferences. Whether it was in physical development, social adjustment, emotional health, or academic performance, there were those children who deviated from the group norm and made the individual case studies that we did not only convenient, but necessary.

Once having said this, it is possible to note some group trends which seem to have some relevance. One of the more striking observations to be made was that the problems that exist in these children were generally of the nonirritating variety. They were not antisocially aggressive. They were not academic problems. They did not generally have emotional problems of sufficient magnitude to disturb their teacher, parents, or peer group. In short, their problems were not ones of commission, but omission. Of course, the findings concerning the adjustment of gifted children in a less favored educational and economic environment might not be so favorable.

These softer, more elusive difficulties only became obvious when one abandoned the frame of reference of the regular classroom and adopted as a reference point the child's own potential. Two of the major difficulties revealed in the present study were those of poor motivation and of intellectual rigidity or sterility. It is impossible to measure the amount of intellectual power going to waste in our present group, but certainly our results suggest it is considerable. Some of these children may show a spurt of creativity and productivity when they reach adolescence or become young adults, but this theoretical spurt cannot be relied upon.

Assigning responsibility for this difficulty of stimulating these children to use their gifts freely and extensively was beyond the scope of the present project but not, we hope, beyond the reach of future research. It is likely that there are many and varied causes for the lack of efficiency of individual gifted children.

These results should discourage those who believe that there is an easy administrative adjustment that will solve the multivaried problems revealed here. It is only when one examines at close range the individual cases that this wider variation of difficulties is revealed in its full significance. The authors hope to publish a series of case studies as a companion piece to the present article to document this point in a later issue of this journal.*

Even if future research determines beyond a doubt that the initial causation of intellectual sterility lies within the family unit or in peer-group relationships, the responsibility of the schools in nowise changes. It is no new task for school systems to have to handle problems that were not of their own making. To recognize the homily that there is no one solution to the adjustment problems of gifted children is not to justify inaction but rather to suggest varied methods and procedures by which we may reclaim the intellectual potential of the most talented of the next generation.

---

* The case studies appeared in *Exceptional Children*, 23, May 1957, 353-363, 396, 398.

SOCIAL STATUS AND SOCIOEMPATHIC DIFFERENCES AMONG MENTALLY SUPERIOR, MENTALLY TYPICAL, AND MENTALLY RETARDED CHILDREN

by Robert V. Miller

UNIVERSITY OF MASSACHUSETTS

The last two or three decades have witnessed some very important and fundamental changes in educational theory and practice in the United States, one of which is the growing recognition of and educational adjustment to individual differences. Equal educational opportunity, formerly interpreted to mean the same method and standard for each child, now is coming to mean maximum opportunity for each child to learn and develop according to *his* needs and capacities. This emphasis fostered an increased interest in special education for mentally deviate groups, the mentally retarded having received more attention in this respect than the mentally superior. Among the numerous gaps of knowledge concerning these two groups, their social characteristics stand high in the hierarchy of importance for a number of reasons, among which are:

1. Social adjustment has become of central importance both as a means (educational placement) and as an end (educational objective) in education.

2. Social abilities and skills are basic determinants of one's self-concept and satisfaction therewith.

3. Though intellectual endowments may set the limits of one's societal role and status, social characteristics are basic in determining one's position within those limits.

[Reprinted from *Exceptional Children*, 23, December 1956, 114-119, with the permission of the Council for Exceptional Children and the author.]

STATEMENT OF THE PROBLEM

OPERATIONAL DEFINITION OF TERMS

This study[1] is concerned only with ascertaining whether significant differences exist between mentally superior, mentally typical, and mentally retarded children in regular (nonspecial) upper-elementary classrooms with regard to sociometrically ascertained social status and certain socioempathic abilities. These three groups, equally spaced on a continuous IQ scale, are operationally defined as follows: mentally superior, IQs of 120-140 inclusive; mentally typical, IQs of 90-110 inclusive; and mentally retarded, IQs of 60-80 inclusive. All IQs were obtained by means of the Primary Mental Abilities Tests, which were given routinely to all fourth graders in the school system by the same school psychologist.

"Social status" in this study referred to a position along a continuum of acceptance-rejection as a friend, determined from ratings by classmates. "Socioempathy" was defined as "an individual's awareness of his own and other's sociometric status in a given group of which he is a member" (3) and was measured in this study by ratings in three different areas.

REVIEW OF LITERATURE

The most relevant research in the area of social status is Johnson's study (10) in which six sociometric questions, one positive and one negative question on each of the topic's best friend, seat companion, and playmate, were asked of 39 mentally handicapped (Revised Binet IQ 69 or below) and 659 typical (group test IQ 70 or above) children from 25 classes in grades one through five. Positive and negative choices were totaled separately and critical ratios between the two groups showed the typical pupils significantly higher in acceptance choices and significantly lower in rejection choices than the mentally handicapped pupils. The latter had a lower percentage of stars (high acceptance choices) and a higher percentage of isolates (low acceptance choices) and rejectees (high rejection choices) than the former. Of Johnson's 698 subjects, nineteen had IQs of 130 and above on the New California Short-form Test of Mental Maturity. This group had the highest mean-acceptance score and the lowest mean-rejection score of any of the

[1] This is a condensation of the author's master's thesis under the same title on file in the library of the University of Illinois.

groups studied (statistical tests of these differences from the other groups were not reported by Johnson). Kirk and Johnson (11) did a comparable study in more "progressive" classrooms and got results very similar to those of the Johnson study. The only other sociometric study with mentally deviate groups of import was that of Hays (7) who found that mentally retarded girls tended to choose friends of the same IQ and MA as themselves. Wardlow and Greene (14), Almack (1), Jenkins (9), and others using comparable sociometric methodology report similar findings with respect to groups of average intelligence. On the other hand, the studies of Bonney (4, 5), Challman (6), and others with average groups indicated that the more intelligent a person, the more he tended to be chosen as a friend.[2] The studies of Terman (13), Hollingworth (8), Witty (15), and others show the personality variables of the superior to be either equal to or greater than the same variables in the typical except in cases of extremely high IQ. Social characteristics were generally in the "equal to" category. Predictions for this study from the generalizations of these latter studies would have the social status and socioempathic abilities at least equal to, if not greater, than those for the typical.

The only study relevant to socioempathic abilities was that of Ausubel, Schiff, and Gasser (3) in which each pupil in two classes at the third-, fifth-, seventh-, eleventh-, and twelfth-grade levels were asked to show on a five-point scale (1) how much he liked each classmate, (2) how much each classmate liked him, and (3) how much the class liked each classmate. Here, predicted and actual scale scores correlated significantly at all grade levels, there was an increase of this ability with age, and the positive end of the scale was used disproportionately. The literature, then, provides us with some strong expectancies (social-status differences between retarded and typical), some controversial findings (how gifted and typical compare on social status), and some gaps of knowledge (nature of socioempathic differences among the three groups). This study purports to shed some light on each of these areas.

RESEARCH HYPOTHESES

The hypotheses stated in null form tested in this research were as follows:

[2] These results are not antagonistic if each child chooses persons slightly more intelligent than himself for friends.

There are no significant differences between our samples of the mentally superior, mentally typical, and mentally retarded in the following respects:

I. The extent to which they were socially accepted;

II. Their ability to judge how their classmates would rate them as friends—prediction of their own social acceptance;

III. Ability to predict the popularity of others;

IV. Ability to judge how easily their classmates learn new things in and out of school; and

V. Their predictions of the extent to which they would be selected as friends.

It was further hypothesized that:

VI. All three groups will proportion their friendship choices equally among the mentally superior, mentally typical, and mentally retarded; and

VII. All three groups will have significant positive relationships between their ability to judge their own social acceptance and their ability to judge other's ease of learning.

SAMPLING AND CLASSROOM PROCEDURES

SAMPLING

There were 120 subjects, 20 in each IQ group at each of two grade levels, fourth and sixth. In a community of 80,000, classrooms were selected having two or more superior (120-140) and retarded (60-80) while the typical were selected randomly and approximately equally from the classes so chosen. The fourth-grade *Ss* were from six different classes; the sixth-grade *Ss*, from seven. The classes were in 11 elementary-school buildings. All pupils included in this study had been in their respective classes for at least six months. The IQs within each of the three groups were distributed as one would expect from their position in the normal curve of the general population. There were 65 boys and 55 girls in the sample.

CLASSROOM PROCEDURES

The sociometric procedures were standardized, consisting of the reading of a prepared introduction to the task and ensuing instructions. The sociometric procedures were administered to everyone in class without singling out the *Ss* in any way. After the introduction, four mimeographed forms, identical except the first sheet was page 1, second page 2, and so forth, were given to each S. On each sheet were the names of everyone in that class, and after each name were the numbers, 1, 2, 3, 4, 5. On page 1, a single number was to be circled after each name according to the following scale:

Scale A
1—if you want that person as a friend very much.
2—if you want that person as a friend.
3—if it doesn't matter whether that person is your friend.
4—if you don't care for that person as a friend.
5—if you don't want that person as a friend at all.

On page 2, a single number was to be circled after each name according to the following scale:

Scale B
1—if that person wants you as a friend very much.
2—if that person wants you as a friend.
3—if it doesn't matter to that person whether you are his (or her) friend.
4—if that person doesn't care to have you as a friend.
5—if that person doesn't want you as a friend at all.

Page 3 was marked according to this scale:

Scale C
1—if the person is very popular; chosen as a friend by many pupils.
2—if the person is quite popular; chosen as a friend by quite a few pupils.
3—if the person is fairly popular; chosen by several others as a friend.
4—if the person is somewhat unpopular; chosen as a friend by only one or two others.
5—if the person is very unpopular; chosen as a friend by no one.

Page 4 was used according to this scale:

Scale D
1—if the person learns new things with great ease.
2—if the person learns new things easier than most pupils.
3—if the person learns new things as easily as most pupils.
4—if the person learns new things less easily than most pupils.
5—if the person learns new things with great difficulty.

Each scale was read orally by the author and was printed on large cardboards placed in front of the room. Further repetitions were made for the few not able to read or remember what the numbers meant. In only a very few cases was individual help necessary. The total class time involved was about an hour per class, including breaks, even with no time limit set to finish. All the classes appeared well motivated and seemingly enjoyed the activity (they were told that it was neither a test nor a race). Students were not permitted to indicate their markings to others and were assured that only the author would see what they marked. The teacher in each class provided the following information on each pupil: sex, age, IQ, number of parents with whom S lives, and an academic achievement rating on a five-point scale.

METHODS AND RESULTS OF ANALYSIS

METHOD OF ANALYSIS

Of all the sociometric data collected in each class, only those pertaining to the pupils in the three groups were analyzed. Each hypothesis was tested for these groups at both the fourth- and sixth-grade levels. The data of the three groups were jointly ranked to test hypotheses I through V. The nature of the ranked data in each of these hypotheses follow:

I. The averages of the friendship ratings given each subject by his classmates.

II. The averages of the differences between how each subject thought others rated him as a friend (page 2) and how they actually did rate him (page 1).

III. The averages of the differences between how popular each classmate was judged to be (page 3) and how popular he actually was (page 1).

IV. The averages of the differences between how each subject judged a classmate's ease of learning (page 4) and how the whole class judged a classmate's ease of learning (page 4).

V. The average predictions by each subject of how much his classmates wanted him as a friend.

The nonparametric Krustal-Wallis H test (12), which tests the null hypothesis for three groups with jointly ranked data, was used to test the above hypotheses.

The formula is: $H = \dfrac{12}{N(N+1)} \sum_1^c \dfrac{R_i}{n_i} - 3(N-1)$

Where R_i = sum of ranks for group i.

$\quad N$ = total number of Ss

$\quad n_i$ = number of Ss in group i.

If the H test was significant at the 5-percent level, the null hypothesis was tested for groups having adjacent sum of ranks[3] using a four-cell median test (X^2 with 1 df), which tests whether one group has significantly more rank scores above (or below) the joint median of both groups than the other group.

In Hypothesis VI the percentage[4] of 1 and 2 ratings on page 1 given to each of the superior, typical, and retarded by each group was tested separately by means of the X^2 test of proportions, testing first with three proportions and then, if necessary, by adjacent pairs.

For Hypothesis VII rank-order correlations were run for each group between their rank in ability to predict how much they were wanted as friends and their rank in predicting how easy or difficult it is for their classmates to learn new things. The t test was used to determine the significance of the correlations.

RESULTS

The following results were obtained:

For Hypothesis I—The superior were most wanted as friends by their classmates. Next most wanted are the typical, then the retarded. The differences were statistically significant in all cases except between the typical and retarded groups at the fourth-grade level. No group was actually rejected, however. These results are harmonious with the conclusions and implications of related studies.

For Hypothesis II—At the fourth-grade level, the superior were significantly more accurate in their predictions of their own social status than either the typical or retarded. No other significant differences were found at either grade level. With regard to the di-

[3] If the three groups were ranked according to their rank totals, it is assumed the extreme groups are significantly different if the H test is significant. The other two-pair combinations must be tested.

[4] This percentage is the number 1 and 2 choices given out of the total number that could have been given, since Ss are in different classes.

rection of errors, the superior tended to underestimate their own status, there being no trend for the estimations of the typical, and the retarded tended to overestimate their social status.

For Hypothesis III—The superior predicted the popularity of their classmates most accurately, the typical next most accurately, and then the retarded. All such differences in socioempathic abilities were statistically significant except at the sixth-grade level where the typical were not significantly differentiated from either the superior

TABLE 1

Summary Table of Results (P Values Given Where Computed)
Differences Significant at the 5-percent Level or Better
Are Indicated By *

Hypoth- esis	Statistic	Fourth				Sixth			
		R-T-S	R-T	T-S	S-R	R-T-S	R-T	T-S	S-R
I	H and X^2	.01*	—	.01*	*	.02*	.02*	.01*	*
II	H and X^2	.05*	.21	.01*	.01*	.13	—	—	—
III	H and X^2	.01*	.02*	.01*	*	.01*	.21	.21	.02*
IV	H and X^2	.03*	.21	.01*	*	.01*	.01*	.01*	*
V	H and X^2	.41	—	—	—	.05*	—	—	.01*

		Fourth			Sixth		
		R	T	S	R	T	S
VI	X^2	.27	.25	.01*	.10	.02*	.04*
VII	X^2	.87	.38	.78	.14	.38	.48

R = Retarded T = Typical S = Superior

Dashes are used where the R-T-S analysis is not significant or where $X^2 = 0$. Asterisks alone are explained in footnote 3. All p values less than .01 are simply noted as .01*.

or retarded groups. With regard to directional tendencies, the superior overestimated the popularity of others while the retarded underestimated the popularity of others. (It was also found that the superior group was rated most popular by their classmates, then came the typical group, and then the retarded. All of these differences were statistically significant.)

For Hypothesis IV—The superior most accurately predicted the ease with which his classmates learn new things, then the typical group, and finally the retarded group. All differences at both grade levels were statistically significant except that between the typical and retarded groups at the fourth-grade level. The directional tendencies are for all three groups to overestimate the ease of learning of others, this being least so for the superior group. (It was also found that superiors were seen by their classmates as the fastest learners, then typical, and then retarded, all differences being significant at both grade levels.)

For Hypothesis V—The only significant differences occurring between the social status each group ascribed to itself was between the superior and retarded groups at the sixth-grade level. The superior estimated themselves more accepted by their classmates than the retarded group.

For Hypothesis VI—The superior chose other superior children as friends significantly more frequently than they chose typical or retarded children. The typical group's choices are equally proportioned at the fourth grade, but shift to significantly more choices of superior children at the sixth-grade level. The retarded group proportion their choices equally between the other two groups at both grade levels.

For Hypothesis VII—Ability to accurately estimate their own social status was not significantly correlated with their ability to accurately estimate other's ease of learning for any of the three groups at either grade level.

The results are summarized in Table 1.

DISCUSSION AND CONCLUSION

The main findings and expectations arising out of such studies as Johnson (10), Johnson and Kirk (11), and Hays (7) with the mentally retarded and Terman (13), Hollingworth (8), and others with the mentally superior indicated that the more intelligent students in an elementary classroom would be better liked as a friend than a child of average intelligence and certainly more so than a retarded child. The results of hypothesis I bear out these expectations for the social-status differences between the three groups studied. Would it not be reasonable to expect that retarded children of 60 IQ or below would be even less accepted and that, as the IQ increased to 150 and above, acceptance as a friend would decrease? Thus, though our results show social status linearly related to intelligence, at the upper limits of the intellectual continuum it could well be curvilinear. Furthermore, it cannot be said from this study that social status is given to the superior *because* of their intelligence. It would be more in keeping with reason and everyday experience to say that friendship choices are based primarily on socially desirable aspects of one's personality; but perhaps the superior are in some way able to acquire these positive personality traits more readily, more fully, and more flexibly.

The question as to whether the retarded are actually rejected or just less accepted deserves consideration. Johnson (10) found they were rejected by having pupils respond to negative sociometric questions. In the present study positive, neutral, and negative choices are available for each person being rated, and it is found that 33 out of the 40 retarded Ss had scale scores less than 3.0 (indifferent to having them as friends), and not one was above 3.3. In other words, the class as a whole was mildly accepting of the retarded.

With regard to socioempathic abilities it should be noted that though we found them to covary with intelligence, we may not say that one is directly or solely causative of the other, since correlation does not establish causation. It is reasonable to assume, however, that the ability to differentiate and ascertain the meaning of environmental cues underlying socioempathy is intellectual in nature or at least has significant intellectual components. In this connection it was found that judging one's own social status hardly differentiated the three groups; judging another's popularity differentiated them more sharply; and judging the learning ability of others differentiated them even more so. It would appear that the reasons for this gradation in differentiation is a function of the greater emotional gradation from the task of judging one's own social status to the task of judging another's learning ease. Another reason might be the gradation in overt, frequently reinforced cues from the latter task to the former task. Thus, socioempathic abilities may have a prerequisite intellectual basis, but are helped or hindered in any particular situation by various other facets of personality called into play by that situation.

Though an insignificant relationship was found between prediction of self status and prediction of the learning ability of others by the same person, little can be said concerning the generality of socioempathic accuracy of the same person over different tasks since the task of judging another's learning ease is not strictly socioempathic in nature. This question is more nearly answered in Ausubel's study (2), in which no relationship was found between a high-school student's ability to judge his own social status and his ability to judge the social status of others.

It seems tenable that social status and socioempathic ability are dependent upon each other to the extent that high social status affords more frequent and more intimate contact with others, allowing greater insight into and prediction of the attitudes and behavior of others. Or conversely, greater socioempathy enables one to behave with others in a manner that gains their friendship. This, of course, is speculation, since the present research at best indicates only that they are highly correlated.

We had expected that the ratings made by the sixth graders would be scattered over more points in the scales than would be true of those made by fourth graders. Such was not true, however. Similarly, one might have expected the superior to be more discriminating (employ a greater variety of ratings in the scales) than would be true of the retarded, but such was found not to be the case. The data on the age, sex, and academic rating of the subjects were consistent with those found for these three groups in numerous studies and were not particularly helpful in interpreting the present results.

Finally, the implications of this research for special classes for the two deviant groups should be considered. In considering the social needs and adjustments involved in the special-class controversy, it can be argued that since the retarded are being least socially accepted in the regular classroom, it would be socially beneficial for them to be in a more accepting group. So these data could be regarded as arguing in favor of special classes for the mentally retarded. The superior, however, seem to be most socially accepted by their classmates and consequently the evidence of this study would contribute in part to questioning a need for special classes for the gifted on the allegation that they are being socially spurned or rejected by their classmates in the regular classroom. This study, of course, has nothing to offer regarding academic or intellectual needs of the superior as bases for special classes.

We have, then, indicated that social status and socioempathic differences *do* exist between mentally superior, mentally typical, and mentally retarded children in the upper elementary grades. It remains for future research to ascertain the causes of such differences and how they might be modified if it is possible and desirable to do so.

REFERENCES

1. Almack, John. The Influence of Intelligence on the Selection of Associates. *School and Society*, 16, 1922, 529-530.
2. Ausubel, David. Reciprocity and Assumed Reciprocity of Acceptance among Adolescents, a Sociometric Study. *Sociometry*, 16, 1953, 339-348.
3. Ausubel, D., H. M. Schiff, and E. G. Gasser. A Preliminary Study of Developmental Trends in Socioempathy: Accuracy of Perception of Own and Other's Sociometric Status. *Child Develop.*, 23, 1952, 111-128.
4. Bonney, Merl. Relationships between Social Success, Family Size, Socioeconomic Home Background, and Intelligence among School Children in Grades III to V. *Sociometry*, 7, 1944, 26-39.
5. ———. A Sociometric Study of the Relationship of Some Factors to Mutual Friendships on the Elementary, Secondary, and College Levels. *Sociometry*, 9, 1946, 21-47.
6. Challman, Robert. Factors Influencing Friendships among Preschool Children. *Child Develop.*, 3, 1932, 146-158.
7. Hays, William. Mental Level and Friend Selection among Institutionalized Defective Girls. *Amer. J. Mental Deficiency*, 1951, 198-203.
8. Hollingworth, Leta. *Gifted Children: Their Nature and Nurture.* New York: The Macmillan Co., 1929.
9. Jenkins, Gladys. Factors Involved in Children's Friendships. *J. Educ. Psychol.*, 22, 1931, 440-448.
10. Johnson, G. Orville. A Study of the Social Position of Mentally Handicapped Children in the Regular Grades. *Amer. J. Mental Deficiency*, 55, 1950, 60-89.
11. Kirk, S. A., and G. O. Johnson. Are Mentally Handicapped Children Segregated in the Regular Grades? *J. Exceptional Children*, 17, 1950, 65-68.
12. Kruskal, W. H., and W. A. Wallis. Use of Ranks in One Criterion Variance Analysis. *J. Amer. Stat. Assoc.*, 47, 1952, 583-621.
13. Terman, L. M., and Melita R. Oden. *The Gifted Child Grows Up.* Stanford, Calif.: Stanford Univ. Press, 1947.
14. Wardlow, M. E., and J. E. Greene. An Exploratory Sociometric Study of Peer Status among Adolescent Girls. *Sociometry*, 15, 1952, 311-318.
15. Witty, Paul. A Study of 100 Gifted Children. *Univ. Kansas Bull. Educ.*, State T. C. Stud. Educ., 1, No. 13.

THE TEMPERAMENT OF GIFTED CHILDREN

by Marcella Ryser Bonsall

UNIVERSITY OF SOUTHERN CALIFORNIA

and Buford Stefflre

MICHIGAN STATE UNIVERSITY

In the past decade there has been a revival of interest in the education of intellectually superior children. This points up the need for further study of the characteristics possessed by these children. Among the many research studies in this area are several which have produced objective testimony showing a favorable moderate divergence of gifted children from the unselected children on characteristic personality patterns in general.

The present study investigates temperament differences between the gifted and other high-school senior boys, to determine the extent to which previously observed temperament differences were a function of "giftedness" and the extent to which they were a function of the socioeconomic background of the gifted. Comparisons were first made of gifted and others at each of the several occupational levels. Then a comparison was made of all the gifted with all others disregarding the occupational level of the home.

The sample consists of 1359 white high-school senior boys in several high schools in a metropolitan area who in the course of a vocational counseling experience completed the SRA Primary Mental Abilities Test (here used as an index of giftedness) and the Guilford-Zimmerman Temperament Survey (here used as a temperament measure), and who gave enough information about the occupation of their wage-earning parent (in most cases the father) to enable the occupation to be classified according to the Alba Edwards Scale.

On the basis of the total score on the Primary Mental Abilities

[Reprinted from the *California Journal of Educational Research*, 6, September 1955, 162-165, with the permission of the California Teachers Association and the authors. Copyright, 1955, by the California Teachers Association.]

Test students were designated as "gifted" if they were in the top 11 percent of published norms. Parent's occupation of all students were classified according to the Alba Edwards six-level scale—professional, managerial and official, clerical, skilled, semi-skilled, and unskilled. Within each of these occupational levels the gifted were compared with the others with regard to scores on each of the ten sections of the Guilford-Zimmerman Temperament Survey. These ten sections are (1) general activity, (2) restraint, (3) ascendance, (4) sociability, (5) emotional stability, (6) objectivity, (7 friend-

TABLE 1

Significance of Differences in Temperament Traits between Gifted and Nongifted

Home level according to Alba Edwards scale	Number of students		Significance of differences in scores on sections of Guilford-Zimmerman Temperament Survey[1]									
	Gifted	Non-gifted	G	R	A	S	E	O	F	T	P	M
Professional	18	160	n	n	n	n	n	†	n	n	n	n
Managerial-official	37	354	n	†	n	n	n	n	n	†	n	n
Clerical	22	266	n	n	*	n	n	n	n	n	n	n
Skilled	8	283	n	n	n	n	n	n	n	†	n	*
Semiskilled	7	157	n	n	n	n	n	n	n	†	n	†
Unskilled	0	37	n	n	n	n	n	n	n	n	n	n
TOTAL	92	1257	*	*	*	n	*	*	n	†	n	*

Key: *n* No significant difference.
 * Gifted superior at the 5-percent level.
 † Gifted superior at the 1-percent level.

liness, (8) thoughtfulness, (9) personal cooperation and (10) masculinity of interest. When these comparisons were subjected to the *t* test to determine the significance of the observed differences the results were as shown in Table 1.

DIFFERENCES FOUND

Those gifted boys whose fathers were classed as professionals manifest greater objectivity at the 1-percent level when compared to nongifted boys having professional fathers.

[1] Sections are designated as follows: G—General Activity; R—Restraint; A—Ascendance; S—Sociability; E—Emotional Stability; O—Objectivity; F—Friendliness; T—Thoughtfulness; P—Personal Cooperation; M—Masculinity of Interest.

The gifted boys from homes where fathers are in managerial or clerical positions demonstrate more restraint, at the 1-percent and the 5-percent level respectively, than do nongifted boys from like occupational backgrounds, and gifted boys from homes where the fathers are in managerial jobs are at the 1-percent level more thoughtful than other boys from like homes. The boys classified as gifted whose fathers were employed in semi-skilled and skilled occupations reveal more masculinity at the 1-percent and the 5-percent levels, than did average-ability boys whose fathers are working at similar jobs.

When gifted boys are compared with all other boys, with the occupational levels of the home disregarded, they show at the 1-percent level more thoughtfulness, and, at the 5-percent level more general activity, restraint, ascendance, emotional stability, objectivity, and masculinity.

EFFECT OF SOCIOECONOMIC LEVEL

This study indicates that the previously found superiority of the "gifted" as regards temperament stems much more from the socioeconomic level at which most gifted children are found than from any other difference in "gifted" children as such. When socioeconomic background is taken into account, relatively few significant differences are found between "gifted" and others, but when the parent background of these children is disregarded, there seem to be differences in seven of the ten areas measured and in all these areas the "gifted" child has superior temperament scores.

Research using different measuring instruments might well have resulted in different findings and it is interesting to speculate on the influence of culture in developing or suppressing "giftedness." Certainly the incidence of giftedness is greatest among the more favored socioeconomic groups and it is these groups which exhibit the temperament traits most valued by our educational institutions. This juxtaposition of high intelligence and valued temperament is not seen as wholly a matter of background, however, since restraint and thoughtfulness seem to be generally characteristic of gifted children. There were no significant differences between the total gifted and the total average students on the following temperament traits, sociability, friendliness, and personal cooperation. Many think the development of these traits should be given special atten‹ tion as it is felt that from this gifted group should come more of the future leaders and that these traits may be important in many leadership situations. In teaching these students it may be important to keep such temperament differences and similarities in mind and check the findings of studies like this one against the situation as seen in the classroom.

Since this study suggests that failure to keep constant the socioeconomic level in making comparisons of the temperament of gifted and other children results in misleading assumptions about the superior adjustment of the gifted, it may be well to restudy some of the findings of Terman and others. Is it possible that Terman in *Genetic Studies of Genius,* in describing the multiple superiority of the gifted child, is simply describing children from the upper socioeconomic levels? If this is so, many of our assumptions about the "differences" of the gifted which call for special educational approaches and methods will need to be reconsidered.

GIFTED ADOLESCENTS' VIEWS OF GROWING UP

by Ruth Strang

COLUMBIA UNIVERSITY

The way in which adolescents perceive themselves and their world determines, to a large extent, their behavior. How they feel about growing up gives important clues to their adjustment during this transition period from childhood to adulthood. Is adolescence for them a period of "storm and stress," a time of uncertainty and insecurity, or a noneventful gradual process, or the gateway to new privileges and responsibilities?

Among any large group of adolescents all of these responses to growing up would be represented in some degree. To obtain

[Reprinted from *Exceptional Children,* 22, October 1956, 10-12, with the permission of the Council for Gifted Children and the author.]

more information about this stage of development, 1124 pupils in grades seven to twelve inclusive were asked to write compositions during class time on the subject "How It Feels to Be Growing Up." The topic was explained in a little more detail and the students asked to sign their names.[1] The compositions gave ample evidence that the writers were giving free, frank, and sincere responses and seemed to enjoy this opportunity to write about themselves. The cooperating teachers gained many insights from reading the compositions.

About half of the population studied came from urban and half from rural areas in the same county. Although a wide range of socioeconomic status was represented, the middle and lower socioeconomic groups predominated. The number of cases, according to IQ level, were distributed as follows:[2]

Grades	IQ	Number of cases
7, 8, 9	95.2 Av.	247
	120-129	121
	130 and over	35
10, 11, 12	94.9 Av.	636
	120-129	65
	130 or over	20

In some categories the relative frequency of responses of the gifted and of the average were quite similar. Other responses were made more frequently by the gifted than by the average; still others, more frequently by those with average IQs. Some responses were made more frequently by the younger than by the older adolescents. Although these differences apply only to this particular sample, it seems probable that the greater differences would be found in other similar groups and that, when percentage differences

[1] Acknowledgment is most gratefully made to Catherine L. Beachley, Supervisor of Guidance and Research, Washington County, Hagerstown, Maryland, for obtaining the interest and cooperation of the teachers in having the children write the compositions and for putting the IQ from group intelligence tests on each composition.
[2] In this article "the gifted" or "the bright students" will refer to students with IQs of 120 or above on a group intelligence test. "Average" will refer to the group with an average IQ of 95. The compositions were read by Dr. Warren Roome, responses categorized, and percentage of responses calculated for each type of response. In the tables, both numbers and percentages are given because the percentages based on the small number of cases in some categories may be misleading.

are at least one third greater for the gifted than for the average, or vice versa, the probability of their having arisen from a chance variability of the sample studied would be extremely low. In the interpretation of these data, comparisons for those categories where the relative frequencies of responses is below 10 percent have been omitted.

SIMILARITY OF RESPONSES

Some feelings about growing up were expressed with similar frequency by average and by gifted students.*

Feelings of dissatisfaction with changes in body growth, functioning, and status were mentioned by about a fourth of each group. Such changes are common to both gifted and average adolescents and are emphasized in books on adolescent psychology. It is not surprising that adolescents should be aware of and concerned about unevenness in growth, individual differences in rate of growth, and attitudes toward themselves arising from these physical and physiological changes.

However, as may be seen in Table 2 [which has been omitted], the gifted expressed *satisfaction* with their body growth and status much more frequently than the average students. These feelings of satisfaction may be attributed to the general superiority of the gifted in physical development and health. The gifted expressed only slightly more concern with clothes, make-up, and other details of personal appearance than those of average intelligence.

Certain references to family relations were common to both average and gifted adolescents. With respect to sibling relations the entire group mentioned both satisfactions and problems. Some enjoyed their younger brothers and sisters and spoke of good relations with older siblings. Almost as many found younger children in the family a trial, a nuisance, or a cause for jealousy, and felt some resentment toward older brothers or sisters. Intelligence does not insure happy family relations. However, roughly half of both groups [data omitted]—but a larger percentage of the gifted—expressed satisfaction concerning relations with parents. This ap-

* Table 1, "Similarity between Average and Gifted Students with Respect to the Frequencies of Certain Response Categories," and Table 2, "Differences between Average and Gifted Students with Respect to the Frequencies of Certain Response Categories," have been omitted in reprinting.—EDITOR'S NOTE.

parently good relation is reinforced by the fact that less than 10 percent mentioned problems of mother-father-child relationships, such as parental differences with respect to discipline or differences in their feelings toward the two parents. Although so many of the gifted (58 percent in the junior high school and 49 percent in the senior high school) made comments that indicated satisfactory relations with parents, almost one fifth of the gifted group in the senior high school, as contrasted with 6 percent of the senior high average IQ group, also mentioned conflicts or lack of closeness or rapport with parents. Good relations with parents may be more difficult for the gifted to achieve in the lower socioeconomic groups than in the middle or upper classes. Still, it is significant that such a large percentage of the gifted, during the years when emancipation from the family is a major goal, seem to be accomplishing this developmental task without excessive emotional wear and tear.

Desire for a particular vocation was mentioned by about one third of both groups. Slightly fewer—one fifth to one fourth [data in omitted table]—expressed feelings or other indications of indecision about their vocation. The indecision of the gifted may stem partly from the wide range of vocational choices open to them. They may also realize that a decision concerning their vocation need not be made in junior or senior high school. If they take the educational program designed to develop their potentialities, they will be prepared to make a decision regarding vocation when the time comes.

Approximately one third of both the average and the gifted gave indications of self-acceptance. One might expect greater self-acceptance among the gifted. This was not indicated by the compositions. Other studies, too, have suggested that gifted students often have feelings of inferiority. Sometimes they compare themselves with the lives of great men and women about whom they read, rather than with their peers.

Nor are the gifted much less *concerned with scholastic success or grades* than are students of average intelligence. About one fifth of both groups expressed concern with school success or grades. They are also not entirely satisfied with their school experiences: about one tenth of the total sample expressed dissatisfaction. Actually many gifted children become bored and disillusioned with school. Their attitudes toward school and achievement will depend a great deal on the morale of the school, the attitude of other students toward them, and the challenges offered by the curriculum and methods of instruction. The pressure of ambitious parents or the indifference of other parents to the education of their gifted children will likewise influence the adolescent's school achievement.

DIFFERENCES IN RESPONSES

In certain respects there were differences between the average and the bright students studied.

The students of average intelligence mentioned more frequently than the gifted *increasing independence and self-direction* as an advantage of growing up. Possibly those with lower intelligence have been more irked by restrictions and, being more dissatisfied with their present status, they look forward to any change. Somewhat allied to this desire for freedom is the wish to own or operate a car—a desire that was expressed by twice as many average as bright students.

At the same time, less able students seem much more *aware of increasing responsibilities*. One possible explanation is that students of average and below-average intelligence are closer to the time when they will leave school and go to work than are the gifted who are planning to continue in school; therefore responsibilities loom larger to them. Another possible explanation is that the bright students, feeling capable of carrying responsibilities, are not anxious enough to write about them.

In interpreting these tables, the relative number of responses given by the average and by the gifted should be considered. The bright students wrote more freely; they gave a larger total number of responses—6.8 categorized responses per composition as compared with 5.9 responses given by the average group.

In the junior high school the bright students more frequently referred to *financial security* and money problems than did the average. In the senior high school the percentage was about the same.

Very marked was the gifted students's *social concern for world peace*. Such precocious interest in more remote and abstract matters, including morality and religion, is characteristic of the gifted.

Contrary to popular opinion (but not to the results of research), the bright students frequently expressed *satisfaction in relations with their peers*. Social giftedness is often associated with verbal ability. However, some mentioned their desire for greater acceptance with their peers and almost half were concerned with boy-girl relations.

The most striking difference on the junior high school level was in *enjoyment of voluntary reading*. In these years, when voluntary reading is at its peak, 42 percent of the bright students as contrasted with 13 percent of the average made some reference to the enjoyment of reading. But in senior high school the difference in voluntary reading was far less marked—23 percent by the average as compared with 31 percent by the gifted. The decrease in interest in voluntary reading of the gifted may be attributable to competition with other adolescent interests, more time devoted to required reading with college entrance in mind, reluctance to be considered a book worm by age mates, lack of intellectual stimulation in the home, and other reasons.

AGE DIFFERENCES AMONG THE GIFTED

Some additional age differences in responses are suggested in Table 3. For categories in Table 3, the frequency for one age level was actually one third or more greater than the frequency at the other age level.

Interest in sports is much more frequently mentioned by the gifted in junior high school than in senior high school. Perhaps this is because other kinds of activities introduced during senior-high-school years, such as school publications and departmental clubs, interest them more than sports. Sometimes, too, the bright child, though equally able to learn athletic skills, learns them relatively more slowly than he does verbal tasks and consequently becomes impatient with his progress.

In *family relations* also some age differences were noted in the groups studied. During junior-high-school years the gifted mentioned concern about their family's problems and welfare more often than they did later. The older brighter students seemed to find less satisfaction in their relations with brothers and sisters than those of junior-high-school age. Among the explanations of this difference is their increasing attention to boy-girl relations, which may crowd out other interests and also put brothers and sisters in the nuisance class. Many individual factors, of course, enter into sibling relations. According to their responses, both age groups have about the same proportion of problems with brothers and sisters. Approximately one fifth to one fourth of the gifted expressed a desire for marriage and children. In the gifted group there was only a slight increase from the junior to senior high school for the bright students, whereas for the average students the frequency of mention

TABLE 3

Differences between Gifted Students at the Junior and Senior High-school Levels with Respect to the Frequency of Certain Response Categories

Category of response	156 junior-high students (IQ 120 or greater)		85 senior-high students (IQ 120 or greater)	
	Number of responses	Percent of relative frequency	Number of responses	Percent of relative frequency
Interest in sports	39	25	7	8
Concern for family's welfare	26	17	6	7
Satisfaction with sibling relations	46	29	15	18
Lack of closeness or rapport with parents	13	8	16	19
Concern with social behavior, making friends	41	26	13	15
Desire for greater peer acceptance	14	9	12	14
Problems about money	19	12	7	8
Concern with military service	5	3	11	13
Concern with morality and religion	25	16	24	28
Enjoyment of voluntary reading	66	42	26	31

in this category increased from 16 percent at the junior-high to 33 percent at the senior-high-school level. This difference between the two intelligence levels may be related to the generally greater precocity of the gifted group: They read earlier, are earlier concerned with religion and with moral values, and also seem to be somewhat more mature socially.

With parents, too, the bright students's relations seem to be better during junior-high-school years than later. More than twice as many of the senior-high-school gifted students mentioned lack of closeness or rapport with parents. Part of this feeling is a natural and desirable accompaniment of gaining independence from the family, but antagonism and misunderstanding underlies some of it. They expressed an awareness of differences between parents in standards and methods of discipline and showed a preference for one parent. However, the numbers in these categories are small and the dominant finding is the fact that about half of the gifted senior-high-school students and still more of the junior-high-school youngsters made some reference to satisfying relations with their parents.

Concern with social behavior, with making friends and getting along with people in general, was mentioned by about one fourth of the bright junior-high-school students. This percentage was almost twice as large as that for the average IQs. But fewer of the gifted in the senior than in the junior high school mentioned this aspect of adolescent adjustment. Perhaps the brighter students had learned to make a better social adjustment; perhaps the senior high school provided social activities that appealed to them; perhaps they have become more absorbed in intellectual pursuits. Perhaps their concern took the form of desire for greater peer acceptance which a number of both age groups mentioned. There are many possible reasons, some highly individual and stemming from early childhood experiences.

Problems about money were mentioned by relatively few of the gifted in their compositions about growing up, and there was a decrease in frequency of mention from the junior to the senior high school. Possibly these students had found ways to meet their increasing need for money or they may have come from socio-economic backgrounds where money was not a problem.

Concern with morality and religion showed a marked increase among the gifted from junior to senior high school. It may be of significance that the increase was larger for the average group than for the gifted—from 9 percent to 23 percent, while the corresponding figures for the gifted were from 16 percent to 28 percent, reflecting the earlier interest of the gifted in such problems.

SEX DIFFERENCES

A further breakdown of the data for 461 students in the eleventh grade confirmed, in general, the relations already mentioned. The responses were tabulated for:

11th-grade boys, IQ *less* than 100
11th-grade boys, IQ *more* than 100
11th-grade girls, IQ *less* than 100
11th-grade girls, IQ *more* than 100

Positive aspects of physical development and fitness seem to mean more to boys than to girls. The brighter eleventh-grade boys mentioned satisfaction with their body growth and status relatively more frequently than did the girls or the boys of average intelligence. The brighter girls expressed the most dissatisfaction.

Family relations seem to be of more concern to girls than to boys. A larger percentage of girls, especially the brighter girls, mentioned having problems with brothers and sisters. Small brothers can be very annoying to older sisters, and perhaps there are more opportunities for conflict between sisters than between brothers. It was the girls, though few in number, who more often complained of conflict or lack of closeness with parents. Girls also mentioned broken homes and concern for the welfare of their families relatively more frequently than did boys. The desire for marriage and children was expressed by 38 percent of the girls over 100 IQ as contrasted with 18 percent of the boys in the same classes. The relationship was practically the same for students with IQs below 100. Girls, in general, are more "family oriented" than boys and are probably more willing to talk about it.

Careers are of concern to gifted adolescent girls, although marriage may be uppermost in their minds. It was surprising that these girls seemed to be thinking about vocations slightly more than boys. Certainly this would not have been the emphasis fifty years ago.

Satisfaction with peer relationships was expressed by slightly more gifted girls than by boys on the same level of intelligence. But, at the same time, the girls more often mentioned a desire for greater acceptance by peers and more concern with or interest in boy-girl relations and in making friends and getting along with people in general. Girls seem to be more socially oriented than boys.

With respect to indications of *self-acceptance,* the percentage of the brighter boys and girls was exactly the same—37 percent. The girls, however, more frequently mentioned a desire to improve their personality. Possibly the boys actually wanted to improve *their* personality but did not consider it the thing to write about.

Voluntary reading showed a marked difference in frequency of mention between the brighter boys and the girls—16 percent of the boys and 41 percent of the girls. Both boys and girls in the upper intelligence groups complained more about homework than those below average. This may have been due to the more rigorous assignments given to students in the college-preparatory curriculum or to kinds of homework that gifted students find exceedingly boring.

The desire for world peace was mentioned slightly more frequently by the brighter girls than by the boys, but concern with military service was referred to primarily by boys. The girls also showed more concern with problems of morality and religion, as indicated by this type of response from 21 percent of the girls as compared with 10 percent of the boys.

CONCLUDING STATEMENT

This study of the spontaneous responses of junior- and senior-high-school students to the topic "How It Feels to Be Growing Up" has confirmed some of the generalizations regarding gifted adolescents. It has also contributed much more detail about the way in which they perceive the growing-up process and ways in which they are alike or different from their age mates of lower intelligence. To read similar compositions written by one's own groups of adolescents would give teachers still more insight into how it feels to be a gifted adolescent.

8

UNDER-
ACHIEVEMENT

❧❦❧

ADEMOCRATIC SOCIETY has an obligation to provide opportunities for individuals to develop and use their talents, and the interests of society require that such opportunities be made attractive. The maximum welfare for a group is achieved when each member of the group contributes as much as he is able. New technological pressures have sharpened our awareness of our short-sighted failure to identify and develop many of our most promising minds to the limit of their potential. Extraordinary talent unchanneled or unevoked is a tremendous waste.

These feelings have caused many educators to be concerned about the achievement of the gifted because the gifted child is seen as the greatest underachiever in school. John C. Gowan has written the most exhaustive review of the literature pertaining to the gifted underachiever, so it would be well to consider his definition (pp. 395-396) at this point. Underachievement is

performance which places the student more than a full standard deviation below his ability standing in the same group. Roughly, this works out to be about 30 percentiles difference, so that we may call gifted children underachievers when they fall in the middle third in scholastic achievement in grades and severe underachievers when they fall in the lowest third.

Although this definition is not uniformly accepted by all investigators, it is used here for clarity and convenience.

Gifted children are the greatest underachievers in our schools because their achievement is further below the limits of their capacity than any other group. The mentally handicapped achieve closer to their capacity than any other group. While those of average intelligence reach higher levels of competence than the mentally handicapped, many still achieve far below their capacity. Likewise, the typical person of superior mental ability can perform somewhat better than the average child even though he may be working far below his potential. The realization that he can quickly accomplish more than his peers often leads to a false sense of worthy accomplishment.

Gifted children have often said that one of their greatest problems is the feeling of "aloneness." Since friendships are often de-

392

termined by intellectual level and ability to think and like the same things, gifted children often find it easy to make acquaintances but difficult to establish real friendships in traditionally grouped classrooms. In their search for acceptance some gifted children feel that they must submerge their information, neglect the use and development of their large vocabularies, and hide their interests and enthusiasms for knowledge.

One's "self-concept" is also thought to have considerable effect on the level of his achievement. The child who is not regarded as bright by those with whom he comes in contact sees himself as slow or incapable of near perfect achievement and retains this concept when he goes to school. The person who believes that his "self" is of only mediocre ability will adhere to all perceptions which encourage that picture of himself and will refuse to believe many things which suggest that he is good, strong, or extremely capable.

Some good in-service research has been conducted in the Portland, Oregon, schools. The faculty committee concerned with their Cooperative Program for Students of Exceptional Endowment became interested in the many high-school students whose IQs indicated superior ability but who did persistently mediocre or poor work in school. Under the guiding hand of research director Robert C. Wilson, the committee investigated some of the reasons for underachievement and compared the characteristics and the backgrounds of these students with those of high-achieving students matched for intelligence, socioeconomic status, and grade in school (grades 9, 10, and 11). The study was limited to 49 pairs of boys since there were not enough underachieving girls to attain significance in the findings. Selected findings from the committee report of March 1957 follow:

The two groups of students tend to agree in viewing teachers as generally competent, sincere, and fair-minded. Their perceptions differ most in that the underachievers see the teacher as more often emotionally undermining rather than supporting. Though the low-achievers in various ways show less achievement-mindedness, three fifths of them express dissatisfaction with their school achievement. But they set their sights lower, and are also less confident of their ability to make high grades, tending to rate their own intelligence as somewhat lower than do the high-achievers. Moreover, many of the underachievers express a negative view of those who make high grades as typically "grinds" who turn away from social activities and athletics. This conception is contradicted by the two groups's reports of their extracurricular and outside activities. These reports reveal the high-achievers to be more active. In general outlook on life, both as to achievement tasks and more personal problems, the high-achievers seem to be somewhat more confident, secure, and optimistic, as well as more concerned with social responsibility. The low-achievers more often show signs of a demoralized outlook, see adult authorities as domineering and victimizing, may be cynical, and sometimes show escapist inclinations toward "excitement" and toward wishful solutions of problems. The low-achievers also somewhat more often describe their family situations as having relatively poor morale, with more parental domination, less sharing, and especially less mutual affection and approval. The parents of the two groups do not differ, however, in their expressed philosophy of child rearing.

The opening article of this section is the comprehensive review of the literature by Dr. Gowan in which he discusses the "Dynamics of the Underachievement of Gifted Students." Dr. Gowan enumerates the 13 common elements he found in the literature relating to the levels of achievement of the gifted. He then goes on to characterize the achiever and the underachiever.

The following three articles summarize specific studies bearing on underachievement. The data presented and analyzed in the first of these three articles was gathered in a Midwestern community with a population under 10,000 by John J. Kurtz and Esther Swenson. Comprehensive reports on 40 students whose achievement was definitely below expectation on the basis of measured intelligence were compared with reports on 40 other students whose achievement was well above expectation on the basis of ability. The sample was drawn from grades four through twelve.

Dr. Jack A. Holmes and Carmen J. Finley were concerned with the hypothesis that certain academic disciplines at the upper elementary level are more important than others in contributing to nonpromotions, promotions, and acceleration. Their study could well be repeated in other localities to determine if a more equal distribution of weight should be placed on success in each subject-matter field. Professor Holmes, a former researcher in physical chemistry, is an educational psychologist on the Berkeley campus of the University of California and Finley is a consultant in administrative research for the Sonoma County California School Districts.

In the last reading, the variables that differentiate achievers from nonachievers among college freshmen, are reported by Robert J. Dowd, a psychologist at the University of New Hampshire.

DYNAMICS OF THE UNDERACHIEVEMENT
OF GIFTED STUDENTS

by John C. Gowan

SAN FERNANDO VALLEY STATE COLLEGE

In recent years, as manpower reserves of talent for scientific and professional occupations have become depleted, more and more attention is being directed to the salvaging of a significant portion of our ablest youth who qualify for the title of gifted underachievers. We are not concerned in this discussion with the economic and social factors which Stice (16) has demonstrated prevented over half of the high-ability high-school seniors in our country from going on directly to college. We are rather concerned with the equally depressing fact, demonstrated by Wedemeyer (19), that of those who go, almost 30 percent of the top decile of intelligence fail to attain significant achievement in scholarship because of emotional, educational, personal, financial, or other problems. Faced with the present economic and political rivalry with Russia, a nation turning out scientists at twice our rate, our country cannot afford this waste of its most vital resource—talent.

It is the purpose of this paper, therefore, to explore recent research on the causes and prevention of underachievement in gifted students. Moreover a developmental hypothesis is proposed to account for agreements in research findings and practical implications for education which seem warranted by these results are appended. By "gifted student" we shall refer to a student who is two or more standard deviations upward from the mean in general intelligence; loosely, an IQ of 130 or above. Recognizing that practically all gifted children are technically underachievers to some extent, we may define "underachievement" for our purposes as performance which places the student more than a full standard deviation below his ability standing in the same group. Roughly, this works out to about

[Reprinted from *Exceptional Children*, 24, November 1957, 98-107, with the permission of the Council for Exceptional Children and the author. A reprint of this article is available from CEC.]

30 percentiles difference, so that we may call gifted children under-achievers when they fall in the middle third in scholastic achievement in grades and severe underachievers when they fall in the lowest third. It should be noted that these definitions are ones made merely for clarity and convenience, and are by no means uniformly used by all those whose research is later to be reported.

It may first be of value to note data concerning the number and percentage of underachievers in secondary schools represented by the previous definitions. Figures have elsewhere (10) been presented to show that in one California high school where 7 percent of the students were gifted, 42 percent of these were underachievers. In another high school where 2 percent of the students were gifted, 16 percent of these were underachievers. In an outstanding independent secondary school, 12 percent of the students were gifted, and 9 percent of these were underachievers. In the same paper, it was suggested that "where the percent of underachievers runs much higher than 15 percent, there may be problems of morale, antisocial trends, or other factors in the school which should receive special attention" (10).

There is considerable research evidence to indicate that achievement both in high school and later stems from habits, interests, attitudes, and motivation established in elementary school. With gifted children, these latter factors seem to be facilitated by special curriculum adjustments.

Terman (18), for example, reported that gifted youth who were accelerated in school outstripped those who had not been accelerated, both in college and in later life success. He concluded that "the exceptionally bright student kept with his age group finds little to challenge his intelligence, and all too often develops habits of laziness that later wreck his college career." The Los Angeles School District (11) in 1931 reported a high-school comparison between 284 opportunity A students and 381 equally gifted controls; the opportunity A group which had been segregated in the fifth through seventh grades, had higher high-school grade averages, earned more honor grades, and had fewer failures. Cohler (4) found in a similar study that the effect of acceleration was improved performance, and stressed the need for vital school experiences to motivate the child. Sanford (15), after a discussion of the bright child who fails, considered boredom, lack of motivation, and home problems as major causes of underachievement. Engle (6), in another study of accelerants, found acceleration generally conducive to more favorable educational and vocational results than nonacceleration. The same results in even more specific terms were reported recently for the Ford scholarship holders (8). It seems evident from the weight of the foregoing reports either that special curriculum methods for the gifted have some value in themselves in reducing underachievement, or that the increased attention, interest, recognition, and personal contact which accompany them result in increased motivation and consequent increased achievement.

A number of investigators have reported on college-level achievement and underachievement of gifted students. Nason (13) found achievement at this level more related to clearness and definiteness of academic and vocational plans and to parental influences than to personal adjustment. Burgess (3), in a study of engineering underachievers, described them in these terms: "less intellectually adaptive . . . less emotional control . . . more dependent in attitudes toward others . . . motivation weak . . . tend not to enjoy the school situation . . . unable to see the value of an education." Dowd (5 and pp. 420-426 in this volume), in a college study of underachievers in the top decile, found no personality difference, but more incidence of males, and concluded that the factors are operative before college entrance. Morgan (12), in a similar study, concluded generally that college achievement of high-ability students is "related to (1) maturity and seriousness of interests, (2) awareness and concern for others, (3) a sense of responsibility, (4) dominance, persuasiveness, and self-confidence, and (5) motivation to achieve." Similar results were secured by Pearlman (14).

Studies on younger gifted underachievers have tended to emphasize home backgrounds, parental problems, and emotional immaturity. A study by Bonsall and Stellfre (2 and pp. 377-380 in this volume) emphasized the importance of not overlooking the socio-economic factor. Basic causes for the behavior of 38 gifted children referred to a metropolitan clinic as maladjusted and reported elsewhere (9) included disagreements between parents over methods of raising the child, transference of problems of parents to the child, overanxiety or overprotectiveness on the part of the parent, fears of the parents regarding the children's health and safety, divorces and separations, and sibling rivalry. The school problems of these gifted children were seen in such symptoms as: ". . . not interested in school, didn't like teacher, work was too easy, didn't have any friends, liked to stay home with mother." Another inquiry (10) into the family backgrounds of high-school underachievers of IQ 130 or better found that they differed significantly from gifted achievers in that the underachievers were predominantly boys, had parents who took little part in community activities, had fewer books in their homes, had less often received private lessons, and expressed a desire in choosing a vocation to get away from the family. The pattern which emerged was one of indifference and rejection on the part of the parent, or behavior so interpreted by the underachiever. In addition he had less time for outside activities, had more problems with time and money, and seemed lacking in ability to conduct himself easily in social situations and to make easy adjustments.

A recent study meriting attention was one made by Barrett (1) in the Toronto, Ontario, high schools. He concluded that the pattern of underachievement is apparent by the fifth grade with weakness in arithmetic characteristic, and parents of underachievers tend to exhibit a neutral or uninterested attitude towards education, to be overanxious, oversolicitous, or inconsistent in their attitude toward the child. In general, such homes show evidence of conflict, authoritarianism by the parent, or domination by the child. In the school situation the underachievers exhibit a predominantly negative attitude towards school, win less acceptance from their classmates, tend to show less interest in reading. While both show feelings of inadequacy, the achievers are aware of their difficulties, and constructive in their efforts, while the underachievers withdraw and refuse to compete.

Another study deserving special attention is that of Gough (9). In an effort to construct and validate an achievement scale on the California Psychological Inventory he investigated personality items among a large number of underachievers. From this group he selected paired groups of gifted achievers and underachievers, dichotomized for both high school and college as well as by sex. While there were a number of personality differences, the major ones were that underachievers were significantly higher on the scale for delinquency; and achievers were higher on the scales for social responsibility and academic motivation. The scale for academic motivation correlated over .50 with scales for good impression, lack of dissimulation, social responsibility, tolerance, social participation, antidelinquency, intellectual efficiency, lack of impulsivity. Gough concluded that ". . . academic achievement among intellectually gifted persons is a form of social behavior, and academic underachievement is a form of a social behavior." He summarizes that underachievement among the gifted is akin to delinquent behavior.

A consonant finding had been previously reported by Terman (17) in comparing 150 of his most successful gifted men with 150 least successful. The A group seemed to have greater enthusiasm for living and activity. They read more books, made more collections, engaged in more hobbies, were more successful in school, and were more popular with classmates and teachers.

The common elements from these research reports indicate that achievement in gifted students versus underachievement seems related to the following factors:

1. Clearness and definiteness of academic and occupational choices versus the opposite.
2. Strong ego controls and strength versus weak ones.
3. Socialization and social interaction versus withdrawal and self-sufficiency.
4. Good use of time and money versus lack of such habits.
5. Reading and arithmetic ability versus lack of such competency.
6. Positive character integration versus psychotic or neurotic tendency.
7. Permissiveness, intraception, and creativity versus authoritarianism in the parental home environment or the gifted individual himself.
8. Parents who motivated and took pains or interest, versus dominant, autocratic, or *laissez-faire* parents.
9. Some tension in task demands in childhood (the imposition of goals which are clear and possible to attain by parents) versus either no goal or impossible ones.
10. Maturity, responsibility, and seriousness of interests versus opposites.
11. Awareness of and concern for others versus disinterest.
12. Dominance, persuasiveness, and self-confidence versus their opposites.
13. Enthusiastic, socialized, activity-oriented view of life, versus apathetic withdrawal.

As such a summarization is inspected critically it appears to be a description of healthy personal attitudes and behaviors which are associated with the accomplishment of growth patterns on schedule. These skills and attributes are connected with cognitive ego development and singularly related to various developmental stages of childhood. As each new adaptation is resolved successfully, a new strength and vitality is incorporated into the ego. An excellent description of this developmental process is given by Erikson (7), especially in his "industry" stage which coincides with early latency period when the child turns outward from the family to peer group recognition in which, in Erikson's words:

He can become an eager and absorbed unit in a productive situation. . . . He develops industry, that is he adjusts himself to the inorganic laws of the tool world. . . . The danger in this stage lies in a sense of inadequacy and inferiority. If he despairs of his tools and skills or of his status among his tool partners, his ego boundaries suffer, and he abandons hope for the ability to identify early with others who apply themselves . . .

Parents who are either too autocratic, too dominant, too protective, or too *laissez faire* arrest the child's development into and through this industry stage, where he learns the joy of real work and accomplishment as an aid to status-getting among his peers and with outside authority figures. As a result he is thrown back for libido rewards to the earlier and more primitive satisfactions of the oral, anal, narcissistic, and oedipal periods. Because boys are slightly less mature than girls, and because parents sometimes expect more of them, their introduction to cultural tasks demands may be more difficult, and hence more problems may accrue.

To be sure, public schooling in the primary grades does much for those children whose parents may not have been successful in aiding the child through these critical adjustments; but while doing well by the generality, it frequently misses meeting the needs of two important groups. First is the minority-group member who does not identify with the alien culture of the school and second is the gifted child whom it does not challenge during this crucial period. Such a hypothesis explains most of the observed differences between gifted achievers and underachievers, as well as pointing up the vital necessity of adequate stimulation of gifted children during the primary grades, instead of forcing them to remain bored and inactive.

In contrast to gifted underachievers, the childhood of the gifted achiever appears to involve a constant, but not severe, pressure towards tasks and responsibilities which are perceived by the child as security or affection-producing and which are neither capriciously administered nor impossible to attain under the aegis of interest—stimulating parental guidance. Thus early experience in realistic goal setting and achieving leads to a personality with strong superego demands and strong ego strength to complete these demands. Such a personality tends in adulthood to have a high sense of social responsibility and large performance needs. He is not without anxieties, but these are oriented toward reality, and tend to be ameliorated by his or others modification of the environment rather than by changes in his attitudes towards it.

The gifted underachiever, on the other hand, appears to be a kind of intellectual delinquent who withdraws from goals, activities, and active social participation generally. As a child his initial attempts at creative accomplishment may not have been seen by others as "worthwhile," but only as "queer" or "different." The blocking of this avenue of rewarding behavior by others, tending as it does to reinforce his often overcritical appraisal of the disparity between his goals and achievements, may blunt his work libido, stifle his creativity, and consign him to a routine of withdrawal and escape as the most tolerable method of insulating his ego from hurt in an alien and disinterested world.

Thus achievement and underachievement in the gifted may be viewed as social and asocial responses of the individual to proper stimulation regarding developmental tasks either tendered or denied by the parental and educational environments.

REFERENCES

1. Barrett, H. G. Underachievement, A Pressing Problem. *Bull. Ontario Secondary School Teachers' Federation*, Oshawa, Ontario, 36, May 31, 1956, 111-112, 151-152.
2. Bonsall, Marcella, and B. Stellfre. The Temperament of Gifted Children, *Calif. J. Educ. Res.*, 6, 1955, 162-165.
3. Burgess, Elva. Personality Factors of Over- and Under-achievers in Engineering, *J. Educ. Psychol.*, 42, February 1956, 89-99.
4. Cohler, M. J. Scholastic Status of Achievers and Nonachievers of Superior Intelligence, *J. Educ. Psychol.*, 32, 1941, 603-610.
5. Dowd, R. J. Underachieving Students of High Capacity, *J. Higher Educ.*, 23, 1952, 327-330.
6. Engle, T. L. Achievement of Pupils Who Have Had Double Promotions in Elementary School. *Elem. School J.*, 36, 1935, 185-189.
7. Erikson, E. H. *Childhood and Society.* New York: Norton, 1950, pp. 219-233.
8. Ford Foundation, Fund for the Advancement of Education. *Bridging the Gap Between School and College.* New York, 1953.
9. Gough, H. G. Factors Related to Differential Achievement Among Gifted Persons (mimeographed). Berkeley, Calif.: Univ. of California, 1955.
10. Gowan, J. C. The Underachieving Gifted Child: A Problem for Everyone, *Exceptional Children*, 21, April 1955, 247-249.
11. Los Angeles City School District, *Fourth Yearbook of the Psychological and Educational Research Division*, No. 211, Los Angeles, Calif., 1931, p. 82.
12. Morgan, H. H. A Psychometric Comparison of Achieving and Non-

Achieving College Students of High Ability. *J. Consult. Psychol.*, 16, 1952, 292-298.

13. Nason, L. J. Patterns of Circumstances Related to Educational Achievement of High School Pupils of Superior Ability. Unpublished Ed.D. thesis, Univ. of Southern California, 1954.

14. Pearlman, Samuel. An Investigation of the Problems of Academic Underachievement among Intellectually Superior College Students, unpublished Ph.D. thesis, New York Univ., 1952 (microfilmed, Ann Arbor, Mich., #4149).

15. Sanford, E. G. The Bright Child Who Fails. *Understanding the Child*, 21, 1952, 85-88.

16. Stice, G., W. G. Mollenkopf, and W. S. Torgerson. *Background Factors and College Going Plans among High Aptitude Public High School Seniors*, Princeton, N. J.: Educational Testing Service, 1956.

17. Terman, L. M., and others. *The Gifted Child Grows Up*, Vol. IV in *Genetic Studies of Genius*. Stanford, Calif.: Stanford Univ. Press, 1947.

18. ———. Earmarking the Talented. *Science News Letter*, April 3, 1954, p. 214.

19. Wedemeyer, C. A. Gifted Achievers and Non-Achievers. *J. Higher Educ.*, 24, 1953, 25-30.

FACTORS RELATED TO OVERACHIEVEMENT AND UNDERACHIEVEMENT IN SCHOOL

by John J. Kurtz

UNIVERSITY OF MARYLAND

and Esther Swenson

UNIVERSITY OF ALABAMA

THE PROBLEM

Old and still persisting is the question of why some students achieve well in school while others achieve poorly. We can answer with some

[Reprinted from *School Review*, 59, November 1951, 472-480, with the permission of the University of Chicago Press and the authors.]

assurance that intelligence is a factor in school achievement, but we must admit with equal assurance that intelligence is not the only factor. It is common knowledge that some students with lesser measured ability do better work in school than other children with greater measured ability. This article reports part of a study concerned with factors, in addition to measured intelligence, that may be related to school achievement. The terms "intelligence" and "achievement" are used here in the narrow sense represented by scores on intelligence and achievement tests.

The study was made in a midwestern city of under 10,000 population as part of a larger research project undertaken there.[1] Five types of achievers were selected on the basis of ranked Otis intelligence test scores and achievement scores on the Iowa Every-

TABLE 1

Rank Order of Group Means according to Intelligence Measure and Achievement Scores

Rank	Intelligence	Achievement score
1	High-high	High-high
2	Minus	Plus
3	Medium-medium	Medium-medium
4	Plus	Minus
5	Low-low	Low-low

pupil Tests of Basic Skills: Test B, Work-study Skills; the Unit Scales of Attainment in Reading; and the Hundred-problem Arithmetic Test.

The five types selected were (1) high achievers of high ability; (2) medium achievers of medium ability; (3) low achievers of low ability; (4) "plus achievers," students whose achievement was well above expectation on the basis of ability rating; and (5) "minus achievers," students whose achievement was definitely below expectation on the basis of ability rating. This report is concerned with the last two groups. The relationships among the groups are shown in Table 1. Altogether, there were 40 students of each type: four of each from grades four through eight, and five of each from grades nine through twelve.

---

[1] The larger report, *Prairie City School Appraisal*, is on file with the Committee on Human Development and the Department of Education at the University of Chicago.

EXPLORATION OF UNDERLYING FACTORS

Along with the test data, reports were available for each pupil on interviews with the children themselves, their parents, and their teachers. These reports contained ratings on attitudes toward the school situation, toward educational achievement, and toward the importance of "an education" in general, as well as information about educational and vocational aims. In addition to these data, there were classroom-observation reports on most of the pupils who had been studied specially; fairly extensive supplementary notes and comments given in the reports of student, parent, and teacher interviews; and several hundred clippings from the local newspaper.

The classroom-observation reports consisted of objective notes dealing with a specific child's behavior in a regular classroom situation, his relation to other persons in the classroom, his general appearance and manner, and any other noteworthy matters witnessed during the period of observation. In a number of instances, the classroom-observation reports concluded with comments which teachers had made to the observer at the end of the class period. The supplementary-interview notes, while mainly consisting in verbal explanations for the interview ratings given, frequently contained a considerable amount of information regarding the home situation, personal relationships of the child in question, and other potentially pertinent data. The newspaper clippings concerned school and community activities involving the children in our study, their friends, or their parents.

This material comprised a considerable body of information requiring some kind of organization for effective use. It was decided to consider the following areas in studying the supplementary data available for a number of students who were representative of the group studied: (1) home conditions, (2) peer relations, (3) physical and mental well-being, (4) academic inclination, and (5) aspirations and prospects for the future. Other areas might have been investigated, but the nature of the data placed some limitation on what could be done. The areas investigated in the present study are all included, in one form or another, in the larger frame of reference developed for the purpose of helping teachers understand children.[2]

[2] *Helping Teachers Understand Children,* by the staff of the Division on Child Development and Teacher Personnel, prepared for the Commission on Teacher Education, Washington, D. C.: American Council on Education, 1945, pp. 431-432.

While space will not permit the presentation of data covering all the areas of investigation listed and all the students studied in grades four through twelve, sample summaries will perhaps illustrate the findings. The data which are presented are for the plus and the minus achievers only.[3] It is not assumed that the children of these groups are essentially different from the children of other groups, but it does seem (and explanation of the data supports the point) that factors which attend school achievement are more sharply brought into focus in instances of plus achievement and minus achievement.

HOME CONDITIONS

Pride, confidence, affection, and parental interest, as shown in instances in which parents read to their children, play with them, build for them, or attend school functions with them, appear to be in greater evidence for plus achievers than for minus achievers. On the part of children, there is a tendency among plus achievers to respect their parents, to take them into their confidence, to be concerned about pleasing them, and to return the love their parents show.

Minus achievers appear to have a comparatively limited place in the home. There does not appear to be so much exchange of affection, or mutual respect, or desire to measure up to expectations. In fact, even expectations appear limited for minus achievers.

We can see also, from the interview excerpts, that the same home may have different meanings for different children of the same family. The climate of affection within the home for a particular child and its various manifestations appear to be related definitely to school achievement.

PEER RELATIONS

The number of friends alone does not, in all cases, distinguish plus from minus achievers, although minus achievers seem more often to be alone. The quality of friends provides sharper distinction. When specific friends are mentioned, plus achievers appear to

[3] It may be of interest to point out that sex composition of the plus and minus groups appears in itself to be significant. Of the 40 plus achievers, 28 are girls and 12 are boys; of the 40 minus achievers, 13 are girls and 27 are boys. This fact, considering that sex was not a factor in the selection of students for study, suggests that the nature of classroom work may be less appealing to boys, although this is not the only possible explanation.

have friends who are also concerned about doing well in school and who are also well regarded by teachers. Minus achievers tend to have friends who are not too well regarded by teachers, who have comparably poor school records, whose attitudes toward school are unfavorable, or who have already left school.

The lines between plus and minus achievers in their peer relations are not so clearly drawn that we should want to depend on this factor in isolation from other factors. It may well be that the interview method used in this study did not supply as adequate a body of information regarding peer relations as one might obtain, for example, through the use of sociometric techniques. Nevertheless, it did reveal apparent differences between the peer relations of plus and minus achievers. How well a child gets along with his age mates appears to be related to school achievement, and the quality of a child's friends appears particularly significant.

PHYSICAL AND MENTAL WELL-BEING

The interview reports suggest that plus achievers have less conflict in their lives than do minus achievers. Although there are exceptions, plus achievers generally present a good appearance and exhibit leadership qualities, originality, and self-confidence. They seem not only to have a comparatively high opinion of themselves but also to enjoy the approbation of others.

In contrast, minus achievers appear comparatively restless, changeable, and unhappy. Problems related to personal appearance are suggested and, at the upper-grade levels, problems of heterosexual adjustment. There is a tendency for minus achievers to lack confidence in themselves, and they do not seem to be highly regarded by other persons.

It is interesting to consider in this regard Lecky's theory of self-consistency,[4] which develops the idea that a person acts in accordance with his concept of himself. As the plus achievers appear to have a higher opinion of themselves than do the minus achievers, it may well be that the students's opinions of themselves (for whatever reasons such opinions have been established) influence their achievement in school. When we recall that plus achievers consistently ranked near the high achievers in the various investigations made in this study and that minus achievers generally ranked near the low achievers (according to self-evaluation and the evaluation

4 Prescott Lecky, *Self-consistency*, New York: Island Press, 1945.

of others in such areas as attitudes, adjustment, personality traits, and educational and vocational aspirations), we have a basis for extending the implications which the additional data on plus and minus achievers suggest.[5] We do not want to lose sight of the fact that mental and physical well-being is only one of several areas explored and that these factors must be viewed in relation to other factors.

ACADEMIC INCLINATION

Notations in this area point to a greater interest or inclination on the part of plus achievers for book learning, in contrast to a greater interest or inclination on the part of minus achievers for nonacademic activities—construction, tinkering, experimentation, or pleasure-seeking. Plus achievers appear to derive more satisfaction from reading and appear happier in the traditional classroom situation, which is typical of the school system with which our study deals. This tendency appears strong enough in some plus achievers to induce them to give reading and study top priority.

In contrast, for some minus achievers almost anything seems preferable to reading and study. We note an absence of evidence that plus achievers dislike doing the kinds of things schooling requires. For minus achievers, a definite disinclination for academic work is apparent. One might speculate that, if the school program were more flexible, differences in achievement might well be decreased, but it would hardly be safe to indicate that such a change alone would solve the problem of achievement discrepancy.

ASPIRATIONS AND PROSPECTS FOR THE FUTURE

Plus achievers appear to have a greater desire for an extended education and more definite plans for attaining it. This appears to show up even in the lower grades. There seems to be encouragement toward this end by parents or teachers or both. Plus achievers also appear more concerned about the possibility of not getting the amount of education they desire. They appear to see a relation between an education and their future life and regard education for more than its job value. They appear to have fairly clear vocational aims, at least in the upper grades, and these aims appear to be reasonable.

[5] John J. Kurtz and Esther J. Swenson, "Student, Parent, and Teacher Attitude toward Student Achievement in School," *School Rev.*, 59, May 1951, 273-279.

As a rule, minus achievers seem to have more limited educational aims. They tend to think about quitting school. Adults appear to have little confidence in, or encouragement for, an extended education for minus achievers. The vocational aims of minus achievers appear comparatively limited, vague, or uncertain. Again, while differences are not clear cut in every case, the tendency is for plus achievers to have higher aspirations for the future than do minus achievers, "higher" referring to educational and vocational levels.

REPRESENTATIVE STUDENTS

If we now examine data pertaining to specific students who are representative of the group studied, we get a kind of balance sheet of a number of factors attending school achievement for the individual child. We shall see that these factors are not all favorable for each plus achiever and not all unfavorable for each minus achiever. We shall note, however, that conditions which seem to surround the lives of plus achievers add up to a more favorable total situation. On the other hand, conditions which seem to surround the lives of minus achievers add up to a more unfavorable total situation. Two eighth-grade boys, one a plus, the other a minus, achiever and two tenth-grade girls, one in each category, serve as examples.[6] The findings are given in Table 2.* The two eighth-grade boys do not seem far apart in some areas. In most of the areas, however, they do. A brief study of the summaries reveals an aggregate of more favorable conditions for the plus achievers and less favorable conditions for the minus achievers. The imbalance between favorable and unfavorable conditions can hardly be mistaken.

Similarly, there is also a clearly discernible difference in the conditions which surround the lives of these two tenth-grade girls. Again, while not everything is unfavorable for the minus achiever and not everything is favorable for the plus achiever, the imbalance of favorable and unfavorable factors is unmistakable. We see here a girl who has a comparatively high ability rating and who has

---

[6] In selecting "representative" plus and minus achievers for this portion of the study, two judges concurred in the selection. The criterion for selection involved a check of "trueness" to type as defined.

* Table 2 has been omitted in reprinting.—Editor's note.

demonstrated willingness to assume responsibility and shoulder a heavy burden when the situation requires it but who is, nevertheless, unsuccessful in the school situation. Considering the circumstances surrounding her life, it is not difficult to understand that her achievement in school is not what it could be. Factors other than measured intelligence appear to exert a determining influence.

It would be futile, perhaps, to attempt to point out some one factor invariably related to school achievement. We could cite a number of students who apparently overcame unfavorable conditions or who were little influenced by favorable conditions. In doing so, however, it would be necessary to point to one or a limited number of factors without obtaining a complete picture of the forces at work. Factors relating to school achievement appear to be numerous and interrelated.

Our findings do not give a complete answer to the question: What factors are related to school achievement? Nor ought we to assume that all influential factors have been explored. As far as this study has gone, results seem to show that not one factor, but a variety of factors in combination, some of which the child is powerless to control, tip the balance in one direction or the other.

SUMMARY OF FINDINGS

In this article some of the underlying factors attending plus achievement and minus achievement have been explored. While the study is merely exploratory, the following statements appear justified.

1. *To what extent do home conditions, as investigated, influence achievement in school?*

In general, the home conditions of plus achievers appear to be favorable. The home atmosphere is pleasant. Parents show interest, affection, and pride in their children. Children respond by being happy, respectful, and eager to please their parents.

On the other hand, the home conditions of minus achievers more often appear to be unfavorable. The home atmosphere is not always pleasant, and there does not seem to be much exchange of affection. Minus achievers seldom appear anxious to please their parents. Their parents do not seem to expect much of them.

2. *Does standing with one's fellows augment a feeling of be-*

longing to the school situation and facilitate school achievement?

The peer relations of plus achievers seem to be somewhat more plentiful, and especially more supportive, than those of minus achievers. Plus achievers seem to choose friends whose standards regarding school achievement, for example, are equally high. Seldom is a plus achiever found to be "utterly alone."

While minus achievers may have friends, their friends usually do not have high standards regarding school achievement or favorable attitudes toward the school situation. A number of minus achievers do not appear to have any close friends at all.

3. *Do physiological efficiency and a feeling of adequacy govern, in part, the quality of school achievement?*

Whatever the reason (and it apparently is not the intelligence quotient), plus achievers are usually regarded as comparatively bright. They tend to possess a feeling of adequacy, to be more alert and attentive in class, and even to exhibit tendencies toward acting superior. Their appearance is favorable, and they seem happy in the school situation.

Minus achievers appear less happy in the school situation. They are often described as changeable or unstable or as having an inferiority complex. In some instances, physical make-up is a cause for concern. In other instances, there appears to be emotional conflict.

4. *Do differences in inclination toward schoolwork, however determined, influence achievement when school programs are rather formal and lacking in diversity of activities?*

Plus achievers appear more academically inclined. At least, they show less aversion for book learning. There is a tendency for them to do more reading and to derive more satisfaction from their reading. They appear to be less averse to doing homework. In some instances, they appear actually to enjoy it.

Book learning appears almost a "pet peeve" of minus achievers. They would rather be doing something with their hands—making things, experimenting, or farming. It seems that they would rather be out of the classroom situation, not necessarily because of indolence, but because of disinclination for academic activity.

5. *Do educational and vocational goals and prospects contribute variably to individual motivation for achievement?*

Comparatively high educational and vocational aims were characteristic of plus achievers, and there appears good prospect of their achieving these aims. Plus achievers appear to relate their school work to future goals. They tend to regard an education for more than its job value.

It does not seem that minus achievers see very far ahead. They appear to have limited educational and vocational aims, and teachers do not appear to have elevated prospects for them.

6. *Is there, then, a complexity of forces underlying human behavior, the aggregate of which prescribes individual achievement?*

While the foregoing generalizations appear justified for groups, any of the areas taken alone might not apply to individuals. For example, a minus achiever might have more favorable peer relations than some plus achievers, even though the group tendency is for plus achievers to have more favorable peer relations.

When the factors are taken in combination, however, plus achievers appear to enjoy decidedly more favorable conditions than do minus achievers. That is, conditions which attend plus achievement appear, in the aggregate, to be more favorable than conditions which attend minus achievement in the aggregate.

UNDERAGE AND OVERAGE GRADE PLACEMENTS
AND SCHOOL ACHIEVEMENT

by Jack A. Holmes

UNIVERSITY OF CALIFORNIA, BERKELEY

and Carmen J. Finley

SONOMA COUNTY, CALIFORNIA, SCHOOL DISTRICTS

This study concludes a series of investigations at the elementary-school level designed to establish relationships between the degree of overage and underage grade placement and relative success in various school subjects. The first two studies, on grades five and six,

[Reprinted from the *Journal of Educational Psychology*, 48, November 1957, 447-457, with the permission of the American Psychological Association and the authors.]

have already been reported (3, 4). This paper presents data for grades seven and eight and then discusses the theoretical significance of the findings.

The hypothesis being tested holds that certain academic disciplines at the elementary level are more important than others in contributing to nonpromotion, promotion, and acceleration.

TABLE 1

Frequency Distributions of Actual Grade-placement Deviations

Direction of deviation	GPD interval	Grade VII Boys f	Grade VII Girls f	Grade VIII Boys f	Grade VIII Girls f
(Underaged)	2.3 + 2.8*	0	1†	0	0
(Accelerated)	1.7 + 2.2	0	0	0	0
↑	1.1 + 1.6	4	9	3	6
	.5 + 1.0	49	72	43	70
Normal	— .1 + .4	125	140	124	123
	— .7 — .2	70	59	83	55
	— 1.3 — .8	28	16	42	25
	— 1.9 — 1.4	12	11	20	8
↓	— 2.5 — 2.0	3	3	3	4
(Overaged)	— 3.1 — 2.6	1	1	0	2
(Retarded)	— 3.7 — 3.2	1	0	0	0
N		293	312	318	293

* The constant K has been subtracted in order to bring these deviations from the mean back into their original form.
† Example: This seventh-grade girl is accelerated by $+2.3$ grades; therefore, according to her chronological age she should have been in the $(7.1 - 2.3)$ or 4.8th grade.

SAMPLES, METHODOLOGY, TESTS

For grade seven, 293 boys and 312 girls and, for grade eight, 318 boys and 293 girls were drawn from pupils enrolled in 68 elementary school districts in Sonoma County (California).

Grade-placement deviation (GPD) was determined by computing the difference between each child's actual grade placement (AGP) and the grade he should have been in according to his chronological age. This latter grade is defined as his chronological-age grade-placement (CaGP). Grade-placement deviation, then, is expressed as:

$$GPD = AGP - CaGP + K$$

where K is a constant (5.0) inserted into the equation to give all GPD values a positive sign.

Table 1 gives the frequency distributions of GPDs for each sex in both grades. Inspection reveals that, according to their chronological ages, the seventh-grade boys *should* have been distributed from grades 5.7 to 10.4 and the seventh-grade girls should have ranged from 4.8 to 9.7; yet, the entire group was actually in grade 7.1.

Likewise, Table 1 shows that, in accordance with their chronological ages, the boys and girls of the eighth grade should have been enrolled in Grades 6.5 to 10.6 and 6.5 to 11.2, respectively; yet, they were all in Grade 8.1.

The California Achievement Test Battery, Intermediate Form DD, was administered to all seventh- and eighth-grade children during the first three months of the school year as part of the general county testing program in 1952. The tests in this battery are: reading vocabulary, reading comprehension, arithmetic reasoning, arithmetic fundamentals, mechanics of grammar, and spelling. Reliability coefficients range from .85 to .95.

FINDINGS

GRADE SEVEN

Table 2 presents the intercorrelations found among the above variables and grade-placement deviation for the boys. The criterion correlates highest with reading vocabulary ($r = .450$) and lowest with arithmetic fundamentals ($r = .259$).

The matrix in Table 2 was submitted to the Wherry-Doolittle Test Selection Method (7) in order to determine which of the test variables made an independent contribution to the variance of the pupils's GPDs. The multiple correlation ($\bar{R}$) rises as the variables, reading vocabulary, spelling, and mechanics of grammar, are successively selected and cumulatively added, but then decreases if any of the other tests are added. Together these three tests yield a multiple $\bar{R}$ of .46, significant at better than the 1-percent level of confidence.

Table 3 presents the intercorrelations for the girls. The criterion (GPD) correlates highest with reading vocabulary ($r = .380$) and lowest with arithmetic fundamentals ($r = .233$). A Wherry-

Doolittle analysis selects only reading vocabulary and spelling as variables making independent contributions to the variance of GPDs for seventh-grade girls. Together, the two tests yield an $\bar{R}$ of .393, significant beyond the 1-percent level.

TABLE 2

Intercorrelations Obtained on 293 Boys in Grade Seven

Variable	1 GPD	2 RV	3 RC	4 AR	5 AF	6 MG	7 SP
1. Grade placement deviation (GPD)		.450	.346	.318	.259	.364	.397
2. Reading vocabulary (RV)			.750	.650	.533	.622	.704
3. Reading comprehension (RC)				.637	.585	.655	.670
4. Arithmetic reasoning (AR)					.667	.569	.538
5. Arithmetic fundamentals (AF)						.564	.496
6. Mechanics of grammar (MG)							.540
7. Spelling (SP)							
Mean	6.98*	6.98	6.75	6.78	6.15	6.70	6.83
Standard Deviation	.68	1.60	1.39	1.01	1.04	1.30	1.65

* Reconverted: K-constant subtracted.

TABLE 3

Intercorrelations Obtained on 312 Girls in Grade Seven

Variable	1 GPD	2 RV	3 RC	4 AR	5 AF	6 MG	7 SP
1. Grade-placement deviation (GPD)		.380	.355	.278	.233	.269	.332
2. Reading vocabulary (RV)			.770	.569	.477	.644	.619
3. Reading comprehension (RC)				.636	.578	.703	.670
4. Arithmetic reasoning (AR)					.618	.574	.489
5. Arithmetic fundamentals (AF)						.572	.492
6. Mechanics of grammar (MG)							.598
7. Spelling (SP)							
Mean	7.13*	7.18	7.23	6.75	6.40	7.30	7.62
Standard Deviation	.68	1.40	1.34	.84	1.16	1.27	1.68

* Reconverted: K-constant subtracted.

TABLE 4

Intercorrelations Obtained on 318 Boys in Grade Eight

	Intercorrelations						
	1	2	3	4	5	6	7
Variables	GPD	RV	RC	AR	AF	MG	SP
1. Grade-placement deviation (GPD)		.434	.440	.430	.327	.381	.439
2. Reading vocabulary (RV)			.781	.691	.564	.667	.699
3. Reading comprehension (RC)				.723	.617	.651	.619
4. Arithmetic reasoning (AR)					.751	.612	.549
5. Arithmetic fundamentals (AF)						.634	.517
6. Mechanics of grammar (MG)							.553
7. Spelling (SP)							
Mean	7.88*	7.78	7.51	7.75	7.05	7.40	7.58
Standard Deviation	.68	1.56	1.57	1.31	1.46	1.38	1.74

* Reconverted: K-constant subtracted, remainder algebraicly added to 8.1.

TABLE 5

Intercorrelations Obtained on 293 Girls in Grade Eight

	Intercorrelations						
	1	2	3	4	5	6	7
Variables	GPD	RV	RC	AR	AF	MG	SP
1. Grade-placement deviation		.348	.365	.302	.298	.279	.327
2. Reading vocabulary (RV)			.774	.641	.571	.652	.634
3. Reading comprehension (RC)				.688	.647	.654	.655
4. Arithmetic reasoning (AR)					.786	.665	.580
5. Arithmetic fundamentals (AF)						.656	.572
6. Mechanics of grammar (MG)							.600
7. Spelling (SP)							
Mean	8.11*	8.18	8.03	7.85	7.65	8.14	8.67
Standard Deviation	.71	1.49	1.41	1.28	1.62	1.42	1.67

* Reconverted: K-constant subtracted, remainder algebraicly added to 8.1.

TABLE 6

Summary Selected Tests and Cumulative $\bar{R}$'s for
Grades Five through Eight

Grade	Boys		Girls	
	Tests	Cumulative $\bar{R}$	Tests	Cumulative $\bar{R}$
Five	Reading vocabulary	.248	Spelling	.170
	Spelling	.268*	Reading vocabulary	.183
	Mechanics of grammar	.275†	Arithmetic fundamentals	.190
Six	Spelling	.365	Reading vocabulary	.302
	Arithmetic reasoning	.393	Spelling	.321
	Mechanics of grammar	.394	Reading comprehension	.326
Seven	Reading vocabulary	.447	Reading vocabulary	.377
	Spelling	.458	Spelling	.393
	Mechanics of grammar	.464		
Eight	Reading comprehension	.437	Reading comprehension	.361
	Spelling	.483	Spelling	375
	Arithmetic reasoning	.497	Reading vocabulary	.379

* Cumulative $\bar{R}$ for reading vocabulary + spelling.
† Cumulative $\bar{R}$ for reading vocabulary + spelling + mechanics of grammar.

DISCUSSION

In order to compare the results obtained in grades seven and eight with those found for grades five and six already published (3, 4), a summary of the selected tests and the cumulative multiple correlations found for both sexes at all four levels is presented in Table 6. Inspection of Table 6 reveals that:

1. Spelling is elected as an important test making a statistically independent contribution to the variance of GPD in all four grades for both boys and girls. The same cannot be said for any other variable in the present battery.

2. Reading vocabulary and spelling are the two most important determiners of GPDs in grades five, six, and seven.

3. The cumulative $\bar{R}$ tends to increase from grade to grade.

4. The cumulative $\bar{R}$ is greater for boys than for girls at each grade level.

5. Mechanics of grammar is selected as an important subject for boys in grades five, six, and seven, but this is not so for the girls.

6. Individual differences in achievement in the *quantitative* subjects (arithmetic reasoning and arithmetic fundamentals, in which boys are supposed to excel) appear to play almost no role in determining whether or not a student shall be retarded, promoted, or accelerated in the elementary schools of this system!

7. Individual differences in achievement in the *linguistic* subjects (reading, spelling, and grammar, in which girls are supposed to excel) have a high premium in regard to GPD.

COULD THESE RESULTS HAVE BEEN LOGICALLY PREDICTED?

Perhaps. The fact is, however, they were not! A class of 75 university students enrolled in a teacher-training program was asked to rate these subjects in the order of their importance for determining GPDs in grades five through eight.

Table 7 presents the rank orders obtained by preferential analysis of the estimates of these university students and compares them with those obtained from a preferential analysis of the $\bar{R}$s of the four grades. The university students stress comprehension and relegate spelling to a low order of importance. Their disagreement with the facts is readily apparent in the almost random relationship of the rank orders of the entries in the two columns, especially for grades five, six, and seven.

THEORETICAL IMPLICATIONS

In essence, these studies recall Keys's observations (5, 6) that acceleration is rare; indeed, the number of pupils that are accelerated in any one grade represent only a fraction of those retarded. The writers agree with Keys's contention that this does not make for the optimum learning situation for the bright, the average, or the dull. The usual argument for the policy of nonacceleration is that the child should be kept with his chronological-age group. Such a social milieu is supposed to foster both maximum mental health and learning. However, these data clearly show that the desired homogeneity for chronological age (or for that matter, subject-matter achievement) is simply not obtained.

Baker (1) and Baker and Traphagen (2) concluded from their studies that often bright pupils may fail in arithmetic, and spelling failure may occur at any level. The relationship of their findings to the present study is clear: bright or dull failure in arithmetic is not important for GPD; and spelling failure, which they found occurs at any ability level, also occurs at any grade level. Its occurrence is of great importance for GPD.

The theoretical implications of the present series of investigations concerning school-grade failures seem clear. The schools should come out openly and tell the students and their parents that success in reading comprehension and arithmetic reasoning is

TABLE 7

Rank-orders for School Subjects Playing Most to Least Important Roles in Determining Grade-placement Deviations

Calculated from college students' estimates	Estimated from the $\bar{R}$ calculations
Grades Five, Six, Seven	
(N = 75)	(Ns = 979 + 869 + 611)
1. Reading comprehension	1. Reading vocabulary
2. Reading vocabulary	2. Spelling
3. Arithmetic fundamentals	3. Mechanics of grammar
4. Arithmetic reasoning	4. Reading comprehension
5. Spelling	5. Arithmetic reasoning
6. Mechanics of grammar	6. Arithmetic fundamentals
Grade Eight	
(N = 75)	(N = 611)
1. Reading comprehension	1. Reading comprehension
2. Arithmetic reasoning	2. Spelling
3. Reading vocabulary	3.5 Arithmetic reasoning
4. Mechanics of grammar	3.5 Reading vocabulary
5. Arithmetic fundamentals	5. Arithmetic fundamentals
6. Spelling	6. Mechanics of grammar

not nearly as important as success in reading vocabulary, spelling, and mechanics of grammar for determining retardation, promotion, or acceleration by the time the child is in grades five, six, and seven. *Or,* the schools should make it their business to give a more equable distribution to the weights they place on success in each of the subject-matter fields.

As a matter of fact, for neither the boys nor the girls in grades five through eight do individual differences in their *combined achievement* in these six subject-matter areas (reading vocabulary, spelling, mechanics of grammar, reading comprehension, arithmetic reasoning, and arithmetic fundamentals) contribute more than 25 percent to the variance of the grade-placement deviations within any one class. On what basis, then, one may ask, are students being grouped together in any one grade? On what basis are they being promoted, retarded, or accelerated?

In a scientific age, the apparent unimportance of success in arithmetic is perplexing. This condition is no doubt widespread in the nation's schools, and it is quite possible that this is one of the major reasons why officials of the armed services complain that a great number of men are not well grounded in arithmetic.

If these data are, in fact, at all representative of elementary schools in general, they point up a pressing need for a re-evaluation of the relative importance of the courses offered in the school curriculum.

In an age of interplanetary exploration, the outcome of the race for world leadership may not depend so much upon the ability of a nation to successfully project a satellite into a precalculated orbit, nor even its ability to launch intercontinental missiles, but, as Professor Edward Teller has so clearly stated, upon its ability to simply take and hold the lead in scientific exploration and production. If the results of the above experiment are at all widespread, and there is reason to believe that they are, then it appears that there must be a revamping of our value judgments on what in the curriculum is of the most worth. More than that, knowledge for its own sake, especially in mathematics and science, must be more enthusiastically supported and *evaluated* as important accomplishments for children in our elementary schools.

REFERENCES

1. Baker, H. J. *Characteristic Differences in Bright and Dull Pupils*. Bloomington, Ill.: Public School Publishing, 1927.
2. Baker, H. J., and V. Traphagen. *The Diagnosis and Treatment of Behavior Problem Children*. New York: The Macmillan Co., 1935.
3. Finley, Carmen J., and J. A. Holmes. Relative Importance of Curricular Areas for Grade-placement Deviation in Grade VI. *Calif. J. Educ. Res.*, 7, 1956, 200-205.
4. Holmes, J. A., and Carmen J. Finley. Relative Importance of Curricular

Areas for Grade-placement Deviation in Grade V. *Calif. J. Educ. Res.,* 6, 1955, 213-218.
5. Keys, N. The Underage Student in High School and College. *Univ. Calif. Publ. Educ.,* 7, 1938, 145-272.
6. ――――. Should We Accelerate the Bright? *J. Except. Child.,* 8, 1942, 248-254.
7. Wherry, R. J. A New Formula for Predicting the Shrinkage of Co-efficient of Multiple Correlation. *Ann. Math. Statist.,* 2, 1931, 440-457.

UNDERACHIEVING STUDENTS OF
HIGH CAPACITY

by Robert J. Dowd

NEW HAVEN STATE TEACHERS COLLEGE

The student of outstanding capacity who fails to achieve scholastically at a level reasonably commensurate with his ability presents a challenge to educators, administrators, and counselors. It is too often true of our educational systems that the pace is geared to the average member of the group, with greatest pressure falling on the slow student, who eventually receives the special attention of deans and counselors when he fails to meet the academic standards. The student of superior capacity, however, is frequently able to maintain a satisfactory scholastic rating when operating at a minimum of efficiency or expenditure of effort, and may even do so when badly maladjusted. Lost in the statistical mass of C students he receives no attention provided his behavior is satisfactory. At the same time, the high scholastic stratum is partly occupied by his intellectual inferiors who profit by the absence of his competition.

It is a matter of concern to the educator and of prime interest to society in general that the potential abilities of our best-equipped youth should be utilized. We are considering here, not the numerous capable individuals who for various reasons have not continued

[Reprinted from the *Journal of Higher Education,* 23, June 1952, 327-330, with the permission of the *Journal* and the author.]

their schooling beyond the level of the secondary school, but those of our college population who possess the most necessary single ingredient of genius—intellectual capacity of high order—but whose academic adjustment is of mediocre or inferior quality.

THE SUBJECTS

This report of an investigation indicates the extent of the problem of underachievement and some of the factors that differentiate achievers and nonachievers who are of a high level of capacity. The subjects of the study were students who entered the University of New Hampshire as freshmen in September 1947. They were the best and poorest achievers in the group of 89 students who composed the highest decile of the class for scholastic aptitude as measured by the American Council on Education Psychological Examination (ACE) total score. The criterion of academic success was the student's grade-point average at the end of the first semester of college work. At this institution marks are A, B, C, D, F, with corresponding point values of 4, 3, 2, 1, 0. The points earned for each course are multiplied by the number of credits carried to obtain the semester point-hour average. Students earning averages of 3.0 and above qualify for the honor roll.

The selected point of underachievement was an average of 2.2, which was the mean grade-point average of the entire freshman class. Students who exceed 90 percent of their classmates for scholastic aptitude may be safely considered underachievers when they fail to exceed 50 percent academically.

Of the original 89 tenth-decile students, 11 left school by the end of the first semester, of whom eight (9 percent) had been forced to withdraw because of failing marks or voluntarily withdrew with low scholastic standards. It was found that 16 (21 percent) of the remaining 78 had earned grade-point averages of 2.2 and below, 31 (39 percent) made averages of 2.3 to 2.9, and 31 (39 percent) made averages of 3.0 or higher.

THE STANDARDS

In order approximately to equate the groups for numbers, the criterion of expected achievement was raised to a grade-point average of 3.1 or better The groups finally determined upon consisted of 19 achievers, with averages from 3.1 to 4.0, with a median of 3.4; and 16 nonachievers whose averages ranged from 2.2 down to 1.4, with a median of 1.7. These individuals represented the entire population of the two extremes of the original group as it had been defined and limited. This method of studying every individual in the group concerned eliminated the chance of errors in sampling procedure. Measures taken to assure complete anonymity helped in securing the cooperation of all the students concerned.

Of the variables controlled in the investigation, the following did not differentiate between achievers and nonachievers:

1. Size of high-school graduating class
2. Amount and kind of extracurricular activities
3. Concern over finances
4. Amount of part-time employment
5. Vocabulary ability
6. Age at entrance into college
7. Scholastic achievement level of aspiration
8. Military service
9. Marital status
10. The Bernreuter Personality Inventory
11. The Bell Adjustment Inventory
12. The Minnesota Multiphasic Personality Inventory

It was found that the second, third, and fourth items actually operated in favor of the nonachievers, because that group expended less time and energy in extracurricular activities and in working at part-time paid jobs, and also indicated greater financial security, than did the achievers. The paper-and-pencil questionnaires failed to discriminate between the two groups, but the small differences that did exist were in almost every case in the direction of better adjustment for the nonachievers.

The variables that differentiated the achievers from the nonachievers are described in the following material:

Women constituted 26 percent of the entire freshman class and 24 percent of the tenth-decile group. Their representation in the achiever and nonachiever groups was not proportional, however, since nine of the 19 achievers and but two of the 16 nonachievers were women. This represents a record for attainment commensurate with ability definitely superior to that of the men in this group.

The achievers ranged from the 67th to the 98th percentile of their respective high-school graduating classes, while the nonachievers ranged from the 35th to the 99th percentile. An inspection of the two distributions indicates that more than one third of the nonachievers were lower in their class than any of the achievers, and that 80 percent of the achievers were at or above the 89th percentile of their high-school graduating class, while only 20 percent of the nonachievers had a standing equally high. It is evident that this factor is associated with scholastic success in the initial college term, since those who stood high in the preparatory class tended to be high in the college class, and those with a relatively low standing in the secondary school tended to remain underachievers in their first college semester.

TEST DATA

While only 21 percent of the achievers were below the freshman-class average on the Cooperative English Test of Mechanics of Expression, 50 percent of the nonachievers were in this range. Above the 95th percentile were 63 percent of the achievers, whereas none of the nonachievers was above that point. The level of skill in English mechanics is evidently related to the level of scholastic performance in a positive and considerable degree.

The Cooperative Reading Comprehension Test yields four scores: vocabulary, reading comprehension, level, and total. The groups are compared on each separate section. Although there was no definite differentiation of the two groups for vocabulary, it was found that 81 percent of the combined groups exceeded the mean, and 25 percent exceeded the 90th percentile, of the freshman class. All of the achievers were at or higher than 6.0 standard score for comprehension, while only 63 percent of the nonachievers made a score that high. Since both groups were above the class average in all cases save one, the difference between the groups existed on a relatively high level. Generally, the students in both groups were in the upper half of the class for reading level, but a large proportion of the nonachievers fell just above the mean, while most of the achievers were in the highest range of scores. On the total score, one fourth of the nonachievers did more poorly than any achiever, and 56 percent of the nonachievers, as compared with 21 percent of the achievers, fell lower than one standard deviation above the mean score for the entire freshman class. These results indicate a definite tendency for the achievers to outperform the nonachievers on this reading test. That reading skill is a strong factor to be considered in connection with achievement, when scholastic ability is held constant, seems evident from these findings.

STUDY HABITS

The achievers studied considerably more than did the nonachievers, the median number of study hours a week for the former being 20, and for the later 13.5. For the achievers Q_1 was 13.75, Q_3 was 22.5, hours; and for the nonachievers these figures were 10 and 18.25 hours, respectively. The average achiever, therefore, studied more hours a week than did three fourths of the nonachievers. However, the least time spent in study was in the case of an achiever with a 3.8 average in five courses, who admitted to only three hours of study a week. He was at the 99th percentile for scholastic aptitude and had an excellent history of scholastic achievement. While these results indicate that there is a very great difference between the groups on this variable, it is not shown that any given amount of study is necessary in order that extremely able students may attain scholastic honors.

The Wrenn Study-habits Inventory yielded a considerable difference between the groups for at least 10 of the 28 items. In general, the achievers were found to employ what Wrenn found to be good techniques and practices of study. Two important factors that are associated with underachievement are unwise distribution of time and the need for an "inspiration" to study. Nonachievers tend to dislike their courses and professors, but it is not known whether personality factors cause these feelings of dissatisfaction or whether the responses solely indicate projection after the fact of failure. Regardless of the origin of these attitudes, the nonachievers are at present dissatisfied with teachers and courses, and may be creating a negative barrier which will be detrimental to their prospects of subsequent achievement. No sex difference was found between male and female achievers, as the responses of both groups indicated that they employed similar techniques of study.

INTEREST INVENTORY

An examination of the profiles obtained from the Occupational Interest Inventory revealed that the nonachievers were frequently following academic curriculums, or held occupational goals, that were inconsonant with their measured interests. In several cases engineering students indicated scientific or computational interests that were at the tenth and twentieth percentiles for the standardization population. It was the judgment of the writer that all of the nonachievers who were technology students showed interest patterns that were at best no more than fairly adequate for the technical and scientific occupations. Several achieving students in liberal arts had similarly inadequate measured interests for the occupations of their choice. It is probable that the technology student with low technical interests is severely penalized scholastically because of the predominantly technical nature of his course content, whereas the wider course offerings in liberal arts permit a change in vocational goals as fields are sampled, without greatly penalizing the student.

Restricted experience and the tendency to follow a vocational course because of extrinsic attractiveness or family pressure would surely account for many cases of inadequate vocational selection. It is considered likely, however, that the pursuit of unrealistic vocational goals may be symptomatic of immaturity, lack of insight, or a lack of purpose that is basically emotional in nature.

The habit patterns of childhood and early youth determine, to a large extent, the subsequent "style of life" or habitual methods of adjustment of the individual, and it is believed that the results of this study illustrate the degree to which such a concept holds true in the case of achieving and nonachieving college students. Some of the basic skills that depend ultimately upon earliest training clearly differentiate the two groups, including reading ability and the use of the English language. The elementary-school pupil who has failed to acquire those skills that are basic to the adequate handling of educational subject matter will be handicapped even when competing with intellectually less able pupils. The factors that operated to inhibit the acquisition of early skills and the learning of successful educational adjustments are obscure, but there is reason to believe that poor emotional relationships in early life may be largely responsible. It is likely that a genetic study of achieving and nonachieving students would indicate the extent to which emotional situations may have had differential effects upon each group, and the manner in which habitual adjustment patterns were initiated and developed.

IN SUMMARY

The following conclusions were drawn as the result of the study:

1. The specific impingements of the college situation are not responsible for underachievement in high-capacity students.

2. The factors which operated to lower academic efficiency in college had also operated to depress achievement in the earlier school environment.

3. The paper-and-pencil personality questionnaires used in this study are of little value in differentiating achieving and nonachieving students of high capacity.

4. There is a definite sex difference in the direction of a greater incidence of extreme underachievement among the male students in the tenth decile for scholastic aptitude.

5. The difference in personality organization between achieving and nonachieving students of high capacity needs genetic investigation, since the factors that depress achievement antecede college years.

9

THE TEACHERS

❦

NOT MUCH is known about selecting good teachers; even less is known about selecting teachers of gifted children. Most schools inaugurating a special class select a teacher of proven competence who is sympathetic toward the program. This method has worked rather well in most instances, but a teacher's competence in one situation does not guarantee her success in another.

If more training facilities were available, administrators would be better able to select teachers for special classes. The last survey (1953) of courses in special education revealed that during the regular school year only two universities in the United States offered a sequence of courses in the area of teaching the gifted. At this same time there were 122 colleges and universities with sequences for teachers in one or more exceptional-child areas. The number of courses offered in summer sessions are not much different from those offered during the regular year. Each year the Council for Exceptional Children publishes a list of courses offered throughout the country which deal with some phase of special education. Cognate courses in psychology, testing, and the like are not included. In 1958, of the colleges responding to the survey, 76 offered one or more courses in special education, but of the nearly 800 courses offered only 34 dealt with the gifted. Of the colleges offering 28 or more courses in the summer only Syracuse University offered more than one course for teachers of the gifted. Syracuse offered "Education of Gifted Children," "Workshop in the Education of Gifted Children," and practice-teaching courses at two different levels. The University of Minnesota, George Peabody College for Teachers, and Illinois State Normal University each offered one course, but such well-known teacher-training centers as San Francisco State, the University of Tennessee, Wayne University, and Columbia University did not offer one such course in the summer of 1958.

The paucity of courses suggests two things. Either not enough is known about teaching gifted children to devote special education courses to that area or schools are not demanding teachers with special training in that area. The fact that many of the traditional courses give attention to the problem of the gifted for

428

several weeks each semester and seminars in various areas devote more and more time to the gifted indicate that teachers, at least, are demanding more information.

The courses that are most frequently offered are "Education of Gifted Children" or a workshop. Kent University offers "Methods and Materials for the Gifted" in addition to "Psychology of the Gifted." The most frequent enrollee is the person with some teaching experience who recognizes a gap in her training.

Where training is available, schools take advantage of it. In Lincoln, Nebraska, the city school administrators select special teachers from their system and offer them scholarships to a University of Nebraska summer session. There they take "Education of the Gifted" as one third of their school load and a "Practicum" in which they have intensive training in working with a selected group of intellectually capable, high-achieving children. The practical experience helps them to become aware of the potential of gifted children. Moreover, it assists them in preparing and experimenting with materials and techniques they will use as directors of the enrichment sessions the following year. When the Lincoln schools do not need new teachers for their special sessions, they send special-assignment teachers and administrators to these courses on a scholarship.

There is little research to indicate the characteristics that differentiate a teacher of the gifted from any other teacher. Certainly the characteristics most frequently listed for teachers of gifted children, such as high intelligence, special aptitudes, deep knowledge of own field, broad knowledge of related fields, knowledge of teaching techniques, flexibility, creativity, and acceptance of student ideas, are desirable in all teachers.

Asking students to describe the best teacher from whom they have learned has not helped much either. Although there are several such lists in the literature, I felt it necessary to make my own survey. Large groups of high-achieving students from a wide variety of high schools in two states were asked to identify the characteristics of an ideal teacher. The students were to identify the five most important traits in a list of 26. The most outstanding traits in order of preference were

Knows subject well.
Encourages students to think.
Makes the course interesting.

Can "get the point across."
Makes the students want to learn.
Keeps the class and course organized.
Maintains the respect of the students.

While these traits seemed to be much more important than the others in the list, the significant finding was that there was little unanimity in the selections. Only one of the traits listed above was selected by a majority of the students as being one of the five most important traits in an ideal teacher: 61 percent of the students thought that knowing the subject well was one of the five most important traits. We have not yet been able to measure the interpersonal relationships that exist between a good teacher and a good pupil.

A teacher of gifted children, in comparison to teachers in traditional classrooms, should be more intelligent, flexible, and creative, and better informed in areas other than her specialty. She should also have a desire to teach gifted children. She needs to be more intelligent because she will have more sharp, quick pupils. She need not, however, be more intelligent than her most intelligent pupil, because she will have had many more experiences from which to draw. She needs to be well informed in a wide variety of areas and flexible and creative because her classes will spend much less time on the "course of study." When the basic requirements have been met, most teachers must, on their own initiative, challenge the students and enrich their program. Because teachers of the gifted will usually have more time to fill effectively whether they are enriching in breadth or depth, they need to be well versed in a variety of areas to help students see the interrelationships of life. The only mandatory requirement, however, is that such a teacher must want to help gifted children learn.

The teacher who has the desire to teach the gifted should not be confused with the teacher who is impatient with slow learners. The gifted need as much patience and understanding as other children. It is a mistake to think of an assignment to a class of gifted children as a job where little teaching is necessary because the pupils learn so well by themselves. Because of the demands for creativity and a broader range of knowledge many teachers find an assignment to a special or honors class the most difficult and challenging work they have ever done.

The readings in this section sum up rather well thoughts on teachers of the gifted. In the first article, Nelda Davis discusses the "Gifted Teacher" and her characteristics before describing some of the formal and informal training available for such teachers. Nelda Davis achieved recognition through *Providing for the Gifted Student,* a curriculum bulletin issued by the Houston, Texas, Independent School Districts, and by several speeches on that topic at national meetings. She is now the Supervisior of Social Studies for the Board of Education in Prince George's County Upper Marlboro, Maryland.

In the second article, Frank T. Wilson, the most frequently quoted authority on the preparation of teachers for the gifted, interprets his survey of "In-service and Undergraduate Preparation of Teachers of the Gifted." A long-time member of the Hunter College faculty, Dr. Wilson has been in a position to receive many inquiries about the preparation of teachers.

In the third article Arthur M. Selvi describes the Connecticut plan for preparing elementary-education majors, who so desire, to organize special activities for enriching the elementary-school curriculum. He suggests five ways in which school administrators can use the few teachers that are worthy of a title such as "enrichment-program teacher" to good advantage. He also discusses the elements of democracy in such provisions.

A survey of the attitude of teachers toward special classes for the intellectually gifted by Joseph Justman and J. W. Wrightstone concludes the section. These members of New York City's administrative research team were able to come up with six conclusions after polling experienced teachers in New York City. They found that younger or newer teachers favored special classes more than the teachers with more than 20 years of experience and that teachers who have had specific experience with special classes show much the same attitude toward such classes, regardless of the number of years of service they may have had as teachers. Unfavorable attitudes are also summarized.

TEACHERS FOR THE GIFTED

by Nelda Davis

PRINCE GEORGE'S COUNTY, MARYLAND, BOARD OF EDUCATION

Since it is true that the teacher is the cornerstone of our educational structure, what then are the qualifications for the teacher of the gifted? Also, in what ways, if any, do the qualifications for the teacher of the gifted differ from those for the teacher of other pupils?

THE "GIFTED TEACHER"

The statement is often made that the teacher of the gifted must be gifted. Unless that opinion is explained, too many teachers take it to mean that she too must have as high an IQ as the highest in her class. With due respect to our profession, it is doubtful that such would often be the case. As with the gifted pupil so with the gifted teacher, IQ is not the only criterion.

Scholarship and a wide cultural background are essential. This does not mean that the teacher can be an expert on every path that a gifted youngster may want to explore. On the other hand to say too often, "I don't know, let's look it up," can invite lack of respect on the part of the pupil for his teacher. This is particularly true of subject fields in junior and senior high school.

Scholarship without an understanding of the individual in the class makes learning a dry husk. A gifted student will find it easier to forgive a teacher who does not know her facts than one who does not understand him. While it is true that all students want this understanding, the gifted, since he is a deviate and varies from the mythical average, has an especial need for a sympathetic attitude from his teacher. It is also harder at times for the teacher to be able to understand him since he is different. Re-

[Reprinted from the *Journal of Teacher Education*, 5, September 1954, 221-224, with the permission of the *Journal* and the author.]

sentment against him because he often does know more in a particular field than the teacher may develop and can become a corroding experience for both.

UNDERSTANDING CHILDREN

In order to keep the proper perspective, the teacher of the gifted also should know average and below-average pupils. A former teacher in Leta Hollingworth's school once told me that her work with the retarded group was a help when she began to teach the gifted. A gifted child is still a child. Perhaps he is different both in quality and quantity of intellect, but understanding the child in general will be helpful in understanding this particular child.

One writer has suggested that "The education of gifted children requires gifted teachers who have the ability to recognize giftedness, to create an atmosphere and environment favorable to its development, to provide conditions that give it a chance to emerge and blossom."[1] In agreeing with this we must also add that it is necessary for the teacher of the gifted to be able to channel the specific qualities of the gifted into worthwhile learning. As an example, one characteristic of these superior pupils is the ability to verbalize. Unless a teacher is alert, breadth of discussion will be limitless, but depth may be lacking.

PUPIL DESCRIPTIONS OF GOOD TEACHERS

Ruth Strang has wisely stated that our most authentic information about qualifications for the teachers of the gifted should come from the gifted pupils themselves. It is interesting to note the similarity in qualities listed by pupils in two different studies, one that Dr. Strang made of fifty pupils in grades six through high school in New York, Pennsylvania, and California; the other made by the writer with the help of Dr. Hedwig Pregler in workshop classes of pupils from grades four, five, and six. Here are some of the pupils' ideas of the qualifications of good teachers:

[1] Paul Witty (ed.), *The Gifted Child,* Boston: Heath, 1951, p. 113.

Sense of humor. She should have a good sense of humor. A teacher should be able to have fun and teach school at the same time.

Encouragement of responsibility. A good teacher should let us talk things over with our friends, and should not always tell us to do things independently.

She should be able to give you your assignment and let you go to work and then not interrupt you.

Knowledge of subject. A teacher, as well as knowing her subject well, must keep her knowledge up to date.

She should read the daily newspaper. It would be very embarrassing if a student should report something very important that the teacher did not know anything about.

Firmness and fairness. She should be strict so the children obey her, but not so strict that the children are afraid of her.

In my opinion I think a teacher should be strict but gentle and she should have a friendly personality.

Understanding of children. A teacher who knows her pupils, not only as boys and girls she sees in school, and tries to teach academic subjects and help to become good citizens, but also as individual people with individual problems is in my opinion an extremely good teacher.

She should be the kind of a teacher that if you have a problem you could go and explain it to her.

Enjoyment of teaching. First of all, I think that to be a good teacher you must want to teach and you must enjoy teaching.

Since the above qualities could be claimed by a good teacher of any group, would we agree that the teacher of the gifted must possess them to a marked degree? Raise the characteristics of a good teacher to the highest point of development, and you will have a gifted teacher for gifted pupils.

PLANNING FOR TEACHER EDUCATION

Mackie and Dunn report that although several states have classes for the gifted and try to select teachers best qualified to teach them, Pennsylvania is the only state that has a special certificate for the teachers of the gifted.[2] Two reasons are given for the

[2] Romaine Mackie and Lloyd Dunn, "State Standards for Teaching Exceptional Children," *J. Teacher Educ.*, 4, December 1953, 273.

lack of certification in this area: (1) relatively few classes for the gifted, and (2) lack of agreement concerning the qualifications needed by a teacher of the gifted.

A significant fact is that only two teacher-education institutions in the United States offer a sequence of preparation in the area of the teaching of the gifted. Since the offering of special preparation for teachers is closely correlated with the supply and demand, it would be reasonable to believe that there are few requests for teachers in this area. Another fact that holds significance for our thinking is that in no state department of education is there a staff member whose major responsibility is education of the gifted children.[3]

It is important to note in the preceding paragraph that the term used is "a *sequence* of preparation on this area." There are many institutions that offer certain courses for the teacher of the gifted, but not a sequence.

Another important source of training that should be noted is the workshop. Some of the universities that have made valuable contributions in this field through their workshops and summer sessions are Kent State University, Boston University, Syracuse University, Pennsylvania State University, Hunter College of the City of New York, George Peabody College for Teachers, University of Kansas, Northwestern University, California (Pennsylvania) State Teachers College, San Francisco State College, Teachers College of Columbia University, Stanford University, and University of Vermont.

OTHER SOURCES OF HELP

The studies made by the Philadelphia Suburban School Study Council under the direction of the Educational Service Bureau, University of Pennsylvania, have been a source of help to all teachers in dealing with the gifted. Working with teacher-training institutions are the various associations for the study of the gifted. The American Association for the Gifted, the International Council for Exceptional Children, the Ohio Association for Gifted Children, the Pennsylvania Association for the Study and Education

[3] Bulletin 1, 1954, U. S. Department of Health, Education, and Welfare, Office of Education (seen in manuscript).

of the Mentally Gifted, and the Metropolitan Association for the Study of the Gifted are some of the organizations that share their findings with interested colleges.†

A bulletin from the Pennsylvania Department of Public Instruction lists the following requirements for certification of teachers of classes for the "mentally advanced" [4]:

A certificate of standard grade for teaching may be extended to include teaching classes for the mentally advanced on the completion of twenty-four semester hours of approved courses on special education in accordance with the following distribution:

1. *Courses Basic to All Special Certification* (6 sem. hrs.)
   *Psychology (or Education) of Exceptional Children
   Diagnostic Testing and Remedial Teaching
   **Mental and Educational Hygiene
2. *Courses Basic to the Teaching of Mentally Advanced Children* (6 sem. hrs.)
   *Arts and Crafts (3 sem. hrs.)
   *Student Teaching in Classes for the Mentally Advanced Children (1 sem. hr.)
   *General Methods for Teaching the Mentally Advanced

The emphasis in these courses should be on the classroom instrumentation of the psychological principles relevant to mentally advanced children.

3. Electives (12 sem. hrs.)
   Clinical Psychology
   Abnormal Psychology
   **Tests and Measurements
   Speech Correction
   Mental Tests (Individual)
   Educational and Vocational Guidance
   Related Courses in Sociology
   **Graduate work in one or more content fields
   ***Teaching experience

* Must be selected within these groups.
** Preferred.
*** Outstanding successful teaching experience in at least two or more different grade levels may be counted at a maximum of six semester hours at the rate of three semester hours a year. At least two years of teaching experience before certification for teaching classes for mentally advanced is highly desirable.
† The National Association for Gifted Children is now helping in this important role.—EDITOR'S NOTE.
[4] Pennsylvania Department of Public Instruction, *Standards for the Organization and Administration of Special Classes,* Harrisburg: the Department, 1945.

It will be noted that the courses suggested would be helpful to any teacher in any typical undifferentiated class. Using them as a basis, an interested teacher-training institution could build a program that would have a wider appeal and yet satisfy the needs of teachers of the gifted. Just as a gifted pupil needs more enrichment, so the teacher of the gifted should have her program more enriched with content material than the requirements indicate. This should be included in the program plans of the institution. There are those who feel that the dynamics of group and individual behavior should be included, and if a choice is necessary, substituted for abnormal and clinical psychology.

PROVIDING IN-SERVICE EDUCATION

Finally, assuming that a school has selected the teachers of the gifted who have the desirable qualifications and have met any and all state requirements, what can the system do in the way of in-service training to aid these teachers?

At the 59th Annual Meeting of the American Psychological Association in Chicago, Albert I. Oliver gave some recommendations for districts working on the education of the gifted that could be used with value in an in-service training program within a school system:

1. Provide a coordinator to centralize activity and to funnel out ideas and materials.

2. Form a planning committee made up of a chairman from each district to develop ideas and serve as interpreters to their local groups.

3. Emphasize the exchange of ideas, practices, and materials, with classroom teachers being prominent in the work.

4. Assure local groups that they have freedom to experiment with their own problems, that group decisions are for the council report. Such reports are vital to providing purpose to activities as well as giving the participants assurance that their efforts have taken definite form.

5. Encourage teachers and administrators to work out plans for procedures as well as find areas of understanding. For example,

administrators in the Suburban School Study Council have been generous in allowing teachers to be released for half days to attend study groups.

6. Above all, do not copy blindly. A single district or a group of districts needs to work out its own salvation using cooperative techniques. Whatever the size of the group or the purpose of the study it is vital to remember—it is the child for whom the school bell tolls.

IN-SERVICE AND UNDERGRADUATE
PREPARATION OF TEACHERS OF THE GIFTED

by Frank T. Wilson

HUNTER COLLEGE OF THE CITY OF NEW YORK

The increasing concern (if not anxiety) about the education of unusually able children in our nation is shown by attempts to improve offerings in many schools in cities, towns, and rural areas, and by much discussion of what should be done. Perhaps the pattern of new action without careful preparation of teachers as to what to do and how to proceed is inevitable in our conservative educational structure. Perhaps, on the other hand, the time is arriving when the horse can be brought around and put in front of the cart, and the order made right and, beginning at the beginning, every teacher will be made ready to nurture the talents, extraordinary abilities, and the enduring interests which one out of five children possesses by virtue of hereditary endowment.

In order to see comparatively what school systems were doing through in-service training of their teachers to meet needs of able children and to what extent teacher education institutions were preparing future teachers at the undergraduate level to make

[Reprinted from *Educational Administration and Supervision*, 43, May 1957, 295-301, with the permission of Warwick and York, Publishers, and the author.]

special provisions for gifted children, a spot-type survey was undertaken. The assumption was made that preparation of teachers in this respect must involve concrete provisions, such as study of the nature and needs of these pupils provided in definite learning situations, for example, in courses or units of courses, conferences, workshops, and the like; field experiences; acquaintance with suitable materials and their appropriate use by able children; and the presence on faculties and staffs of persons equipped with special skills and understandings to supervise students and teachers in respect to able children, and to render other significant leadership regarding the education of the gifted.

A questionnaire concerning these concrete provisions was sent to 64 city school systems and to 62 institutions preparing teachers, which a previous comprehensive study[1] had indicated had shown special interest in the problem. Although these numbers are not large they represent widely spread educational units of the nation, the school systems being located in 34 states and the institutions in 31.

A considerably greater number of replies were received from school systems: 40, as compared with 29 from institutions. The replies returned by school systems came from 24 states; those made by institutions from 17. The percentages of returns was unusually good: 62 percent and 47 percent, respectively.

The returns indicate that (1) the majority of school systems made little use of special courses in their in-service training, although eight of them referred to courses as being available. Only four institutions mentioned courses, and these were described as electives for undergraduates and graduates. (2) However, 25 institutions reported units on the gifted in undergraduate courses; 15 named "exceptional children," as the area in which course units were given, and six indicated educational psychology. Seven respondents reported that these courses were elective; four, that they were required. A few indicated the length of units to be from two to four hours. These findings indicate little change from reports received in the 1952 comprehensive survey referred to above, which showed that consideration of the education of the gifted was provided mainly in units of courses and that one half of the reported units were one week or less in length.

[1] Frank T. Wilson, "The Preparation of Teachers of Gifted Children," *Exceptional Children*, 20, November 1953, 78-80.

Conferences seemed to be the more frequently used plan for in-service stimulation of improvement in the education of the gifted, almost 70 percent of school systems reporting them. While most of the conferences were described as having been arranged for faculty meetings, institutes, and the like, three were for parents; five, as organized committees; two, as study groups, and one, as a council. Six of the 15 workshops were referred to as summer activities, which varied in length from two to four weeks, and were held in nearby colleges. In most of them the entire time was devoted to problems of the gifted. Six other workshops were held during the school year and two additional ones were described as workshop study groups.

TABLE 1

The Number of Respondents Reporting Provision of Field and Laboratory Experiences

	School systems	Institutions				
		Observa- tion	Participa- tion	Case studies	Student teaching	Other
Blank	25	18	19	18	16	24
"None"	9	3	4	4	2	0
Provisions	6	8	6	7	11	5
TOTALS	40	29	29	29	29	29

Table 1 * shows the reported use of field and laboratory experiences. The six responses from school systems which reported use of this type of preparation indicated visitation in three instances, observation in a local junior high school in one, a Ford fellow in one, and research programs in two. Although most of the replies from institutions were blank or "none," there were several particulars that are of interest. Observations of gifted students varied from one visit per term to twelve times for one month. Three of the six reporting participation had definite arrangements with schools specializing with gifted pupils. The others "encouraged" such experiences "as possible," for example, in practice-teaching work. Case studies of gifted children were

* Formerly Table 4. Tables originally numbered 1, 2, 3, and 6 were omitted in reprinting.—EDITOR'S NOTE.

vaguely indicated as possible projects in connection with course requirements. Student teaching of the gifted depended in the main upon the presence of able children in heterogeneous classes where students were assigned. Three of the five "other" experiences reported were in connection with graduate students, the other two reported that undergraduates might choose projects on the gifted.

Table 2 gives data on preparation in the use of materials. Nine of the school systems reported provision of materials to teachers through libraries (three), bibliographies or outlines (two), or curriculum guides or files (seven), and three mentioned their own publications describing programs or research on the gifted. These materials seemed to be mainly for teachers's use. Three systems in-

TABLE 2

The Number of Respondents Reporting Special Attention to the Selection and Use of Materials Suitable for Gifted Pupils

	School systems	Institutions
Blank	22	16
"None"	3	2
Special Preparation	15	11
TOTALS	40	29

dicated provisions of books, supplies, and the like for use by children in the enrichment of their activities. The eleven responses from institutions were to the effect that use of materials was covered in regular courses or in the special units on the gifted, in extracurricular activities students might devote to such purposes, and by examination of descriptive materials used with the more able.

Both groups were queried as to the presence on their staffs of specialists on the gifted, with the suggestion that a person specially trained in psychology or education might be considered a specialist. Eight of the responses from school systems indicated at least one specialist. Seven reported supervisors of various titles. Five said that the responsibility was "for all," the "entire staff sensitive," "all alert," or specialists "on call." Five of the institutions listed individuals who had doctorates in psychology or special education.

Note of leadership activities by the staffs regarding the education of the gifted was requested and findings are given in Table 3. The 25 particulars given by school systems included 11 instances of publications or preparation of substantial mimeographed material and special reports on the gifted. Eight reported memberships in organizations giving attention to the education of the gifted, and eight mentioned talks, addresses, and radio and television programs. Seven had held teacher conferences, three of which were with parent groups, on topics about the gifted.

TABLE 3

The Number of Respondents Reporting Leadership Activities in Regard to the Gifted by Staff Personnel

	School systems	Institutions			
		Conferences	Committees	Service	Publications
Blank	12	14	18	12	16
"None"	2	4	4	2	12
Activities	25	11	7	15	1
TOTALS	40	29	29	29	29

Eleven institutions reported attendance by staff personnel at or participation in area conferences, one of them sponsoring lectures and courses on the gifted. Seven mentioned that staff members served on area committees working on problems of the education of the gifted, 15 referred to help given schools as consultants, lectures given, and talks on the radio about the gifted. One college mentioned publications made in this field by a faculty member.

DISCUSSION

Discussion of these findings and their implications regarding the preparation of teachers, particularly at the undergraduate level, will be found in the 1958 Yearbook of the National Society for the Study of Education.[2] Some rather significant observations

[2] National Society for the Study of Education, "Preparation of Teachers To Meet the Needs of the Gifted," *Education of Gifted Children, Fifty-Seventh Year Book,* Chicago: Univ. Chicago Press, 1958.

are apparent from glancing at the data of this paper. One, for example, is the consistently large proportion of blank and "none" responses. In but one or two instances more than one half of those who responded to various items left them blank or wrote "none." These were: (1) 27 school systems out of 40 reported the use of one of more conferences on the gifted in their in-service programs for teachers; (2) 25 institutions out of 29 indicated the use of units on the education of the gifted in connection with undergraduate courses. While not impressive, these two instances suggest, perhaps, an awareness of need, and may presage further moves of more veritable value to prepare teachers to meet the needs of able children more constructively and adequately.

As compared with the considerable effort being made by public-school administrators to assist teachers in service to serve their gifted children, teacher-education institutions seem unprepared, at the undergraduate level, to attempt anything but the most elementary and limited measures. In fact, the data seem to show that administrators are moving by conferences, workshops, and supervision to re-educate their teachers, whom institutions had sent to them with scarcely any practical techniques or understanding of the educational needs of gifted children. The findings reported in the earlier survey[3] seem to have been rather starkly underlined: administrators of schools want teachers who are prepared and willing to meet the varying needs of their gifted pupils, so they are setting up in-service experiences to provide the preparation that the teacher-education institutions were not giving students in their undergraduate training.

Suggestions as to steps which institutions might take to prepare students in undergraduate years more adequately to serve gifted and talented children are given in the Yearbook mentioned above. Most surely some group discussion and thinking by institutional staffs which are ready to take steps would be in first order. Our fraternity has met the challenge to serve handicapped children of all variations. It will rise eventually to this emerging challenge to make suitable provision, also, to prepare students to serve gifted children. May we teacher-education staffs press forward in this most important endeavor.

[3] Wilson, *loc. cit.*

PREPARING TEACHERS FOR THE EDUCATION OF THE GIFTED *

by Arthur M. Selvi

TEACHERS COLLEGE OF CONNECTICUT

The question of what to do—if anything—for the education of the gifted comes up again and again in current educational literature. It comes up in the discussion of the aims of education, particularly when referring to the concept of self-realization; it comes up in studies of educational psychology dealing with motivation, individual differences, success experience; in methodology, with special reference to classroom management, individualized procedures in instruction, and the like. We are bound to encounter this question when we try to define "democratic education." Here the discussion follows somewhat along the following propositions.

Democracy in education presupposes equality of educational opportunity for all children;

Equality of educational opportunity means that the best possible opportunity for educational growth should be offered to all children so that they may avail themselves of it according to their capabilities and interests;

In a classroom where democratic procedures prevail, the enlightened teacher does just that. Appealing to individual interests he helps each child attain in cooperation with others a full measure of intellectual, emotional, and social growth.

This is what the book says. This is what the professor reiterates. Everyone looks pleased, for the answer has been found. All we have to do now is to put these principles into practice.

Alas, here is where all kinds of difficulties set in. The everyday

* Presented in Atlantic City, N. J., on February 17, 1953, at a joint meeting of the American Association of School Administrators and the American Association for Gifted Children.

[Reprinted from *Educational Administration and Supervision*, 39, December 1953, 493-499, with the permission of Warwick and York, Publishers, and the author.]

school situation falls a bit short of the ideal situation mentioned in the discussion. The classroom teacher, enlightened though he may be, also fails to measure up to the "ideal teacher" of whom the theorist is speaking. There is, unfortunately, a great gulf between theory and practice, the same difference, in fact, that there is between "ideal" and "real," and the teacher can never be an "ideal," an abstract entity; he is a real human being. He is tied down to earth by practical considerations and is limited in his acts by the very nature of that reality of which he is a part. For instance, it is just in the nature of things that Teacher cannot be in the four corners of the room at the same time; cannot help and guide all children at the same time nor all of the time; cannot think of all the problems, answer all questions, plan several individual or group projects—all at the same time. The enthusiastic young teacher fresh out from college may try to do it, to be sure, and literally fall to pieces as a result. Fortunately, the experienced supervisor may have taught him, during his period of apprenticeship, that this cannot be done, that those professors at the college, though well intentioned, often live in the clouds; that one of the essential requisites of a teacher is to be able to cope with the classroom situation, to have those children well "under control." A good teacher must have that combination of poise, knowhow, and almost hypnotic power which creates in the classroom a slightly rarefied atmosphere conducive to relaxation. When the children's reflexes are thus slowed down a bit, mollified, put at ease, then classroom activities can be organized in an orderly manner.

The teacher reads a story and then begins to discuss it. He has barely formulated a question when Jane's hand shoots up, waving frantically. This is fine. It is a good thing to have bright children in the class. Jane's answer is a good one. Other questions are asked and up goes Jane's hand every time. Eventually the teacher will say, "I know, Jane, you have an answer, but won't you let us hear Bobby, who hasn't yet said a word?" Certainly, this is indeed the democratic procedure. Even if Bobby is slow, even if he has failed to grasp the question, he should be heard, and Jane's raised hand will have to be disregarded. Jane will have to mark time a bit, and to slow down to Bobby's pace since Bobby cannot keep pace with her. Soon Jane will become uninterested, fidgety. Teacher will have to find something for her to do. He might give Jane a special assignment—ah, but will there be time to discuss this special assignment with Jane? Perhaps it might be more expedient to find her some "busy work," send her on errands around the school building, ask her to take telephone calls in the office, put her on hall duty, so she can come to class ten minutes late and leave ten minutes early.

Obviously, this does not seem to be the best way to deal with the gifted. A number of alternatives have been suggested in this connection. They are, as listed in the Educational Policies Commission's booklet, *Education of the Gifted* (1950):

1. Acceleration
2. Grouping
3. Enrichment
4. Elective courses

It will not be necessary at this time to examine in detail each of these schemes. To simplify matters, we might reduce these four plans to two; namely, "acceleration" and "grouping," since "enrichment," as mentioned in the publication, is "a policy rather than a plan" and can be attempted through "differentiated instruction" in a regular classroom or by resorting to acceleration or grouping. As for the elective courses, they resolve themselves, ultimately, into "grouping" of some kind.

It might perhaps be pointed out that acceleration, as a plan to deal with the gifted, seems to be gaining less and less favor chiefly because it may lead to social and emotional maladjustments for the child who becomes farther and farther removed from his own chronological age group.

Grouping, while resorted to fairly frequently, especially in larger school systems, may vary from a simple plan of having A and B sections in each grade to more elaborate schemes, some of which amount to segregation of the gifted, who are sent to special schools.

It will be largely up to the administrators to weigh the pros and cons of each plan and to decide on the course to follow. We might, however, attempt here to outline some ways in which enrichment programs can be worked out in practice. To do this, the school administrator must have, to begin with, (1) available teachers who are equipped to take charge of these enrichment programs, under whatever plan is desired; and (2) a workable plan, dependent upon the local situation such as building facilities, budget, community support, and so forth.

Let us begin, then, with the question of preparing teachers with special qualifications. This may be the proper place to present a plan which is at the present time being considered for adoption at the Teachers College of Connecticut. The plan, as submitted to the College Curriculum Committee, reads in part as follows.

> In order to enable Elementary Education majors, who so desire, to be prepared to organize special activities for the enrichment of the elementary school curriculum, a proposal is being made to institute special *Elective Programs* at our College.
>
> Students who complete satisfactorily all the requirements in a special area will receive upon graduation a statement from the College attesting to this special preparation. A limited number of students will be admitted to these programs each year. Admission will be based upon previous training, personal qualifications, and interest. Students admitted to an Elective Program will take in lieu of their free electives a recommended group of related courses.

The following Elective Programs are suggested at the present time:

*E.P. in a foreign language**
(French is given here as a pattern)

M.L.1 (Languages and Folklore of Other Lands)
French 26A (Review of French Grammar and Composition)
French 26B (Survey of French Literature—Part I)
French 26B (Survey of French Literature—Part II)
French 51 (Advanced Composition and Diction)
French 96B (Methods of Teaching French in Elementary Schools)

*E.P. in science**
** Phys. Sc. 1 (Introductory Physical Science)
** Phys. Sc.•51 (Advanced Physical Science)
** Bio. 30 *or* Bio. 76 (Field Biology and Conservation)
Bio. 2A (General Zoology—Part I)
Bio. 2B (General Zoology—Part II)
Bio. 3 (General Botany)

* To be admitted to the E.P. in a foreign language, students must already possess a fair command of the spoken and written language and a good pronunciation.
* Students electing this program will not take Biology 1.
** Currently required of all elementary-education majors.

Bio. 27A (Anatomy and Physiology—Part I)
Bio. 27B (Anatomy and Physiology—Part II)
Geol. 51 (Introductory Geology)
** Ed. 51B (Elementary Curriculum Materials—Science)
It is suggested that students enrolled in an Elective Program be permitted, whenever possible, to assume special assignments during their senior training.
Elective Programs in other areas than the above may be developed as the need for them arises.

It may be proper to mention at this time that one of the enrichment areas for which an Elective Program is under study is the "Expressive Arts," with special emphasis on music, art, and interpretive dancing.

Now, assuming that other colleges might institute similar programs and that a number of "Enrichment Program Teachers" have thus been made available, the school administrator will be confronted with the question of how he might best be able to use these teachers. Here are but a few suggestions:

1. They might be used as regular classroom teachers, but would be always on call as resource persons, to help other teachers to plan and carry out special activities when desired;

2. They might take charge, for several periods of time during the week, of a special class of gifted children taken from several rooms, while his own homeroom pupils have a library period under the supervision of the librarian;

3. They might exchange classes for one or several periods with other teachers;

4. They might be used as roving teachers in a given system to substitute for others in case of illness and have charge of special classes when not on call otherwise;

5. They might be used exclusively as specialists and move from room to room in a given system.

A more complex plan might be attempted in a school where several of the teachers are equipped with a special preparation in a given area. Let us assume, for the sake of simplicity, that enrichment programs are to be administered in the fifth and sixth grades of a school and that there are two sections in each grade. In this hypothetical situation let us assume that of the four teachers involved, Teacher *A* has special preparation in science; Teacher *B* in French; Teacher *C* in music; and Teacher *D* has done some work in remedial reading. The principal might without too much difficulty plan to devote the last forty minutes of each school day to what might be officially called the visiting hour, or individual-interest hour. During this period, all children with pronounced interest and ability in science would flock to Teacher *A*'s room where they would find some laboratory equipment and materials and become engrossed in the scientific methods of inquiry; the children with a gift for tongues would all go to Teacher *B* and experience the thrill of learning to express themselves in a foreign language. Others will go to Teacher *C* and learn some songs or rehearse a play. Finally, those whose achievements in the fundamental processes leaves something to be desired, might all gather around Teacher *D* for a storybook hour to improve their reading and work occasionally on spelling or remedial arithmetic.

Are these procedures undemocratic? Hardly. Not any more than having some of the boys on the baseball team, others on the basketball team, and others still sitting in the bleachers.

Unfortunately, while in physical education we are ready to condone the paradox that those who need it the least get the most, we have been all too willing to go overboard in the opposite direction when it comes to ministering to the intellectual needs of children. Here we have been, perhaps unconsciously, prone to encourage the leveling off of individual differences for fear of making intellectual snobs out of the brighter children. Many children are sensitive to this kind of pressure and are ready to respond to the urge to "stick with the group," to "conform," reluctant to stand out and be different from others. Ultimately, this amounts to intellectual cowardice.

In an attempt to clarify this complex situation, it might be useful to bring into the picture a component of the democratic process which is often being overlooked. The following simile may serve to illustrate the point.

If we were to suggest that for the sake of democracy the nation's wealth should be distributed equally amongst its citizens, we would expect that such a proposal would be overwhelmingly voted down. For we know that democracy does not stand solely on a principle of equality, nor is it based exclusively on economics. It is not equality, but equality of opportunity we want. In the field of economics, the principle of equality of opportunity results inevitably in some sort of inequality in the distribution of the national wealth—yet the democratic principle is not impaired so long as it is understood that regardless of how much they own, all citizens are equal in human dignity and have the same rights to life, liberty, and the pursuit of happiness.

What goes with regard to differences in wealth may be applied to differences in intellect. Wealth, in itself, is no more objectionable than intelligence, in itself. We see, then, that in the meaning of democracy there is an all-important element which permeates the economic, the political, and the social components—an element whose importance can never be stressed enough. It is the ethical component which resolves itself in the attitude with which we regard our fellowmen, regardless of the differences which may result from equality of opportunity.

For this reason it is of the utmost importance that the teacher of the gifted in our schools be able to convey, along with the richer intellectual and emotional experiences he provides for these children, an understanding of the greater social responsibility and ethical integrity which democratic leadership entails.

THE EXPRESSED ATTITUDES OF TEACHERS TOWARD SPECIAL CLASSES FOR INTELLECTUALLY GIFTED CHILDREN

by Joseph Justman

NEW YORK CITY BOARD OF EDUCATION

and J. W. Wrightstone

NEW YORK CITY BOARD OF EDUCATION

For many years, the New York City schools have organized special classes for intellectually gifted children on the elementary-school level. These IGC classes, as they are known, enroll only children with IQs of 130 or over. In view of the fact that the organization of IGC classes constitutes a departure from normal school prac-

[Reprinted from *Educational Administration and Supervision*, 42, March 1956, 141-148, with the permission of Warwick and York, Publishers, and the authors.]

tice, the extent to which they are accepted by the teaching staff becomes an important factor in assessing their contribution to the functioning of the gifted child. As a means of determining the acceptance of the IGC classes by teacher personnel, a questionnaire sampling teacher attitudes was administered to 121 teachers in four schools in which IGC classes had been a part of the school organization for at least five years. This paper reports the findings of an analysis of teacher responses to the questionnaire.

THE QUESTIONNAIRE

The questionnaire administered to the teachers called for the indication of teacher acceptance of a series of thirty statements on a five-point scale as follows: strongly agree, agree, undecided, disagree, strongly disagree. The majority of the statements were phrased in a negative fashion. A few were so worded that they were positive or complimentary in tone. Typical statements included the following:

Children enrolled in IGC classes would have made more progress had they remained in regular classes.

Teachers are chosen for IGC classes because they are personal favorites of the principal.

Children enrolled in IGC classes are above average in social adjustment.

In addition to the thirty items of this type, each teacher was also asked to indicate whether "all things considered, IGC classes should be retained or abolished."

THE RESPONDENTS

In order to achieve objectivity, an effort was made to maintain complete anonymity of response. However, each questionnaire did carry a series of questions designed to elicit certain personal information. Thus, it was possible to determine the number of years of teaching experience each respondent had completed, and whether or not the respondent had served as the teacher of an IGC class.

Analysis of the returns revealed that the 114 teachers of the total group of 121 who supplied this information reported a mean of approximately twenty-two years of experience. Approximately 18 percent of the group reported more than thirty years of experience, while approximately 16 percent reported that they had completed less than ten years of service.

In all, 116 of the 121 teachers responded to a question seeking to determine specific experience with IGC classes. Of the group 44 (37.9 percent) indicated that they had taught such classes, while 72 (62.1 percent) replied that they had not.

While this information provides a limited picture of the experimental background of the teachers, of far greater interest is the relationship existing between years of teaching experience, and specific experience with IGC classes [Tables 1 through 3 have been omitted].

The relationship between years of teaching experience and specific experience with IGC classes approaches statistical significance on the 0.05 level. It is apparent that length of service is a factor which is taken into consideration by supervisors charged with the responsibility of assigning teachers to such groups. In general, teachers with longer service are assigned to IGC classes.

THE FINDINGS

GENERALIZED ATTITUDES

An analysis of teacher responses to the general question concerning retention or abolition of IGC classes indicated that, of 118 teachers responding, 77 (65.2 percent) voted for retention of the IGC classes, while 34 (28.8 percent) felt that such classes should be abolished. A small proportion of the group failed to express a choice.

In general, the greater the number of years of service reported by the teachers, the greater the tendency to vote for abolition of IGC classes. This relationship approaches significance at the 0.05 level. Moreover, teachers who have actually been assigned to IGC classes tend to vote that they be retained in the school's organizational structure; teachers who have never been assigned to an IGC group, as a rule, vote for abolition of such groups. In this instance, the relationship is significant at the 0.05 level. Evidently, both length of service and specific experience with IGC groups contribute to the generalized attitudes reported. A more definitive statement of differences in teacher attitudes must be sought in their responses to individual items of the questionnaire.

RESPONSES TO INDIVIDUAL ITEMS

In order to determine the relative contribution of length of service and specific experience with IGC classes to teacher attitude, the nature of the responses (favorable or unfavorable) to each item of the questionnaire given by each of the following groups of teachers was determined:

1. Teachers with IGC experience reporting less than twenty years of teaching service (11);

2. Teachers without IGC experience reporting less than twenty years of teaching service (30);

3. Teachers with IGC experience reporting twenty or more years of teaching service (31);

4. Teachers without IGC experience reporting twenty or more years of teaching service (41).

In each instance, the number in parenthesis refers to the total number of teachers in the group.

When either favorable or unfavorable responses to the individual items of the questionnaire given by teachers with and without specific IGC experience who report less than twenty years of experience are considered, in only one instance is there a significant difference in the responses of the two groups of teachers. Evidently, in so far as both favorable and unfavorable responses are concerned, teachers with less than twenty years of service show much the same attitudes, whether or not they have had specific experience with IGC classes.

When favorable responses to the individual items of the questionnaire given by teachers with and without specific IGC experience who report more than twenty years of service are considered, one notes that, for every item, the proportion of teachers giving favorable responses is greater in the group of teachers reporting IGC experience. Moreover, the responses of the two groups differ significantly in seventeen instances. The indications are that specific experience with IGC classes is an important factor entering into the formation of attitudes to such classes on the part of teachers reporting more than twenty years of service.

A consideration of unfavorable responses gives rise to much the same impression. In this instance, in the case of 25 of the items of the questionnaire, a greater proportion of unfavorable items is given by the group without IGC experience. When the data are examined for statistical significance, the responses of the two groups of teachers prove to differ significantly in six instances. This lends additional weight to the conclusion that, for the teachers showing more than twenty years of service, specific experience with IGC classes is an important factor entering into their attitudes to such classes.

In order to verify these findings, Table 4, which contrasts the responses of teachers with and without IGC experience reporting varying years of service, was prepared.

In exactly one half of the thirty items comprising the question-naire, the proportion of teachers giving favorable responses is greater in the group of teachers reporting less than twenty years of experience. In three instances a significant difference in the responses of the two groups of teachers appears. When unfavor-able responses are considered, a significant difference arises in only one instance. It is quite clear that specific experience with IGC classes is more important than years of service in determining teacher attitude toward such classes.

TABLE 4

Number of Items Received Favorably and Unfavorably by Larger Proportion of Teachers in Service Groups Reporting IGC or No IGC Experience

	Favorable responses	Unfavorable responses	Significant Differences	
			Favorable	Unfavorable
With IGC Experience				
Less than 20 years	15	10	2	1
20 or more years	15	20	1	0
Without IGC Experience				
Less than 20 years	30	4	16	0
20 or more years	0	26	0	3

When the responses of teachers without IGC experience are considered, the proportion of teachers giving favorable responses is greater in the group of teachers reporting fewer years of serv-ice for all 30 items comprising the questionnaire. When the data are analyzed for statistical significance, the responses of the two groups prove to differ significantly in 16 instances. The indica-tions are that, when teachers have had no opportunity to work with IGC classes, years of service represent an important factor determining teacher attitude toward such classes.

For 26 of the items of the questionnaire, a greater proportion of unfavorable responses is given by the group showing twenty or more years of service. While it is true that a significant differ-ence in responses appears in only three items, the obtained results tend to reinforce the observation that when teachers who have had no opportunity to work with IGC classes are compared, those showing greater years of service (older teachers will express the lesser degree of acceptance of such classes).

The differences in the attitudes between teacher groups is summarized below, presenting those items which gave rise to significant differences.

Younger teachers and teachers with IGC experience tend to maintain that:

1. The attitude in IGC classes is *not* too competitive.

2. Intellectually gifted children get better training for leadership in an IGC rather than in a regular class.

3. Children of IGC classes tend to be above average in social adjustment.

4. Children of IGC classes get along well with children from other classes in work and play situations.

5. Children enrolled in IGC classes do *not* tend to become conceited about their abilities.

6. Teachers of IGC classes have to spend more time in preparation for class.

7. You get more cooperation from parents of children enrolled in IGC classes.

8. Parents of children in IGC classes take more interest in the work of their children than other parents do.

9. The IGC class gets *no* more than a fair share of school supplies and equipment.

Older teachers and teachers without IGC experience tend to maintain that:

1. Too many children are placed in IGC classes who really do not belong there.

2. Children in IGC classes would have made more progress had they remained in regular classes.

3. Placement of a child in an IGC class tends to aggravate such personal problems as he may have.

4. Children in IGC classes do not develop respect for adults as do children in regular classes.

5. Children in IGC classes tend to "show off" at every opportunity.

6. Having small IGC classes is unfair to other teachers.

7. Parents of children in an IGC class try to interfere with the teacher's work.

8. Parents try to pull strings to get their children enrolled in an IGC class.

9. IGC classes tend to neglect the fundamentals.

In general, then, younger teachers and teachers with IGC experience show markedly more favorable attitudes than teachers with relatively greater service who have not had an opportunity to work with IGC classes. Not only does the latter group tend to reject the basic philosophy upon which the organization of IGC classes is predicated, but they feel that the enrollment of the child in such classes leads to his personal and social maladjustment. This group of teachers, too, expresses considerable resentment towards parents of children placed in IGC classes and, in addition, maintains that undesirable administrative practices result from the organization of such classes.

CONCLUSIONS

Teachers who have had specific experience with IGC classes show markedly more favorable attitudes toward such classes than teachers who have not been assigned to such groups.

Teachers who report less than twenty years of experience show markedly more favorable attitudes toward such classes than those who have served in the schools for twenty or more years.

Teachers who have had specific experience with IGC classes show much the same attitude toward such classes, regardless of the number of years of service they may have had as a teacher.

Teachers reporting less than twenty years of service show much the same attitude toward IGC classes, regardless of their specific experience with such classes.

Teachers reporting more than twenty years of service show marked differences in attitude toward IGC classes, depending upon whether or not they have had specific experience with such classes.

Unfavorable attitudes toward IGC classes take the form of: (1) rejecting the basic philosophy underlying the formation of IGC classes; (2) maintaining that enrollment of a child in an IGC class is conducive to personal and social maladjustment; (3) resenting the activities of parents of children placed in IGC classes; and (4) contending that organization of IGC classes leads to undesirable administrative practices.

IO

EVALUATION
AND RESEARCH

◈

OBJECTIVE EVALUATIVE reports have appeared in the literature only infrequently. Since we can not really progress very far by restating biases and prejudices, it seems imperative to emphasize the research that has been conducted. In this final section, readings here are representative of the evaluations that have been published.

To evaluate the effectiveness of a class or a course one must know its specific objectives and find some way of evaluating how realistically or to what degree these objectives have been reached. The farther these objectives depart from those of academic competence, the more difficult they are to measure. Valid, objective, standardized tests have not been devised to measure goals such as "applies his knowledge of such subjects as history to the understanding and solution of community, state, national, and world problems." It is even more difficult to assess the accomplishment of students in becoming "worthy community members in adulthood" while the students are still in school. Frequently the development of leadership is stated as an objective; yet no record could be found of an evaluation of special-class provisions which reported data regarding leadership training.

Actually evaluations center around (1) achievement, (2) personal and social adjustment, and (3) attitudes of children, parents, and school personnel towards the program under consideration.

The evaluation of special provisions for improving the achievement of the gifted is particularly difficult because standardized achievement tests leave quite a bit to be desired. The tests measure the objectives of the basic curriculum for the general population. They therefore fail to reflect the extra enriching experiences enjoyed by the fast learner. When the achievement of the rapid learner is measured by a test suited for his age mates, his ability places him near the ceiling of the test where one or two raw score points makes a great difference in his converted score. When the achievement of the rapid learner is measured by a test suited for youths several years older (his mental age), we are not sure of the results because the tests were standardized for the older students.

When achievement tests are used, it is desirable to show the

458

effectiveness of an enriched program by comparing the results of the experimental group with those of a control group. To measure the value of the *program* for improving achievement, comparable students with comparable teachers should be used. In the larger cities such situations are not difficult to arrange. In smaller communities students taught according to one method by teacher *A* can be compared with other students taught by teacher *A* when another method is used if the students are of equal ability or if appropriate statistical controls are used. It is much better to use the foregoing method rather than to compare students in one community with students in another, because there is too much variability in students, teachers, and communities. When the community and the teacher are the same, statistical methods can be used to control such student variables as level of intelligence, prior achievement, socioeconomic background, and other factors bearing on achievement.

Growth in creative performance, another aspect of achievement, has received much less attention than the acquisition of facts, understandings, and command of basic skills. Lack of instruments for the purpose of determining or rating creative work probably has been responsible for this shortage of significant research. The suggestions of DeHaan in Section 2 have been employed in Quincy, Illinois, and Portland, Oregon, but primarily to identify those with talent. If the development of creative talent is an objective of the schools, certainly ways of measuring the emergence of such talent need to be devised.

Many studies, although they are often considered less reliable than studies of achievement, have evaluated the personal and social adjustment of gifted individuals or groups of individuals for whom some special provision has been made in the educational setting. These studies might be classified as those using (1) teachers's ratings, observational records, or check lists; (2) standardized personality tests, questionnaires, or sociometric measures, and (3) projective techniques and/or clinical observations. Clinical observations are the most valid and reliable; standardized and sociometric measures fall into second place. Observational records and ratings, however, have been of considerable value in many instances.

Teachers's ratings are frequently referred to in the literature. Mueller's research, reported by Worcester in Section 6, is a good example of such work as are the reports of Lewis in Section 2.

Lewis, however, was not concerned with program evaluation. While the articles in Section 7 were not concerned with program evaluation, they do illustrate some of the frequently used methods of assessing personal and social adjustment.

In evaluating programs where improved academic achievement is the major objective, determining the improvement of social or personal adjustment is not so necessary as determining whether or not the individuals in the program fall within an acceptable adjustment range; if they do, a control group is not as essential as in the measurement of achievement. The attitudes of children, parents, and school personnel are usually assessed by questionnaires, but occasionally more standardized instruments and/or personal interviews are used.

One of the more comprehensive efforts to determine the opinions of those most directly involved in a citywide program has been made by the evaluators of the Portland, Oregon, Cooperative Program. This group collected the opinions of principals in the schools which had special classes, children who were in special classes, teachers of both special and regular classes, and parents of children in special classes. The principals were questioned about administrative arrangements, identification procedures, classroom enrichment, special-interest classes, effects of the program, and public acceptance, and were given an opportunity to express general opinions on the program. The responses were generally favorable to the program, then in its fourth year, and indicated that its outcomes were desirable. Perhaps it is significant to note that only one out of the ten principals felt that a "complete education for gifted pupils can be provided through classroom enrichment."

The questionnaire for children in the special program was given to 972 elementary-school children and dealt with interest in school, the degree to which there was opportunity for new and different work, interpersonal relationships, comparative amount of learning, what was liked best about special classes, how the class could be improved, the desire to participate in the program another year, interference with routine schoolwork, requirements for making up work missed in home room, opportunity to help other pupils in special classes and other classes, and any other remarks that pupils might wish to make. The questionnaires given to teachers and parents sought their views on many of the same areas. The responses by all groups substantially favored the program and only minor changes were suggested for forthcoming years.

The article by Justman and Wrightstone in the preceding section is a good example of assessing teacher attitude towards a specific program.

As one surveys the literature two problems become increasingly apparent. There is a scarcity of published program evaluations, and of those published the methods of investigation differ so widely that a comparison of results is extremely difficult. Publication of more evaluative studies are needed to substantiate some of the existing data and to identify procedures that may have proven to be unusually valuable for others preparing evaluations. If some of the existing procedures could be used in other communities, a cross validation of tremendous significance would be obtained. Probably one of the biggest problems is that the evaluations are not planned as the provisions are instituted, and consequently the investigative design cannot be modified to secure desirable comparisons when the program is well in progress.

The first eight readings in this section are representative of the evaluation that has taken place recently. The last three articles summarize our present knowledge and point the direction for new research.

In the first two articles Walter Barbe, Professor of Education and Director of the Reading Clinic at the University of Chattanooga, reports portions of his Ph.D. dissertation at Northwestern University. In the dissertation he attempted to evaluate Cleveland's major work program by sending a follow-up questionnaire to all high-school graduates of the program between 1938 and 1952. He received a 77-percent return. In the portion of the survey described in the first article he analyzes the best- and least-liked aspects of the program. About two thirds of the respondents felt that the program aided them in making a good adjustment. Whether the others felt that the program hindered them or did not have any particular influence, or both, could not be ascertained from the questionnaire. In the second article he describes the educational level attained by the respondents. He feels that the major work classes fulfilled their function in increasing the college attendance of the gifted, especially when one considers the socioeconomic backgrounds of the sample. Unfortunately, the questionnaire did not allow a thorough exploration of the reasons why some of the subjects did not continue their education further than they did.

The third article is a report by Horace Mann of two sociometric measures and a questionnaire used to assess the freindships of children in the Colfax program of partial segregation. The sociometrics were phrased for both acceptance and rejection and were used with both workshop and regular pupils. The questionnaire was distributed to parents of the workshop children to determine whether choices made at home were similar to those made at school. The results are in opposition to the belief that "because we group children together we have trained them to accept each other for what they are." Mann not only welcomes but encourages repetitions of this study in other settings.

The article by Justman in this section is an excellent example of the experimental method and control of certain variables in evaluating the part of a special-progress class in fostering academic achievement in mathematics, science, social studies, work-study skills, and creative expression in the language arts.

Harold Smith also reports the achievement of special-class pupils, but he compares the subjects in St. Louis with older, national norm groups of normally distributed intelligence rather than with a matched control group of comparable chronological age and IQ. Smith assessed the ability of these elementary-school pupils on tests for secondary-school youth. These students registered quite adequately in areas measured by the achievement tests and showed improvement in scores on standardized personality tests after entering the special classes. Not to be overlooked, even though it was not mentioned by Smith, was the teacher's satisfaction with achievement of pupils in areas not measured by the standardized tests.

In evaluating the effects of an accelerated collegiate program, Marie Flesher and Sidney Pressey used the questionnaire method to learn the opinions of paired accelerates and nonaccelerates toward employment while in school, acceleration, extracurricular activities, schooling beyond the undergraduate degree, marital status, employment, and participation in community affairs. The use of the control group of matched, nonaccelerated students lends stature to the study as does the ten-year lapse between graduation and the questionnaire. It should be noted that preparation for this study began when the subjects entered college.

The report by the Ford Foundation concerning 1350 students who entered college early presents a somewhat different type of evaluation. Here, statistics and formal measures have been de-emphasized in favor of impressions formed by key individuals— scholars, comparison students, school and college administrators, parents, and (the lay report of) the professional evaluators. The fact that, after Ford financial support was withdrawn, the program was continued in all but one university is in itself an indication of its success.

In the hopes of stimulating an "increasingly solid foundation of pertinent experimentation" the Division of School Psychologists of the American Psychological Association submitted questions that, in the judgment of their committee on gifted children, were in urgent need of research exploration. These questions were published in the *American Psychologist*. This article and the following two articles by Dr. Gowan and Dr. T. Ernest Newland summarize what is known about gifted children and suggest areas which require additional investigation. Gowan's article reviews the research pertinent to the questions set forth by the committee of school psychologists. Dr. Newland elaborates on the committee's outline and treats other aspects not dealt with by them. Dr. Newland is a diplomat in clinical psychology in the APA and an authority on psychological assessment and the psycho-educational problems of exceptional children.

≈§§≈

EVALUATION OF SPECIAL CLASSES FOR GIFTED CHILDREN

by Walter B. Barbe

UNIVERSITY OF CHATTANOOGA

The major work program of special classes for gifted children in the public schools of Cleveland, Ohio, has been in operation for over thirty years. Recent literature on the gifted has decried the absence of evaluation studies of this type of program. In this study, the evaluation of the program in Cleveland by its former students will be reported. By means of a questionnaire, which was mailed to all high-school graduates of the program in Cleveland between the years 1938 and 1952, the following information was obtained.

There were 703 questionnaires mailed and 456 were returned. Allowing for "address unknown" returns and addressees later identified as deceased, this represented a 76.9 percent return. Of the responses 237 were from women and 219 were from men. Since all of the respondents were formerly students in a program of special classes for the gifted, the author believed that they were in a particularly good position to evaluate this method of education for the gifted.

The respondents were asked: "What is your opinion of special classes for gifted children?" The data collected are reported in Table 1. The number of respondents who approved the program with enthusiasm were in the majority. Those who approved with hesitancy make up the next largest group. Only 7.9 percent of the respondents either disapproved or strongly opposed the program.

BEST-LIKED ASPECTS OF THE PROGRAM

Since so many of the former major work students endorsed the program with enthusiasm, it was interesting to discover what as-

[Reprinted from *Exceptional Children,* 22, November 1955, 60-62, with the permission of the Council for Exceptional Children and the author.]

pects of the program were best liked. This was, in a sense, an evaluation of the enrichment procedures. While it was doubted that many of the subjects would be familiar enough with educational terminology to label these differences "enrichment," by allowing them to state freely the aspects which they liked best, it was believed that there would be an indication as to the effectiveness of certain enrichment procedures.

TABLE 1

Opinion of Former Major Work Pupils on
Special Classes for Gifted Children

	Number of respondents	Percent of total respondents
Approve with enthusiasm	215	47.2
Approve with hesitancy	169	37.0
Undecided	29	6.4
Disapprove	25	5.5
Strongly oppose	11	2.4
No reply	7	1.5

TABLE 2

Best-liked Aspects of Major Work Program
in Order of Preference

Male respondents	Female respondents
Opportunity to express individuality	Foreign Language
Curriculum differences	Curriculum differences
Freedom from regimentation	Opportunity to express individuality
Stimulation and challenge	Freedom from regimentation
Classmates	Classmates
Foreign language	Stimulation and challenge
Student-teacher relationships	Small classes
Small classes	Student-teacher relationships

There was definite disagreement between the men and the women on the importance of French in the curriculum. The women definitely favored it, while the men appeared not to favor it. The opportunity to express individuality was stated as the best liked aspect of the major work program by 18.7 percent of the men respondents and by 15.8 percent of the women. Curriculum differences, which might have been called enrichment procedures, were listed by 14.8 percent of the men respondents and 18.2 percent of the women. Freedom from regimentation was listed by 13.2 percent of the men respondents and 10 percent of the women. About 10 percent of both the male and the female respondents listed their enjoyment of the type of students in the class as the aspect of the program which they liked the best. Presented in Table 2 are the best-liked aspects of the program.

LEAST-LIKED ASPECTS OF THE PROGRAM

The major aspects which were least liked by both the males and females in this study were lack of social contacts with other

TABLE 3

*Least-liked Aspects of Major Work Program
in Order of Dislikes*

Male respondents	*Female respondents*
Attitudes of other students and teachers	Lack of social contacts with other pupils
Lack of social contacts with other pupils	Attitudes of other students and teachers
Foreign language	Not attention enough to skill subjects
Not rapid enough advancement	Single teacher in elementary school
Teachers	The arts program
Not enough attention to skill subjects	Foreign language
More than one grade in each room	Teachers

pupils and attitudes of other students and teachers. Approximately two out of every five reported one of these two things. Since 1938 there has been a definite attempt in the major work program to provide the gifted students with more opportunities for contacts with other pupils. That this condition is not the same as it was previously was apparent when the differences between the earlier and later groups were noted. Of 115 respondents who graduated between 1938 and 1941, 22 percent stated that they liked least the lack of opportunity to mix with other students. Of 85 respondents who graduated between 1950 and 1952, only 16 percent made this same objection. Apparently, the changes which have been made in the program have made this problem less severe. The least-liked aspects are presented in Table 3.

DESIRED CHANGES

All of the respondents replied to a question asking if they had any suggestion for change in the major work program, over one half of both the male and female respondents reported "none." Of those who had some suggestions for change, the following were listed in decreasing order of frequency.

By male respondents:
1. More mixing with other pupils;
2. Change in teachers (better trained, etc.);
3. More acceleration;
4. Vocational guidance;
5. Revision of curriculum (include shop, commercial subjects, etc.).

By female respondents:
1. More mixing with other pupils;
2. Vocational guidance;
3. Change in teachers (better trained, etc.);
4. More freedom;
5. Revision of curriculum (include commercial subjects, etc.).

About 10 percent would like to have seen more mixing, particularly at social functions. Responses indicating dissatisfaction with the lack of opportunity for contact with other pupils were listed. Suggested several times was a better integration of school social activities to give major work pupils opportunity to mix with others.

About 3 percent believed that the teachers should be given more special training. Types of response to this item included suggestions as to more careful selection of teachers, more training for teachers, and a change of attitude of the teachers toward gifted children.

A great many other suggestions were made, such as "drop the name major work," "throw it out entirely," "change French to Spanish," and "have committee of students and teachers to work out problems."

INFLUENCE OF THE PROGRAM ON LATER ADJUSTMENTS

Approximately 65 percent of the men who have been out of high school three or more years believed that the major work program aided them in making a good adjustment. Of the most recent male graduates only 46 percent reported this. In the total group, 61.1 percent of the males believed that the major work program aided them in making a good adjustment.

There appeared also to be a difference between the responses of the recent female graduates and those who had graduated earlier, but this difference was very slight as compared with the difference of nearly 20 percent in the male group. About 74 percent of women graduates, as contrasted with 61 percent of the males, believed that the program aided them in making a good adjustment.

About two out of three of the respondents, then, believed that the major work program aided them in making a good adjustment. Whether this means that the others felt the program hindered them from making a good adjustment or that they did not believe the program had any particular influence either way, or both, cannot be ascertained from the data.

SUMMARY AND RECOMMENDATIONS

A questionnaire was mailed to all of the living, locatable high-school graduates between 1938 and 1952 of special classes for gifted children in the Cleveland, Ohio, public schools. Information was requested concerning their attitude toward special classes for gifted children, the best- and least-liked aspects, their suggestions for improvement, and opinion of the influence of the program on their later adjustment.

According to the returns, the major work program of special classes for gifted children has been very successful. The majority of them (84.3 percent) favored, with varying degrees of enthusiasm, special classes for gifted children. More than 50 percent of both the men and women had no suggestions for improving the program. This generally agreed with the percentage who approved of the program with enthusiasm (47.2 percent). It reflects a general satisfaction with the program as it was at the time they were in school.

The male respondents stated as the best-liked aspects of the program: the opportunity to express individuality, curriculum differences, and freedom from regimentation. The female respondents listed as the best-liked aspects of the program: foreign language, curriculum differences, and freedom from regimentation.

Of those who replied to a question concerning the least-liked aspect of the program, the most frequently mentioned factors in both the male and female groups were: (1) attitudes of other students and teachers, and (2) the lack of social contacts with other pupils. While the majority of the respondents had no suggestions for improving the major work program, of those who did, more mixing with other pupils was listed most frequently by about 10 percent of the total group.

Having been members of these special classes for gifted children was reported by 61 percent of the male respondents and by 74 percent of the female respondents as having aided them in making a good adjustment. This contradicts the usual complaint against homogeneous grouping to the effect that such children have a more difficult time adjusting to other groups.

From the responses of these former major work students, it is possible to give a rather clear definition of enrichment as it existed in the major work program. This definition might be: Enrichment in the major work program consisted of opportunities to express individuality in an atmosphere free from regimentation and offering stimulation and challenge. It included curriculum differentiation such as the teaching of French, as well as good student-teacher relationships, and classmates who were intellectual equals.

WHAT HAPPENS TO GRADUATES OF SPECIAL CLASSES FOR THE GIFTED?

by Walter B. Barbe

UNIVERSITY OF CHATTANOOGA

If gifted children who are identified early in childhood and who are provided with a special education do not take advantage of the op-

[Reprinted from the *Educational Research Bulletin,* 36, January 1957, 13-16, with the permission of the Bureau of Educational Research and the author.]

portunities of higher education, the reasons should be ascertained. A recent survey by the writer to determine the educational achievements of just such a group of young people—the graduates of the major work program in Cleveland—has revealed some interesting facts.

For thirty years, Cleveland has provided special educational opportunities for superior children. The program is not one of acceleration but one of enrichment. Its purpose is to encourage gifted children to participate in many learning activities commensurate with their grade level and their ability. The subject matter studied by the members of these groups in the elementary and high schools differs chiefly in the intensity with which the major work pupils pursue their studies. French is taught in the elementary school in addition to the usual subjects. High-school students make the ordinary subject choices (a large percentage choose college-preparatory subjects), and their programs differ from the regular high-school programs only as each subject teacher may choose to vary it.

Each major work class in the elementary school includes three grades. Although a child may be chosen for this program in the second half of the first grade, the usual combinations are second, third, and fourth, and fourth, fifth, and sixth. At the high-school level, there is only one grade in each special class.

Candidates for the major work program are selected on the basis of group intelligence tests given to all children in the Cleveland public schools and the Stanford-Binet test given to those ranking high on the group tests. A child may enter the special classes at any grade from the first through the twelfth.[1]

To gather information needed for the study here reported, a questionnaire was sent to all the graduates of the major work program within the past fifteen years. Replies were received from 456 men and women—a 77-percent return. Of the 23 percent who did not reply to the questionnaire, certain observations may be made. It is likely that a large percentage of these had not attended college and were less successful in their occupations and life adjustments than were the respondents. Even considering these possibilities, however, since such a high percentage of return was obtained, there is little reason to believe that the results would be materially affected.

---

[1] Walter B. Barbe and Dorothy N. Norris, "Special Classes for Gifted Children in Cleveland," *Exceptional Children*, 21, November 1954, 55-57, 71. Reprinted on pp. 221-227 in this volume.

These young people, whose average age is twenty-six, are aware of the advantages of higher education, for 91 percent of the men and 63 percent of the women—an average of about 77 percent [2]—attended college at least one term. About 40 percent of those who replied are still in college, while others interrupted their college work and have not returned. The percentage of women attending college is much smaller than that of the men, but it is interesting to note that during the eight-year period from 1942 to 1950 the percentage increased 20 percent. Since over half of the men (53 percent) were in the armed forces, there is a great possibility that had it not been for the veterans's educational benefits, the percentage of men who attended college would have been much less. The majority of the major work graduates attended collegiate institutions in the Cleveland area, such as Western Reserve, Fenn, and Cleveland College; a large number attended other Midwestern universities; and a small number attended Eastern colleges.

In the Terman and Oden report, *The Gifted Child Grows Up,* 90 percent of the men and 86 percent of the women entered college.[3] If the most recent graduates of the major work program were excluded from the study here reported, about 97 percent of the men and 65 percent of the women entered college. While a larger percentage of the men in the present study attended college than the percentage in Terman's study, the situation is reversed for the women. About 23 percent fewer women in the present study attended college than did those in Terman's study. This lack of interest on the part of the women is difficult to explain. Since many of these young people were first-generation Americans, however, a partial explanation may be inferred from lack of sympathy in higher education for women held by many foreign groups.

The number of years of education beyond high school reported by the greatest number of the 456 people in this study was four, about 25 percent reporting this. The fact that the four-year college degree is terminal education for many professional groups would explain the predominance at this level. It is interesting to note that 20 percent of the total group had more than four years of education beyond high school. Of the total group 202, or 44 percent, hold college degrees. Bachelors's degrees are held by 147, M.A.'s by 38;

---

[2] The plans of the most recent graduates are included, although at the time the data were gathered they had not had the opportunity to begin college.
[3] Lewis M. Terman and Melita H. Oden, Stanford, Calif.: Stanford Univ. Press, 1947, p. 148.

M.D.'s by three; Ph.D.'s by four; and other degrees by ten. Of the men and women who replied to the questionnaire 90 did not attend college. This is 20 percent of the total sample. The following table lists the reasons given for not attending college by the indicated percentages of the total sample:

Reason	Percent of total group
Financial	9
Marriage	3
Nurses's training	3
Work	2
Second World War	*
Miscellaneous	3

* Less than 0.5 percent.

Obviously many of these reasons overlap. For instance, those who stated "marriage" and "work" possibly would have gone to college if financial difficulties and marital obligations had not prevented them. The fact that some chose to list their jobs rather than state that it was financial difficulties is understandable.

It is significant that 46 percent of the 90 persons who did not attend college indicated a lack of finances as the deterrent. To this percentage must be added those students who interrupted their college training before it was complete; 10 percent of the total group is in this category. The reasons for permanently interrupting their college careers given by these people are presented in the following table.

Reason	Percent of total group
Financial	2
Work	2
Others	3

Not one of the people who answered the questionnaire said that he did not want to go to college. This could be one of the outcomes of his special education and the realization that he could profit from college education and the desire to receive this training. However, attitudes on the part of some of the major work students and their parents may have had some influence on those who did not attend college.

The financial problem, while it is a major one, is not so severe that it cannot be overcome. The fact that 77 percent of the group being studied did attend college, even though they were largely from families of the lower-middle class which can hardly afford the present high cost of a college education, indicates that it is possible for the student with ability to finance a college education. Undoubtedly veterans's educational benefits greatly aided many of the men in this respect. Moreover, two out of every five of those who attended college received financial aid in the form of scholarships or assistantships, either from schools, civic groups, charitable organizations, or the government. This large proportion indicates the need for such assistance.

Since all of the people in the present study are of superior intelligence and were identified as gifted early in childhood, there appears to be little reason why they would not attend college. The fact that they were a part of a special-education program which placed a high value upon learning should also have contributed to the realization on the part of these individuals of the value of advanced education. Their achievements should be expected to be good, for they were provided with challenging educational experiences for many years in the major work program.

HOW REAL ARE FRIENDSHIPS OF GIFTED AND TYPICAL CHILDREN IN A PROGRAM OF PARTIAL SEGREGATION?

by Horace Mann

STATE UNIVERSITY OF NEW YORK, COLLEGE FOR TEACHERS

Whenever educators come together to talk about what should be done for gifted youngsters in our schools, the discussions seem to

[Reprinted from *Exceptional Children*, 23, February 1957, 199-200, with the permission of the Council for Exceptional Children and the author.]

bog down in a morass of arguments over what kind of placement we should provide. Those favoring special classes argue that the special class is most democratic, most effective in challenging the gifted, and most "lifelike" in that we tend as adults to select as close friends our intellectual peers. Those favoring the alternate provision of enrichment in regular programs claim that this particular placement is most democratic, most effective in challenging gifted youngsters, and most "lifelike" in that the world into which the gifted graduates is not a homogeneously grouped one. It is not surprising, therefore, that many educators have sought to develop programs which resolve the criticisms arising from either of these arrangements. One such educator, Dr. Hedwig Pregler, has organized in a program of partial segregation, at the Colfax School in Pittsburgh, Pennsylvania, a compromise provision which attempts to meet the criticisms of those favoring placement in a special class and those favoring placement in a regular class for the gifted.

Here, at this kindergarten to sixth-grade school, with an enrollment of over 1000, gifted children with Binet IQs of 130 and above, spend 50 percent of their school day in a regular class with typical children participating in art, music, physical education, and other cultural activities, while the other 50 percent of their day is spent in workshop rooms, with other gifted children doing either individual or group enrichment projects as well as academic learnings.[1]

Dr. Pregler contends that in such an arrangement gifted children have an opportunity to develop and maintain friendships with typical children in their regular classes, as well as receive the challenge and stimulation which comes from working with their intellectual peers in the workshops.[2] In an attempt to validate Pregler's premise that gifted children develop and maintain friendships with typical children in such a program the present study was undertaken.

PROCEDURES

Since the study asked "How real are the friendships of gifted and typical children in this program of partial segregation?", the

[1] Hedwig O. Pregler, "Provision for Mentally Superior Child," *Pittsburgh Schools,* 26, January-February 1952, 69, 70.
[2] Pregler, "The Colfax Plan," *Exceptional Children,* 20, February 1954, 198-201, 222. Reprinted on pp. 215-220 in this volume.

procedures developed were designed to measure the social position the gifted children hold among gifted as well as typical classmates. The procedures consisted of two sociometrics and a parent questionnaire. The first sociometric asked three acceptance-oriented and three rejection-oriented questions:

1. Which children attending this school would you *like* to have near you at a school party?
2. Which children attending this school would you *like* to have help you catch up on your school work after you have been absent?
3. Which children who attend this school would you *like* to have on your side or team in playing games?

The children were told that they might choose from any of the pupil population, kindergarten to sixth grade, attending Colfax. To obtain rejection-oriented responses, the questions substituted the words *"least like"* for the word *"like."*

The second sociometric was designed primarily to examine the likelihood of a gifted child choosing a typical child in those classes to which they went together. Two acceptance-oriented and two rejection-oriented questions were asked:

1. Which three children who attend this school would you *like* to have give you their criticism concerning the art work you have done?
2. Which three children who attend this school would you *like* to have give you their criticism concerning the music work you have done?

Again, the substitution *"least like"* was made for *"like."*

Finally, a questionnaire to be sent to parents of the workshop children was developed. The first part asked three questions:

1. Which children does your child invite to your home when he is given the opportunity to have someone stay overnight?
2. Which children does your child call upon when he needs someone to help him with his studies?
3. Which children does your child call upon when he wants someone with whom to play?

The second part of the questionnaire asked the parent to indicate in each of the above cases where their child had met the children listed.

Two things were to be examined through the parent questionnaire. The first was the consistency of social status a gifted child attained in and out of school. Was the most popular gifted child in school, the most popular out of school? The second thought to be examined was the belief that Pregler held on admission to Colfax School. Ordinarily gifted children in many communities are transported to a special class from various parts of the city. At Colfax, however, only those children residing within the school district which Colfax normally serves are accepted for admission. Pregler feels that such a policy tends to develop and reinforce further the friendships that gifted children made.

FINDINGS

The first sociometric was given to children drawn from the fourth, fifth, and sixth grades—in all, 281 children. Of this number, 67 were gifted children. These 67 came from two workshops at Col-

TABLE 1

Acceptance Choices of Gifted Children

| | Children being chosen | |
Gifted child choosing	Gifted	Typical
Intermediate workshop	199	18
Senior workshop	186	62

fax—the intermediate and the senior workshop groups. The intermediate workshop group consisted of 31 gifted children drawn from the fourth and the lower half of the fifth grades. The senior workshop group consisted of 36 gifted children drawn from the upper fifth and sixth grades.

An analysis of the results gave strong evidence that while gifted children did have visible social and academic contacts with typical children, this contact was far from real. Table 1 dramatically illustrates this.

Here gifted children, as members of the intermediate workshop, chose other gifted children 181 times more than typical children. In the senior workshop they chose other gifted children 124 times more than typical children.

Typical children too, when they choose friends, seemed to prefer their own. Table 2 indicates that typical children from the intermediate regular classes chose other typical children 524 times more than gifted children. In the senior regular classes they chose other typical children 806 times more than gifted children.

These results might lead one to assume that since gifted and typical children preferred their own groups, they would tend, when asked whom they *"least liked,"* to reject one another. This assumption however is not borne out by the results indicated in either Tables 3 or 4. In Table 3 it may be seen that gifted children in the in-

TABLE 2

Acceptance Choices of Typical Children

| Typical child choosing | Children being chosen | |
	Typical	Gifted
Intermediate regular class	542	18
Senior regular class	868	62

TABLE 3

Rejection Choices of Gifted Children

| Gifted child rejecting | Child being rejected | |
	Gifted	Typical
Intermediate workshop	173	20
Senior workshop	137	35

TABLE 4

Rejection Choices of Typical Children

| Typical child rejecting | Child being rejected | |
	Typical	Gifted
Intermediate regular class	627	20
Senior regular class	956	35

termediate workshop reject other gifted children 153 times more than typical children. In the senior workshop they reject their own 102 times more than typical children.

Table 4 indicates that typical children from intermediate regular classes reject other typical children 607 times more than gifted children. In the senior regular classes they reject their own 921 times more than gifted children.

In all instances, gifted and typical children significantly chose and rejected more of their own group.

The results of the second sociometric which was given to the 67 workshop children tended to reinforce the findings on the first sociometric. In the intermediate workshop, gifted children preferred other gifted children to criticize their work in music and art 71 percent of the time; in the senior workshop they preferred gifted children to criticize this work 65 percent of the time.

It should be noted that at no time during the administration of these sociometrics were typical and gifted children in the same room.

The final procedure, the parent questionnaire, was sent to the homes of the 67 workshop children. Parents were asked to fill in the questionnaire without consulting their youngsters. The 93-percent return revealed that there was a substantial relationship between

TABLE 5

Returns of Questionnaire Responses Indicating Meeting Place of Out-of-school Friends

Type of friend	School General (Percent)	Workshop (Percent)	Neighborhood (Percent)	Family (Percent)	Miscellaneous (Percent)
Comes to my house	13.59	44.20	22.18	15.01	5.02
Study	1.81	87.64	5.99	4.56	0.00
Recreation	12.51	16.08	51.79	17.86	1.76

the friends the workshop children had in school and those they had in the community. When the acceptance choices of workshop children on the first sociometric were compared with the children listed by the parents as their child's most chosen associate in each of the three situations, a correlation of + .42 was found for intermediate workshop children and + .39 for senior workshop children.

Since the relationship between the in-and-out-of-school friendships that gifted children had was substantial, the investigator's apprehension that had he given the sociometrics when gifted and typical children were in the same room the results would have been different were mitigated.

Table 5 indicates that the results of the second part of the parent questionnaire, which asked where their children met each of the children listed, verified Pregler's contention that the Colfax policy of not admitting children from outside the district which the school ordinarily services tends to develop and reinforce friendships among children in the workshops.[3] Here we see that the workshop provided the most frequent locale for meeting the friends the workshop children made except in the case of their "recreation" friends, where the neighborhood took precedence.

SUMMARY AND CONCLUSIONS

This much becomes clear, then, from our analysis of the findings. The sociometrics indicated: (1) As a group the workshop children tended to accept and reject more workshop children than typical children; (2) as a group, typical children tended to accept and reject more typical children than workshop children; (3) in both cases there was a significant difference in the acceptance-rejection scores obtained by workshop children from typical children with whom they shared a common homeroom and those obtained from gifted children with whom they shared a workshop.

The parent questionnaire indicated: (1) There was a substantial relationship between the friends the workshop children had in school and those they had in the community. The higher the school-acceptance score the more frequent the mention of the child's name on the parent questionnaire; (2) the workshop provided the most frequent locale for meeting the friends gifted children made.

One might say therefore that while the workshop, the room in which the gifted children work together, helped to develop and reinforce friendships in and out of school, the regular class, which provides a place where gifted and typical children mingle and which is the really unique contribution of the Colfax Plan, did not actually produce relationships significant enough to be classified as friendships. This again calling attention to the fallacy of believing that "because we group children together we have trained them to accept each other for what they are."[4]

Perhaps, if studies similar in methodology were done in complete segregation and in complete integration programs, a firm basis would be provided for general conclusions concerning the best provision for gifted children in our schools.

[3] Author's conversation with Pregler.
[4] Pregler, "The Gifted," *Special Class Teacher*, November 1955, p. 10.

ACADEMIC ACHIEVEMENT OF INTELLECTUALLY GIFTED ACCELERANTS AND NONACCELERANTS IN JUNIOR HIGH SCHOOL

by Joseph Justman

NEW YORK CITY BOARD OF EDUCATION

One way of meeting the challenge presented by intellectually gifted children has been the formation in New York City of homogeneously organized special classes in which pupils complete the normal span of junior high school work in two, rather than three, years. These classes enroll children with intelligence quotients of 130 and higher who show superior academic achievement and who also possess personal characteristics of initiative, enthusiasm, willingness to work, reliability, regular attendance, and capacity for sustained work. It has been felt not only that the special class will serve as a medium for stimulating the pupil to better academic achievement but also that the formation of such groups will help the child attain better personal and social adjustment.

A previous paper (1) has presented evidence concerning the role of the special class in furthering the personal and social adjustment of the intellectually gifted pupils which it enrolls. The present study seeks to assess the part that the special-progress class plays in fostering academic achievement in mathematics, science, social studies, work-study skills, and creative expression in the language arts.

PROCEDURE OF THE STUDY

The study involved a comparison of matched pairs of intellectually gifted pupils drawn from special-progress and normal-progress classes. Pupils were matched on the bases of school attended, grade, sex, chronological age, mental age, and intelligence quotient.

[Reprinted from the *School Review*, 62, March 1954, 143-150, with the permission of the University of Chicago Press and the author.]

The Pintner General Ability Test, Intermediate Test, Form B, was utilized as the measure of intellectual status in forming equated groups. The subjects of the study were drawn from a group of 95 matched pairs of special-progress and normal-progress pupils from 11 normal-progress and 11 special-progress classes in nine junior high schools located in comparable middle-class neighborhoods in New York City. The number of matched pairs of pupils to whom the various appraisal instruments in the test battery were administered varied between 70 and 83.

ACHIEVEMENT IN MATHEMATICS, SCIENCE, AND SOCIAL STUDIES

RESULTS ON TESTS

In the areas of mathematics, science, and social studies, the X Forms of the appropriate subject tests of the Cooperative Tests for grades seven, eight, and nine were used as measures of pupil performance. Table 1 summarizes the performance of special-progress and normal-progress pupils on the three measures.*

Pupils enrolled in special-progress classes show significantly higher attainment, not only on the total test, but on all the subtests of the Cooperative Mathematics and Science Tests. On the social studies test, the special-progress group shows significantly higher attainment on two of the three subtests, while the difference in favor of the special-progress group approaches statistical significance at the .05 level on the third subtest.

In interpreting these findings, it must be remembered that the two groups are not equated in all important aspects which might conceivably affect pupil achievement. While the factor of intellectual status has been adequately controlled, no attempt was made to establish the equivalences of the two groups in ability in the three subject areas at the beginning of the survey period. As a result, the observed differences cannot be attributed solely to influences stemming from placement in a special-progress group.

Still another factor must be considered in assessing the relative performance of the two groups. The special-progress pupil, since he completes the junior-high-school grades in two, rather than three, years, is exposed to a much wider range of subject matter in these

* Tables 1, 2, and 3 have been modified in reprinting.—EDITOR'S NOTE.

three areas than is the normal-progress pupil in an equivalent span of time. In the present instance, at the time the Cooperative Tests were administered, the special-progress pupil had virtually completed 75 percent of his work in mathematics, science, and social studies. The normal-progress pupil, on the other hand, was reaching the completion of eighth-grade work (66 percent) in these areas. This difference is undoubtedly reflected in the attainment of the two groups.

TABLE 1

Mean Scores and Significance of Mean Differences of Matched Normal-progress and Special-progress Pupils on Cooperative Mathematics, Science, and Social Studies Tests

Test	Matched pairs (N)	Differ- ence between means**	Standard deviation of dif- ference	t
Mathematics:				
Skills	82	3.72	8.69	3.855*
Facts, terms, and concepts	82	2.30	4.55	4.545*
Applications	82	1.92	6.86	2.520†
Appreciation	82	2.30	4.86	4.259*
Total test	82	10.24	19.40	4.750*
Science:				
Informational background	83	6.60	11.93	5.038*
Terms and concepts	83	2.91	7.35	3.606*
Comprehension and inter-				
pretation	83	3.76	5.80	5.903*
Total test	83	13.27	19.64	6.155*
Social studies:				
Informational background	79	2.38	11.90	1.777
Terms and concepts	79	2.13	7.11	2.663*
Comprehension and inter-				
pretation	79	2.15	5.02	3.805*
Total test	79	6.66	17.10	3.462*

* Significant at the .01 level.
† Significant at the .05 level.
** Favoring the accelerated group.

EFFECT OF INCLUDING NINTH-GRADE CURRICULAR ITEMS

In order to illuminate the role of curricular differences in contributing to the obtained results, pupil performance on the individual items of the three measures was analyzed. In addition, the grade level at which the individual items of the tests would normally appear in the New York City course of study in mathematics, science, and social studies was determined. The special-progress group achieved significantly higher scores on 17 of 25 ninth-grade items included in the mathematics test; on 19 of 60 ninth-grade items appearing in the science test; and on 11 of the 59 ninth-grade items included in the social studies test. The normal-progress pupils, on the other hand, achieved significantly higher scores on none of the ninth-grade items in mathematics and science and in only two of the items in social studies. It is evident that, in part, the relative superiority of the pupils drawn from special-progress classes may be attributed to their better performance on those items which may be looked upon as specific to ninth-grade instruction in the three subject fields.

In order to arrive at a more exact determination of the role of this curricular difference, new scoring keys for the Cooperative Tests were prepared, and the papers of both groups of pupils were rescored in order to secure a measure of relative achievement in seventh- and eighth-grade mathematics, science, and social studies. Table 2 presents the mean raw scores of both groups on each of the three tests (exclusive of ninth-grade items) and the statistical significance of the mean differences.

Comparison of the results presented in Table 2 with those summarized in Table 1 indicates that the differences between the two groups are reduced through the elimination of those test items which are specific to ninth-grade instruction. In mathematics, two sections of the test, both of which tend to emphasize the more computational aspects of the subject, no longer give rise to reliable differences between the two groups of pupils. On those sections of the test which purport to measure knowledge of facts, terms, and concepts and pupil appreciation of mathematical processes (both of which encompass verbal materials to a relatively greater degree than those measuring skills and applications), pupils enrolled in special-progress classes continue to show reliably better performance than matched pairs drawn from normal-progress classes, even when ninth-grade items are eliminated.

In the field of social studies, not only are the differences between the two groups reduced through the elimination of ninth-grade items, but the direction of the difference on one section of the test is reversed. In this area, none of the obtained differences is statistically significant.

In the field of science, however, the obtained mean differences on each section of the test, as well as on the total test, remain statistically significant. In each instance, the functioning of those pupils enrolled in special-progress classes is better than that of their matched pairs drawn from normal-progress classes. The New York City course of study in science at the junior-high-school level is organized on a modified spiral plan. Many seventh- and eighth-year

TABLE 2

Mean Scores and Significance of Mean Differences of Matched Normal-progress and Special-progress Pupils on Cooperative Mathematics, Science, and Social Studies Tests (Exclusive of Ninth-grade Items)

Test	Matched pairs (N)	Difference between means**	Standard deviation of difference	t
Mathematics:				
Skills	82	1.22	6.10	1.799
Facts, terms, and concepts	82	2.24	3.97	5.079*
Applications	82	1.21	5.92	1.839
Appreciation	82	1.93	4.27	4.089*
Total test	82	6.60	15.18	3.192*
Science:				
Informational background	83	3.87	5.46	6.418*
Terms and concepts	83	1.65	4.76	3.137*
Comprehension and inter-				
pretation	83	1.62	4.49	3.608*
Total test	83	7.14	10.73	6.025*
Social studies:				
Informational background	79	1.74	8.84	1.738
Terms and concepts	79	0.73	5.72	1.127
Comprehension and inter-				
pretation	79	− 0.08	2.44	0.325
Total test 1	79	2.39	12.66	1.668

* Significant at the .01 level.
** Favoring the accelerated group.

units of work are repeated, on a higher level, during the ninth year. As a result, the ninth-year student receives the benefits accruing from repetition of course work.

In order to eliminate the effect of this repetition of course content, the performance of the matched pairs of special-progress and normal-progress pupils on those items which appear only in the seventh and eighth years of science instruction was compared.

Again it was found that special-progress pupils are significantly superior to their matched normal-progress pairs on those items of the test which relate solely to the seventh- and eighth-year courses of study in science. All differences in the mean scores are significant at the .01 level, except that for knowledge of terms and concepts, which is significant at the .05 level. The superior functioning in science of pupils enrolled in special-progress classes cannot be attributed solely to completion of additional course work or to repetition of course work, although these curricular factors are undoubtedly operative. In general, it would appear that these curricular factors are of relatively greater importance in social studies and in mathematics than they are in science.

EFFECT OF READING SKILL

Another factor which may contribute to the better performance of pupils drawn from special-progress classes on the total test is their relative superiority in reading skills. In order to test this hypothesis, the contribution of ability in reading to the pupils's performance in mathematics, science, and social studies was investigated through an analysis of covariance technique, which makes it possible to compare the performance of special-progress and normal-progress pupils equated in reading ability as well as in intellectual status.

In the case of all three tests, comparison of the special-progress and normal-progress groups is based upon material common to the course of study which both groups complete. The results indicate that the attainment of special-progress pupils is uniformly better than that of normal-progress pupils of equivalent intellectual status and reading ability in all but one aspect of performance in both mathematics (application) and science (knowledge of terms and concepts). In social studies, the greater attainment may be attributed, in large measure, to their initially superior achievement in reading.

ADVANTAGE OF SPECIAL-PROGRESS GROUPS

The indications are that the relative superiority in mathematics and science manifested by pupils drawn from special-progress classes is an outgrowth, in part, of two factors—their initial superiority in reading skills and the greater amount of course content which they complete by virtue of their accelerated program. In the field of social studies, when an attempt is made to equate the influence of these two factors, the relative performance of matched special-progress and normal-progress pupils does not differ appreciably. These two factors, however, when considered both independently and jointly, do not wholly account for the superiority of the special-progress group in mathematics and science. It would appear, then, that some advantage in these two areas is associated with pupil enrollment in a special-progress group or that the observed superiority results from other factors in the situation that have not been controlled.

WORK-STUDY SKILLS

To measure the pupils's mastery of work-study skills, the Iowa Every-Pupil Tests of Basic Skills, Test B: Work-Study Skills, Advanced Battery, Form N, was utilized. A comparison of scores made by 70 matched pairs of special-progress and normal-progress pupils for whom results were available is presented in Table 3.

TABLE 3

Mean Scores and Significance of Mean Differences of Matched Normal-progress and Special-progress Pupils on Iowa Work-study Skills Test

Test item	Matched pairs (N)	Difference between means**	Standard deviation of difference	t	Co-variance F
Map reading	70	3.08	6.55	3.909*	9.27*
References	70	.70	3.07	1.892	.21
Index	70	1.04	3.72	2.321†	4.03†
Dictionary	70	.45	2.80	1.335	1.69
Graphs	70	1.07	4.37	2.034†	3.04
Total test	70	6.34	12.25	4.312	11.40*

* Significant at the .01 level.
† Significant at the .05 level.
** Favoring the accelerated groups.

The scores of pupils attending special-progress classes are consistently higher than those obtained by their matched pairs drawn from normal-progress groups. The data reveal that the special-progress pupils earn significantly higher scores on three of the five subtests of the Iowa Work-study Skills Test and on the total test scores.

As in the subject-matter fields, one important factor contributing to performance in this area is the mastery of reading skills which pupils bring to the testing situation. Here, too, the contribution of reading ability of the pupils to achievement was investigated through an analysis of the covariance technique. The results are also presented in Table 3. In this area, too, the indications are that the relative superiority of the special-progress group is an outgrowth, in part, of their initial superiority in reading skills. It should be noted, however, that this greater initial reading skill does not wholly account for the relatively better performance of pupils drawn from special-progress classes. It would appear, then, that some advantage in this area is associated with enrollment in a special-progress group.

CREATIVE EXPRESSION IN LANGUAGE ARTS

Collecting the samples

An evaluation of pupil functioning in the area of language arts presents several difficulties that do not enter into a survey of pupil achievement in other fields. In order to obtain complete spontaneity of expression, two samples of creative writing, an original poem and an original story, were obtained from each pupil in the survey. In both instances, an attempt was made to secure a modicum of uniformity in a situation which, of necessity, must remain relatively unstructured and amorphous.

Although no attempt was made to delimit or define the nature of the poem which the pupils were called upon to write, the title of the poem was fixed. Without any previous announcement to the pupils, paper was distributed, and they were asked to write an original poem to be titled "The Stranger." Thirty minutes were allotted for the task.

Thirty minutes were also allowed for the development of the original story, to be based upon a picture shown to the pupils. The picture, semistructured in character, portrayed a teen-age girl touching the spread of a freshly made bed, as seen through a partially open door. In actuality, the picture was interpreted in a variety of ways: the teen-age girl was considered a young child by some children and a mature mother by others; the bedspread became a snow-covered lawn seen through an open window; the open door was looked upon as a window or a porch.

Little difficulty was encountered in the actual collection of the samples. In the case of both the poem and the story, all the pupils submitted finished products within the set period.

RATING THE SAMPLES

In order to evaluate pupil performance, scales for rating pupil products were prepared. Three teachers of junior-high-school English, who were relieved of classroom duties for a period of one week, rated the poems and the stories. Rating of pupil products was undertaken after a preliminary orientation period in which the judges, in order to familiarize themselves with using the scales and to reduce differences in the ratings, rated similar poems and stories written by pupils not included in the survey. The poems and stories by pupils included in the survey were rated independently by each of the three teachers. The results of these independent judgments were averaged to arrive at a pupil's final rating.

RESULTS

A comparison of the mean ratings obtained by 74 matched pairs of pupils drawn from special-progress and from normal-progress classes on the original story and 73 matched pairs on the original poem is presented in Table 4 [which is omitted].

In each of the areas in which ratings were assigned, pupils enrolled in special-progress classes show better performance on stories than their matched pairs drawn from normal-progress groups.

In over-all rating and in two of these areas, feeling tone and vividness of diction and style, the mean ratings on stories obtained by the special-progress group prove to be significantly better than those of the normal-progress pupils. It would appear, then, that there is relatively little difference between the two groups in the selection and development of the stories that were submitted. In mastery of the more technical aspects of prose composition (exclusive of mechanics of English), however, the group of pupils attending special-progress classes is superior to that in normal-progress classes.

The ratings assigned on all qualities, with the exception of the area of mechanics of English, to the poems submitted by pupils attending special-progress classes are significantly better than those obtained by their matched pairs enrolled in normal-progress groups. In the field of poetic composition, special-progress pupils are clearly superior to pupils drawn from normal-progress classes, not only in selection and development of basic poetic themes, but in mastery of the more technical aspects of literary creativity.

CONCLUSIONS

The segregation of intellectually gifted pupils in a special class is generally accompanied by academic achievement superior to that normally attained by equally gifted pupils who remain in normal-progress groups. To be sure, in several of the areas to which attention is here directed, the better attainment which special-progress pupils manifest must be attributed, in part, to the greater amount of course work which they complete and to the selection, for such classes, of pupils who show greater initial mastery of reading skills. However, these two factors, operating independently or jointly, do not wholly account for the superiority of the special-progress group. The indications are that some of the advantage is associated with pupil enrollment in a special-progress group.

The acceleration of intellectually gifted pupils by a period of one year on the junior-high-school level is not accompanied by loss in those areas to which the program of appraisal was directed. On the contrary, a concomitant gain in academic achievement may be noted. On the basis of the evidence resulting from this study, it is clear that the segregation of intellectually gifted pupils in homogeneous special-progress groups on the junior-high-school level has some value.

REFERENCE

1. Joseph Justman. Personal and Social Adjustment of Intellectually Gifted Accelerants and Non-accelerants in Junior High Schools. *School Rev.*, 61, November 1953, 468-478.

A SUMMARY REPORT OF EXPERIMENTAL CLASSES FOR GIFTED CHILDREN: ST. LOUIS PUBLIC SCHOOLS

by Harold C. Smith

ST. LOUIS, MISSOURI, SPECIAL SCHOOLS

In September 1955, the St. Louis Public School System launched an experimental study of gifted children at the sixth-grade level. An outline of organizational procedures follows:

1. Identification of the Experimental Group
   a. As a screening device, all second-semester fourth-grade pupils were given the Otis Quick Scoring Mental Abilities Test (Beta) during the 1953-1954 school year.
   b. Those children scoring 110 or above on the Otis Test were given the Revised Stanford-Binet Intelligence Scale (Form L or M). (800 Binet Tests were administered by the Test Service Section of the Board of Education during the 1954-1955 school year.)
   c. Some 260 of these children were identified as having IQs of 125 or above, and were designated as the experimental group (the minimum IQ has been since raised to 130).
2. Organization of Classes
   a. These 260 gifted pupils were assigned to nine special classes. Each is located in an elementary school in a regional area of the city.
   b. Experienced teachers were selected and assigned to the classes on the basis of excellence of teaching record, personal qualifications, and the quality of academic teacher preparation.
   c. Additional supplies and equipment were placed in the rooms for gifted children, such as a room library of reference materials, a microscope, a typewriter, and a science kit.
3. Courses of Study
   a. The regular sixth-grade courses of study were used as a guide and constituted the minimum basic essentials of instruction.

[Mimeographed paper, reprinted with permission of the author.]

b. The courses of study materials were to be enriched in all areas with special emphasis upon science, social studies, creative writing, and literature.

c. The study of French was introduced as a part of the enrichment program, with emphasis upon functional conversational French.

The Educational Research Division of the Board of Education has been conducting a study of these classes for gifted children under the direction of Dr. Earl G. Herminghaus. Nine regular sixth-grade elementary classes were used in the study for comparative purposes.

In addition to the mental tests described above, the testing program included pretests and post-tests using the Iowa Every Pupil Test of Basic Skills, the Iowa Tests of Educational Development, and the California Test of Personality. These batteries were administered simultaneously to the experiment classes and to the regular sixth-grade classes.

Probably one of the more significant gains as indicated by these criteria was in the general area of social adjustment. The pretest results indicated that the experimental groups were somewhat below the regular sixth-grade groups. At the end of the year the classes for gifted children ranked well above the regular sixth grade, having gained 16 percentile points during the year in Basic Social Concepts (Iowa Tests of Educational Development series). As measured by the California Test of Personality, gains in the experimental classes were ten times that of the regular classes in social adjustment.

At the conclusion of the 1955-1956 school year, Dr. Herminghaus reported in part as follows:

Comparison of total group scores on pre-experiment and postexperiment tests showed substantial gains in all areas. Mean gains were generally accompanied by a decrease in the standard deviations, which would appear to indicate that the groups become more homogeneous, with less variance from the means. This was particularly true of the experimental group.

In the Iowa Tests of Educational Development series, designed for secondary schools, ninth-grade norms are the only ones available for judging the achievement of these sixth-grade experimental-group pupils. Judged by these standards, a great deal of progress was shown during the year. In every test, the mean of the experimental group on the post-tests was above the 50th percentile for the ninth grade. Greatest gain was in general vocabulary, where postexperiment test scores were at the 77th percentile for the ninth grade. In three other areas, means were above the 70th percentile.

Experimental group scores on the California Test of Personality showed substantial gains on the post-test with ratings superior to the sixth-grade group on all areas of the test. Judged by norms established by pupils in grades seven through ten, total adjustment was at the 50th percentile; personal adjustment and social adjustment were near the 50th percentile. It is perhaps significant that the largest gain was made in the area of social adjustment, where pretest results indicated that the regular sixth-grade group had ranked superior to the experimental group at the beginning of the experiment.

It may be concluded from these results that during the school year 1955-1956 the experimental group of sixth-grade gifted children showed a high degree of academic proficiency, corresponding, on the whole, to that of ninth graders; their personal and social adjustment, as measured by the California Test of Personality, improved and appeared to be satisfactory in terms of their grade level.

Our tentative conclusions tend to refute the rather widespread opinion that gifted children should not be separated from normal children for instructional purposes. However, in our experimental program we have located these classes in regular schools and the pupils in the gifted classes are integrated into regular school activities in all areas except classroom instruction.

At the beginning of the school year 1955-1956, there were 116 pupils participating in the newly established gifted children's program who were at that time classified as six high. Of this number, 76 were still enrolled and present for retesting at the time of their graduation from the eighth grade in January 1958. At that time all tests of the Iowa Tests of Educational Development series were administered to the group.

Percentile ratings based on beginning-of-the-year ninth-grade norms indicate that the average score of these gifted children, upon their graduation from eighth grade, corresponds with that of the top 3 to 6 percent of beginning ninth-grade students.

A comparison of their mean scores with those of high-school students beginning the second semester of grade twelve (the highest norms available for the test) shows that they rank well above the average achievement of such students. After seeing the program in operation, the qualifications for the program and the course of study were modified. In addition to the previous requirements, students had to be achieving at grade level and be socially adjusted and emotionally stable to qualify for the program. When it was observed that enrichment in breadth alone was not meeting the needs of the students, the courses of study were accelerated so that sixth-, seventh-, and eighth-grade enriched courses in arithmetic, science, and literature were completed in two years. The eighth grade then includes (high-school level) algebra one and two, English one and two, French one and two, and general science.

The Langton First-year Algebra Test, Form AM, was administered to the January 1958 graduates. Scores on this test, converted

TABLE 1

ITED Scores for January 1958
Graduates; Gifted Children's Program

	September 1955	January 1958	
	9th-grade percentile	9th-grade percentile	12th-grade percentile
Social concepts	39	94	64
Natural sciences (background)	69	94	62
Social studies	60	95	72
Natural sciences	61	97	75
Literary materials	59	97	78
General vocabulary	63	94	66

into percentile norms, indicated that the mean score of all pupils in the group was at the 61st percentile for students who had completed one year of algebra.

The Cooperative French Test, Elementary Form Q, was also administered at this time. Mean scores of all pupils on the three parts of this test and total scores indicated that, in general, achievement was well above the 80th percentile for end-of-first-semester high-school French.

As of September 1958, we have added new fifth-grade classes so that we now have four classes (fifth, sixth, seventh, and eighth grade) in the selected schools for this program. Tentative conclusions on the basis of this study indicated few changes in the program. However, we expect to make adjustments and revise the program as indicated by further research.

WARTIME ACCELERATES TEN YEARS AFTER

by Marie A. Flesher and Sidney L. Pressey

THE OHIO STATE UNIVERSITY

During World War II acceleration was the most hotly debated of all educational topics, and most colleges and technical schools had some form of accelerated program. When the war ended, most of these programs seemed quickly to have been dropped, and most educators seemed desirous to forget the topic as quickly as possible. However, the Korean war, and likely indefinite continuance of the draft or related measures in view of continuing international tensions, makes the matter again of at least potential importance. Moreover, the few studies which have been made of wartime programs of acceleration have shown not the anticipated unfortunate effects, but rather the reverse! Thus the writers studied intensively the 104 women who in the four colleges of Arts, Education, Commerce, and Agriculture of The Ohio State University completed a four-year undergraduate program in three years or less, from 1941 through 1945 (4). The average academic record of these 104 accelerates was found to be better than the records of 104 other women graduating in the same period who entered at the same age, made approximately the same scores on the test of general ability given at entrance, and took the same type of program, but who spent the usual four years (three years and nine months, or four years if graduation was in August) in obtaining an undergraduate degree. The accelerates also participated reasonably in extracurricular activities. A follow-up, a couple of years after graduation, showed them beginning their careers in as promising fashion as the paired "regular" cases.

Terman's notable continuing studies of his gifted child group have added impressive new evidence of the value of rapid progress in school of able young people (5, 6). The Ford Foundation proj-

[Reprinted from the *Journal of Educational Psychology*, 46, April 1955, 228-238, with the permission of Warwick and York, Publishers, and the authors.]

ects have re-emphasized the values of acceleration at the college level. Under all these circumstances, a further follow-up of the writer's wartime accelerate cases seemed desirable, to see how they were doing approximately ten years after graduation, and how they then regarded their accelerated programs. This paper is a brief summary of such a study.

CASES AND METHOD

When the above-mentioned 104 women accelerates were first being studied, it was hoped that a follow-up might be made. Hence their names, as well as the names of students paired with them but taking the usual three years nine months or four years to complete an undergraduate program, were saved. In 1946, another 41 young women completed an undergraduate degree in three years or less; they were "paired" with 41 other women students. The present study is concerned with the total 145 accelerates and their paired cases who graduated from 1941 through 1946 and is based upon data gathered in the spring of 1954. The subjects at that time averaged around thirty-two years of age and had graduated an average of ten years previously.

A simple straightforward two-page questionnaire was prepared, which could be very quickly filled in, almost entirely by checking. It was mimeographed on University stationery and was sent to the total of 290 alumnae. It began with the following statement:

Dear Ohio State University Alumna:
You were a student at OSU during the Second World War, when certain adjustments of program were made. Campus life was in many respects different from normal times, and some students worked in war industry. An appraisal of such wartime adjustments and conditions as seen in retrospect seems desirable, especially since the cold war and possible crises might again bring educational changes. Your answers to the following questions can be very helpful; most require only a check after the answers you think correct.

Then followed questions about employment while in school, acceleration, extracurricular activities, further schooling after the undergraduate degree, marital status, employment, and participation in community affairs. Special effort was made to phrase the entire document so that the recipients would not know that acceleration was a special matter of concern. And indeed the aim was, as the introductory statement said, to obtain broad appraisals regarding student life at the University in the war period.

One of the 290 students was found to have died, and persisting search failed to locate the addresses of ten others. The inquiry forms were mailed to the remaining 139 accelerates and the 140 who completed their work in the regular time. Since the post office did not return them as undelivered, it is assumed that the addressees received them, though a few may have very likely been accepted by a member of the family, or otherwise not come to the attention of the addressees. A stamped, addressed envelope for return was enclosed with the inquiry form.

The forms were mailed on April 7, 1954, and a follow-up was sent to those from whom replies had not been received on June 11. By August 1, 81 percent (112 cases) of the accelerates had returned filled-in forms, and so had 71 percent (100 cases) of the regulars. A greater return from the accelerates might be attributed to their greater interest because they were aware of having adjusted more to the wartime situation. A further finding can perhaps be explained similarly. At the end of the questionnaire was the statement: "If you would like a report of the results of this study, give your name and address. But if you prefer, return the form unsigned." Some 80 percent of the accelerates, but only 68 percent of the regulars, gave their names and addresses.

Though the 76-percent return on the questionnaire (for the two groups together) might be considered good, the question may always be raised as to whether selective factors may seriously have biased the results. Replies ranged from the highly favorable to the strongly and anonymously critical; it is believed that they are reasonably representative of the total group solicited. The great majority of replies seem to have been carefully considered; additional written commentaries often extended to the backs of the blanks. In general, these alumnae seemed pleased to have had their opinions asked, and were interested in the topics.

RESULTS

The first question asked was "During the period when you were an undergraduate, were you ever employed? If so, indicate when.

While in school?—" and so on. Table 1 summarizes the answers. It shows that the great majority found it possible to earn some money during the years when they were going to college. That slightly fewer of the accelerates did so might be the result of not only more unremitting school-going or heavier loads but also less need, since completing a degree in three years obviously costs less than taking a year more. And, since accelerates and their controls began school at the same age, the accelerates finished a year younger.

TABLE 1

Percentages of 112 Accelerates and 100 Regulars Who Were Employed as Undergraduates

	Acc.	Reg.
Period of employment:		
At some time	79	86
While in school	73	68
During vacations or quarters; not during school	31	65
Full time	12	30
Part time	69	73
Attitudes toward employment:		
Put a strain on health	3	7
Interfered with schooling	7	8
Unfortunately limited social life	19	18
Was a good experience	93	87

Yet more interesting are the last four lines of the table. Only rarely did either group consider that employment put a strain on health, and slightly fewer of the accelerates than of the regulars so thought. Nor did either group feel that employment interfered with schooling. Only a few thought that it unfortunately limited social life, with no significant difference between the two groups. The great majority—and slightly more of the accelerates—thought that employment during the school years was a good experience.

The first part of Table 2 shows the percentages of the acceler-ate and the regular groups who ever took a four-quarter schedule, obtained credit by examination, took extra-heavy course loads, or tried any combination of the above three methods of expediting progress through a college program. A few of the students who took four years for a degree did at some time take one of these steps;

but they then were out of school, were ill, or for some reason did not actually shorten their over-all time in college. On the other hand, 92 percent of the accelerate group spent four quarters in school at least once; over half took extra-heavy schedules; 29 percent got some credit by examination; and over half used two or more of such methods. In the judgment of the writers, there should be more use of credit by examination; and four-quarter schedules should then become less necessary (4, 7).

Even though there may have been too much continuous going to school and too much heavy course work, the second part of the

TABLE 2

Experience with and Judgments of "Acceleration" (Percentages)

	Acc.	Reg.
Experienced acceleration:		
Four-quarter yearly schedule	92	11
Credit by examination	29	12
Extra-heavy course schedule	57	15
Two or more of the above	57	6
Attitudes toward acceleration:		
A strain on health	7	15
Prevented best school work*	12	15
Undesirably limited social life*	9	16
A desirable challenge	62	40
Desirably saved time	79	34

*Included here are a few judgments that undesirable results occurred at times, though not generally, and a few replies of doubtful or not sure.

table indicates that very few of the accelerate group thought accelerated programs put a strain on health, not many judged that acceleration "prevented the student from doing as good work as he normally would" or that accelerated programs "undesirably limited social life." Instead, those not accelerating thought, more frequently, that such undesirable outcomes followed. And two thirds of the accelerate group thought that acceleration presented a desirable challenge, while over three fourths felt that desirable time was saved. Apparently few of the accelerates looked back on their college programs some ten years or so earlier with any feeling that damage had so been done them; rather, most felt that their acceleration had been advantageous.

It has been held that accelerated programs cause too unremitting work and interfere with student activities, these being evaluated as making major contributions to a student's real growth in the college period. The writers's studies during and immediately after the Second World War showed the accelerates only slightly less active than students taking the regular four years for an undergraduate degree. But we felt it was desirable to get the reaction of the alumnae on these aspects of the program, as they saw them ten years after. About as many of the accelerates engaged in activities related to the war as did the regulars. But more of the regular students went into the usual student activities—doubtless because they had more time, and partly probably because student activities are organized in terms of the conventional four-year autumn-winter-spring schedule. A few more of the regular students felt that these activities took too much time and energy and slightly more of the accelerates felt that they were too frivolous, both groups agreeing that they were of value.

It is important to keep in mind that the accelerates and their paired regulars have been out of school the same length of time but that the accelerates were approximately a year younger, since accelerates and controls were selected as graduating in the same year and entering at the same age but the accelerates had been in school one year less. Thus, in the same time since graduation and though they were a year younger, twice as many of the accelerates have earned a further degree. In fact, the accelerates have earned 32 degrees: 24 master's, one LL.B.; one M.D.; four Ph.D.'s; and two physical and occupational therapy certificates. In contrast, the only further degrees the regulars obtained were 12 master's.

Slightly more of the regulars are married, slightly more of those married have children; slightly more of the accelerates have been divorced or separated. The accelerates married about a year younger; being a year younger as a group, they have been married about the same time. Whether such slight differences in the marriage, divorce, and child-bearing rate are significant, especially in view of the differences in age, can hardly be judged. Slightly more of the regulars are housewives, and appreciably more of the accelerates are employed—substantially more of the married accelerates are also working. The numbers participating in community activities are approximately the same. In short, the two big differences are the substantially greater number of accelerates obtaining advanced degrees and the substantially greater number continuing some sort of a career after marriage. The accelerates included a physician, an attorney, three chemists, and a bacteriologist.

As mentioned earlier, in various places there were opportunities for the respondents to comment and a special invitation so to do at the end of the blank. The comments varied. Some accelerates felt that the program, although desirable, was so only in an emergency. Others were delighted at the saving of time, and considered that such possibilities of timesaving should always be available. Some complained of summer attendance, but others liked the contact then with more mature students. Accelerates who had been out in full-time employment tended to like the businesslike atmosphere of a four-quarter schedule; one remarked that simply the four ten-day periods between quarters gave her more vacation than she had had on the job. Some complained of heavy work, but others liked it, and said they worked better under some pressure.

There were sundry comments about curricula and instructional methods. Several alumnae wished that, somewhere, they had been taught to type; a number of married women wished they had had courses in homemaking and child care. Some of these young women felt that their curricula should have prepared them more adequately for their vocation. Others wished that their programs had been broader, and, in fact, a number of the regulars had "accelerated" a bit (for instance, gone to a summer session) to enrich their schedules with extra electives; three had obtained two undergraduate degrees in four years. It was pleasant to find, in this time of widespread criticism of schools and colleges, that many of the comments were favorable; most alumnae looked back upon their college years as pleasant and profitable.

GENERAL SIGNIFICANCE OF THE FINDINGS

The present findings regarding acceleration, as viewed by students ten years after graduation, seem in substantial accord with results obtained earlier, and by other investigators (1,3,4,5). It seems clear that many students of good ability can complete the usual four-year undergraduate program in less time without any unfortunate outcomes. Several in the present study finished in two calendar years. Further, most of the accelerates in this study (and most others) chose accelerated programs and carried them forward without any special counseling in the matter; a few should have been warned away from acceleration, and a majority might have planned better. The writers have found, as has the Fund for the Advancement of Education (1,4), that with careful selection and guidance, outcomes are even better. It seems especially desirable that more use be made of credit by examination, for secondary-school work beyond entrance requirements, also sometimes for crediting independent study (4,7). But the question now is, how are such findings to be explained?

The accelerates in the present study were not notably superior in general ability to the average graduating student—they had tested only about ten percentiles higher on the test of general ability given at entrance to college. The possibility comes to mind that perhaps many undergraduate programs are sufficiently easy, studded with vacations, sometimes repetitious, that some timesaving could become more general, or the programs be made more substantial.

But the accelerates in important respects actually did better than the controls: in academic record, number obtaining advanced training, and number continuing a career. If they had been men, presumably yet more of them would have thus pushed ahead. Previous research of the writers, and the findings of Terman regarding his gifted group, indicate that accelerates are more likely to be successful and even distinguished in their careers (4,5). How are these anomalous findings to be explained: better schooling in less time, and better career too?

In most studies above referred to, the accelerates were equated with controls in initial ability, but not in ambition and energy. The person with more drive may more often accelerate, and work harder in school and job. Certain other studies have been broad enough or so planned that they somewhat allow for these factors, and still the accelerates did better. Might acceleration in itself have beneficial effects?

The accelerates not infrequently mentioned the challenge of such an intensive program, and the stimulus to confidence and ambition resulting from success in it. An opportunity into desired advanced training and career a year sooner can be very appealing to able young people. Earlier graduation may obviously leave more time and funds for further training. Certain other possible factors seem worth mention. May it perhaps be that in the growth years the organism is in subtle respects more ready for the broad learnings of undergraduate curricula, that as it becomes mature it is constitutionally set for adult career, and that careers begun early enough to be fully energized by the vigor of young adulthood are most likely to be successful? These last are indeed hypotheses. But there seems much to suggest that they have some soundness (2,4, 5,6).

SUMMARY

This paper reports a follow-up, some ten years after graduation from college, of a group of young women who completed a four-year undergraduate program in three years or less during World War II, and of cases then paired with them as to year of graduation, ability and age at entrance, and nature of college program. A previous study had shown the accelerates doing slightly better academic work than their controls and participating about as much in campus activities. The questionnaire was directed to after-graduation careers of the two groups, and their retrospective judgments about their college programs.

A brief inquiry form was mailed to all cases (139 accelerates and 140 regulars) for whom addresses could be found. Returns were obtained from 112 accelerates and 100 regulars (81 percent of the first and 71 percent of the second group).

The onetime accelerates reported almost as much employment while in school; and few accelerates or regulars felt that such employment unfortunately affected health, schooling, or social life. Most thought such work experiences of value.

The most common method of acceleration was a four-quarter schedule, but a considerable number of students also obtained credit by examination, took heavy course loads, or used some combination of the above three methods. Very few accelerates thought their accelerated programs unfortunately affected health, schoolwork, or social life. A majority felt acceleration a desirable challenge and a saving of time. The nonaccelerates were more critical and dubious about acceleration.

About as many accelerates as nonaccelerates took part in extracurricular activities related to the war, but somewhat fewer accelerates participated in the usual undergraduate activities. Since there are few such activities in the summer, and most are organized on the presumption of a four-year program, the accelerates might be considered participating relatively well.

Slightly fewer of the accelerates have married and had children, but it must be kept in mind that they are a year younger than the regulars. The accelerates married almost a year younger, or about the same time after graduation. About the same number in each group are now active in community affairs. Twice as many of the accelerates have earned further academic degrees, as compared to the nonaccelerates. Almost twice as many of the married accelerates are continuing a career.

The above findings are explained as possibly in part due to a greater ambitiousness and energy on the part of the accelerates, but probably also a result of certain challenges and advantages of accelerated programs. The considerations involved seem of fundamental importance in planning secondary and higher education, more so for men, and in furtherance of their careers, than for women as in this study.

REFERENCES

1. Ford Foundation. *Bridging the Gap between School and College.* New York: The Fund for the Advancement of Education, 1953.
2. H. C. Lehman. *Age and Achievement.* Princeton, N. J.: Princeton Univ. Press, 1953.
3. G. Melcher. *An Evaluation of the Northeast Accelerated Junior College,* Kansas City, Mo.: Board of Education, 1953.
4. S. L. Pressey. *Educational Acceleration: Appraisals and Basic Problems.* Columbus, Ohio: Ohio State Univ. Press, 1949.
5. L. M. Terman and M. H. Oden. *The Gifted Child Grows Up.* Stanford, Calif.: Stanford University Press, 1947.
6. L. M. Terman. The Discovery and Encouragement of Exceptional Talent. *Amer. Psychologist,* 9, 1954, 221-230. Reprinted on pp. 41-57 in this volume.
7. Mazie E. Wagner. *Anticipatory Examinations for College Credit: Twenty Years' Experience.* Buffalo: Univ. Buffalo Studies, 20, No. 3, December 1952.

ᢏᢧᢖᢁᢧ

THEY WENT TO COLLEGE EARLY

Fund for the Advancement of Education

On the basis of the evidence gathered to date on the experience of 1350 early-admission scholars in the 12 participating colleges and universities over a period of five years during which two groups of scholars have graduated, it is now possible to make much firmer judgments about the results of the experiment—and about the wisdom of early admission in general—than was the case in the summer of 1953, when the Fund published its first preliminary report on the program.

What does the evidence add up to? What were the conclusions of the independent evaluators? How do the scholars, their comparison students, their parents, the schools from which they came, and the colleges to which they went, feel about the early-admission program in particular and the idea of early admission in general? What are the implications of the results to date for secondary and higher education as a whole?

This final chapter will attempt to answer these questions on the basis of the evidence accumulated thus far.

THE JUDGMENT OF THE SCHOLARS
AND COMPARISON STUDENTS

In their senior essays, the 1951 and 1952 scholars and comparison (older but matched on aptitude) students who successfully completed their undergraduate work were asked to express their judgment about the wisdom of early admission on the basis of their own experience and observations.

The scholars were asked these questions:

[Reprinted from Chapter 5, *They Went to College Early*, New York: Fund for the Advancement of Education, 1957, pp. 60-92, with the permission of the Fund.]

In retrospect, how do you feel now about the advantages and disadvantages of having entered college early? On balance, do you think it was profitable in your case?

What advice would you give to a friend of yours who was considering the advisability of entering college at an earlier age than usual?

Do you think the early admission idea should become a regular part of the admission policy of American colleges?

The comparison students were asked this question:

In your opinion, what are the advantages and disadvantages of acceleration? On balance, do you think the idea is wise or unwise? Under what circumstances?

The responses of the scholars and comparisons are shown in Table 1.

As the table indicates, nearly nine out of ten of the scholars who were about to graduate said that on balance it had been profitable for them to enter college early, and about eight out of ten comparisons who were about to graduate expressed themselves as generally favorable toward the early admission idea.

Rather marked changes in attitude are observed when the answers to the four questions by the 1952 scholars and comparisons are compared to the responses of the 1951 group. The 1952 scholars expressed far fewer reservations than their 1951 counterparts about early admission, whether they were asked about it as a personal experience, or in terms of advice to a friend, or in terms of a general policy for American colleges and universities. (One scholar, in an emphatically affirmative answer to the latter question, wrote: "What I cannot understand is how early admission was once a regular part of American education and then abandoned. As you can imagine, I never miss the name of a great American who went to college early. Cotton Mather entered at twelve. Jonathan Edwards graduated at seventeen. This list could go on and on.")

The 1952 comparison students also expressed far fewer reservations than their 1951 counterparts about the early-admission idea. This increase in the "wholly favorable" category was not accompanied by any comparable shift in the proportion of students expressing wholly unfavorable judgments, except that a much smaller proportion of the 1952 scholars rejected the idea that early admission become a regular part of the admission policy of American colleges, and a somewhat larger proportion of the 1952 comparisons were definitely opposed to the acceleration of qualified students. Thus, the responses indicate an even stronger endorse-

TABLE 1

The Over-all Judgment of Scholars and Comparisons about Early Admission

RESPONSES BY THE SCHOLARS	1951	1952
Was early admission profitable in your case?		
Yes, very much so	42%	75%
Yes, with reservations	46	15
Neither profitable nor unprofitable	7	5
No, definitely not	4	3
No response	1	2
Would you advise a friend to enter college early?		
Yes, definitely	12%	27%
Yes, with reservations	75	61
Only in exceptional cases	8	5
No, definitely not	3	3
No response	2	4
Do you think the early-admission idea should become a regular part of the admission policy of American colleges?		
Yes, definitely	41%	66%
Yes, with minor modifications	31	15
Yes, with severe limitations	12	16
No, definitely not	15	2
No response	1	1

RESPONSES BY THE COMPARISONS	1951	1952
Do you think acceleration of qualified students is wise?		
Yes, definitely	12%	32%
Yes, with reservations	67	44
Only in exceptional cases	11	10
No, definitely not	9	13
No response	1	1

ment of the early-admission idea by the 1952 scholars and comparisons than by their 1951 counterparts.

In their appraisal of the advantages and disadvantages of early admission, the scholars and comparison students were virtually in complete agreement. The advantage both cited most frequently was a much greater academic challenge in college than in high school; 58 percent of the 1951 scholars and 82 percent of the 1952 scholars cited this as an advantage. The corresponding figures for the comparison students were 61 percent and 72 percent. The views expressed by the scholars and comparison students on this point were interesting and revealing. Many of the scholars said that early admission to college had "rescued" them from an unchallenging highschool experience. This view was expressed in several different ways. One scholar said flatly: "The one year which I missed in high school was, as I was informed by my friends who remained there, a complete waste of time." Another said: "I loved high school because of the extracurricular activities and my friends, but I was wasting my time academically. College classes were much more of a challenge." A third put it this way: "The [early-admission program] picked me up when I still had great interest and ambition, which I feel I would have lost in the next two years. . . . [It] put me into a challenging intellectual atmosphere at precisely the time when I was best equipped to accept it."

The tenor of some of the scholars's comments on this point suggested that their criticism was aimed not at their high schools but at the "lockstep," which frequently keeps able students from entering college when they are ready to, regardless of chronological age or the number of years of prior schooling. This distinction was clearly made by a scholar from a reputable high school in a large Eastern city who wrote:

I found at college an intellectual challenge and satisfaction which I wanted out of high-school work at that time, but which I could not seem to obtain, even though I feel that the high school I attended offered the best high-school education that one could receive in ———.

It also was made by the scholar who wrote:

High schools are of necessity (and rightly so) geared to the average student, since he forms the majority of our population. Yet if we are to maintain our position of world leadership with any degree of dignity and self-respect at all, we must not neglect the education of those who are our future leaders and who are at present marking time in an educational atmosphere which is not challenging.

Several of the comparison students made the same point. One wrote: "I have known many accelerated students who would have been seriously frustrated and perhaps permanently damaged by having to spend two additional years in conventional high school." And another, on the basis of personal experience, wrote: "I see no reason, academically, why qualified students should not be able to accelerate their education. From my own experience, I believe that much of the time in the last year of high school is wasted in that the material could either have been taught earlier, or is repeated in college courses."

The next most frequently mentioned advantage on the part of both scholars and comparisons was the opportunity for acceleration, which they described in various ways—an earlier start on professional study, an earlier start on a career, an earlier marriage, or an opportunity to finish college before being called up for military service. Several of the students who cited this as an advantage mentioned that the time saved looked less significant from the vantage point of senior year than of freshman year. Pearson [Richard Pearson, Associate Director of the College Entrance Examination Board] concluded that most of these students were more concerned with avoiding wasting time than with saving time.

The scholars and comparisons also agreed with respect to the major disadvantages of early admission. The most frequently cited disadvantage was that early admission makes personal and social adjustment to college more difficult. This was cited by 58 percent of the 1951 scholars and 65 percent of the 1952 scholars. The corresponding figures for the Comparisons were 95 percent and 83 percent. Here again the comments of the scholars were interesting and revealing. Said one:

> On looking back over my past four years here, I am quite glad that I entered college early. However, I honestly believe I am expressing the feeling of one who has "made the grade" and not the feeling of one who has to do it over again. I sincerely believe, however, that in four years' time I have gotten much more out of school than the average student, but it was a tough climb.

Another summed up the matter in these words: "That there are difficulties involved cannot be denied, and many individuals may find the adjustment problems very difficult to overcome, but for the majority I feel these will not be insuperable, or even trying."

Several of the scholars reported that early admission had actually enhanced their social and emotional development. As one scholar put it:

From my first moments on campus, college represented a new and exciting experience. I had no difficulty adjusting to this new life, partly because of the sincere interest which the faculty and upperclassmen took in us. . . . The newly acquired self-responsibility was a challenge which stimulated my social and emotional maturation.

The fact that the 1952 scholars endorsed early admission with far fewer qualifications than the 1951 group, yet cited the personal and emotional adjustment problem as a disadvantage with much greater frequency than the 1951 group, appears to be somewhat contradictory. Pearson concluded that the 1952 scholars, in making an over-all appraisal of their college experience, assigned less weight to this disadvantage than their 1951 counterparts.

The reservations expressed by the scholars and comparisons in qualifying their endorsement of the early-admission idea were of such a nature as to indicate that they had given the questions thoughtful consideration before answering them. For example, in their answers to the questions about the wisdom of early admission, the reservations dealt not only with the advantages inherent in the program, but also with the kinds of students and the kinds of colleges where the policy was most likely to be successful. In general, both the scholars and the comparisons who expressed these reservations felt that the early-admission policy should be adopted only by colleges capable of wise selection and proper handling of such students, and should apply only to students who demonstrated exceptional ability and a high degree of social and emotional maturity. One scholar wrote: "What is really needed . . . is a more effective high-school system, but until the answer to this comes, colleges should provide some sort of an escape hatch for the students who are ready to handle advanced work."

After analyzing the scholars' reservations, Pearson concluded:

The impression one forms in considering these comments is that the important thing is enrichment of the educational program and recognition of individual ability, rather than any particular partiality for the idea of early admission per se. These students recognize that the offering of advanced college-level courses at secondary schools would probably be limited to a relatively few schools among the total number in the country. To the extent that this is possible, the need for a regular policy of early admission is limited. To the extent that this is not possible, a regular program of early admission is essential. We believe it is clear from these comments that the scholars look upon early admission as a rather specific exception within the general framework of American education, although from their point of view the exception would be a most important one.

The qualities mentioned by both scholars and comparison students as desirable in applicants for early admission included mature appearance, sense of responsibility, emotional stability, self-reliance, adaptability, high motivation for college, and social maturity. Many of the students who pressed for appraisal of these qualities admitted their elusiveness and confessed their inability to describe just how an admission officer could determine their presence or absence in a specific applicant. "Their point," Pearson observed, "is that intellectual readiness for college does not presuppose emotional readiness for college and somehow the latter must be weighed in the balance."

Both scholars and comparison students were sharply split on the relative importance of intellectual readiness and emotional readiness. Some described the ideal student as one who is in the top 5 or 10 percent of his class scholastically, scores extremely high on college entrance examinations, and is active in extracurricular activities and sports. There was general agreement that if such an individual were a sophomore or a junior in high school and was frustrated by an unchallenging academic diet, he would be clearly admissible by these high standards. However, it was far less clear from the essays whether favorable early-admission action should be taken in the case of a student who was strong intellectually but had a poorer chance of successful college adjustment. One scholar wrote: "My own prejudice is that only intellectual adequacy to do the work is really relevant; I resent the present attempts of my own university to impose social and intellectual orthodoxy by its admission policy." Another scholar wrote that at his college "social maturity is much less important than academic preparation." Two other students suggested that the intellectually strong youngster who was not well adjusted at secondary school was a likely prospect for early admission because he probably would be no worse off in college.

Pearson observed in his report,

Quotations such as these contrast quite sharply with the qualities of personal and social maturity which were mentioned quantitatively more often among the essays. A conceivable reconciliation of these somewhat divergent points of view is that intellectual competence is the *sine qua non* for early admission; given this, the final decision should rest on a relative assessment of the applicant's challenge and adjustment at high school and his likely challenge and adjustment at college.

The scholars and the comparison students were unanimous in urging a minimum of special treatment for early-admission students. Many also urged that college counseling services should be improved. Reports on this aspect were very favorable on some campuses and sharply critical on others. There was a general feeling on the part of most scholars that a strong counseling system was essential at any college admitting youthful students—not a system uniquely for them, but one which they could share with the rest of the student body.

Finally, the scholars and the comparison students stressed the need for a "good fit" between the individual students and the individual college.

Pearson noted in his report,

This requirement came out in an amusing way in a number of essays where special and fervent pleas were made for confining early admission to small liberal arts colleges, or to large universities, or to highly selective colleges, or to engineering and technical schools. If one were to be guided by the sum total of these suggestions, one would conclude that early admission is a necessary feature at *all* American colleges and universities.

THE VERDICT OF THE INDEPENDENT EVALUATORS

THE PEARSON EVALUATION

The principal conclusions reached by Pearson after his analysis of the senior essays can be summarized as follows:

1. The evidence is that adjustment difficulties were by no means limited to early-admission students, although more scholars than comparisons reported such difficulties. The conclusion is that early admission was a contributing factor—but not the sole factor—in the existence of adjustment difficulties among the scholars. Although the scholars were faced initially with a greater adjustment problem than the comparison students, they were able to effect as successful an over-all adjustment as the comparison students.

Borrowing from Toynbee, the response to challenge, rather than the challenge itself, becomes a measure of success of the experiment, and in these terms we would record our conclusion that the experiment was a success for the students whose essays we have considered in this report.

2. The scholars's definition of early admission as an exception to general educational practice underscores a concern that the able student will be hurt unless special arrangements are made to recognize and develop his ability. From this point of view, early admission or indeed any program of enrichment is viewed as giving the able student the same opportunity as that routinely offered to other students. Similarly, the problem of trying to describe the student for whom early admission would be wise is by no means dissimilar from the problem faced by the admissions officer in attempting to select candidates for regular admission. Finally, the obligation of the college to insure a successful educational experience for the early-admission student differs only in detail from the college's obligation toward normal-age students.

This suggests that the important lesson from the early-admission experiment is that the American educational system cannot afford to overlook the individuality of the students with whom it deals. Whether these students are normal age or underage, or whether they have completed a formal program in secondary school, is probably of less importance than their capabilities and aspirations as individuals. The contribution of the schools and the colleges to society is likely to be gauged in terms of how well these are recognized and developed, rather than in terms of formal structures and prescribed programs.

THE FARNSWORTH EVALUATION

Dr. Farnsworth [Dana Farnsworth, Director of the University Health Service at Harvard] and his colleagues, after studying the social and emotional adjustment of the 1951 scholars, concluded that the scholars adjusted to campus life as well as their comparison students and classmates and that the reasons for failures among the scholars were the same as for college students in general.

They suggested that the following guideposts might be helpful to admissions officers in selecting candidates for early admission, noting that most of them apply equally to the selection of regular freshmen:

1. Such students must be carefully selected on an individual basis for the individual college. They should be of the type most apt to benefit from the type of education which the college has to offer.

2. Such students should have above-average academic achievement and superior intelligence.

3. Such students, except in unusual cases, should have completed the eleventh grade.

4. Personalitywise, they should show evidence of emotional maturity at least consistent with their chronological age, good ability in interpersonal relations, and freedom from excessive parental pressure toward early admission. Students who have had frequent changes of schools without similar moves by the family, who come from families with severe discord, or who are using college entrance as an escape from serious personal problems are poor risks.

5. Students who have had psychiatric illnesses should have had adequate treatment.

6. Students with characteriological disorders should not be admitted. However, a distinction must be made between misbehavior as representative of a long-standing characteriological disorder and misbehavior as a manifestation of adolescent rebellion. These latter cases, if the difficulties have been overcome, either as a result of the natural maturing process or of psychiatric treatment, should not be excluded.

7. In the selection of students for liberal arts courses, such students should have appropriate educational values, or the capacity to acquire such values.

8. Close scrutiny should be given by large urban universities to students from rural areas.

9. In selection, it is all too easy to err in not admitting the unusually intellectually gifted student or the chronic dissenter who is not "well rounded." While "well-rounded" students are highly desirable, if this is used as the main criteria for admission, these unusual students may be passed over. Such students may make great contributions in the future. As one dean said: "There should be room in our stable for all kinds of horses."

COMMENTS OF SCHOLARS'S PARENTS

The colleges and universities participating in the early-admission program have not made a systematic effort to determine how the scholars's parents feel about the program, but two colleges (Goucher and Louisville) conducted special canvasses of the parents of their 1951 scholars shortly after their graduation. These results, although based on a very small and incomplete statistical sample, tended to confirm the general impression reported by the colleges that the parents on the whole have been favorable toward the program.

In the Goucher survey, 26 of the 27 parents responding said that if they had the choice to make again they would send their daughters to college early. Many of the parental opinions reflected the same balancing of advantages and disadvantages as the scholar essays. One mother, who said she would again choose early admission for her daughter, remarked nonetheless that the girl had lost contact with her high-school classmates and added on the drawback side: "It was, too, a lonely pinnacle of fame in the adolescent community." Another expressed the opinion that entering college early "'helped to build up her self-confidence and initiative." Another wrote: "She was made more resourceful and self-reliant; had to think and act independently." And another: "I believe she matured in many ways sooner than if she had completed high school."

In the Louisville survey, 11 of the 12 responses expressed parental approval of the early-admission program. The one exception, written by the mother of a scholar, said in part:

I would never influence a boy or girl again into giving up the last year in high school. . . . [My son] entered engineering school at the age of 16. He needed the chemistry, physics, and math he would have had his last year in high school. He was lost as far as the work was concerned and very unhappy. He had always made good grades. . . . As far as [my son] is concerned the early entry was not right and I've regretted it.

Another Louisville mother, who had two children in the program, wrote:

Since I wasn't sold on the program when I first heard about it, I'm happy to have the opportunity now to say I'm wholeheartedly in favor of it since our two children have tried it. . . . They both seem happier and better adjusted at the University than they did in high school. They are certainly not either one geniuses but I really believe now that they would have been wasting their time if they had stayed in high school another year. They have even had more social life at the University.

Apart from the Goucher and Louisville surveys, a number of participating institutions have reported their general impressions on the matter of parental attitudes. Utah said it believed that most parents consider going to college early to have been a successful and valuable experience for their children. Fisk reported the reaction of parents to have been "quite favorable." Lafayette said a few of the parents felt that it would have been better for their children to have finished high school, but that most were well satisfied with the results.

Oberlin reported that the reactions of parents have been difficult to evaluate. It noted that where a scholar was successful the parents were highly cooperative and pleased but that where it did not work out "the reactions ranged from a mature acceptance to a projection of all the blame on the college." (In a number of these cases, it reported, the scholars had been strongly encouraged to apply for the Fund scholarships by their parents.)

Wisconsin, on the other hand, reported that the attitude of its scholars's parents has been "one of the most interesting and heartening aspects of early admission." The parents were pleased and grateful when their sons and daughters did well, Wisconsin added, but "what is more important, when the boys did badly, the parents were extremely helpful and cooperative, and to this we probably owe many of the successful recoveries from trouble the scholars have made. . . . It is interesting that three families have sent two scholars each."

THE ATTITUDES OF HIGH-SCHOOL PRINCIPALS

As with parental attitudes, the participating colleges have not made a systematic effort to gather data about the attitudes of the high schools from which the scholars were chosen. However, Goucher and Louisville polled the secondary schools from which their 1951 scholars came, and several of the other colleges have obtained, through correspondence and discussion, a general picture of the reactions of principals and guidance officers.

The available evidence suggests that the character of high-school reaction is mixed, ranging from strong approval to strong disapproval, and that to some extent it is in the process of change.

Ten of the 12 participating colleges have reported to the Fund on their experience with high-school principals and guidance officers, often in relation to the difficult task of scholar selection. According to these reports, many of the college officials have encountered considerable resistance to the early-admission program. Sometimes this has been vocal. Sometimes, as one college commented, it has not: "The general reaction has been to ignore the plan entirely."

Many teachers and principals in secondary schools have been strongly opposed to the early departure to college of some of their best potential juniors and seniors. As one principal frankly told a college official: "We don't like the idea of the colleges taking our leaders out of high school at the end of the tenth or eleventh grade."

The dean of one of the participating colleges, reporting considerable high-school resistance to the early-admission program, voiced the opinion that,

[it] is based partially on a genuine concern for the emotional and social development of the individual and a belief that he will be harmed by taking him out of his chronological peers and placing him with his intellectual peers. It may also result partially from the reflection upon the job of the secondary school which is seen in the program.

This dean noted that there appeared to be a marked difference among high schools, depending on the quality of their own instruction.

Those schools which were well-established and doing very good jobs saw this as another indication of the fine work they were doing in having their students qualify for admission after only two or three years with them. On the other hand, the weaker schools tended to see this as a criticism of the programs which they were performing and a reflection that they were doing so poor a job that an additional year or two with them made little difference in the college success of the student.

Some of the colleges and universities have reported cases of active high-school interest in and cooperation with the experiment. For example, one large university reported that the majority of high schools from which its scholars came were quite enthusiastic and continued to be so, except in the case of a few scholars who failed to stay. Another university, noting that a few high schools have sent it a large proportion of its scholars, remarked: "Their views on the program are, of course, colored by the experience of their boys; since they have sent us applicants year after year, they presumably approve the plan."

One university said that some principals in its state

have realized early admission could take some burdens from their shoulders, by removing some of the pressure for college preparation of a few students. If, for example, a boy shows potentiality as a scientist, but goes to a school which does not teach mathematics beyond algebra, early admission offers him a way to get his trigonometry without straining the resources of the school.

A number of the participating institutions reported that high-school attitudes, first largely negative, have changed, presumably as a result of experience with early admission, and that there has been a growing acceptance of its possibilities during the last few years.

Aside from these general observations by the colleges the only direct evidence as to the attitudes of high-school principals and guidance officers is afforded by the results of the Goucher and Louisville surveys. The responses to these surveys ranged all the way from strong approval to strong disapproval of early admission, with most of the principals emphasizing that they felt it was wise only for students of exceptional academic ability and social maturity. For example, of the six principals responding to the Louisville survey, two said they approved of the idea, one said the wisdom of early admission depends entirely on the student concerned, another said the idea had both good and bad points, and two disapproved of the idea on the ground that the early-admission student misses much by not completing high school. Following are samples of the range of comments:

Students who enter college too young seem to lack social maturity and often are not accepted by the more mature college students. I often wonder how much these students lose by not remaining with their classes and probably taking over positions of leadership during their senior year.

Whether or not it is wise for a high-school student to enter college at the end of his junior year depends entirely upon the student concerned. . . . In brief, both the academic progress and the social development of the student must receive equal consideration in making the decision. In our opinion only a relatively small percentage would qualify socially.

I think the [early-admission] program has been a distinct service to the students from this school, and I believe I would like to see the program renewed and the selections be made on an individual basis.

The pattern of responses to the Goucher survey was quite similar to that of the Louisville survey. The principals and guidance officers of high schools that had sent the largest number of students into the early-admission program tended to be the most favorably disposed toward it. The tenor of the replies suggested that there were two major reasons for this tendency: (1) Since the senior classes in such high schools were generally large, the scholars were not "missed" as much as they were in small high schools, and (2) since the academic standards of these schools were generally high, the principals tended to be much less sensitive to the implication that the scholars were offered a much greater academic challenge in college.

The reply of the scholarship counselor in a large Eastern high school that has sent nine students into the early-admission program aptly illustrates this tendency. Asked to cite the major advantage of early admission from the student's point of view, she replied: "The student stops 'marking time' and gets on with the real work that he wants to do. If he's mature enough, he gets real satisfaction out of the greater challenge of college work." Asked to cite the major disadvantage of the program from the school's point of view, she wrote: "The school is deprived in the sense that these early-admission students leave gaps in their class. The school no longer benefits from the stimulation of their superior work and attitudes, and generally from their participation in the extracurricular life of the school." She added, however, that "since our early admission people are so few in number, we feel no significant deprivation; and since we feel that the boys and girls themselves are benefited, we are very happy to see them succeed in college."

Principals of other large Eastern high schools which have sent relatively large numbers of students into the early-admission program made similar observations.

The principal of a Massachusetts high school which has furnished eight scholars wrote:

Most high schools like to have bright students in their enrollment. Occasionally key posts are left vacant (by the departure of early-admission students), but they are usually filled by another capable student. Occasionally we find a brilliant student who is bored by his contemporaries; he finds their activities childish. A change in environment could be helpful.

In preparation for this report, the Fund asked each of the participating colleges and universities to study the records of the first two groups of scholars to graduate and to judge whether early admission had been wise in each individual case. The results of this appraisal were as follows:

Opinion	1951 group	1952 group
Wise	79.6%	76.4%
Opinion divided	14.6	17.1
Unwise	5.8	6.5

As the table indicates, the faculty judgment at the participating institutions was that early admission was wise in the case of eight out of ten scholars in the 1951 group, and in the case of three out of four in the 1952 group. (It must be remembered that the judgments covered only those scholars who had survived through senior year.)*

THE FUTURE OF EARLY ADMISSION

In *Bridging the Gap between School and College,* the Fund said that the preliminary results of the early-admission program were "decidedly encouraging." On the basis of the evidence presented in this report, it now feels that the results to date have been impressive.

Although the period of Fund support has ended, 11 of the 12 colleges participating in the experiment have incorporated the early-admission idea into their regular admissions policy. (Wisconsin has not yet taken any action on the matter.) At least one of the colleges—Goucher—has set up a special scholarship program for early-admission students. At the other colleges, early-admission students

* Reports from the 12 institutions, which followed here, have been omitted. —EDITOR'S NOTE.

are permitted to compete for scholarship aid on equal terms with other entering freshmen.

There are some indications that the early-admission idea is gaining wider acceptance. The College Entrance Examination Board reports that 29 of its 169 member colleges had early-admission programs in the academic year 1955-1956. Only six of these were participants in the Fund-supported experiment. It is interesting to note that 27 of the 29 also had programs of advanced placement, thus providing able high-school students two different kinds of opportunity for college-level work before graduation.

It is much too early yet to predict the future of the early-admission idea, but the evidence in this report clearly indicates that under the proper circumstances it represents a promising approach to the problem of enabling the very best students to realize their full potential. The risks of entering college early have been the subject of much popular concern, and properly so. But too little thought has been given to the risks run by an able student in an unchallenging environment in *not* entering college early. As one of the scholars wrote in his senior essay:

There is some danger that a young student's talents will be harmed by being thrust among older students who do not accept him. But the greater danger is that he will be allowed to stagnate in secondary school and will arrive in college lacking imagination and ambition, these having been "educated" out of him. The harm to him and society is great.

Richard Pearson observed in his report that,

the important lesson from the early-admission experiment is that the American educational system cannot afford to overlook the individuality of the students with whom it deals. Whether these students are normal age or underage, or whether they have completed a formal program in secondary school is probably of less importance than their capabilities and aspirations as individuals. The contribution of the schools and colleges to society is likely to be gauged in terms of how well these are recognized and developed, rather than in terms of formal structures and prescribed programs.

Yet there is some danger that in the decades ahead, when American colleges and universities become engrossed in the problems attendant upon steeply rising enrollments, the capabilities and aspirations of the "unusual" student are likely to be neglected. College admissions officers, confronted with the happy prospect of having many more applications for admission than there are places to be filled, may well tend to "play it safe" and to avoid the risks involved in admitting unconventional students, particularly those who are younger than most and who have had a less-than-normal high-school preparation. It will be all too easy to say, "We'll get them next year anyhow, and another year in high school won't hurt them." But the evidence clearly indicates that the superior student *can* be hurt by being detained in an intellectual environment he has outgrown. As one scholar wrote in his senior essay:

> I don't advocate anything so radical as a society composed exclusively of eggheads, but it seems downright cruel to force a gifted child to suffer needless years of boredom (and boredom can be suffering, I know) when he can have an opportunity (whether or not he utilizes it is obviously up to him) to meet some fine minds on a college faculty which might be able to salvage at least part of his intellectual potential before the habit of mental laziness has completely encrusted him.

The notion that the superior student does not need special attention because he is bright enough to look out for himself is still widely prevalent, but an increasing number of thoughtful educators and laymen have begun to challenge it and the assumption that regardless of ability and energy each student must move with his chronological age group through eight years of elementary school, four years of high school, and four years of college. Coupled with this has been a critical re-examination of the meaning of educational equality in a democratic society—a questioning as to whether it means equal amounts of education for all or equal opportunity for each individual to develop his talents as fully and freely as possible.

There is also a growing awareness that the health and vigor of our society—and indeed even its very life—depend on making the most of all the capacities of all of our people. And it has become increasingly clear that if we are to make the most of these capacities, we must not fail to provide for the fullest possible development of our ablest young people. The Fund for the Advancement of Education believes that the early-admission experiment has clearly demonstrated its promise as a means to that end.

NEEDED RESEARCH ON GIFTED CHILDREN

by Harriet E. O'Shea*

PURDUE UNIVERSITY

Many social scientists are concerned with the welfare and development of gifted individuals. There has been much research on retarded children and on children with behavior problems but relatively little is known about the gifted child. It is the conviction of
the Subcommittee on Needed Research on Gifted Children that society cannot afford to block or damage the functioning of gifted
children; if they function at their optimal level, they undoubtedly
constitute one of the major reservoirs of real wealth in the country.

The subcommittee has endeavored to locate and formulate
troublesome, unanswered questions about gifted children, questions
for which the lack of experimental answers is probably directly interfering with such children's receiving optimum guidance in
homes, schools, and the community. Each psychologist who is interested in gifted children will undoubtedly make additions to this
list of important and puzzling questions. The subcommittee has
studiously avoided shaping any experimental designs to explore
these questions. Each experimenter's design will be his own. This report has been approved by Division 16's Committee on the Gifted,
by its Executive Committee, and by the entire Division of School
Psychologists. It is the hope of the Division that activities devoted
to the developmental progress of gifted children and to their education may be lifted rapidly out of areas of uncertainty and controversy by way of an increasingly solid foundation of pertinent
experimentation.

By gifted children, the subcommittee means children whose

* The report was drawn up by the Subcommittee on Needed Research on Gifted
Children of the APA Division of School Psychologists. Its members were
Gertrude Hildreth, George Myer, Lee Meyerson, Paul Witty, and Harriet E.
O'Shea, chairman.

[Reprinted from the *American Psychologist,* 9, February 1954, 77-78, with
the permission of the American Psychological Association and the authors.]

rate of mental growth is 1.4 or 1.5 mental years per calendar year or faster.

The subcommittee hereby submits questions concerning gifted children that in its judgment are urgently in need of research exploration. The experimental design and procedure are conceived of as being the province of the research worker to determine. It is anticipated that each of the questions listed below will prove to encompass a family of research projects.

I. Educational administrative procedures.
   A. What are the relative merits (emotional, social, and intellectual effects) of various administrative plans for the gifted such as the following?
      1. Keeping the child with his chronological age group and "enriching the curriculum."
      2. Locating the individual close to his mental-age level in school class with chronologically older children.
      3. Retaining the child in his chronological age group for some subjects and advancing in others.
      4. Establishing special classes for children who have high rates of mental growth.
      5. Utilizing no special administrative plan for the gifted.
   B. What preceding or concomitant conditions can be recognized that are correlated with varying results from a given administrative plan such as any of the foregoing or any combination of such plans?
   C. Which of these administrative procedures (or others not listed or any combination of procedures) has the best over-all results for the gifted child?
II. What is the effect (emotional, social, and intellectual) upon the gifted child of organizing his school work?
   A. In terms of greater quantity of work of the same level of difficulty as that which he has been doing.
   B. In terms of introducing additional new subject matter (both in classroom and extramural).
   C. In terms of advancing to higher levels of organization and abstraction in whatever experience is provided for him.
III. Relationship between ability and performance.
   A. To what extent is there "concealed failure" among gifted children; that is, are they operating below their appropriate

achievement level although not failing by the school's standards?

B. What personality correlates are there to such "concealed failure"?

C. What factors have contributed to such "concealed failure"?

D. What are the over-all effects of various procedures intended to raise the gifted child's performance to its optimum level?

IV. What is the teacher's distinctive role in training the gifted?

A. What effects upon a gifted child result from various characteristics of his teacher?

B. Are special qualifications necessary in the teacher of the gifted and if so, what are they?

V. Lifework.

A. Is it desirable or undesirable to explore vocational interests and aptitudes earlier in the life of the gifted child than in the life of other children?

B. What are the effects of beginning vocational planning and vocational preparation at various times in the life of the gifted child?

VI. Personal relationships.

A. Do close personal relationships become established between children of widely different mental age?

B. Does the gifted child have to have companions at or close to his mental age in order to experience close personal relationships?

VII. Special frustrations.

A. Are there special frustrations that impinge upon the gifted child that less often affect other children:

1. in his family,
2. in his neighborhood,
3. in the classroom,
4. in extracurricular activities,
5. in job placement?

VIII. Special satisfactions.

A. Does the gifted child experience special satisfactions?

B. If so, what are they and what are their effects upon the gifted child?

IX. What factors account for any undesirable personality traits that may be found among the gifted?

X. Status as a group.

   A. Do the gifted in effect constitute a minority group receiving some of the typical hostilities directed toward such a group?

   B. What are the effects upon the gifted of such treatment when it does occur?

   C. Are there recognizable elements in a community that attack gifted children?

   D. What are the effects of various procedures instituted to make favorable changes in attitudes toward gifted children?

 XI. Does the gifted child have special needs with respect to his ultimately developing desirable citizenship traits, needs either in terms of the subject matter or in terms of the age at which subject matter (classroom and extramural) is introduced?

WHAT DOES RESEARCH TELL US?

by John C. Gowan

SAN FERNANDO VALLEY STATE COLLEGE

In 1954 a committee of school psychologists from Division 16 of the American Psychological Association, including Gertrude Hildreth and Paul Witty, proposed a list of needed research for children whose mental growth was greater than 1.4 mental years per calendar year.* An abridged restatement of these questions has been made below together with brief notices of representative research, plus a summary of common findings. Such a framework would seem helpful in establishing what we know and do not know about gifted children.

   1. *What are the relative merits of administrative plans for the gifted including enrichment, acceleration, special classes, and no special provisions?* Which method gives the best over-all results?

   Despite the wide claims made for enrichment, there are

---

* Recent reviews of research include (19) and (41).

[Reprinted from the *Psychological Newsletter*, 9, March 1958, 140-144, with the permission of the *Newsletter* and the author.]

practically no research results to substantiate its superiority. One of the reasons is the difficulty of devising experiments; another is that when enrichment procedures are found at their best, other methods are also employed. In contrast, there is a great deal of evidence regarding the value of acceleration. Tyler (41), citing research by Flesher and Pressey (15), Worcester, (45), Birch (4), Justman (24,25), Kemper (26), and Jones and Ortner (23), summarizes that "evidence continues to pile up that the effects on gifted children of acceleration are favorable rather than the reverse." Passow (35), in supporting acceleration, cites the evidence of Hobson (21), Lamson (27), Engle (14), on the elementary level, and Wilkins (44), Unzicher (42), and Moore (32), on the secondary level as attesting his statement. In no other area of gifted-child education has there been so much change as in this one. There have been fewer evaluative studies of the effects of grouping in recent research, although some of the earlier explorations seem conveniently to have been ignored. The grouping practices cited in the Twenty-third Yearbook of the National Society for the Study of Education (34) all report superior achievement cutting across grade levels. Another excellent but forgotten study is the evaluation of the old Los Angeles Opportunity A rooms (28). A comparison between 284 Opportunity A people and 381 equally gifted controls in high school showed higher grade-point averages from the A group, more A's, and fewer failures. More recent evaluation of the Cleveland major work program by Barbe (1, 2) confirms the same hypothesis. In conclusion it may be said that modern research supports the idea that the three methods work better in conjunction than alone.

2. *What is the effect of organizing the gifted child's schoolwork (a) in terms of greater difficulty, (b) additional new material, (c) higher levels of difficulty and abstraction?*

This area has not interested researchers of recent years, or it has been incorporated into other research work.

3. *To what extent do gifted children fail to achieve up to their potential and what personality correlates are involved?* What home factors have contributed to such failures? What are the effects of the procedures of section 1 on this area?

There has been a great deal of research and interest in this area, with the result that we know considerably more about underachievers and motivational failure than formerly. The basic research of McClelland on motivation in children (30) has yielded much value. The studies of Terman (40) and Brandwein (9) should also be mentioned. Several ongoing studies in motivation or achievement are in progress such as that undertaken by the Horace Mann-Lincoln Institute in New York. Specific underachievement studies have been reported by Barrett (3), Bonsall and Stefflre (7), Burgess (11), Cohler (12), Dowd (13), Gough (17), Gowan (20), Horrall (22), Nason (33), Pearlman (36), Sanford (37), and Wedemeyer (43). The latter found that 30 percent of the top decile in intelligence fail in college to attain significant achievement. Figures have elsewhere been presented to show that between 12 percent and 42 percent of gifted children were underachievers in various high schools, using the criterion that achievement lower than the top third for students in the top 2 percent represented underachievement (20). The key personality factor in this area is sociability: to achieve is a social response; to fail to achieve is an asocial response. Home environments are found to have played a large part in the formation of the personality of the underachiever. One study, after listing 13 common elements from a summary of such research, summarizes the personality of the achiever as "a description of healthy personal attitudes and behaviors which are associated with growth patterns on schedule." It continues: "Achievement and underachievement in the gifted may be viewed as social or asocial responses of the individual to proper stimulation regarding developmental tasks either tendered or denied by the parental or educational environments."

4. *What is the teacher's distinctive role in this area?* What effects result from various characteristics of the teacher? Are special qualifications desirable? What are they?

Studies in this area have been fewer in number but productive of results. Goodrich and Knapp (16), in investigating the origins of American scientists, found that they had been produced in larger numbers in small liberal arts colleges where there had been close interaction between students and dedicated teachers. Brandwein (9) noted a special teaching factor aiding in the "questing" persistence developed in young potential scientists. MacCurdy's study of 600 national science-talent-search winners (29) turned up the information that the teacher predisposing students to science has served the gifted student as a father figure, is well trained, experienced, professional, permissive, progressive, and a good example. Each of these studies is well worth reading *in toto*. From them one gains the impression that there is much transference from teacher to pupil, and that habits of logical inquiry, independent thinking, persistent questing, and initiating action are absorbed directly from the teacher's personality as the subject matter skills are absorbed from his ability and background. It is significant that almost all the recent research in this area has been concerned with science.

5. *When is it found desirable to explore vocational influences and what effects are found?*

Except with respect to college-going factors, not much research has accumulated in this area, and almost nothing has been done about determining optimal ages. Barbe (2) in a study evaluating results of the Cleveland major work program, points out that they need much occupational guidance, and that many do not go on to college or professional life. Bloom (5), in a paper entitled "The Early Identification of Potential Scientists," makes a plea for early identification and stimulation. Brandwein (8) echoes this same theme, and Brumbaugh (10) avers that the gifted child aged 6 to 11 can make specific occupational choices. Evidence accumulates that lack of stimulation of gifted children is one of the important factors in underachievement and drop-out problems. Further research on the effects of early vocational stimulation of gifted children is needed.

6. *Do close personal relationships become established between children of widely different mental ability?* Does the gifted child have companions close to his mental age?

Mann's doctoral thesis on this subject (31) would appear to establish that gifted children do not easily make friends with those of average mentality and that "birds of a feather flock together." An earlier thesis by Steinson (38) strongly indicated this probability. An important application for elementary schools is that since gifted children in their peer-group relations identify first with those most like themselves, they need the presence of other gifted children early in the primary grades if they are to make a smooth transition to easy social relationships and not become isolates.

7-8. *Are there special frustrations or satisfactions that gifted children experience?*

Self report studies of gifted children have been the method of procedure here. A doctoral study by Bonsall (Sea) (6) summarized the reactions of 137 gifted children toward elementary schooling and found their happiest experiences were in group activities where they had opportunity to achieve; unhappiest experiences were caused by classmates who made them feel socially inferior. They reported that the advantages of acceleration outweighed the disadvantages and wished for more individualization of instruction, more effective group work, and more chance for creativity. Strang (39) did a similar study which revealed areas of special concern to gifted children to include independence, responsibility, financial security, world peace, and satisfactions in relation to peers.

9-11. *What special factors account for undesirable personality traits found in gifted children?* Do gifted children constitute a minority group recipient of typical hostilities? What is the effect of this? Are there certain elements which attack gifted children? What are the effects of various procedures instituted to make favorable changes in attitudes toward gifted children?

There appears to have been no significant research in any of these areas.

In summary, it seems that research has furnished educators with considerably more information regarding gifted children than they are at present using profitably. Much has recently been discovered which could serve as a scientific basis for the considerable improvement of our programs for the education of the gifted child. It takes time for old beliefs and misconceptions to die out, but a careful perusal of the literature results in the feeling that most of the facts necessary for constructing a better program for education of the gifted are now in our possession, and that we are now waiting only on funds and leadership.

REFERENCES

1. Barbe, W. B. Evaluation of Special Classes for Gifted Children. *Exceptional Children,* 22, 1955, 60-63. Reprinted on pp. 464-469 of this volume.
2. ———. Occupational Adjustments of the Mentally Gifted, *Vocational Guidance Quarterly* 5, Winter 1956-1957, 74-76.
3. Barrett, H. G. Underachievement, A Pressing Problem, *Bull. Ontario Sec. Sch. Teachers' Fed.,* Oshawa, Ontario, 36, May 1956, 111-112, 151-152.

4. Birch, J. Early School Admissions for Mentally Advanced Children, *Exceptional Children*, 21, 1954, 84-87.
5. Bloom, Samuel W. The Early Identification of Potential Scientists, *School Science and Mathematics*, 55, April 1955, 287-295.
6. Bonsall, Marcella Ryser. Reactions of Gifted High School Pupils to Elementary Education, *Calif. J. Educ. Res.*, 6, May 1955, 107-190.
7. ——— and B. Stefflre. The Temperament of Gifted Children. *Calif. J. Educ. Res.*, 6, 1955, 162-65. Reprinted on pp. 377-380 of this volume.
8. Brandwein, Paul. New Patterns in the Education of Gifted Children in Mathematics and Science. *Kentucky School J.*, 35, November 1955, 20-21.
9. ———. *The Gifted Student as a Future Scientist*. New York: Harcourt Brace, 1955.
10. Brumbaugh, F. N. Earning a Living as the Bright Child Sees It, *Instructor*, 65, June 1956, 56.
11. Burgess, Elva. Personality Factors of Over- and Under-Achievers in Engineering. *J. Educ. Psychol.*, 42, February 1956, 89-99.
12. Cohler, M. J. Scholastic Status of Achievers and Non-achievers of Superior Intelligence. *J. Educ. Psychol.*, 32, 1941, 603-610.
13. Dowd, R. J. "Underachieving Students of High Capacity," *J. Higher Educ.* 23, 1952, 327-330. Reprinted on pp. 420-426 of this volume.
14. Engle, T. L. Achievements of Pupils Who Have Had Double Promotions in Elementary School. *Elem. School J.* 36, November 1955, 185-189.
15. Flesher, Marie, and S. L. Pressey, Wartime Accelerates Ten Years Later. *J. Educ. Psychol.*, 46, April 1955, 228-238.
16. Goodrich, H. B., and R. H. Knapp, *Origins of American Scientists*. Chicago: Univ. Chicago Press, 1952.
17. Gough, H. G. *Factors Related to Differential Achievement Among Gifted Persons* (mimeographed). Berkeley: Univ. California, 1955.
18. Gowan, J. C. Dynamics of the Underachievement of Gifted Students. *Exceptional Children*, 24, November 1957, 98-101. Reprinted on pp. 395-402 of this volume.
19. ———. *Resumé 5: 1956 Addition to Annotated Bibliography on Education of Gifted Children*. San Francisco, Calif.: State Advisory Council on Educational Research.
20. ———. The Under-Achieving Gifted Child: A Problem for Everyone. *Exceptional Children*, 21, April 1955, 247-249.
21. Hobson, J. R. Mental Age As a Workable Criterion for School Admission. *Elem. School J.*, 48, February 1948, 312-321.
22. Horrall, Bernice. Academic Performance and Personality Adjustments of Highly Intelligent College Students. *Genet. Psychol. Mono.*, 55, February 1957, 3-83.

23. Jones, E. S., and G. K. Ortner. Advanced Standing for Superior Students, *NEA J.*, 43, 1954, 107-108.
24. Justman, J. Academic Achievement of Intellectually Gifted Accelerants and Non-accelerants in Junior High School. *School Review*, 62, March 1954, 142-150. Reprinted on pp. 480-489 of this volume.
25. ————. Personal and Social Adjustments of Intellectually Gifted Accelerants and Non-Accelerants in Junior High School, *School Rev.*, 61, November 1953, 468-478.
26. Kemper, J. M. Saving Time in the Transition from Secondary School to College. *Educ. Rec.*, 37, October 1956, 310-311.
27. Lamson, Edna. A Study of Young Gifted Children in Senior High School, Contrib. to Ed. #424, New York: Columbia Univ. Teachers College Bureau of Publications, 1930.
28. Los Angeles City School Districts, Psychological and Educational Research Division, Extracts from *The Third Yearbook* No. 185, 1929, and *The Fourth Yearbook* No. 211, 1931.
29. MacCurdy, R. D. Characteristics and Background of Superior Science Students. *School Rev.*, 64, February 1956, 67-71. Also *Science Educ.* 40, February 1956, 3-24.
30. McClelland, D. C. (ed.). *Studies in Motivation*. New York: Appleton-Century, 1955.
31. Mann, Horace. How Real are Friendships of Gifted and Typical Children in a Program of Partial Segregation? *Exceptional Children* 23, February 1957, 199-201. Reprinted on pp. 473-479 of this volume.
32. Moore, Margaret. A Study of Young H. S. Graduates, Contrib. to Ed. #583, New York: Columbia Univ. Teachers College Bureau of Publication, 1933.
33. Nason, L. J. *Patterns of Circumstances Related to Educational Achievement of High School Pupils of Superior Ability*. Unpublished Doctor of Education dissertation, Los Angeles, Univ. of Southern California, 1954.
34. National Society of the Study of Education, *The Education of Gifted Children*, Part I, Yearbook, Chicago, 1924.
35. Passow, A. H. *The Enrichment of Education for Gifted Children* (mimeographed). New York: Horace Mann-Lincoln Institute, Columbia Univ. 1957, 20-21.
36. Pearlman, S. *An Investigation of the Problems of Academic Underachievement among Intellectually Superior College Students*. Unpublished Ph.D. thesis, New York: New York Univ., 1952.
37. Sanford, E. G. The Bright Child Who Fails. *Understanding the Child*, 21, 1952, 85-88.
38. Steinson, S. W. *The Characteristics of Mentally Superior Children*, Unpublished master's thesis, Los Angeles: Univ. of California, 1942.

39. Strang, Ruth, "Gifted Adolescents's Views of Growing Up," *Exceptional Children,* 23, October 1956, 10-15. Reprinted on pp. 380-389 of this volume.
40. Terman, L. M. and others. *Genetic Studies of Genius:* Vol. I, *Mental and Physical Traits of a Thousand Gifted Children;* Vol. II, *The Early Mental Traits of Three Hundred Geniuses;* Vol. III, *The Promise of Youth: Follow-up Studies of a Thousand Gifted Children;* Vol. IV, *The Gifted Child Grows Up; Twenty-Five Years Follow-Up of a Superior Group,* Stanford, Calif.: Stanford Univ. Press, 1925-1947.
41. Tyler, L. E. "Studies on Motivation and Identification of Gifted Pupils," *Rev. Ed. Res.,* 27, October 1957, 291-299.
42. Unzicker, S. P. A Study of Acceleration in the Junior High School, *School Rev.,* 40, May, 1932, 346-356.
43. Wedemeyer, C. A. "Gifted Achievers and Non-Achievers," *J. Higher Educ.,* 24, 1953, 25-30.
44. Wilkins, L. H. S. Achievement of Accelerated Pupils, *School Rev.* 44, April 1936, 268-273.
45. Worcester, D. A. *The Education of Children of Above-average Mentality,* Lincoln, Neb.: Univ. Nebraska, 1955.

ESSENTIAL RESEARCH DIRECTIONS
ON THE GIFTED

by T. Ernest Newland

UNIVERSITY OF ILLINOIS

It would appear that this is a rather direct encroachment on the splendid treatment of this subject by the subcommittee of the division of school psychologists of the American Psychological Association (6). Some of these observations will be only elaborations of their outline; others will, it is hoped, treat with aspects not dealt with by them.

That the area of the gifted cries out for more perceptive, in-

[Reprinted from *Exceptional Children,* 21, May 1955, 292-296, with the permission of the Council for Exceptional Children and the author.]

tensive, and sustained consideration by our major social planners seems at once apparent. But all too few persons appear to be conversant with the extent of society's crying needs for the more effective realization of the potentialities of the gifted. And all too many either ignore or are unaware of the crimes perpetrated, albeit unwittingly, on the gifted by society's agency—education. Further impeding a fuller realization of the possibilities of the gifted is the seemingly studious refusal on the part of many to accept, among other things, the social and psychological validity of both individual and social achievement goals in place of purely normative goals for individuals already known to differ greatly in their capabilities.

It is unfortunate that international tensions have been injected into our thinking to increase our sensitivity to the need for more study of intelligent planning for the gifted. For him who would read, it has been clearly shown for over 25 years that a socially dangerous percentage of gifted individuals has failed to go on for the advanced work which would materially enhance their contributions to our society. We now have a national Commission on Human Resources and Advanced Training under the stimulus of which new data have been collected which essentially corroborate leads uncovered by earlier research and which sharpen the picture considerably. Wolfle, in his recent book, *America's Resources of Specialized Talent* (8), indicates this social loss when he says:

> Fewer than half of the best 25 percent of all high-school graduates now graduate from college. Only six out of ten of the potentially most promising 5 percent of high-school graduates earn college degrees (p. 8).

Society's increasingly felt needs for more top-level specialists, who presumably will come largely from the ranks of the gifted, are well depicted in this important contribution. The situation as described by Wolfle confronts us with expressed and implied demands for both basic and technological research on the gifted. More is needed than many realize.

DEFINING THE GIFTED

In order that we may have a common frame of reference, the "gifted" will be regarded as those children whose Binet IQs are, not too roughly, 120 and above and those adults whose measured general-learning aptitude places them in the top 5 to 10 percent of the adult population. We shall regard the term "gifted" as applying to those who are called "talented" as well as to those called "mentally superior." Witty's proposal (7) that we regard as gifted "any child . . . whose performance, in a potentially valuable line of human activity, is consistently remarkable" can well be included here. It is emphasized, however, that there may be a greater commonality, at least potentially, among these seemingly divergent characterizations than frequently is reflected in our literature. The possible effects of acculturation in necessitating such seemingly divergent characterizations constitute an area that could well be explored quite vigorously.

The psychometric aspect of the definition of gifted children which is suggested is intentionally broader than that used by many. The reasons for this are both philosophical and psychological. Our social needs being what they are, it is indefensible for us to continue to rely upon the *laissez-faire* and *post hoc* definitions which hold, in effect, that one is gifted if he can show, or has shown, himself to be so. In terms of our large social needs, we need to think of the gifted, particularly from the standpoint of intellectual potential, as constituting more than the top one tenth of 1 percent, or the top 1 percent of our population. Once such a broader conception of even this aspect of the gifted is accepted, responsibilities of the public schools are somewhat more sharply defined and, at the same time, considerably broadened. This broadening of the definition is essentially a matter of social philosophy.

There are psychological grounds, also, for favoring the use of a larger IQ range as part of our basis for identifying the gifted. An Otis IQ is not a Binet IQ is not a WISC IQ is not a Kuhlmann IQ. And, to the psychologically uninitiated, an IQ is not the IQ he probably thinks it is, especially when the psychometrically measured intelligence of a child inadequately reflects the basic learning potential of that child. By making the Revised Binet IQ of 120 our cut-off point for the gifted, rather than the 130, 140, or higher which is used by man, we are increasing our chances of picking up children of higher potential who, for any of a number of possible reasons, have been characterized at less than their true capacity. This manner of thinking takes on added significance as we address ourselves to the problems of locating the gifted earlier in their lives.

Some in public-school work, in so far as their reflecting a public-school responsibility for the gifted is concerned, seemingly have stuck their heads in the sands of ambiguous or extremely deviant definition, saying either "People can't agree on just who the gifted are," or "According to So-and-so, the gifted are those 165 (or 150, or 185). Since we don't have children that high, we don't have any problem with the gifted." It is quite possible that the research persons working with the gifted, or with a part of them, unwittingly have contributed to some confusion as to who "the gifted" are. In the last three *Review of Educational Research* summaries on the gifted, (4,5,9), no fewer than 51 different terms were used to characterize the populations on which research was reported in 126 studies. While some of this multiplicity of terminology may well be attributed to the corrupting influence of the reviewer himself, the variety of characterizations of "the gifted" in the original articles would be only somewhat better.

Most definitely, I do not intend to imply that a single uniform definition of the gifted should be adhered to by all who do research in this area. Rather, a seeming paradox is recommended. As a research area, the gifted should be more broadly regarded, intellectually, socially, and artistically. Specific inquiry into any subgroup of the total area, however, is both possible and warranted. Once information is so obtained, however, both the reporter and the consumer of such research are obligated to be fully sensitive to the possible specificity of such findings and to be on their guard against unwarranted generalizations.

The discussion thus far having been predominantly IQ-oriented, we plead guilty to succumbing to convenience. To follow a similar pattern of thought with respect to creative behavior and with respect to social behavior is neither appropriate nor possible here. That the school's concepts of these areas of the gifted might well be broadened probably could easily be defended. That we should be sensitive to future Galtons, Bachs, Miltons, Mark Twains, Franklins, Hoovers, and Toynbees goes without question; lesser potential lights, too, can be identified early and helped to make their needed contributions to society.

Our designation here of research needed on the gifted necessarily will be brief and quite superficial. We shall only point at problem areas or specific problems and raise a few questions that seem relevant to them. A few implications will be suggested. These suggestions will pertain to both theoretical and technological research.

SOCIOEMOTIONAL NEEDS

Much educational tinkering and testimonial compiling and some more formal research have occurred with the gifted. These activities have been carried out in connection with methodologies that appeared to someone to have face validity, usually from a limited frame of reference. It is interesting to note, in this connection, that we have very little, if any, research information on the socioemotional needs of the gifted. It seems reasonable to assume that it would be initially on such information that decisions regarding appropriate educational methodology should be made. If such an assumption be granted, the need for research on the social status of the gifted is at once apparent.

Queries such as these cry out for answer: What factors determine the social status of the gifted in his group or groups? Are these same factors operative for both males and females? Are these same factors operative at different age levels, say, at five, eight, 12, 15, 20 years of age, or even older? If a given set of, say, five factors is operative, what are the relative weights of each, at different age levels? Are these weights the same for both sexes? Take, for instance, the matter of being academically "smart" in school. Many of us would guess this characteristic to have a high positive loading in the cases of children in their first year or so in school, later to have, perhaps, a negative loading, and still later, perhaps to have again a positive loading, but perhaps less so than for the early school years. How about the attenuating effect of the manner in which the child is "smart"? How about physical characteristics? Would these and/or other yet-to-be-identified factors have varying weights depending upon the level of the child's intelligence? Would the ways in which these factors operate vary with the kind of educational setting of the child—in "regular" classes (with varying kinds of teachers), in accelerated, or enriched, or enriched-accelerated programs, or in special-class programs? The answers to these and related questions could well indicate the possible over all suitability of, say, acceleration at one level, followed by enrichment at a later one, and, perhaps, more acceleration at a still later time, or of some pattern yet to be discovered. A number of cross-sectional studies of such problems, conducted with view to the comparability of the findings, could well be repeated at subsequent, predetermined intervals on the same populations and thereby constitute a major longitudinal developmental study.

WHAT IS GIFTEDNESS?

But we could appropriately back up a bit and face up to the fact that we do not actually know the psychological structure of giftedness. Psychologically, what are the components of giftedness as contrasted with nongiftedness? We get only a partial picture with our tests of intelligence. How about tenacity or perseverance? Drive? Physique? Emotional characteristics? Creativity? Having identified the major psychological components, why do some appear to wane? Where do earlier-identified tenacity, drive, and creativity go? To make a factor analysis of the research scientist, as Cattell (1) has done, is helpful in that it suggests a generalizable methodology and in that it tells us some important things about such people, but we, as well as he, can recognize the need for this type of study of other kinds of behavior of the gifted, and we can wonder concerning the stability of such patterns from childhood to realization. Clearly the need is pointed up for a longitudinal study structured similarly to Cattell's, or for a series of cross-sectional studies with common frames of reference.

Even though the investigation of the nature and nurture of the creative behavior of the gifted could yield returns of major proportions, the systematic and objective study of this area has been, most unfortunately, inadequate. It is quite possible that we have been lulled into the complacency of studying, instead, the significant part presumably played in creativity by certain elements of general intelligence and that, at the same time, we have been frightened away from the problem by its complexity and seeming unpredictability. At the upper age levels, some attempts have been made at measuring aspects of it, but at the earlier and more crucial age levels we have practically virgin territory. A 20-minute pencil and paper, machine-scoring technique for identifying this complex phenomenon in young children not being immediately at hand; we seem loath to undertake the more laborious approaches that may be necessary for its measurement. Even if it were so easily measurable, we would have a number of questions remaining. Does it grow? If so, what are the characteristics of its growth? Does it, as many fear, wither on the vine? If so, what factors or conditions cause it to lose in effectiveness or to be stunted? Is it amenable to training and/or resuscitation? He who throws light on these and related questions will do much for the gifted—and for society. But creativity will have to be conceived of in terms of a number of facets—scientific, social, literary, and artistic.

In the past few years, at least because of an educational and clinical emphasis, we have paid attention, quite properly, to the wide differences that are found among the gifted. In much educational literature the fact of exceptions among the gifted has itself become a generality that has tended to cloud the generalization that correlation among traits, not compensation, is the law of nature. Man has difficulty adjusting to his real world of paradoxes, and seems almost unable to reconcile the fact of trait variation within a gifted child, or among gifted children, with the larger and socially important fact of correlation of traits. Perhaps it is time again, even if only in the interests of the reading public, to study the extent and nature of the overlap between mentally superior and talented populations, with particular attention to this condition in early childhood. Is the disparateness between these two groups, which seems so real to some, attributable to differences in the kind and amount of intelligence possessed by them and/or to differences in some other trait or condition, e.g., emotionality or some other manifestation of acculturation? Old hat to some? Perhaps. But, with our improved measurement methodologies, perhaps a concept of eye-opening proportions—especially to those impaired in psychological orientation.

There is another aspect of the gifted that is intriguing and challenging from the clinical and educational-psychological standpoints. It can be illustrated most easily by means of an incident which, without doubt, numerous psychologists and educators have had. The phenomenon occurred during an individual psychological examination of a little boy who had earned a WISC IQ of 154, with no apparently significant difference between his verbal and performance quotients. To some, the boy behaved as a gifted child. IQ-wise, this would be suggested. Evaluating his performance qualitatively, it appeared that he performed on certain items in a way in which one would not expect a child of so high an IQ to behave. Certain conceptualization processes were considerably less adequate than his total performance would lead one to expect. To illustrate, his reply to "How are a cat and a mouse alike?" was "They both have four legs"—a lower, more elementary response than categorizing them both as animals. Other responses in this and other tests were of the same quality. (This seeming disparity is found, of course, in other children.) Generalizing this phenomenon into a research problem, the question becomes something like this: With children whose measured intelligence in terms of total performance on such an examination suggests a higher over-all level than is manifested in the conceptual level demonstrated in certain parts of the examination, is it possible to train them to a conceptual level more nearly in harmony with that suggested by the total examination? More intensive methods of differential testing, analysis, and appropriate remedial methods may need to be developed. Even though this type of problem is not unique to the gifted, society may have more at stake in so far as they are concerned.

Research on the gifted has concerned itself little with the area of social leadership. It is true that we have learned that the gifted tend to hold more than their share of school and campus offices and that they later take certain other roles of social leadership. Yet the schools have given little thought to extra-school social situations in which the gifted can be evaluated. This pertains not only to the leadership which the gifted may actually exercise there but also to the leadership for which the schools could help train such children. With few exceptions, the social leadership possibilities of work with the gifted have been either neglected or avoided with respect to situations centering on the less-structured neighborhood playground or poolroom and the more structured operations of the scouts, church, or camp programs. With the exception of some "guess-who" sociometric and socioempathic approaches, some of them still being developed, methodologies appropriate to this kind of research are either very time consuming or are yet to be developed. The problems of situation control or sampling, or observer training, or of complexity and definition of the behavior being observed combine to frighten away from this type of research the weak at heart or the hasty doctoral candidate. Society badly needs to know what research can discover here.

RESEARCH IN THE EDUCATIONAL AREA

Research on educational methodology has been of two sorts— enumerative and evaluative. While much of the reporting of such enumerative research probably has had an exhortatory value, one cannot help but wonder if some of it does not serve the purpose of placating the conscience of the educator. Evaluative research has been directed at difficult, complex problems where significant variables have been impossible to control within the limits of the customary doctoral thesis or dissertation. Populations have been varied, teaching methods so different, and investigative procedures so incomparable in the studies which have been made that it is practically impossible to integrate the findings on any sound basis. While it is true that many of the findings have been interesting and some have been significant, we have yet to have carried out major definitive research on educational methods with the gifted. Assuming that experimentation in the strict sense is not feasible, at least a five- to ten-year research program involving a large number of studies employing comparable definitions, research techniques, and definitions of goals is needed before we settle the haggling of both lay and professional persons concerning what is good schooling for the gifted. Yet this can not be properly done until we know more of the social picture of the gifted.

It may well be argued that too much of the research on the gifted has been done in schools and universities for teachers and professors. There is need for research geared heavily to those outside the ivory towers. The type of study now to be proposed should be made for the purpose of getting facts which will sharpen the perceptions of the lay public, as well as no small number of educators, to the need for special social and educational provisions for the gifted, as well as to the financial feasibility of such provisions.

In spite of the fact that there exists an abundance of data on the size of the problem of educating the gifted, facts of retardation and academic mortality and the later performances of those gifted who survive, a surprisingly large number of persons have remained highly impervious to such facts and their educational and social implications. We acutely need to make a variety of studies at the community, public-school level. These studies will be intended not to uncover new truths, even though some may be encountered, but rather to demonstrate the nature of the educational and social problems at the local levels. With careful thought to the devices and definition used, such local research can contribute significantly to the community's realization of the number of gifted children who live there and how retarded they are in terms of their *own* potentials. Research on their strength of motivation to obtain continuing education, college or noncollege, as well as on their possibilities of being financially able to pursue further training has public news value. Follow-up studies of the performances of the gifted are of interest to the public. Witness the recent *Time* article (3) reporting the study by Mrs. Catherine P. Chambers of the post-public-school performances of some gifted in the St. Louis schools. In view of recent releases by the Commission on Human Resources and Advanced Training, it is not unreasonable to expect local editors to be highly sensitive to the news value of such findings.

Generally speaking, we have failed to be practical in indicating the financial feasibility of making more adequate educational provisions for our gifted. To this end, we need more research on the costs of such provisions. There undoubtedly are others, but so far only one published study on the costs of special classes for the gifted as compared with those for regular classes appears to have come to light (2). Costs of other provisions for the gifted will not be computable in terms of class costs, but they can be compared to other basic educational expenditures. Other cost computations are feasible and deserving of study and publicizing—costs of productive years lost through retardation, scholarship needs and expenditures, and reports of the extent to which industry, for instance, is moving in the direction of helping promising students. But industry consistently has been more sensitive to the value of research than has education.

SUMMARY

Society always has needed the contributions of the gifted. Their contributions have been varied, occurring at least in the intellectual, scientific, artistic, social and technological areas. As a country, we are awakening both to their needs and to the fact that we are failing to help the gifted contribute to meeting these needs. Without implying any regimentation of those who would do research in this area, a broader definition of the gifted is advocated on both philosophical and psychological grounds. Research needs appear to be particularly acute with respect to matters such as the socioemotional needs of the gifted, the psychological constitution of giftedness, the conceptualization processes of the gifted, the extra-school leadership behavior of the gifted, the effectiveness of educational methodologies with the gifted, social loss aspects of the neglect of the gifted, and the costs of making different kinds of educational provisions for the gifted. The lack of comparability of subjects, procedures, and data among the studies lessens the impact which such studies should have.

Research ranging from the theoretical to the purely practical is needed on the gifted. This makes possible the utilization of a wide range of research talent. Major and integrated planning, however, is badly needed. For the larger problems, doctoral dissertation research is not an adequate means, although a series of such studies, carried out as part of a common structure, can fill in some of our needs. At present, no organization interested in the gifted has indicated readiness to serve as catalyzer or integrator of such major research. Perhaps some structure or organization devoted to the scientific or more objective aspects of the problems in this area can be caused to evolve in order more adequately to meet the research needs in the area of the gifted.

REFERENCES

1. Cattell, Raymond B. The Personality and Motivation of the Research Scientist. Submitted to the New York Academy of Sciences, Wenner-Gren Foundation Prize Committee, October 15, 1953.
2. Division of Special Education, *Status of the Gifted in Ohio.* Columbus, Ohio: Ohio Department of Education, 1951.
3. "Neglected Brain Power." *Time,* January 17, 1955, p. 56.
4. Newland, T. Ernest. "The Mentally Gifted." *Rev. Educ. Res.* 11, June 1941, 277-287.
5. ———. "The Gifted." *Rev. Educ. Res.,* 23, December 1953, 417-431.
6. O'Shea, Harriet E. (Chairman). Needed Research on Gifted Children.

Amer. Psychol., 9, February 1954, 77-78. Reprinted on pp. 522-525 of this volume.

7. Witty, Paul. The Gifted Child. *Exceptional Children,* 19, April 1953, 255-259.

8. Wolfle, Dael. *America's Resources of Specialized Talent.* New York: Harper and Brothers, 1954.

9. Woods, Elizabeth C. The Mentally Gifted. *Rev. Educ. Res.,* 14, June 1954, 224-230.

INDEX

INDEX

Page numbers in **bold-face** type refer to entire articles by an author.